# Uncle John's
# GIANT

## AUSTRALIAN
## BATHROOM
## READER®

# *Uncle John's*
# GIANT

## AUSTRALIAN
## BATHROOM
## READER®

The Bathroom Readers' Institute

Ashland, OR
&
San Diego, CA

UNCLE JOHN'S
GIANT AUSTRALIAN
BATHROOM READER

For information, write to
The Bathroom Readers' Institute
5880 Oberlin Drive, San Diego, CA, USA 92121
unclejohn@advmkt.com

Cover design by Michael Brunsfeld
San Rafael, CA (brunsfeldo@attbi.com)

National Library of Australia
Cataloguing and Publication data

Uncle John's giant Australian bathroom reader.

Includes index.
ISBN 1 59223 160 8.

1. Wit and humor.  2. Anecdotes.  3. Curiosities and
wonders.  4. History - Miscellanea.  5. Science -
Miscellanea.  I. Bathroom Readers' Institute (Ashland, Or.).
II. Title : Uncle John's bathroom reader.  (Series : Best
selling bathroom reader series).

828.07

Typeset in 10 pt Goudy by Midland Typesetters,
Maryborough, Victoria
Printed in Australia by Griffin Press, South Australia

**Project Team: Bookwise International**
Patricia Genat, Managing Director
Robert Sarsfield, Publisher
Rosemary McDonald, Australian Managing Editor
**Project Team: Portable Press**
Allen Orson, Publisher
JoAnn Padgett, Director, Editorial and Production
Cindy Tillinghast, Staff Editor
Amanda Wilson, Editorial Assistant
Laurel Graziano, International Sales Director

# THANK YOU

The Bathroom Readers' Institute sincerely thanks the people
whose advice and assistance made this book possible

Jeff Altemus
Susie Arnott
Claudia Bauer
Emily Bennett
Julie Bennett
Molly Bennett
Jesse & Sophie, B.R.I.T.
Michael Brunsfeld
Nenelle Bunnin
Liz Connolly
Claire Craig
John Dollison
Alice Drew
Susan Elkin
Kathy Gerrard
Penelope Houston
Sharilyn Hovind
Gordon Javna
John Javna
Larry Kelp
Lonnie Kirk
Lenna Lebovich
Jennifer Lee
Eric Lefcowitz

Rosemary McDonald
Jack Mingo
Arthur Montague
Jay Newman
Allen Orso
Ross Owens
JoAnn Padgett
Mustard Press
Julie Roeming
Kelly Rogers
Leo Rosten
Robert Sarsfield
Russel Schoch
Jill Sheridan
Jennie Simpson
Bennie Slomski
Andrea Sohn
Paul Stanley
Amanda Wilson
Peter Wing
Ana Young
…and all the bathroom
readers!

# CONTENTS

*Extra-long articles suitable for an extended sitting session are marked with an asterisk.*

x

## WORDPLAY

## THE ANSWER ZONE

# INTRODUCTION

G'day and thank you once again for supporting Uncle John. The reception given to our first *Uncle John's Great Big Australian Bathroom Reader* has been truly amazing. We, (the folks at the Bathroom Readers' Institute), are so proud that you have opened your bathroom doors and raised your toilet seats in a special salute to the books we produce that we have decided to create a second Australian bathroom reader—the *Uncle John's Giant Australian Bathroom Reader*. But wait there's more...it looks like there will now be annual visits from us, like unwanted relatives from the overseas!

This book will have you flushed with excitement. With over 500 pages of sport, trivia, humour, science, fun facts, Australiana and lots, lots more, you're bound to find the perfect article just when you need it.

We would love to hear your thoughts about this book and what you would like to see in future editions. So send us your bits of weird trivia, strange-but-true history, or anything else you would like to see included in future Bathroom Readers.

Please contact us about this book at unclejohn@advmkt.com. (We are in the process of setting up a more permanent seat...I mean site...in Oz.) If you would like to become a member of the Bathroom Readers' Institute, contact us at www.bathroomreader.com. No charge. No spam. Just a monthly newsletter, the opportunity to stay in touch, and (when our Australian location is established) the chance to go to the source for more products from Uncle John's.

So John now! And as always, go with the flow (which as you know goes counter-clockwise down-under)!

Uncle Al
Publisher
Portable Press

# FELINE FACTS

*Cats are one of Australia's most popular pets. Here are
six things you may not know about them.*

## THE INSIDE POOP
Nearly all domestic cats bury their faeces—but in the wild,
only timid cats do. Aggressive cats in the wild actually
leave their droppings on tiny "advertising hills" that they create.
This leads researchers to believe that domestic cats see themselves
as submissive members of their human families and environments.

## FAMILY FLAVOUR
Does your cat lick its fur clean after it rubs against you? That's its
way of "tasting" you—becoming familiar with the taste and scent
of the people in its life.

## CAT & MOUSE
Why do cats play "cat and mouse" with their victims? Experts
believe it's because they're not hungry. Wild cats, who eat
nothing but the food they catch, rarely, if ever, play cat and
mouse.

## PURR-FECT
Do cats purr because they are happy? Probably not, researchers
say; even dying cats and cats in pain purr. The researchers think a
cat's purr is a sign it is receptive to "social interaction."

## THE BETTER TO SEE YOU WITH
Unlike human eyes, a cat's eyes have pupils that are shaped like
vertical slits. These vertical slits work together with the horizontal
slits of the cat's eyelid to give it greater control over how much
light it allows into its eyes.

## WHISKED AWAY
Because a cat's whiskers are sensitive to the slight air currents that
form around solid objects (such as furniture and trees), they help
it to "see" in the dark. This is especially helpful when the cat
hunts at night.

On average, three people die each year from shark attacks.

# WHERE-ING CLOTHES

*Ever wonder how fabric designs and clothing styles get their names?*
*Some are named after the places they were created or worn.*
*For example…*

**C**ALICO. In the early 1700s, a fabric from India became so popular with the British public that they stopped buying English cloth and English weavers began losing their jobs. The weavers rioted. (In fact, they started attacking people wearing the cloth.) The result: Parliament banned imports of the fabric, and English weavers began making it themselves. They named it after the place it was originally made, the Indian town of Calicut. Eventually, *Calicut* cloth evolved into *calico* cloth.

**PAISLEY.** These amoeba-like patterns were originally found on shawls imported into England from India in the 1800s. Scottish weavers in the town of Paisley began producing their own versions of the design.

**BIKINI.** Daring two-piece swimsuits were introduced at end-of-the-world parties inspired by America's 1946 A-bomb tests on the Bikini Atoll in the Pacific.

**BERMUDA SHORTS.** Bermuda, an island in the Atlantic, was a popular warm-weather tourist resort in the 1940s. But female vacationers had to use caution when they relaxed—a law on the island prohibited them from walking around with bare legs. The fashion solution: knee-length shorts, worn with kneesocks.

**CAPRI PANTS.** Fashion designer Emilio Pucci met a beautiful woman while vacationing on the Isle of Capri in the 1950s. The encounter inspired a line of beach fashions that featured these skintight pants.

**JODHPURS.** These riding pants were created by English horsemen living in Jodhpur, India.

# FAMOUS
# FOR 15 MINUTES

*We've included this feature—based on Andy Warhol's comment that
"In the future, everyone will be famous for 15 minutes"—in almost
every Bathroom Reader. Here it is again, with new stars.*

**THE STAR:** Oliver Sipple, an ex-marine living in San
Francisco
**THE HEADLINE:** "Man Saves President Ford's Life by
Deflecting Assassin's Gun"
**WHAT HAPPENED:** President Gerald R. Ford was visiting
San Francisco on September 22, 1975. As he crossed the street,
a woman in the crowd, Sara Jane Moore, pulled out a gun and
tried to shoot him. Fortunately, a bystander spotted Moore and
managed to tackle her just as the gun went off. The bullet missed
the president by only a few feet.

Oliver Sipple, the bystander, was an instant hero—which was
about the last thing he wanted. Reporters investigating his private
life discovered that he was gay—a fact he'd hidden from his family
in Detroit. Sipple pleaded with journalists not to write about his
sexual orientation, but they ignored him. The next day, the *Los
Angeles Times* ran a front-page story headlined "Hero in Ford
Shooting Active Among S.F. Gays."
**THE AFTERMATH:** The incident ruined Sipple's life. When
his mother learned that he was gay, she stopped speaking to him.
And when she died in 1979, Sipple's father would not let him
attend the funeral. Sipple became an alcoholic. In 1979, he was
found dead of "natural causes" in his apartment. He was 37.

**THE STAR:** Hiroo Onoda, a Japanese army lieutenant during
World War II
**THE HEADLINE:** "Japanese Soldier Finally Surrenders…
29 Years After the War"
**WHAT HAPPENED:** In February 1945, Allied forces overran
Lubang Island in the Philippines. Most of the occupying Japanese
soldiers were captured, but a few escaped into the hills. There they

---

Heavy fact: Gram for gram, earthworms make up half of all animal life.

waited to be "liberated," unaware that Japan had surrendered. They survived by living off the forest and raiding native villages for food. Villagers called them "the mountain devils."

The U.S. and Japanese governments knew there were holdouts on the island, and for more than 25 years they tried to reach them by dropping leaflets, organising search parties, and bringing relatives to coax them out of hiding. But nothing worked.

By 1974, there was only one soldier left: 53-year-old Hiroo Onoda. One day, he spotted a young Japanese man drinking from a stream in the hills. The stranger turned out to be Norio Suzuki, a university dropout who'd come to the island specifically to find Onoda. Suzuki explained that the war had been over for 27 years and asked Onoda to return with him to Japan. But Onoda refused —unless his commanding officer came to the island and delivered the order personally. Suzuki returned to Japan, found the commanding officer, and brought him back to Lubang Island, where Onoda finally agreed.

**THE AFTERMATH:** Onoda was regarded as a curiosity in the world press, but in Japan he was a national hero. More than 4,000 people greeted him at the airport when he returned to Japan. He sold his memoirs for enough money to buy a 1,161-hectare (2,870-acre) farm in Brazil, stocked with 1,700 head of cattle.


**THE STAR:** Roy Riegels, captain of the football team at the University at California, Berkeley during the 1929 season
**THE HEADLINE:** "Blooper of the Century: Cal Captain Runs Wrong Way, Gives Away Rose Bowl Game"
**WHAT HAPPENED:** It was the 1929 Rose Bowl game: U.C. Berkeley was playing Georgia Tech, and the score was 0-0 in the second quarter. Cal had the ball deep in Georgia Tech territory, but in four attempts, they failed to score. Now Tech took over the ball...but on first down, the Georgia quarterback fumbled. In the confusion, Roy Riegels recovered the ball and started running for a touchdown. The only problem was, he was running *the wrong way*.

Benny Lom, Cal's centre, realised what was happening and chased Riegels, shouting and screaming. But Riegels outran him, carrying the ball 64 metres (70 yards) down the field. Lom finally tackled him—15 cm (6 inches) from the California goal line.

**THE AFTERMATH:** On the next play, Tech nailed Cal for a safety, making the score Georgia 2, California 0. They added a touchdown in the third quarter, but failed to make the extra point. Now the score was Georgia 8, California 0. In the fourth quarter, California scored a touchdown and made the extra point—but that was it. Final score: Georgia Tech 8, California 7. Riegels's blunder had cost Cal the game. The next day, Riegels was the most celebrated sports figure in the country. In fact, he's still known as "Wrong Way" Riegels.

**THE STAR:** William Figueroa, a 12-year-old student
**THE HEADLINE:** "New Jersey Student Makes Vice President Look Like a Foole"
**WHAT HAPPENED:** In June 1992, Vice President Dan Quayle visited a Trenton, New Jersey, elementary school where a spelling bee was being held. Quayle took over. Reading from a cue card, Quayle asked Figueroa, a sixth-grader, to spell the word "potato." The boy spelled the word correctly, but Quayle insisted that he change it, because "potato" was spelled with an "e" at the end. "I knew he was wrong," Figueroa later told reporters, "but since he's the vice president, I went and put the 'e' on and he said, 'That's right, now go and sit down.' Afterward, I went to a dictionary and there was potato like I spelled it. I showed the reporters the book and they were all laughing about what a fool he was."
**THE AFTERMATH:** Figueroa became an instant celebrity. "Late Night with David Letterman" had him on as a guest, and he was asked to lead the pledge of allegiance at the 1992 Democratic National Convention. Afterwards, an AM radio station paid him $50 a day to provide political commentary on the Republican National Convention. He was also hired as spokesperson for a company that makes a computer spelling program.

\*     \*     \*     \*

## NOTABLE AUSTRALIAN QUOTES

"Balmain boys don't cry."

—Neville Wran

Technically, snow is considered a mineral.

# FAMOUS PHRASES

*Here's another of our regular* Bathroom Reader
*features—the origins of familiar phrases.*

## NOT UP TO SCRATCH
**Meaning:** Inadequate, subpar
**Background:** In the early days of boxing, there was no
bell to signal the beginning of a round. Instead, the referee would
scratch a line on the ground between the fighters, and the round
began when both men stepped over it. When a boxer couldn't
(or wouldn't) cross the line to keep a match going, people said he
was "not up to the scratch."

## CAUGHT RED-HANDED
**Meaning:** Caught in the act
**Background:** For hundreds of years, stealing and butchering
another person's livestock was a common crime. But it was hard
to prove unless the thief was caught with the dead animal...and
blood on his hands.

## CAN'T HOLD A CANDLE TO (YOU)
**Meaning:** Not as good as (you)
**Background:** Comes from England. Before there were streetlights,
when wealthy British nobles went walking at night they brought
along servants to carry candles. This simple task was one of the
least-demanding responsibilities a servant could have; people who
weren't able to handle it were considered worthless. Eventually,
the term "can't hold a candle" came to mean inferiority.

## GIVE SOMEONE THE BIRD
**Meaning:** Make a nasty gesture at someone (usually with the
middle finger uplifted)
**Background:** Originally referred to the hissing sound audiences
made when they didn't like a performance. Hissing is the sound
that a goose makes when it's threatened or angry.

# Q & A:
# ASK THE EXPERTS

## STAR-GAZING
**Q:** *What are those silvery, star-like spots I sometimes see in my eyes?*
**A:** "These spots may look like tiny flickers of light or swarms of fireflies. Usually they last only a second or two. You may see them after receiving a blow to the head, or after doing a somersault or making some other sharp head movement.

What happens is that the sudden movement increases the pressure in the blood vessels in your eyes for a few moments. That triggers the nerves in your eyes, fooling your brains into thinking you're seeing spots of light." (*Know It All*, by Ed Zotti)

## POSSESSED
**Q:** *Why do cats' eye shine in the dark?*
**A:** "[It's] due to the reflection of light by the *tapetum lucidum*—a part of a membrane layer between the retina and the outer covering of the pupils that enables [cats] to see even when there is very little light. In the domestic cat the tapetum lucidum is brilliant green or blue in colour and has a metallic luster." (*Why Do Some Shoes Squeak? and 568 Other Popular Questions Answered*, by George W. Stimpson)

## SHOUT
**Q:** *What is the origin of "shout" for buying a round of drinks?*
**A:** The term comes from the last century when there was a need in a crowded pub to be heard over the other patrons to buy a round of drinks. As it was standard practice to share the cost of the drinks, everyone had a turn at shouting out the order to the barman.

## COOL AS A CUCUMBER
**Q:** *What is the origin of "cool as a cucumber" meaning anyone who is self-possessed & unemotional?*
**A:** The term refers to the fact that on a hot day, the inside of a cucumber in the garden is six to ten degrees cooler than the outside air.

# THE BEER-SOAKED BLOKE

*The birth and hoped-for death of a legend.*

**THE SOCIAL LUBRICANT**
It's been around since Neolithic times. The Romans loved it. Queen Elizabeth I was a fan and so was Shakespeare, but it's as Australian as a kangaroo. It's bitter, it's brown, it's brewed, and it's just below *Beelzebub* in the *Oxford English Dictionary*.

> Beer: An alcoholic liquor obtained by the fermentation of malt (or other saccharine substance) flavoured with hops or other bitters.

It's also known as ale. Saxon ale was dark, murky, full of protein and bits of barley mash—the original liquid lunch. The brew was flavoured with a variety of ingredients. "The wicked weed called hops" was introduced into England at the start of the 15th century by soldiers returning from the Hundred Years' War in Flanders, and hopped beer caught on fast. It was the daily drink in England until the 18th century and often the only safe drink. Children drank it freely. A gallon of beer (about 4 litres) was the daily allowance for a workingman; a schoolboy might get two and a half gallons a week. Novelist Anthony Burgess described Shakespeare's London like this:

> Nobody drank water...Ale was the standard tipple and it was strong. Ale for breakfast...Ale for dinner...Ale for supper. The better sort drank wine, which promoted good fellowship and swordfights. It was not what we would call a sober society.

Nor was Colonial Australia.

**LET'S DRINK TO THE HARD-WORKING PEOPLE**
Rum was the first drink in the New South Wales penal colony, but beer drinking was encouraged to lessen the consumption of "ardent spirits." The first Australian beer was brewed by John Boston, who arrived in Sydney in 1794. The British Government

sent him to the new colony to cure fish and make salt, but Boston showed a keen nose for market forces and decided to brew soap and beer instead. Demand was enthusiastic and small breweries soon proliferated. Supplies were erratic. Barley was often unavailable and brewers had to use whatever grain they could get. Not surprisingly, Australian beer earned a terrible reputation. Publicans would often water down the beer and "enhance" it with anything from tobacco juice to vitriol to opium. On one notorious occasion in 1855, a party of A-list guests at a Queen's Birthday ball in Melbourne fled to the toilets in agony after drinking her majesty's health with the explosively laxative "Murphy's Swipes" brew.

## BIRTH OF A LEGEND
This hard-drinking, male-dominated society produced what was to become one of Australia's most famous icons: the beer-soaked larrikin. Rough, tough, crude and cocky, he became the poster boy for Australian beer. He probably had his heyday half a century ago when opening hours were restricted. He was forced to rush straight from work to the pub and drink as much as he could as quickly as he could before being thrown out on the streets at 6 pm. This unfortunate social experiment became known as "the 6 o'clock swill." It took effort, but it enabled the Boozy Bloke to consume enough beer to make the current Australian 100 litres yearly average seem modest in comparison.

## BEER TODAY, GONE TOMORROW
Premium beer is now the fastest growing market segment. Carlton United Breweries, which produces more than half the beer drunk in Australia, brews 50 different types of beer for home and export (even the Mesopotamians only had 19). To monitor this complex operation, Carlton, one of the world's top five brewers, spent $17 million in 2000 to upgrade the filtration room of their Abbotsford (Melbourne) brewery. Sales of low-alcohol beer have doubled over the past ten years. But the Australian Tourist Board is worried. They are not convinced the Boozy Bloke isn't lurking somewhere in the corner of the bar waiting to embarrass the nation. They want to kill the beer-soaked cliché off. "The ads for Australian beer brands are humorous but they don't always present a very clear picture of the sophisticated restaurants and lifestyle of

Australia." A brewery spokesman replied, "We're marketing a lager, not a fine wine."

## BUMS ON SEATS

Here's a suggestion: Shakespeare, who wrote beer jokes before lifestyle was invented and did as much as anyone to popularise the comic drunk, had a father in the beer trade. John Shakespeare was appointed Ale-Conner (tester) for Stratford-upon-Avon in 1557. One of his tasks was to pour a pool of beer on a stool and sit in it for half an hour. If his leather breeches stuck to the stool when he stood up, the ale had too much residual sugar and wasn't fit to drink. What simple, cheap, effective quality control.

## DIEHARD

Australian Tourist Board take note: perhaps you could find a corner in a little brewery somewhere with a wooden stool and a pair of leather breeches. Install the Boozy Bloke. Let him live out his days with a stubbie in his hand, sitting in his favourite drop, telling stories of the good old days, while his breeches test the beer. Hire out leather breeches and let the punters have a go. It could bring the tourists flocking and could save some breweries 17 million bucks! You could be national heroes for providing the only fitting retirement for a cliché that just won't die: the authentic beer-soaked Aussie Bloke.

\*     \*     \*     \*

## LIFE'S LIKE THAT

Before performing a baptism, the priest approached the young father and said solemnly, "Baptism is a serious step. Are you prepared for it?"

"I think so," replied the man. "My wife has made appetizers and we have a caterer coming to provide plenty of biscuits and cakes for all our guests."

"I don't mean that," the priest responded. "I mean, are you prepared spiritually?"

"Oh sure," came the reply. "I've a keg of beer and a case of whiskey."

# HOORAY FOR HOLLYWOOD

*Hollywood is so closely identified with the "decadent"*
*film industry, that it's hard to imagine that it started out*
*as a prim Victorian town…but it did.*

**H**ISTORY. In 1886, Kansas prohibitionists Harvey and
Daeida Wilcox "bought a 49-hectare (120-acre) citrus
farm in sleepy Cahuenga Valley, a suburb of Los Angeles,
for $70/hectare."

They built an elaborate Victorian house in the middle of a
fig orchard, then began subdividing the property. Liquor wasn't
allowed, and only "well-educated, worldly, decent" people were
offered the property.

In 1903 the subdivision was big enough to become the city of
Hollywood. But that didn't last long. In 1910, the citizens voted
to make Hollywood an official district of L.A. The reason: They
wanted access to L.A.'s water system. Since then, one historian
laments, "Hollywood has been reduced to a mere 'northwest sector
of the city of Los Angeles.' "

**NAME.** While her California house was being built in 1886,
Daeida Wilcox went East to visit her family. On the train, she
met a woman who described a lovely Illinois summer estate,
called Hollywood, that was sprinkled with holly trees.

Wilcox was taken with the idea. She repeatedly tried to grow
holly on her citrus farm before deciding that the climate wasn't
suitable. Perhaps to console herself, she named their ranch
"Hollywood" anyway. In 1887 she registered the name with the
Los Angeles recorder.

**MAIN INDUSTRY.** In the early 1900s, the film industry was
centred in both New York City and Fort Lee, New Jersey. But
soon movie companies were headed west.

**The First West Coast Studio.** In 1907, Col. William Selig was
producing crude silent movies in Chicago, "whenever the sun was
shining—which was not frequently enough to make [his business]
a profound success." He happened to read a promotional pamphlet

---

Amazing fact: 20% of the people in human history who lived beyond age 65 are still alive today.

sent East by the Los Angeles Chamber of Commerce that mentioned the city was "bathed in sunshine some 350 days of the year." This impressed Selig, and he sent two men—Francis Boggs and Thomas Parsons—to see if it was true.

To give the area a test, Boggs and Parsons set up a temporary studio in L.A. and began making pictures, recruiting actors off the streets of the city. When they'd completed several pictures, they left to test another location—Colorado—where they compared the climate and photographic possibilities to those on the coast. The West Coast won. Not only was there almost unlimited sunshine, but the varied scenery—mountains, rivers, deserts, and ocean—was unbeatable. Boggs and Parsons shared their discovery with other filmmakers in the east, and in early 1909, Selig went to Los Angeles to build the first L.A. film studio.

**The First Hollywood Studio.** Ironically, it was the Wilcoxes' puritanism that brought moviemakers to Hollywood. When the couple subdivided their estate, one plot of land wound up in the hands of a tavern owner, who opened a bar there. The outraged Victorians passed a law prohibiting booze, bankrupting the bar. So when the Nestor Moving Picture Company arrived from New Jersey in 1911, it was able to buy the abandoned tavern cheap and convert it into the first Hollywood studio. Within a week, the company had produced Hollywood's first film, *Her Indian Hero*, a Western featuring real Native Americans. Within three months, it was sharing Hollywood with 14 other film companies—despite the "Actors Not Welcome" signs posted all over town.

## HOLLYWOOD FACTS

• Early filmmakers who moved West weren't just looking for a place in the sun; they were looking for a place to hide. So many were violating Thomas Edison's motion picture patents that a legal battle known as the Patents War erupted. Southern California was the perfect refuge—as far from the federal government as possible and close enough to the Mexican border for a quick getaway.

• The famous "HOLLYWOOD" sign in the hills above the film capital originally said "HOLLYWOODLAND." It was built in 1923 to promote a real estate development. The last four letters fell down during WW II.

# THE LAST LAUGH: EPITAPHS

*Some unusual epitaphs and tombstone rhymes,
sent in by our crew of wandering BRI tombstone-ologists.*

*Seen in Massachusetts, USA:*
**In Memory of Peter Daniels,
1688-1746**
Beneath this stone, a lump of clay,
Lies Uncle Peter Daniels, Who
too early in the month of May
Took off his winter flannels.

*Seen in Ribbesford, England:*
**Anna Wallace**
The children of Israel wanted bread,
And the Lord he sent them manna.
Old clerk Wallace wanted a wife,
And the Devil sent him Anna.

*Seen in Westminster Abbey:*
**John Gay**
Life is a joke, and all things show it;
I thought so once and now I know it.

*Seen in Death Valley, USA:*
**May Preston**
Here lies the body of fat May Preston
Who's now moved to heaven
To relieve the congestion.

*Seen in Falkirk, England:*
**Jimmy Wyatt**
At rest beneath this slab of stone
Lies Stingy Jimmy Wyatt;
He died one morning just at ten
And saved a dinner by it.

*Seen in Thanet, England:*
**Against his will, here lies
George Hill**
Who from a cliff, fell down quite stiff.
When it happened is not known,
Therefore not mentioned on this stone.

*Seen in Shutesbury, USA:*
**To the Four Husbands
of Miss Ivy Saunders**
Here lies my husbands, One, Two, Three,
Dumb as men could ever be.
As for my fourth, well, praise be God,
He bides for a little above the sod.
Alex, Ben and Sandy were the first three's names,
And to make things tidy I'll add his—James.

# HAPPY BIRTHDAY!

*It may come as a surprise to learn that celebrating birthdays is
a relatively new tradition for anyone but kings and queens.*

**B**IRTHDAY CELEBRATIONS. The first people known
to celebrate birthdays were the ancient Egyptians—starting
around 3000 B.C. But only the queen and male members
of the royal family were honored. No one even bothered *recording*
anyone else's birthdates.

• The ancient Greeks expanded the concept a little: they
celebrated the birthdays of all adult males…and kept on
celebrating, even after a man had died. Women's and children's
birthdays were considered too unimportant to observe.

• The Greeks also introduced the birthday cake (which they got
from the Persians) and birthday candles (which may have been
used to honour Artemis, goddess of the moon, because they
symbolised moonlight).

• It wasn't until the Middle Ages that German peasants became
the first to celebrate the birthdays of everyone in the family.
Children's birthday celebrations were especially important.
Called *Kinderfestes*, they were the forerunner to our toddler
birthday parties.

**THE BIRTHDAY SONG.** Mildred and Patty Smith Hill, two
sisters from Louisville, Kentucky, published a song called "Good
Morning to All" in a kindergarten songbook in 1893. They wrote
it as a "welcoming" song, to be sung to young students at the
beginning of each school day.

In 1924, a songbook editor changed the lyrics to "Happy
Birthday to You" and published it without the Hill sisters'
permission. The new lyrics made it a popular tune, but the Hill
family took no action…until the song appeared in a Broadway play
in 1933. Then Jessica Hill (a third sister) sued for copyright
infringement. She won, but most singers stopped using the song
rather than pay the royalty fee. In one play called *Happy Birthday*,
for example, actress Helen Hayes *spoke* the words to avoid paying it.

Today, whenever "Happy Birthday" is sung commercially, a
royalty still must be paid to the Hills.

---

About a quarter of the oxygen in your bloodstream is used by your brain.

# A TOY IS BORN

*You've bought them. You've played with them. Now
the BRI will satisfy your curiosity about where
they came from and who created them.*

## WIFFLE BALLS

In 1953 David Mullaney noticed that his son and a friend were playing stickball in the small backyard of their Fairfield, Connecticut, home...but they were using one of Mullaney's plastic golf balls instead of a rubber ball. It seemed like a good idea; that way the ball couldn't be hit or thrown too far.

Intrigued, Mullaney began experimenting with the golf balls. He cut holes in some with a razor blade and discovered that, with the right configuration, players using a lightweight plastic ball could even throw curves and sliders. In 1955, he began manufacturing his new creation, marketing it as a Wiffle Ball—a name he adapted from the baseball term "to whiff," or strike out.

## SUPERBALLS

In the early 1960s, a chemist named Norman Stingley was experimenting with high-resiliency synthetics when he discovered a compound he dubbed "Zectron." He was intrigued: When the material was fashioned into a ball, he found it retained almost 100% of its bounce—which meant it had six times the bounce of regular rubber balls. And a Zectron ball kept bouncing about 10 times longer than a tennis ball.

Stingley presented the discovery to his employer, the Bettis Rubber Company, but the firm had no use for it. So, in 1965, Stingley took his Zectron ball to Wham-O, the toy company that had created Hula Hoops and Frisbees. It was a profitable trip. Wham-O snapped up Stingley's invention, named it "Superball," and sold 7 million of them in the next six months.

**Scientific Curiosity.** Stingley wasn't the only "scientist" interested in Superballs. During the Superball craze, aficionados in Australia made a giant Superball and dropped it from a skyscraper to see if it would bounce all the way back up.

Unfortunately, the experiment went awry: when the ball hit the ground, it split in half and one part went crashing down the street, bouncing off cars and buildings until it crashed through the front window of a store.

## PIGGY BANKS

"For almost 300 years," writes Charles Panati in *Extraordinary Origins of Everyday Things*, "the predominant child's bank has been a pig with a slot in its back." Yet, he points out, pigs have no symbolic connection to saving money. So why did people pick a pig?

According to Panati, "The answer is: by coincidence. During the Middle Ages, mined metal was scarce, expensive, and thus rarely used in the manufacture of household utensils. More abundant and economical throughout Western Europe was a type of dense, orange clay known as pygg. It was used in making dishes, cups, pots, and jars, and the earthenware items were referred to as pygg.

"Frugal people then as now saved cash in the kitchen pots and jars. A 'pygg jar' was not yet shaped like a pig. But the name persisted as the clay was forgotten. By the 18th century in England, pygg jar had become pig jar, or pig bank. Potters, not usually etymologists, simply cast the bank in the shape of its common, everyday name."

## TROLL DOLLS

In the early 1950s, a Danish woodcarver named Thomas Dam made a wooden doll as a birthday gift for his teenage daughter. The doll, Dam's interpretation of "the mythical Scandinavian elves visible only to children and childlike grown-ups," was so popular with local kids that a Danish toy store owner insisted he make more of them. Eventually, to keep up with European demand, Dam began mass-producing them out of plastic.

In the early 1960s, they were exported to the United States as Dammit Dolls...and quickly became a teenage fad, adapted to everything from key chains to sentimental "message" dolls. But since Dam had no legal protection for the design, dozens of manufacturers jumped on the troll-wagon with knockoffs called Wish Niks, Dam Things, Norfins, etc.

The original Dammit Dolls are now collectors' items.

---

Q: How long is the world's longest human foot? A: 69 centimetres (27 inches).

# OL' BLOOD 'N' GUTS

*General George Patton was famous for his one-liners
as he was for his military victories in World War II.*

"In war, just as in loving, you've got to keep on shoving."

"To be a successful soldier you must know history....What you must know is how man reacts. Weapons change but man who uses them changes not at all. To win battles you do not beat weapons—you beat the soul of the enemy man."

"Wars may be fought with weapons, but they are won by men. It is the spirit of the men who follow and of the man who leads that gains the victory."

"The most vital quality a soldier can possess is self-confidence, utter, complete, and bumptious."

"Never tell people *how* to do things. Tell them *what* to do and they will surprise you with their ingenuity."

"A pint of sweat will save a gallon of blood."

"Untutored courage is useless in the face of educated bullets."

"Take calculated risks. That is quite different from being rash."

"A piece of spaghetti or a military unit can only be led from the front end."

"Use steamroller strategy; that is, make up your mind on the course and direction of action, and stick to it. But in tactics, do not steamroller. Attack weakness. Hold them by the nose and kick them in the pants."

"There's one thing you men can say when it's all over and you're home once more. You can thank God that twenty years from now when you're sitting by the fireside with your grandson on your knee, and he asks you what you did in the war, you won't have to shift him to the other knee, cough and say, 'I shovelled crap in Louisiana.'"

**Sigmund Freud had a morbid fear of ferns.**

# AUSTRALIAN RULES THE WORLD

*AFL is not just a matter of life and death—it's far more serious than that.*

O nce upon a time a young Australian athlete called Tom Wills was sent to finish his education at Rugby school in England, where a version of the ancient village game of football was played. Tom returned to Victoria in 1856 and told his cousin Henry Harrison that Rugby football was "unsuitable for grown men engaged in making a living." They decided to make their own rules up.

## THE GAME BEGINS

The first game of Australian Rules football was played on 7 August, 1858, between Scotch College Melbourne and Melbourne Grammar School. It lasted three weeks, including postponements. The playing field had no defined area, the goals were a mile apart and each team had 40 players. The game had enormous scope but clearly the rules needed some fine-tuning. Tom and Henry set to work and by 1866, the basic rules were sorted out. In 1867, the round ball was replaced by an oval one. Tom wanted a game for cricketers to play in winter. Australian Rules is the only football game played on a cricket oval; it's the only game to have four goalposts at each end; the teams are uniquely big; and the scoring is bewildering to the uninitiated.

## MARN GROOK

"Aussie Rules" or "footy" soon caught on in Victoria. Fans loved the speed of play, the big kicking, and the spectacular leap to catch the soaring ball known as the "mark." Thousands of Irish immigrants came to the Victorian goldfields in the early 1800s and Aussie Rules is often compared to Gaelic football. The games are similar enough to allow Irish and Australian teams to play test matches under "compromise rules," but Australian Rules football was established 18 years before the Gaelic Athletic Association

Sydney's streets were first lit at night by gas on 24 May, 1841.

was formed. Tom Wills was undoubtedly inspired by the Aboriginal game of "Marn Grook" (gameball) that he played as a boy. "Marn Grook", played with a stuffed possum-skin ball, was an expansive, exciting game that could last for hours. Like Aussie Rules, it featured drop kicks and high leaping and favoured tall athletic players.

## CAPTAIN BLOOD

Aussie Rules turned out to be no less bruising than Rugby. In 1939, Canadian journalist Paul Malone wrote, "Australian football makes American football look like a ladies' game. Furthermore, the Australian game makes even English Rugby, which looks like murder to Americans, appear softer than somewhat." In the 1920s Jack Dyer "Captain Blood" broke the collarbones of more than a dozen opponents with his shoulder charge. The AFL has a special category of inductees into its Hall of Fame known as *Legends*, selected for their "particularly significant positive impact on the game." Jack Dyer was officially inducted as a *Legend* in 1996. As was Hadyn Bunton, who showed that, aggression apart, the ethics of the game were unquestionable. He was signed by Melbourne's Fitzroy club in 1929 and promptly banned for a year when it was discovered the club had tempted him with a pair of boots. Unfazed, he went on to win the "fairest and best" medal six out of the next nine seasons.

Oddly, though support for Aussie Rules was fanatical in Victoria—a big game could attract upwards of 100,000 spectators and local rivalries were fierce—the game resisted export. It took almost a century to gain a firm foothold in Rugby-loving New South Wales and Queensland. Rugby became and remained more popular in the former British Empire countries of South Africa, New Zealand and Australia than it ever did in Britain. Rugby is a body-contact sport best played on a nice grassy pitch, such as may be found in the schools of the rich in England or in the wide open spaces of the New World. Soccer is more adaptable. Skills can be picked up kicking a ball around the streets and a game can be played on a gritty bit of asphalt. Balls can be, and have been, made from anything—leather, plastic, a blown-up condom with string wrapped tightly round, a tin can, even an enemy's head!

## THE PEOPLE'S GAME

Most modern codes of football are derived from British village football, a folk custom steeped in violence and vulgarity. The Romans must take some blame. Their armies in Britain played a war-game called *Harpastum*, not unlike American football and Rugby League, in which opposing teams tried to force the ball over the enemy's line. When the Romans went home, they left their game behind. It mutated into parish battles fought over a ball. A game could last all day, village battling village. Everyone joined in. Then, as now, beer was involved. It was the people's game and the monarchy didn't like it. The first banning was in London in 1314. Edward II objected to "a great noise in the city caused by bustling over large balls." Edward III followed with another ban in 1349 because "bowmanship was neglected." In Manchester, "lewd and disordered persons" could cop a stiff twelve-penny fine for playing with balls. The bans went on for 300 years. Football flourished.

It was rehabilitated as a respectable pastime in Victorian England when schools decided that team games were "A Jolly Good Thing" for growing boys (girls didn't get a look-in). The Old Boys wanted to carry on playing after school so they got together in their gentlemens' clubs and drew up some rules. Between 1850 and 1875, five distinct football codes were established. All five codes are still going strong: Rugby (which split into League and Union in 1907), association football (soccer), American football (which was exported as a college game), Gaelic football and Australian Rules.

## AUSTRALIAN RULES THE WORLD

Tom Wills' ambition was to take Australian Rules to the world. He died in 1880 without achieving it. Henry Harrison tried to carry on his work. They might be surprised to see what big business their game has become in the 21st century. They might be astounded to see that not only are women allowed to play, they actually have their own leagues now (since 1981). They would undoubtedly be gratified that the International Australian Football Council was formed in 2001 to promote their game around the world. But they might well ask why it took so long. One and a half centuries? It was a long time coming. But at last, perhaps, *Australian Rules the World?*

21% of the world's gambling machines are in Australia, with only 0.003% of the world's population.

# THE MYTH-ADVENTURES OF CHRISTOPHER COLUMBUS

*Who was Christopher Columbus and what did he really do?*
*Much of what we were taught in school is untrue.*

**THE MYTH:** Columbus was born in Genoa, Italy.
**BACKGROUND:** The only documentary proof is a will written in 1498, purportedly by Columbus, that begins with "I, being born in Genoa…"
**THE TRUTH:** According to his son Fernando, Columbus never revealed where he was born; he preferred to call himself "a man of the sea." And historians doubt whether the 1498 will is genuine. Meanwhile, dozens of places claim to be Columbus's birthplace:

- **Corsica.** The town of Calvi claims both his birth and his remains; Columbus has a tombstone there.
- **France.** In 1687, French lawyer Jean Colomb claimed Chris was his ancestor.
- **England.** A book published in 1682 in London states that Columbus was "born in England, but lived in Genoa."
- **Spain, Armenia, Poland, and even Norway.** Norwegians say his real name was Christopher Bonde.

**THE MYTH:** Christopher Columbus was named…Christopher Columbus.
**BACKGROUND:** This name first appeared in 1553, long after his death, in a book by Petrus Martyr.
**THE TRUTH:** He was never called Columbus in his lifetime. In fact, when Columbus was alive he was known by at least five other names:
- **Cristoforo Colombo.** Most historians believe he was born

---

The screwdriver was first used to help knights put on their armour.

Cristoforo Colombo.

• **Christovam Colom.** When he settled in Portugal and became a successful merchant-seaman, he was known as Christobal (or Christovam) Colom (or Colombo).

• **Cristobal Colon.** He adopted this name after he moved to Spain (also Christoual or Colamo). This was his name during his voyages and what he's still called in Spanish countries.

• **Christophorus Colonus.** This is the name preferred by his son Fernando, who wrote a biography of his dad. Other Latin forms of the name: Christoforus Colom, Cristoferi Colom.

• **Xpoual de Colon.** This is what he was called in his agreement with the King and Queen of Spain before his first voyage across the Atlantic. After 1493, he signed his name Xpo FERENS, using only his first name, in the fashion of royalty. Later he began to sign his name like this:

.s.
.S. A .S.
X M Y
: Xpo FERENS/

Nobody in the past 500 years has been able to explain what this signature means.

**THE MYTH:** Columbus's boats were officially named the *Nina*, the *Pinta*, and the *Santa Maria*.

**BACKGROUND:** Blame historians for spreading the story. For example, in *Three Ships at Dawn*, Augustus Heavy wrote: "*Pinta*, meaning 'Lovely Lady,' was called that because she floated so gracefully; *Nina*, meaning 'Baby,' was named that because it was so small; and the devoutly religious sailors called the last ship the *Santa Maria* in honour of Saint Mary."

**THE TRUTH:** In Columbus's time, if a ship had a name, it was unofficial—usually something that the crew came up with.

• The *Pinta* might have been called that in honour of the Pinto family in Palos, where the ships were readied for the voyage. But "Pinta" also meant "Painted Lady"—a prostitute.

• The *Nina*, smallest of the three ships, had previously been known as the Santa Clara. "Nina" means "Little Girl—sailor slang for a woman who's easy with sexual favours.

• And the *Santa Maria*? The crew knew it by its newer name, *Marigalante* meaning "Dirty Mary."

---

# DEFINITIONS

*In previous Bathroom Readers we've included some uncommon words, and their meanings, to help build weak vocabularies. Here's another batch.*

**Ambivert:** A person who's half introvert and half extrovert.

**Backclipping:** Shortening a longer word into a smaller one, like *chrysanthemum* to *mum*.

**Boomer:** A male kangaroo.

**Callipygian:** Having shapely buttocks.

**Chad:** The little circles of paper your hole-punch makes.

**Furfurrate:** What dandruff does when it falls from your scalp.

**Genuglyphics:** Painting or decorating a person's knees to make them more erotic.

**Hypocorism:** Baby talk.

**Infix:** A word placed inside another word to change its meaning, as in *fan-f——tastic.*

**Izzard:** The name of the letter "z."

**Kith:** Your friends.

**Lecanoscopy:** The act of hypnotizing yourself by staring into a sink filled with water.

**Liveware:** People who work with computer software and hardware.

**Nidus:** A place where bacteria multiplies.

**Otoplasty:** A surgical procedure to fix ears that stick out.

**Otorhinolaryngologist:** An ear, nose, and throat doctor.

**Pandiculate:** To yawn.

**Paradog:** A military dog that's been trained to parachute out of airplanes.

**Paranymph:** The bridesmaid or best man at a wedding.

**Pica:** A desire to eat nonfoods (like dirt).

**Pilomotor reaction:** What your hair does when it stands on end.

**Pip:** What an unhatched chick does to break through its eggshell.

**Pullet:** A female chicken one year old or younger.

**Puwo:** An animal that's half poodle and half wolf.

**Taresthesia:** The tingling sensation you get when your foot falls asleep.

**Tautonym:** A word consisting of two identical parts, like *tutu.*

**Ucalegon:** A neighbour whose house is burning down.

**Zoonoses:** Diseases humans can get from animals.

---

A scallop has 35 eyes—all of them blue.

# IN THE BLINK OF AN EYE

*In the time it takes to read this four-page article, you'll blink at least 30 times. Or at least that's what Jay Ingram says in his fascinating book,* The Science of Everyday Life. *Here are some of the more fascinating tidbits on blinking and the eye from Ingram's book and others.*

## IT CLEANS & MOISTENS!

Although eyeballs vary slightly, the typical eyeball is about 2.5 centimetres (1 inch) in diameter and 7 grams (¼ ounce) in weight.

• The front, non-white part of the eye—the *cornea*—is covered by a transparent membrane called the *conjunctiva*, which functions along with the lachrymal (or tear) gland, to keep the eyeball moist.

• When we blink, the tear gland releases tears and the eyelid washes the eyeball clean while moistening it at the same time.

• From there the liquid collects in tear ducts at the sides of our eyes, and it eventually drains back into our bodies by way of the back of the nasal passages.

• Beyond keeping the eyeball moist, the blink serves other important functions. It protects the eyeball from nearby objects, like an oncoming finger. But primarily it acts as a cleaning device, washing out dust and dirt particles and killing germs and bacteria.

• A blink is an involuntary reaction, much like breathing and if you choose to not blink, your body will usually take over and do it for you when your eyes get dry enough.

## FAST, FAST, FAST RELIEF!

• How often one blinks varies from person to person, but most scientists agree that we blink an average of 17,000 times in a day.

• That translates to roughly one blink every five seconds and rounds up to six-and-a-quarter million times in one year.

• Each blink lasts about three-tenths of a second.

• Author Jay Ingram: "Slow motion replays show that the eyelid begins to drop, builds up speed to a maximum, then begins to slow again before your eye is actually closed."

---

Elvis's nickname for his sexual organ was "Little Elvis."

- The eye-closing part of a blink lasts, on average, one-tenth of a second.
- Ingram, again: "The eyelid stays closed for about one-twentieth of a second, then it starts accelerating back upward again, leaving a film of tears behind. The odd thing is that even though your eye is partly or completely closed for three-tenths of a second or more, you aren't aware of missing anything."

## BLINKIN' PSYCHOLOGY

- We tend to blink faster when we're excited or nervous. For instance, someone who's on television tends to average between 31 and 50 blinks per minute—twice the normal rate.
- But why? A chemical called dopamine is responsible. It's released in the brain when we're under stress...which triggers body arousal—faster heart rate, quicker breathing, and more rapid eyelid movement, or blinking.
- Knowing this, psychotherapists have long thought that excessive blinking in a patient can reflect, among other things, a deep-seated desire to hide. As a result, blink rates are used to gauge subjects taking polygraph tests as well. The normal blink rate is about twenty times per minute. A faster rate signifies anxiety, emotional distress, or that the "fight or flight" response is kicking in—all indicators that someone may be lying.

## INSIDE INFO

- FBI Special Agent, Joe Navarro, has gone so far as to identify a specific type of blink that he directly associates with someone about to lie.
- In an online interview, Navarro explains: "On NBC's *Today Show*, Matt Lauer talked about how Madonna had lied to him about her announced pregnancy just the other day. He showed the video and her response but he missed something to ponder about. She did what I call the eyelash flutter when asked, 'Are you pregnant?' "
- It's different under high speed camera from the eye-blink, we can see that it does not close completely and the speed is amazing. I first observed this eyelid behaviour in 1985, and find that people who are troubled by a question or an event do this, especially if they have to answer and are about to lie.

**All kangaroos use their tails when they jump.**

- "I tell attorneys to look for the eyelash flutter when they have people on the stand; it means they really do not like the question at all. I even had a case where the individual picked out the route of escape for me when I went through several routes with him; I just waited for the flutter to pick out the way."

## DEMOCRACY GOES ON THE BLINK

- With the advent of video closeups, political analysts have looked for signs in the blinking of politicians. Somebody with a video recorder and a stopwatch discovered that Richard Nixon blinked twice as much as normal when answering hostile questions about Watergate and that Bill Clinton's blinking rate went up from 51 blinks per minute to 71 when discussing Monica Lewinsky.
- During the television debates between Michael Dukakis and George Bush, somebody else discovered that both candidates blinked faster when questions were directed to them.
- Most recently, Boston College neuropsychologist Joe Tecce noted that George W. Bush blinked an average of 82 blinks a minute, indicating severe stress. Al Gore, on the other hand, blinked at a rate of 48 blinks a minute. Based on the previous six elections, where the slower blinker won, Tecce believed it was a sign that Gore was more likely to keep his head and win the election. However, as the election showed, the eyes didn't have it.
- The extremes of blinking in presidential debates? Bob Dole is "the fastest blinker among all world leaders I've studied," says Tecce. He clocked a record 147 blinks per minute in his 1996 debate with Clinton. The slowest? Ross Perot, who managed a meditative 9 bpm in the three-way 1992 debate.

## DOCTOR, MY EYES

- Excessive blinking in children is one of the symptoms that paediatricians watch for. It can mean a number of things, including allergies, chronic exposure to cigarette smoke, extreme anxiety or eye problems.
- Rapid and habitual blinking is often the first symptom that appears in children who are developing Tourette's Syndrome. On the other hand, sometimes it's just a habit that a kid does because it gets him adult attention.

"The" is the most used word in the English language.

## WITH A NOD AND A WINK

• Blinking eyes have many times been used as a signal. American prisoners of war appearing before movie cameras communicated secret messages in Morse code during the Vietnam War.

• While frozen within a block of ice, magician David Blaine answered questions by blinking once for yes and twice for no.

• However, the most extraordinary use of blinking for communication has to be writer Jean-Dominque Bauby. Profoundly paralysed by a stroke, he lost all movement in his body except his left eyelid. Using 200,000 blinks and a very patient friend, Bauby wrote his memoirs. The book became an instant bestseller in France, but Bauby all-but-missed the excitement—he died two days after it was published.

## HISTORY PASSES IN A BLINK OR TWO

• The Roman emperor Gaius screened gladiators based on whether they could go unblinking into the face of extreme danger. It wasn't a foolproof test—only two of 20,000 passed it.

• It was a blinking surgeon during the French Revolution who first demonstrated that a head lived for a short time after decapitation. Unfortunately, the head in question was his own. Antoine Lavoisier (1743–1794), a French chemist who discovered oxygen, was beheaded during the Reign of Terror. Ever the scientist, before being beheaded he told a friend that he would continue blinking for as long as possible after the guillotine struck to see how long he would remain conscious. His friend reported that Lavoiser's disembodied head blinked for about 15 seconds.

\* \* \* \*

## NOTABLE AUSTRALIAN QUOTES

"I've always hated my personality—it's one of the most unfortunate I've ever encountered."

**—Percy Grainger (composer)**

"Of course I can sell. Anyone who's persuaded a two-year-old to eat spinach can make a sale."

**—Sandra Yates (magazine publisher)**

Water babies: Baby sea lions have to be taught how to swim.

# 10 CANDY BARS YOU'LL NEVER EAT

*These tidbits about extinct candy bars come from Dr. Ray Broekel,
"candy bar historian" and publisher of a newsletter called the
Candy Bar Gazebo.*

**T**HE AIR MAIL BAR. Introduced in 1930 to honour the first airmail flight in the U.S.—in 1918, from Washington, D.C. to New York City. Ironically, the first flight never made it to New York. After takeoff, the pilot noticed someone had forgotten to fill the fuel tank. Then he got lost over Maryland and had to land in a cow pasture. The Air Mail candy bar had a similar fate.

**FAT EMMA.** In the early1920s, the Pendergast Candy Company in Minneapolis introduced a candy bar with a nougat centre. They planned to call it the Emma bar. But when it wound up twice as thick as expected (they accidentally put too much egg white in the mixture), they changed the name to Fat Emma. Later, Frank Mars copied the idea to create the Milky Way bar.

**THE SAL-LE-DANDE BAR.** The first candy bar named after a stripper—Sally Rand, whose "fan dance" at the 1933–34 Chicago World's Fair shocked and titillated the nation. In the 1960s, another stripper bar was available briefly: the Gypsy bar, named after Gypsy Rose Lee.

**THE RED GRANGE BAR.** Endorsed by Red Grange, the most popular football player of his day. After starring at the University of Illinois, he joined the Chicago Bears in 1925 and helped keep the National Football League in business. Unfortunately, he couldn't do the same for his candy bar.

**THE VEGETABLE SANDWICH BAR.** One of the weirdest "health" bars ever made, this 1920s vegetable concoction contained cabbage, celery, peppers, and tomatoes. Its makers claimed it aided digestion and "will not constipate."

**THE ZEP CANDY BAR.** "Sky-High Quality." One of several candy bars that capitalised on the popularity of "lighter-than-air"

---

Galileo went blind studying the sun through telescopes.

dirigibles in the 1930s. This one featured a sketch of a Graf Zeppelin on the wrapper. It was taken off the market after the Hindenburg exploded in 1937.

**THE CHICKEN DINNER BAR.** One of the best-selling bars you've never heard of. It was introduced in the 1920s and remained on the market for about 50 years. The original wrapper featured a picture of a roasted chicken on a dinner plate—a bizarre way of suggesting it was a nourishing meal and encouraging consumers to associate it with prosperity ("a chicken in every pot"). The manufacturer, Sperry Candy Co., even dispatched a fleet of Model A trucks disguised as giant sheet-metal chickens to deliver the candy to stores. Several years after the bar's debut, Sperry dropped the chicken from the wrapper. But it kept the name.

**THE BIG-HEARTED "AL" BAR.** George Williamson, owner of the Williamson Candy Company, was a good Democrat and a good friend of New York governor Al Smith, Democratic nominee for president in 1928. Smith lost in a landslide to Herbert Hoover, and his candy bar soon followed.

**THE SEVEN UP CANDY BAR.** Got its name from having seven connected pieces, each with a different centre. The bar came out in the 1930s, before the 7-Up Bottling Company began producing its soft drink—so the Trudeau Candy Company owned the trademark rights to the name. Eventually the 7-Up Bottling Company bought the bar and retired it, so they had exclusive use of the name no matter how it was spelled—*Seven Up or 7-Up*.

**THE "IT" BAR.** The #1 female sex symbol of the silent movie era was Clara Bow—known as the "It Girl." (She had that special quality her movie studio called "It.") In 1927 the McDonald Candy Company of Salt Lake City tried cashing in on her popularity with a candy bar featuring her face on the wrapper. It did well for a few years, then disappeared along with Bow. (She wasn't able to make the switch to talkies, because although she was lovely to look at, her Brooklyn accent made her impossible to listen to.)

*Also Gone:* The Betsy Ross bar, the Lindy (for Charles Lindbergh), Amos 'n' Andy, Poor Prune, Vita Sert, and Doctor's Orders.

---

During the Middle Ages you could be accused of witchcraft if your pets disobeyed you.

# OLD TOM—NO ORDINARY KILLER WHALE

*A true story about killer whales and humans working together.*

## LOOKING FOR CLUES

On the south coast of New South Wales, in the pretty little town of Eden, you'll find the skeleton of a killer whale on public display—the skeleton of Old Tom.

Nothing remarkable about that you might think, but if you look at the skeleton you will notice that the huge sharp teeth on one side of the jaw have been worn right down to the bone—a most unusual occurrence in an animal that feeds almost exclusively on the soft tissues of whales and seals. But then, Old Tom was no ordinary killer whale…

## A WHALE OF A TALE

In the late 1800s, the hunting of whales was widespread throughout the world and big business for the town of Eden. Whaling stations were dotted up and down the coasts of eastern and western Australia, hunting the humpbacks and southern right whales that migrated from feeding grounds to breeding areas each year. The whalers weren't the only ones interested in the whales; pods of killer whales also preyed on these whales.

It was only in Eden, however, that a highly unusual and very special relationship developed between the whalers and the killer whales—the killer whales began to actively help the whalers find and kill other whales. Old Tom was the leader of these killer whales and this is his story.

## IT WASN'T A FLUKE

Records show that when Old Tom and his pod of killer whales spotted a whale off the coast of Eden, some of the killer whales would swim to the whaling station to alert the whalers while other killer whales would remain with the whale to make sure that escape was impossible.

At the whaling station, the killer whales would jump right out of the water or slap their large tail flukes so that the whalers soon learnt that this was their cue that whales were offshore.

As the whaleboats in those days were large, ungainly craft powered by oars, Old Tom would grab the anchor rope with his teeth and tow the whalers out to the besieged whale. The whalers would then harpoon the whale while the killer whales kept jumping onto the whale's back trying to stop the whale from surfacing so it could breath.

## AHAB SHOULD HAVE BEEN SO LUCKY

Harpooned whales usually took off, pulling the whalers and their boat for great distances before the injured animal ran out of strength and died. To stop this, Old Tom would grab the harpoon rope in his jaws to slow the whale down by using his weight as a drag.

It was all this work with the ropes that eventually ground down Old Tom's teeth right to the bone, as his skeleton bear's witness today.

After the harpooned whale had died, it was anchored with a buoy and left for the killer whales to take their share of the bounty. Killer whales have a preference for the soft tissue of whales—mainly the tongue and lips—and as the whalers did not use these parts, this alliance was seen as being of mutual benefit to both the whalers and the killer whales.

In essence the partnership meant that the whalers killed more whales thus increasing their profits and the killer whales got to eat more frequently—a win-win situation for both parties.

Legend has it that when Old Tom died (reputedly after 90 years of assisting the Eden whalers) the rest of the pod disappeared and was never seen again. It wasn't long after Old Tom's death that the Eden whaling station went out of business and closed, supposedly as a result of changed economic conditions and the increasing scarcity of whales. But locals say that the whalers just lost interest—without Old Tom to help them their hearts just weren't in it anymore.

# PRETTY FLAMINGOS

*They're America's beloved symbol of bad taste—as designs for lawn ornaments, lamps, cups, and so on. BRI member Jack Mingo tells us how these strange-looking birds became as American as apple pie.*

## THE FLAMINGO BOOM

During the 1920s, Florida was the hottest vacation spot in the United States. Tens of thousands of real estate speculators and tourists swarmed to the semitropical state…and many brought home souvenirs bearing pictures of a bizarre pink bird that lived there—the flamingo.

In the North, these items—proof that their owners were rich enough to travel to exotic places—became status symbols. Everyone wanted them. So manufacturers started incorporating flamingos into a variety of new product designs.

They were so popular that by the 1950s, the image of a flamingo was as much a part of middle-class America as Wonder Bread or poodles.

## THE LAWN FLAMINGO

In 1952, the Union Plastics Company of Massachusetts introduced the first flamingo lawn ornament. It was "flat and unappealing."

• To boost sales, the company decided to offer a more lifelike, three-dimensional flamingo. But the second generation of lawn flamingos "was made of construction foam and fell apart rather quickly," recalls a company executive. "Dogs loved to chew it up."

• Finally, in 1956, Union Plastics hired a 21-year-old art student named Don Featherstone to sculpt a new lawn flamingo. "I got a bunch of nature books and started studying them," says Featherstone. "Finally, I sculpted one, and I must say it was a beautiful looking thing."

• The first atomic-pink molded plastic lawn flamingo went on sale in 1957. It was an immediate success; in the next decade, Americans bought millions of them. But by the 1970s, lawn flamingos were, "gathering dust on the hardware store shelves along with other out-of-date lawn ornaments such as the scorned sleeping Mexican peasant and the black jockey." In 1983, The

*New York Times* ran an article titled "Where Did All Those (Plastic) Flamingos Go?"
• Then suddenly, lawn flamingos were flying again. 1985 was a record year, with 450,000 sold in the United States. Why the resurgence? Critics suggested a combination of nostalgia and the popularity of the television show "Miami Vice." "They are a must for the newest hot social events—'Miami Vice' parties," reported a California newspaper in 1986.
• Featherstone never got any royalties for his creation. But he did become a vice president of Union Plastics...and in 1987, he was honoured when the company started embossing its flamingos with his signature. "I'm getting my name pressed into the rump of every flamingo that goes out the door," he announced proudly.

## FLAMINGO: THE BIRD
**History.** Flamingos, looking pretty much as they do today, were roaming the earth 47 million years before humans came along.
• They were well known in Egypt during the pyramid-and-sphinx period. A flamingo played a prominent role in Aristophanes' 414 B.C. play *The Birds*.
• The American flamingo is extinct in the wild—captive flocks (most with wings clipped so they don't fly away) at zoos and bird sanctuaries are the only ones left.

**Body.** Flamingos' knees don't really bend backward. But their legs are so long that the joint you see where it seems the knee ought to be is really the flamingo's ankle, and it bends the same way yours does. The knee is hidden, high up inside the body.
• The flamingo is the only bird that eats with its head upside down—even while it is standing up.

**Colour.** While flamingos are known to sometimes eat small fish, prawns and snails, they are primarily vegetarians. They consume vast quantities of algae, and this is what makes them pink. Without the "food colouring," flamingos are actually white.
• Flamingos in captivity are, as a result of algae deprivation, quite a bit paler than their wild cousins. Zoos attempt to keep their flamingo flocks in the pink by feeding them carotene to compensate for the algae they'd get in their natural habitats.

The average bird's eyes take up 50% of the space in its skull.

# SECRETS OF DISNEYLAND

*Well, they're not really secrets—more like gossip. But most people
don't know much about the history and operations of the original
mega-theme park. And it's pretty interesting stuff.*

## INSPIRATION

In the 1940s, a couple of Walt Disney's top animators were
real train buffs. They got Uncle Walt interested in the hobby
and he set up a miniature steam railroad that circled his house and
gardens (note: see *Bathroom Reader #2*, p. 62), big enough to ride.
After several train-theme parties, Walt got the idea that if his
friends got such a kick from this one ride, maybe a whole
amusement park would lure vacationers who were visiting
Hollywood to star-gaze.

## HOW WALT GOT THE MONEY

Walt proposed the idea to his brother Roy, the Disney
stockholders, and their bankers…but they rejected it. In fact, they
thought he was nuts. (In those days, amusement parks were sleazy
places full of carnival side-shows, rip-off games, and cheap
mechanical rides.)

So Disney was on his own. He went on a relentless search for
financing. He sold his Palm Springs home and cashed in his
$100,000 life insurance policy to finance his research. He lined
up corporate sponsors, who were willing to pay for exhibits and
restaurants in exchange for name recognition.

But the turning point came when he made a deal with
American ABC-TV. At the time the ABC, a relatively new
network, was a distant third in the ratings. It was desperate for the
high-quality, high-name-recognition programming Disney could
provide. But Disney had already turned down offers from other
networks. Why should he join forces with a loser like the ABC?
The answer: financing for his amusement park. In exchange for
doing the show, Disney received a substantial sum of money and
the ABC agreed to call the show "Disneyland," virtually making
the weekly show a one-hour commercial for the park. But perhaps

more important, later, in an "unrelated" deal, the ABC purchased a 34% interest in Disneyland, Inc., the company set up to build the park. (Ironically, Disney now owns the American ABC.) When Roy saw the package Walt had put together, he changed his mind and hopped on the Disneyland bandwagon. In 1954, ground was broken in an Anaheim orange grove.

## OPENING DAY

In the wake of its enormous success, people have forgotten that Disneyland's opening day was a disaster. Nearly 33,000 people—twice as many as the number invited—packed the park with the help of forged tickets and surreptitiously placed ladders. Not all the rides were operational, and the restaurants ran out of food after a few hours. In some parts of the park, concrete and asphalt hadn't hardened properly, and women walked out of their high-heel shoes.

Also, there had been a plumber's strike during construction, and there weren't enough drinking fountains. The press thought it was a ploy to get visitors to purchase soft drinks. What they didn't know was that, in order to be ready for opening day, Walt had to choose between installing toilets or drinking fountains.

Thanks to nationwide TV coverage emceed by Ronald Reagan, the entire country learned of the mess. The next day's headlines read, "Walt's Dream A Nightmare," and Disney seemed to agree: For the rest of his life he referred to opening day as "Black Sunday."

## LAND OF ILLUSIONS

When Uncle Walt bought the property for Disneyland in Anaheim in the early 1950s, he couldn't afford to buy all the land he wanted. So, in order to fit everything in, he used movie makers' tricks to make everything look bigger.

One trick was to use things that are familiar, but make them smaller than normal. Unless you look carefully and measure with your eyes, you'll assume, for instance, that the Disneyland train is normal size. It isn't. It is built to 5/8 scale. Many of the Disney buildings use the same trick, but that's just the beginning.

If you look carefully at some of the Disney buildings, especially those on Main Street, you'll notice there's something a little odd about them. They are not only smaller than normal, but their second and third stories are smaller still. This is known in art and in movie making as "forced perspective." By tapering the upper stories, the designers fool your eye into believing that they are bigger and taller than they really are.

This is done especially skilfully on Sleeping Beauty's Castle, even to the point that the bricks get smaller and smaller with each level.

In making Disney World this was less of a problem, because by that time the company could afford to buy an area bigger than most cities. It used many of the same tricks, but on an even bigger scale.

## DISNEYLAND DEATHS

According to an article in *Egg* magazine, at least 53 people have died at Disneyland. According to *Egg*:
• The first Disney death was apparently a suicide: In 1964, after an argument with his girlfriend, a passenger on the Matterhorn stood up on the ride and was catapulted onto the tracks when his car came to a sudden stop. He never regained consciousness, and died four days later.
• The Matterhorn killed again in 1984, when a 48-year-old woman fell out of the ride and was struck by the following car. (For the rest of the day the Matterhorn was closed due to "technical difficulties.")
• Two people have been killed in accidents in Tomorrowland's PeopleMover ride, two others drowned in the river surrounding Tom Sawyer's Island. Another person was run down by the Monorail when he tried to sneak into the park without paying; and a park employee was crushed by a moving wall in the "America Sings" attraction.
• The park's first homicide occurred in 1981, when a man was stabbed after touching another man's girlfriend. (Disneyland was found negligent in the death and fined $600,000 after a park nurse neglected to call paramedics—and instead had the victim driven to the hospital in a park van.)
• Not all of Disneyland's deaths happen inside the park: In 1968, 44 people were killed in two separate helicopter accidents travelling between Disneyland and Los Angeles International Airport; and in 1987 a teenage male was killed during a gunfight in the parking lot.

# WHAT'S IN A NAME?

*You know these corporate and product names, but probably not where they come from. Well, the BRI will fix that. Here's a little trivia you can use to entertain store clerks next time you're shopping.*

**Kodak.** No meaning. George Eastman, founder of the company, wanted a name that began and ended in the letter K.
"The letter K has been a favourite with me," he explained. "It seems a strong, incisive sort of letter."

**Chanel No. 5 Perfume.** Coco Chanel considered 5 her lucky number. She introduced the perfume on the fifth day of the fifth month of 1921.

**Lucky Strikes.** Dr. R. A. Patterson, a Virginia doctor, used the name to sell tobacco to miners during the California Gold Rush in 1856.

**Ex-Lax.** Short for *Excellent Laxative*.

**Reebok.** An African gazelle, "whose spirit, speed, and grace the [company] wanted to capture in their shoes."

**Avon Products.** Named for Stratford-on-Avon, William Shakespeare's birthplace.

**Random House.** America's biggest publisher started out in the 1920s, offering cheap editions of classic books. But founder Bennett Cerf decided to expand the line by publishing luxury editions of books selected "at random."

**Kent Cigarettes.** Herbert A. Kent, a Lorillard Tobacco Company executive, was so popular at the office that the company named a cigarette after him in 1952.

**Toyota.** Sakichi Toyoda made the first Japanese power loom. His son Kiichiro expanded into the automobile business.

**Xerox.** The Haloid Company originally called its copiers "electrophotography" machines. In the 1940s, they hired a Greek scholar at Ohio State University to think up a new name. He came up with "Xerography" for the process (after the Greek words for dry and writing) and called the copier itself a *Xerox* machine.

# TANG TWUSTERS

*Ready for a workout? Here are 20 difficult tongue twisters. Try to say each of them five times fast...and don't pay any attention to the people banging on the bathroom door, asking what's going on in there.*

If you must cross a coarse cross cow across a crowded cow crossing, cross the coarse cross cow across the crowded cow crossing carefully.

Does this shop stock short socks with spots?

The sixth sheik's sixth sheep's sick.

"The bun is better buttered," Betty muttered.

Seven sleek sleepless sleepers seek sleep.

Sixty-six sickly chicks.

The sun shines on shop signs.

The shady shoe shop shows sharp sharkskin shoes.

A noise annoys an oyster, but a noisy noise annoys an oyster more.

Rush the washing, Russell!

The seething sea ceaseth seething.

Awful old Ollie oils oily autos.

Mummies munch much mush.

This is a zither.

Ike ships ice chips in ice chip ships.

She says she shall sew a sheet.

Feed the flies fly food, Floyd!

Miss Smith dismisseth us.

Ted threw Fred thirty-three free throws.

Rex wrecks wet rocks.

The praying mantis is the only insect that can turn its head.

# THINGS THAT SSS-STING AND SSS-SNAP!

*It's true. Australia really is a land of things that make you sss-shiver with fright. Is it just a coincidence that so many of these things begin with the letter 'S'?*

## SNAKES

Take your pick from the line-up of venomous snakes that live in Australia: brown snakes, tiger snakes, black snakes, death adders (there's a name to send you into a total panic!), copperheads, sea snakes and taipans.

There are two species of taipan in Australia. At up to 3 metres (10 feet) long, the coastal taipan is the longest venomous snake in Australia. The inland taipan, or fierce snake, is limited to a small area of western Queensland, which is just as well! It has the most toxic venom of any snake in the world.

Brown snakes sound innocuous, but don't be fooled. These aggressive, 2-metre (6.5-foot) long snakes are now responsible for most of the snakebite deaths in Australia. They might have relatively small fangs, but these deliver a potent venom that causes progressive paralysis and blood clots.

## SPIDERS

Australia also leads the way when it comes to spiders. Funnel-web spiders are large and dark in colour. They can be found mainly along the east coast of Australia, from Tasmania to mid-Queensland. They weave silk trip-lines out from their burrow to warn them of the approach of possible prey. Funnel-web spiders often fall into swimming pools. They have been known to survive for nearly 30 hours underwater, so don't assume that the funnel-web spider floating in your pool is dead! Bites from a male funnel-web spider can cause serious illness or death, but there is an antivenom available. To date, there have been 13 deaths recorded from funnel-web spiders. Trapdoor spiders and mouse spiders are often mistaken for funnel-web spiders, but to those of us who won't be waiting around for a formal introduction—a spider is a spider!

Red-back spiders are found throughout Australia, especially in urban areas. They like to build their webs in dry, sheltered places, and are the infamous spider of Australian "dunny" stories. The equally notorious American black widow spider is a close relative of the red-back spider. Like the black widow spider, only the female red-back spider is dangerous. Its venom acts quickly on the nerves, but antivenom is available.

Funnel-web spiders and red-back spiders have the dubious distinction of being among the most dangers spiders in the world.

## SCORPIONS

It's easy to pick out a scorpion. It has a long, sting-bearing tail and a pair of pincers on long arms. Scorpions also have plenty of eyes (six to twelve) but, strangely, they do not have very good eyesight. Found throughout Australia, they live under logs and rocks, and usually move around at night. Scorpions are deadly in some parts of the world. In Australia, however, their sting is painful but usually not dangerous. It can be treated by applying a cold pack to the sting and seeking medical advice if the pain persists.

## STONEFISH

To the unsuspecting eye, it looks like a piece of rock or coral. But be very wary before you reach out to investigate it further. The reef stonefish is considered to be the most venomous known fish in the world. It can be found in the Indian and Pacific oceans north to China, east to Hawaii and south to Australia. It has tough, warty skin, which may be covered in slime, and 13 spines in its dorsal fin, which can inject a highly toxic venom. This causes intense pain and can result in death. An antivenom was developed in 1959 but, to date, there have been five deaths recorded. One death reported from Japan was that of a man who tried to put a stonefish in a bag!

## STINGRAYS

Gliding along the sea floor like a cloaked creature, or buried under the sand in shallow water, the smooth stingray is the largest of all the stingrays. Although it is not usually aggressive, the sting is definitely in its short tail. The one venomous spine halfway along its tail can kill or severely wound people. Found worldwide in tropical and subtropical waters, at least 17 deaths have been recorded from stingrays.

## SEA WASP
You might know this by its more common name: the box jellyfish. Found in the coastal waters of Northern Australia, the stinging cells in its dangling tentacles can cause a variety of symptoms— from trouble breathing and swallowing to cardiac arrest. There is an antivenom available for box jellyfish stings, but someone who has been stung has very little chance of surviving unless they are treated immediately. The box jellyfish is considered the world's most venomous creature.

## STINGING NETTLES
Bushwalkers and gardeners beware! Australia has the nastiest stinging nettles in the world! The hairs and bristles on the plant contain formic acid that stings when you touch them. But remarkably, stinging nettles also contain healing properties for conditions such as baldness, prostate problems and rheumatic pain.

## SHARKS
Out of all the creatures beginning with "s" the shark is sure to evoke the most fear. There are about 350 species of shark worldwide of which 165 species are found in Australian waters. They vary in size from the whale shark, which can reach up to 20 metres (66 feet) in length, to the small dogfish that is less than 30 cm (12 inches) long. Sharks live for approximately 25 years and generate new teeth every eight days. But get back into the water as only a small number of them are dangerous to people.

# BOX-OFFICE BLOOPERS

*We all love bloopers. Here are a bunch of movie mistakes to look for in popular films. You can find more in a book called* Film Flubs, *by Bill Givens.*

**M**ovie: *The Wizard of Oz* (1939)
**Scene:** Dorothy, the Tin Woodsman, and the Scarecrow dance down the Yellow Brick Road singing, "We're Off to See the Wizard."
**Blooper:** A crew member can be seen in the background among the trees. (For years, rumours circulated in Hollywood that the crew member had committed suicide and hung himself from one of the trees on the set. The rumours were false.) *Note:* Also pay close attention to the length of Dorothy's hair. Because the scenes were filmed out of sequence, her hair changes from mid-length to long to short as the movie progresses.

**Movie:** *Spartacus* (1960)
**Scene:** Peter Ustinov gets off of his horse.
**Blooper:** His jockey shorts are visible under his tunic as he climbs down.

**Movie:** *The Alamo* (1960)
**Scenes:** The battle sequences.
**Bloopers:** Though the movie is a Western, you can see several mobile trailers in the distance. (And in another scene, you can see a stuntman falling into a mattress.)

**Movie:** *Children of a Lesser God* (1986)
**Scenes:** Several occasions in which Marlee Matlin (who is deaf and portrays a deaf character) and co-star William Hurt sign to each other during conversations in which Hurt is speaking.
**Blooper:** The sign language has nothing to do with the movie— it's about Matlin's and Hurt's private life. (At the time the movie was made, Matlin and Hurt were having an affair.)

**Movie:** *Rambo III* (1988)
**Scene:** Rambo steals a "Russian" helicopter.
**Blooper:** A small American flag is clearly visible on the helicopter's rotor housing.

English word with the most different meanings in the dictionary: Set, with 464. (2nd place, Run.)

# FAMILIAR NAMES

*Some people achieve immortality because their names become commonly associated with an item or activity. You already know the names—now here are the people.*

**A**lfredo di Lellio. A Roman restaurateur. His fettuccine with butter, cream, and Parmesan cheese became famous in the 1920s after Hollywood stars Mary Pickford and Douglas Fairbanks ate in his restaurant every day during their honeymoon.

**John Langon-Down.** An English doctor of the late 19th century. He was the first doctor to describe, in medical literature, the genetic defect now known as Down's Syndrome. Down called it "mongolism," because physical characteristics related to the condition reminded him of the features of people of Mongolia.

**Queen Mary I of England and Ireland.** A fanatical Catholic, she brutally repressed Protestants in her realm. Her reputation earned her the nickname "Bloody Mary," and inspired a cocktail made with vodka and tomato juice.

**Vyacheslav Mikhailovich Molotov.** Soviet foreign minister, 1939-1949 and 1953-1956, and rabid Stalinist. Finnish resistance fighters battling Russian tanks in the 1940s named their primitive gasoline-filled bottle bombs "Molotov cocktails" in his "honour."

**Sir George Everest.** The surveyor-general of India from 1830 to 1843, he named the world's tallest mountain after himself.

**Dr. A. M. Latan.** A quack dentist and peddler of health tonics in Paris during the 1840s. He travelled the city in an opulent coach—usually with a man marching in front, blowing a horn to attract attention—selling his wares as he went. Parisians shouted "Voila, le char (car) de Latan"—later shortened to "charlatan."

**Mickey Finn.** A 19th-century saloon keeper who ran Chicago's Lone Star and Palm Saloons. When customers got too rowdy, he slipped drugs into their drinks to knock them out. Today, giving someone a knockout drink is called "Slipping them a Mickey."

**Sam Ellis.** A tavern keeper on what was later called Ellis Island.

**Edward Stanley, 12th Earl of Derby.** A British nobleman of the late 1700s and early 1800s. An avid horse lover, he hosted a 2.4-km (1.5-mile) horse race in 1780 that he called the "Derby Stakes." Today the term "derby" is used to represent any horse race or other sporting event that has a strong local following.

**Gabriel Daniel Fahrenheit.** German scientist of the late 17th and early 18th centuries. Invented a new thermometer that used mercury instead of alcohol. Its new scale—which marks water's freezing point at 32° and its boiling point at 212°—was named Fahrenheit after him and became popular in English-speaking countries.

**Anders Dahl.** In 1789 Alexander von Humboldt, a German explorer, discovered a new species of flower while on an expedition to Mexico. He sent some of the plant's seeds to the Botanic Garden in Madrid, where the curator promptly named the plants *Dahlias*—after his close friend Anders Dahl, a famous Swedish botanist who had died earlier that year.

**George Nicholas Papanicolaou.** Pioneered the use of cervical tissue smear samples in detecting uterine cancer. Today that test is known as a "Pap smear."

**Josiah Wedgwood.** An English potter of the late 1700s. He developed a line of china famous for its white designs on a blue background, which later became known as "Wedgwood" china.

**David Douglas.** A 19th-century Scottish botanist and explorer of the western United States. He discovered a new species of tall evergreen trees that bear his name: Douglas firs.

**Draco.** A magistrate and lawmaker who wrote the first code of laws of ancient Athens in the seventh century B.C. The code was one of the strictest set of laws ever written; it gave the death sentence for nearly every crime—even petty theft. Today any punishment that seems too severe for the crime can be labelled "draconian."

**Caspar Wistar.** A professor of "anatomy and midwifery" who held regular Sunday tea parties for a wide variety of scientists. One of his frequent guests was Thomas Nuttall, curator of the Harvard University Botanical Garden. In appreciation, Nuttall named a species of climbing plant "wistarias" in Wistar's honour. But because of a spelling mistake, the plants became known as "wisterias."

# THE TRUTH ABOUT THE PANAMA CANAL

*The Panama Canal was a triumph of engineering—but it was also a triumph of political conspiracy. As one Political wit said in the 1970s: "The Panama Canal belongs to us. We stole it fair and square."*

**T**HE MYTH: The Panama Canal was an American idea. **THE TRUTH:** The idea of a building a canal through the Panama Strait was more than three centuries old before anybody actually did anything about it.

The possibility was first discussed just decades after Columbus landed in the New World, when the Spaniards realised how far around South America they had to go to get to the Pacific Ocean. Panama seemed to be an ideal spot for a canal, since it measured only 50 miles from coast to coast.

But the issue was put to rest in 1552 by King Philip, whose religious advisors reminded him that the scriptures warned: "What God has joined together let no man put asunder." Philip agreed.

"If God had wanted a Panama Canal," he announced, "He would have put one here."

**America's First Effort.** In the 1850s, the U.S. sent a survey team to Panama to see if it was possible to build a canal. But the idea was dropped when the team reported that there wasn't "the slightest hope that a ship canal will ever be found practicable across any part of it."

**The French Effort.** That didn't stop the chief promoter of the Suez Canal from trying. In 1880 Ferdinand de Lesseps, backed by a group of French investors, began building a canal across the Isthmus of Panama. American President Rutherford Hayes was outraged that this was happening in "our" territory and decreed that France should cede control of the canal to the United States.

Before the issue became an international incident, however, the French project collapsed under the weight of corruption, poor planning, and the harsh Central American jungle environment: floods, earthquakes, yellow fever, and malaria. The French

The London Bridge has never fallen down.

abandoned their partly dug canal and left most of their heavy machinery to rust in the jungle.

**THE MYTH:** The U.S. signed a treaty with the legitimate government of Panama to build and lease the Canal Zone.
**THE TRUTH:** Panama wasn't even a country when the U.S. decided to build a canal there—it was a territory of Colombia.

**Background.** In 1898 the battleship *Oregon*, stationed off the California coast, was ordered to Cuba to prepare for battle in the Spanish American War. The voyage around South America took two months. Clearly, a faster route was needed.

When the war was over, President Theodore Roosevelt began pushing for a canal. He was partial to a canal through Nicaragua: Even though that route was longer, it appeared to be an easier dig, since it would run through Lake Nicaragua.

But Panama had its partisans in the fierce Senate debate about the canal. When the French—who wanted to unload the canal they'd begun—dropped the price for their unfinished assets from $109 million to $40 million, America decided on Panama.

**The Colombia Problem.** There was just one problem: Roosevelt found that the people he called "Dagos" in Colombia were asking too much for using their territory.

He decided the solution was simple—if the existing country was a problem, create a new country that would be more willing to compromise. The U.S. Army teamed up with a former director of the French canal company, who stirred up a "revolt" against Colombia. Meanwhile, the American battleship *Nashville* positioned itself off the Colombian coastline with guns ready, in case Colombia objected.

**Friendly Nation.** As soon as a new revolutionary government was announced, the U.S. recognised it and pushed through a deal: for $10 million, an annual fee of $250,000, and a guarantee of "independence," the United States received rights to the 10-mile-wide canal zone "in perpetuity." Since the new country of Panama was not much wider than that 10-mile-zone, the U.S. effectively controlled the country. Colombia did protest, but there wasn't much it could do. The canal was finished in 1914.

# THE PLUMBER'S HELPER

*While you're sitting on the dunny, take a moment to examine it. Do you notice a problem? If so, you're in luck: BRI plumber's helper is here. We can't guarantee or even recommend this advice, of course (we're writers, not plumbers), but it sounds good.*

**T**he Problem: Running water.
**What It Could Mean:** The chain connecting the handle to the flush valve—the hole at the bottom of the tank where the water enters the bowl—is too long. Remove a few links of the chain so that it hangs with only a little slack.
**Other Possible Causes:**
• The "float mechanism" that shuts off the water isn't working; it's letting water leak into the overflow pipe. If your mechanism is a "float ball" attached to a horizontal rod, bend the rod so that the ball hangs lower in the tank. If it's a plastic cylinder called a "float cup," adjust it so that it hangs lower in the tank.
• Your "flush valve" is leaking. This is most likely the problem if you have to jiggle the toilet handle a lot, or if the toilet hisses regularly. Your best bet is to replace the rubber bulb mechanism. Replace the flush valve with one that's the same size.

**The Problem:** A wet floor around the base of your toilet.
**How To Fix It:** Add several tablespoons of food colouring to the water in the bowl and in the tank. Wipe the floor around the toilet dry, and then wait for the moisture to reappear.
  Mop up the area again, this time using white paper towels. If the moisture is coloured, your toilet is leaking. If it isn't, you probably have a condensation problem, or a leak from another fixture.
• To fix a leaky toilet tank, drain it and use a wrench or screwdriver to tighten the nuts at the base of the tank. (If the washers around the bolts look worn, replace them.) Don't overtighten; if you do you'll risk cracking the tank.
• If the toilet still leaks, the flush valve may be loose. The only way to fix it: remove the tank from the bowl and tighten the valve.

**The 100 Years War lasted 116 years.**

# LAST WISHES

*Think it's tough planning ahead now? Try imagining
what your dying wish will be. Here are some odd
last requests from nine well-known people.*

**Eleanor Roosevelt:** Fearful of being buried alive, the former first lady requested that her major veins be severed to eliminate the possibility of regaining consciousness after burial.

**Harry Houdini:** The famous escape artist asked to be buried in the "trick" coffin he used in his magic act—with letters from his mother tucked beneath his head.

**William Shakespeare:** Wanted his oldest daughter, Susanna, to inherit his favourite bed. He left his wife "my second best bed."

**President Andrew Johnson:** The first president to be impeached asked to be wrapped in an American flag, with a copy of the U.S. Constitution placed beneath his head.

**J. Paul Getty:** Requested a burial on the property of the Getty Museum in Malibu. However, his lawyers never applied for burial permits, so his remains had to be refrigerated and stored in a nearby mausoleum for *three years* until the necessary paperwork was completed. (Getty left his son J. Paul, Jr. "the sum of $500, and nothing else.")

**W. C. Fields:** Wanted a portion of his estate to be used for a "W. C. Fields College for orphan *white* boys and girls." (The request was never honoured.)

**P. T. Barnum:** Wanted to keep the Barnum name from dying with him...so he left his grandson, Clinton Seeley, $25,000—on the condition that he change his middle name to Barnum. Seeley did.

**Janis Joplin:** Asked friends to have a farewell party for her at her favourite pub, the Lion's Share, in California—and left $2,500 in her will to finance it.

**Albert Einstein:** No one knows what his last wishes were. On his deathbed, he said something in German to his nurse—but she didn't speak German.

# SIR DONALD BRADMAN

*He was Australia's greatest cricketer but how much do you really know about "The Don?"*

## ON THE REBOUND

Don Bradman was born in Cootamundra, NSW, on 27th August, 1908, and was the youngest of five children. When he was two years old, he and his family moved to Bowral in the Southern Highlands. His family were all keen cricketers and he developed his skills by throwing a golf ball against a small brick wall and hitting it on the rebound with a cricket stump. Sounds easy? Give it a try and you will see that it is no mean feat.

## TENNIS, SQUASH OR CRICKET?

The young Don excelled at ball sports and was also a champion tennis and squash player. He won the South Australian squash championships in 1939 in a five-set match that lasted over an hour. He was so exhausted by the time it ended that he never played competition squash again! He soon had to make a choice between tennis and cricket—thankfully for Australia (and the world!) he chose cricket.

## BRADMAN'S BIG BREAK

Bradman played his first cricket match when he was 11 years old and scored 55 runs at the Bowral oval that now carries his name. He scored his first century at the age of 12 and never looked back. Legend has it that his father took him to the Sydney Cricket Ground in 1921 to watch a test match and he turned to his father and said, "I shall never be satisfied until I play on this ground."

His big break came in 1928 when he was chosen to play in the test against England. It wasn't an auspicious start. He made 18 runs in the first innings and only one run in the second and, not surprisingly, was dropped from the second test. But things soon turned around for the young Don and in the third test he scored his first test century. He was never dropped again!

If you bury a traffic ticket, it will decompose in about four weeks.

## RECORD BREAKER

The more Don Bradman played the more records he broke. On the 1930 tour of England he scored 334, the highest test score at the time. He scored 452 for NSW against Queensland setting a new first-class innings score. He was only ever run out four times, only once after reaching the age of twenty-one. Of his 338 innings, 16 were ducks while 37 were upward of 200 runs. He scored a massive 211 centuries, played 80 tests matches and scored a whooping 6,996 test runs. He was so good that the English devised a method called "bodyline" in an attempt to curb his scoring. Fast bowlers bowled short-pitched bouncers that were aimed at the head and body. A group of short legs made up the field behind the stumps on the leg side and batsmen were forced to hit the ball to the fieldsmen or get hurt. It didn't slow Bradman down but it was soon declared illegal.

Bradman was Australia's captain between 1936 and 1948 during which time his side won 11 tests to England's three. During World War II, cricket was not played but Bradman emerged again at the end of the war to boost the morale of those affected. His 1948 team were virtually invincible and went on to become known as the "invincibles." It is still regarded today as one of Australia's best cricket teams.

Bradman ended his career in England in 1948. His test record of 99.94 was such that he needed to score only 4 runs in his last test innings to average 100—but he was bowled for a duck.

## BEACON OF HOPE

What was it about Bradman that inspired a nation? Australia was gripped by the Depression when he burst onto the cricket scene and people needed someone to inspire them. When Bradman was batting during a match, crowds would gather in cities around newspaper offices to watch his run tally on specially erected scoreboards. According to newspapers at the time, Bradman was "not only a beacon of hope for the unemployed, but a symbol of the fitfully-emerging Australian nation."

Bradman was knighted for services to cricket by the Governor General of Australia in 1949 but was always quoted as saying, "I would have preferred to remain just mister." He died on 25 February, 2001, at the age of 92.

# LUCKY STRIKES

*Some of the most important historical discoveries have been complete accidents. Here are four examples.*

**The Discoverer:** A peasant farmer digging a well
**What He Found:** Lost cities of Pompeii and Herculaneum
**Lucky Strike:** In 1709 a peasant who was digging in the area that had been destroyed when Mount Vesuvius erupted in 79 A.D. brought up several pieces of sculpted marble from statues and other objects. When word of his discovery spread, an Italian prince bought the land and began the first large-scale excavation of the site. Today more than three-quarters of ancient Pompeii has been uncovered; the rest remains buried underneath the modern city of Pompeii.

**The Discoverers:** Some quarrymen digging in a cave
**What They Found:** Neanderthal man
**Lucky Strike:** In 1856 workers excavating a cave in Germany's Neander Valley unearthed a human skeleton more than 100,000 years old. The remains provided some of the earliest evidence supporting the theory that modern humans evolved from apes.

**The Discoverers:** A group of French army engineers in Egypt
**What They Found:** The Rosetta stone
**Lucky Strike:** In July 1799, French army engineers working near the Egyptian town of Rosetta noted that a section of the wall they were about to demolish had both Greek script and hieroglyphics carved into it. On a hunch, they saved it. The stone turned out to be the first Egyptian hieroglyphic document ever found that was accompanied by a translation into a modern language. With the aid of this "Rosetta stone," scientists finally cracked the code of the hieroglyphics—which had been indecipherable for more than 1,300 years.

**The Discoverer:** A Bedouin boy looking for a lost goat
**What He Found:** The Dead Sea Scrolls
**Lucky Strike:** In 1947 a Bedouin boy searching for his goat on cliffs near the Dead Sea idly tossed a rock into a cave. He heard some pottery shatter. Investigating, he found a number of large clay jars containing hundreds of scrolls, many of which were early versions of the Bible at least 1,000 years older than any other known copy.

**The Roman emperor Nero played the bagpipes.**

# WHO WERE HARLEY & DAVIDSON?

*Here's the story behind two of the best-known names in motorcycle history.*

The first motorcycle was developed by Gottlieb Daimler, one of the founders of Daimler-Benz (maker of the Mercedes Benz) in Germany in 1885. Ten years later, two German brothers, Hildebrand and Alois Wolfmuller, began manufacturing motorcycles to sell to the public.

In 1901 news of the Wolfmullers' motorcycles reached the USA. Four young friends—21-year-old William Harley and the Davidson brothers, William, Walter, and Arthur—decided to build a small engine in the Davidsons' backyard and attach it to one of their bicycles. Legend has it that the engine was made from household castoffs, including a carburetor made of a tomato can.

After working out the bugs on their prototype, they built three more motorised bicycles in 1903 and began riding them around town. Their bikes were simple but reliable—one of them ultimately racked up 100,000 miles. People began asking if they were for sale.

The Harley-Davidson Motorcycle Company legally incorporated in 1909. More than 150 U.S. manufacturers eventually followed suit, but Harley-Davidson has outlasted them all. It's now the only American motorcycle company and sells more than 50,000 motorcycles a year.

## THE HARLEY IMAGE

In the mid-1980s, Harley's "rough rider" image began hurting sales. So the company took steps to change it. They encouraged Harley execs to wear white or red shirts to biker rallies to dispel the notion that Harley riders wear only black. They formed the Harley Owner's Group (H.O.G.) and the Ladies of Harley club to offset outlaw biker clubs. And they licenced the Harley name and logo to $100 million worth of products as diverse as wine coolers, cologne, and removable tattoos. Still, the company prefers customers with permanent Harley tattoos: "If you can persuade the customer to tattoo your name on their chest," one executive admits, "they probably will not switch brands."

# FREE ADVICE

*Why pay for advice when you can get it for free?*
*Here are some pearls of wisdom from some of the best.*

"Never kick a fresh turd on a hot day."
—**Harry S. Truman**

"Never say anything on the phone that you wouldn't want your mother to hear at the trial."
—**Sydney Biddle Barrows, the "Mayflower Madam"**

"You can get much further with a kind word and a gun than you can with a kind word alone."
—**Al Capone**

"Never trust a man unless you've got his pecker in your pocket."
—**Lyndon Baines Johnson**

"To succeed with the opposite sex, tell her you're impotent. She can't wait to disprove it."
—**Cary Grant**

"Sleeping alone, except under doctor's orders, does much harm. Children will tell you how lonely it is sleeping alone. If possible you should always sleep with someone you love. You recharge your mutual batteries free of charge."
—**Marlene Dietrich**

"Anything worth doing is worth doing slowly."
—**Gypsy Rose Lee**

"Don't try to take on a new personality; it doesn't work."
—**Richard Nixon**

"There's nothing to winning, really. That is, if you happen to be blessed with a keen eye, an agile mind, and no scruples whatsoever."
—**Alfred Hitchcock**

"Rise early. Work late. Strike oil."
—**J. Paul Getty**

"Don't let your mouth write a cheque that your tail can't cash."
—**Bo Diddley**

"Never eat at a place called Mom's. Never play cards with a man named Doc. And never lie down with a woman who's got more troubles than you."
—**Nelson Algren**

"What is worth doing is worth the trouble of asking someone to do it."
—**Ambrose Bierce**

# THE MYTH-ADVENTURES OF THOMAS EDISON

*Most people believe that Thomas Edison invented the lightbulb. He didn't. In fact, although he was a great inventor, there are a number of myths we commonly believe about Edison. Let's correct a few.*

**THE MYTH:** Edison was the father of electric light.
**THE TRUTH:** Electric lighting had been made practical decades before Edison began his famous research. Although incandescent light (the kind that's made by charging a wire filament until it glows white hot with energy) had not yet been perfected, by the 1870s *arc* lighting (light that's created when a spark "arcs" across two highly charged electric rods) was already in use in lighthouses and in the street lamps of some major cities.

The only problem was, they used too much energy and generated too much light (300 times as much as the household gas lights of the day) to be practical in homes. A less-powerful source of light was needed.

**THE MYTH:** Edison invented the incandescent lightbulb.
**THE TRUTH:** Incandescent lightbulbs had been around as a laboratory curiosity since 1823, and the first incandescent bulb was patented by Joseph Swan, an English inventor, in 1845.

By the time Edison began experimenting with lightbulbs in 1878, scientists around the world had already spent 55 years trying to perfect them. Edison wasn't trying to invent the lightbulb; he was trying to find a long-lasting *filament* that would make the lightbulb practical for the first time.

Incandescent lightbulbs operate on the principle of electrically heating a tiny filament until it glows white hot with energy, creating light in the process. The main problem at the time: most substances either melted or burned up when heated to such a high temperature, causing the bulb to burn out after only a few seconds.

Vacuum bulbs, which had some of their air removed, solved part of the problem; by reducing the amount of oxygen in the bulb, they lengthened the time it took for the filament to burn up. Even so, in 1878 even the best bulbs only lasted a short time...and *that*'s where Edison came in.

**THE MYTH:** He perfected the incandescent bulb by himself.
**THE TRUTH:** He failed on his own, and had to bring in experts. Edison thought the secret to building a better light bulb was to design a switch inside the bulb that would function like a heater thermostat, turning off the electricity when the filament got too hot, and turning it on again as soon as the filament cooled off—a process that would take only a fraction of a second.

Edison thought (and announced) that he could develop the switch in a few weeks—but he guessed wrong. It didn't work at all. More a scientific tinkerer than a scientist, his strategy had always been to blindly build prototype after prototype. He ignored work that other researchers had done and, as a result, often unwittingly repeated their failed experiments. That's what happened with the lightbulb. After a month of trying on his own, he threw in the towel and hired Francis Upton, a Princeton physicist, to help him.

As soon as Upton signed on, he had the lab's researchers study old patents, electrical journals, and the work of competing inventors to see what progress they had made. He also shifted the focus of the work from testing prototypes to methodically experimenting with raw materials (in order to understand their scientific properties and see which ones made the best filaments). Without this important shift in strategy, Edison's lab might never have developed a practical bulb at all...and certainly would have fallen behind competing labs.

**THE MYTH:** Edison made his critical breakthrough on October 21, 1879—known for many years as "Electric Light Day"—when he had kept a lightbulb lit for more than 40 hours.
**THE TRUTH:** The story is a fake. According to lab notes, nothing important happened on October 21—and it took another full year to produce a 40-hour bulb. The October 21 date was made up in late December 1879 by a newspaper reporter who needed a good story for the Christmas season.

# INNOVATIONS IN YOUR HOME

*You probably have some of these products around the house. Here's how they were created.*

C OPPERTONE SUNTAN LOTION
**Background:** In the early part of the 20th century, suntans were the mark of the lower classes—only laborers who worked in the sun, like field hands, had them. But as beaches became more popular and swimming costumes began revealing more skin, styles changed. Suntans became a status symbol that subtly demonstrated that a person was part of the leisure class.
**Innovation:** The first suntan lotion was invented in the 1940s by Dr. Benjamin Green, a physician who'd helped develop a sunblock for the military to protect soldiers from the sun. After the war, Green became convinced civilians would buy a milder version of his product—one that protected them from the sun while letting them tan. He called his lotion Coppertone, because it produced a copper-coloured tan on the people who used it.

## RUNNING SHOES WITH "WAFFLE" SOLES
**Background:** In the late 1950s, Phil Knight was a track star at the University of Oregon. His coach, Bill Bowerman, was obsessed with designing lightweight shoes for his runners. "He figured carrying one extra ounce for a mile," Knight recalls, "was equal to carrying an extra thousand pounds in the last 50 yards."
When Knight began his graduate work at the Stanford Business School, he wrote a research paper arguing that lightweight running shoes could be manufactured cheaply in Japan and sold at a low price in the United States. Then he actually went to Japan and signed a deal with a Japanese shoe company called Tiger. He and Bowerman each invested $500 to buy merchandise, and the Blue Ribbon Sports Company (later Nike) was founded.
**Innovation:** Bowerman developed Nike shoes to meet runners' needs. *Swoosh: The Story of Nike* describes the origin of the celebrated "waffle" shoe: "It occurred to Bowerman to make spikes

out of rubber…One morning while his wife was at church, Bowerman sat at the kitchen table staring at an open waffle iron he had seen hundreds of times. But now, for some reason, what he saw in the familiar pattern was square spikes. Square spikes could give traction to cross-country runners sliding down wet, muddy hills.

"Excited, Bowerman took out a mixture of liquid urethane… poured it into about every other hole of the waffle iron in…just the right pattern, and closed the lid to let it cook. Legend had it that he opened the waffle iron and there was the waffle sole that became Nike's first signature shoe. But what really happened that morning is that when he went to open the smelly mess, the waffle iron was bonded shut…[He] switched to a plaster mold after that."

## THERMOS JUGS
**Background:** In the 1890s, British physicist Sir James Dewar invented a glass, vacuum-walled flask that kept liquids hot longer than any other container in existence. Dewar never patented his invention; he considered it his gift to the scientific world.
**Innovation:** Reinhold Burger, a German glassblower whose company manufactured the flasks, saw their potential as a consumer product. Dewar's creations were too fragile for home use, so Burger built a sturdier version, with a shock-resistant metal exterior. He patented his design in 1903 and held a contest to find a name for the product. The contest was more of a publicity stunt than anything else, but Burger liked one entry so much that he used it: "Thermos," after the Greek word for heat.

## S.O.S. SOAP PADS
**Background:** In 1917 Edwin W. Cox was peddling aluminium cookware door-to-door in San Francisco. He wasn't making many sales, though; aluminum cookware was a new invention, and few housewives would even look at it.
**Innovation:** In desperation, Cox began offering a free gift—a steel-wool soap pad he made in his own kitchen by repeatedly soaking plain steel-wool pads in soapy water. (His wife used them in their own kitchen and loved them; she called them "S.O.S." pads, meaning Save Our Saucepans.) The gimmick worked—sort of. Housewives still weren't interested in the cookware, but they loved the soap pads. Eventually he dropped pots and pans and began selling soap pads full-time.

# WILL THAT BE ONE HUMP OR TWO?

*Camels may have a tough time passing through the eye of a needle, but they have no trouble at all populating the toughest terrain in the outback.*

**M**AKE WAY!
Hard to believe as it might be, koalas and kangaroos may soon lose their status as Australia's most well-known critters to a lumbering, rancorous beast with a lineage that goes back 40 million years—none other than the camel.

### DUTIFUL DROMEDARIES
Camels are no more native to Australia than the dung beetle is. The dung beetle was brought in solely to keep cattle droppings under control. Camels were more multipurpose. The first camels were imported into Australia in 1840 to assist in opening up the outback. That they did. They came in as pack animals, the usual lot in a camel's relationship with man. For years, camel caravans supplied goods to Alice Springs. Central Australia's Overland Telegraph Line was built on the humps of camels, so to speak, and, if not for camels in those early days, hardly a wagon load of wool would have been shipped from the railhead at Oodnadatta. Add to that, if not for the camels there may have been no railroad. They proved so useful in the railroad's contruction, when the line from Oodnadatta to Alice Springs was finally completed in 1929, the link was named the Ghan Express, after the Afghani cameleers.

Camels didn't just help open the outback for settlement. Beginning in 1880 and up until 1949, law and order in the outback as likely as not came riding in on a camel, thanks to the suggestion of a police inspector, B.C. Besley.

### CAMELS GO WALKABOUT
By the turn of the 20th century, the camel population was up to 7,000 and today, according to Peter Seidel of the Central Australian Camel Industry Association, may number a staggering 500,000, most

---

Vampire bats use rivers to navigate. They smell the animal blood in the water and follow it.

of them roaming wild. Why now wild? The simple answer: highways, byways, rail and air. Once other means of transportation had replaced them, the camels were released to the wild. Because camels will eat just about anything and can weigh in at 680 kg (1,500 lbs), perhaps the canny Australians thought the camels might decide to eat the rabbits that had become one of Australia's greatest pests.

## MOVEABLE FEASTS

For years the camels went their own way—eating, breeding and doing whatever else camels do when left to their own devices. Eventually, however, their increasing birthrates stimulated reassessment of their presence in the outback—that, and an eye to world food markets—Saudi consumption of camel meat had outstripped African supply and demand was growing. The Central Australia Camel Industry Association was formed and Australians were as quickly shipping camel meat to the United Arab Emirates as the New Zealanders were shipping lamb to North America.

## HOW WOULD YOU LIKE YOUR STEAK DONE?

The meat is said to look and taste like beef. It may not need marinating in battery acid, but it does need some diligent tenderizing or it's as tough as a barbecued boot. That in mind, the market remains steady. The Australian government's agriculture officials got into the act, putting out information sheets extolling the potential market to farmers. One government paper notes the value of the average camel landed in Victoria at about $600.

The time-consuming tasks of corralling them in the wild and then calming them enough to have them tolerate being shipped were not mentioned in the paper. Officials could hardly know that camels at the best of times will bite, kick and spit their cud on the unwary. They could hardly know that camels carry grudges. Those soft brown eyes belie a nastiness that often dominates their personality. Indeed, history records that John Horrocks, the man who brought the first camels to Australia back in 1840, died as a result of a run-in with one.

## FOOD FOR THOUGHT

Beyond a caravan to a meat locker, farmers found other uses for Australia's camels. Cattle ranchers now use them to buffet feed crops for their cattle, the notion being that camels eat the noxious weeds that inhibit growth of the feed crops. Down the road may come the issue of what happens when they've eaten all of the noxious weeds or decide the feed crops look more appetising.

## CAMELS' CLASS ACT
Never short on enterprise, an Australian camel breeder sold some racing camels to a sheik from Dubai. Talk about selling refrigerators to the Eskimos! The story made the news worldwide and suddenly everyone outside of Australia knew the island had camels. The fact of the matter is Australians have been racing camels since the early 1970s. Doubtless they had heard of the Turkish sport, camel wrestling, but being more used to crocodile wrestling, they decided racing the camels, in the manner of Arab royalty, would be more their own sporting style. Call it a touch of class.

## AT THE POST
In Australia, camel racing has now grown in popularity to the point that a formal racing circuit has been established with a prize pool of more than $100,000 a year. Crowds for the races easily reach 10,000 people. The big race, the Boulia Desert Sands run in Queensland, is the camel version of the Melbourne Cup, Kentucky Derby, Hambletonian, and Epsom Derby all rolled into one. The Boulia has a $30,000 purse. Not a bad return from a bunch of feral interlopers!

## NEW NATIONAL TREASURES
Camel kebabs and a day at the races—the star turns for the koalas and kangaroos may definitely be over.

\*     \*     \*     \*

## NOTABLE AUSTRALIAN QUOTES
"I'm an immensely shy and vulnerable woman. My husband has never seen me naked. Nor has he expressed the least desire to do so."

—Dame Edna Everage

Queensland was the first Australian state to introduce compulsory voting.

# DIRTY TRICKS

*Why should politicians have all the fun? You can pull off some
dirty tricks, too. This "dirty dozen" should inspire you to new lows.*

## POUND FOOLISH
Pay a visit to the local dog pound or RSPCA, wearing a chefs hat and an apron. Ask to see one of the kittens or puppies that are available for adoption. Pick it up and act as if you're weighing it, then set it down and ask to see one that's "a little more plump."

## SOCK IT TO 'EM
Tired of looking for that one sock you lost in the laundry? Pass on your anxieties: Stick the leftover sock in with someone else's wash-load. Let them look for the missing sock for awhile.

## SOMETHING FISHY
If you have a (clean) aquarium, toss some thin carrot slices into the tank. Later when you have guests over, grab the slices out of the tank and eat them quickly. If you do it quick enough, your victims will assume you're eating a goldfish. (If you accidentally grab a *real* goldfish, toss it back in, grab the carrot slice, and complain to your victims that the first fish was "too small.")

## LOST YOUR MARBLES?
Pry the hubcap off a friend's car, drop two or three steel ball bearings inside, and replace the hubcap. Then watch them drive off. The ball bearings will make an enormous racket for a few seconds, until they become held in place by centrifugal force. They'll stay silent until the victim applies the brakes, and then they'll shake loose again.

## TV GUIDE
Got a friend who's a couch potato? Carefully remove the cover of their *TV Guide* (or weekly newspaper TV schedule), then glue it to an older schedule, so the TV listings are wrong. It'll drive a true TV fanatic crazy.

## RETURN TO SENDER
Embarrass a coworker by buying a magazine they would *never* read (*High Times*, *Guns & Ammo*, and *Easy Rider* work well), and glue the mailing label from one of their regular magazines to the cover. Then stick it in the cafeteria or restroom where other coworkers can see it.

## PRACTICE DRILLS
The next time you visit the dentist, scream really loud the minute you get seated in the dentist's chair. You'll send the patients in the waiting room running for cover.

## MAD HATTER
If your friend wears a favourite hat, find out the manufacturer and buy two or more others of varying sizes. Then periodically switch them with your friend's hat. He'll be convinced his head is changing sizes. (Another hat trick: Fill your victim's hat with baby powder.)

## AT A WEDDING
If you're a close friend of the groom, paint a message on the sole of his shoes (the raised part near the heel that doesn't touch the ground) without telling him. When he kneels at the altar, the message will be visible for everyone to see.

## PARK PLACE
The next time you're walking through a crowded parking lot, pull out your car keys and act as if you're looking for your car. Walk in between cars across the rows; motorists looking for a parking space will race to keep up with you.

## PARTY IDEA
Using superglue, glue someone's drink to the bar or to a table.

## WAKE UP CALL
Gather as many alarm clocks as you can find and hide them in different places in your victim's room. Set one alarm so it goes off very early in the morning, and set the others so they go off every five minutes afterward. Guaranteed to make your victim an early riser.

**Big splash: Most hippopotamuses are born under water.**

# WILDE ABOUT OSCAR

*Wit and wisdom from Oscar Wilde, one of the 19th century's most popular—and controversial—writers.*

"The only way to get rid of temptation is to yield to it."

"It is better to have a permanent income than to be fascinating."

"The soul is born old but grows young. That is the comedy of life. And the body is born young and grows old. That is life's tragedy."

"Seriousness is the only refuge of the shallow."

"Children begin by loving their parents. After a time they judge them. Rarely, if ever, do they forgive them."

"There's no sin...except stupidity."

"Experience is the name everyone gives to their mistakes."

"Formerly we used to canonise our heroes. The modern method is to vulgarise them. Cheap editions of great books may be delightful, but cheap editions of great men are absolutely detestable."

"All women become like their mothers. That is their tragedy. No man does. That's his."

"Society often forgives the criminal; it never forgives the dreamer."

"It is better to be beautiful than to be good, but it is better to be good than to be ugly."

"The only portraits in which one believes are portraits where there is very little of the sitter and a very great deal of the artist."

"The youth of America is their oldest tradition. It has been going on now for three hundred years."

"One should always play fairly—when one has the winning cards."

"Discontent is the first step in the progress of a man or a nation."

"The well-bred contradict other people. The wise contradict themselves."

The story of Cinderella has been made into a movie 58 times.

# A HANDY GUIDE TO THE END OF THE WORLD (Part I)

*Most cultures have a tradition that predicts the end of the world...and many of their prophecies could apply to our era. The good news is that they're not all fire and brimstone. Here are three examples from Eastern cultures, reprinted from* Uncle John's Indispensable Guide to the Year 2000.

**B**UDDHISM
**Background:** Founded in the sixth century B.C. in India. One of its primary teachings is observance of the 10 moral precepts (standards of conduct).
**Signs the End Is Near:** According to the Buddha in the *Sutta-pitaka* (Buddhist scriptures and sermons):
• The 10 moral courses of conduct will disappear...and people will follow the 10 *immoral* courses instead—"theft, violence, murder, lying, evil-speaking, adultery, abusive and idle talk, covetousness and ill will, wanton greed, and perverted lust." Poverty "will grow great."
• "The Dharma [universal law, or truth] will have disappeared from the world...as a counterfeit Dharma arises."
**When the World Ends:** Good news! A new Buddha "by the name Maitreya" will arise. This new Buddha will "replace the counterfeit Dharma of materialism and selfishness...and give new teachings to solve the social problems of the world."

## ZOROASTRIANISM
**Background:** A Persian religion based on the belief that the universe is filled with good and evil spirits. There will be an ultimate battle between these forces, and evil will be eliminated.
**Signs the End Is Near:** The *Zand-i Vohuman Yasht* predicts:
• "(At the) end of thy tenth hundredth winter...the sun is more unseen and more spotted; the year, month, and day are shorter; and the earth is more barren; and the crop will not yield the seed;

and men...become more deceitful and more given to vile practices; they have no gratitude."
• "Honorable wealth will all proceed to those of perverted faith...and a dark cloud makes the whole sky night...and [it will rain] more noxious creatures than water."
**When the World Ends:** Saoshyant, the Man of Peace, comes to battle the forces of evil. "The resurrection of the dead will take place—the dead will rise...the world will be purged by molten metal, in which the righteous will wade as if through warm milk, and the evil will be scalded."

At the end of the battle, the Final Judgement of all souls begins. Sinners will be punished (apparently for 3 days), then forgiven, and humanity will be made immortal and free from hunger, thirst, poverty, old age, disease, and death. The world "will be made perfect once again."

## HINDUISM
**Background:** "Hindu" is a Western term for the religious beliefs of numerous sects in India dating back to 1500 B.C. Their goal: "liberation from the cycle of rebirth and suffering."
**Signs the End Is Near:** The world falls into chaos and degradation; there's an increase in perversity, greed, conflict. According to Cornelia Dimmit's translation of the *Sanskrit PurAnas:*
• "When deceit, falsehood, lethargy, sleepiness, violence, despondency, grief, delusion, fear, and poverty prevail...when men, filled with conceit, consider themselves equal with Brahmins...that is the *Kali Yuga* [present era]."
**When the World Ends:** A savior (avatar) will appear. "The Lord will again manifest Himself as the Kalki Avatar...He will establish righteousness upon the earth and the minds of the people will become pure as crystal....As a result the Sat or Krta Yuga [golden age] will be established."

\*　　\*　　\*　　\*

## NOTABLE AUSTRALIAN QUOTES

"Sport is a loathsome and dangerous pursuit."
—**Barry Humphries**

Spotted skunks do handstands before they spray.

# IT'S A MIRACLE!

*The tabloids are full of stories of people who see images of Jesus in everything from a lima bean to a smudge on a car window. Could they be real? Here are the details of five sightings. Judge for yourself.*

**T**he Sighting: Jesus in a forkful of spaghetti, Stone Mountain, Georgia
**Revelation:** Joyce Simpson, an Atlanta fashion designer, was pulling out of a petrol station in Stone Mountain when she saw the face of Jesus in a forkful of spaghetti on a billboard advertising Pizza Hut's pasta menu. Simpson says at the time she was trying to decide whether to stay in the church choir or quit and sing professionally. (She decided to stick with the choir.)
**Impact:** Since the sighting, dozens of other people called Pizza Hut to say that they, too, had seen someone in the spaghetti. But not all the callers agreed that the man in the spaghetti was Jesus; some saw Doors singer Jim Morrison; others saw country star Willie Nelson.

**The Sighting:** Jesus in a tortilla, Lake Arthur, New Mexico
**Revelation:** On October 5, 1977, Maria Rubio was making burritos for her husband when she noticed a 3-by-3-inch face of Jesus burned into the tortilla she was cooking. Local priests argued that the image was only a coincidence, but the Rubio family's faith was unshaken. They saved the tortilla, framed it, and built a shrine for it in their living room.
**Impact:** To date more than 11,000 people have visited it.

**The Sighting:** Jesus on a soybean oil tank, Fostoria, Ohio
**Revelation:** Rita Rachen was driving home from work along Ohio Route 12 one night in 1986 when she saw the image of Jesus with a small child on the side of an Archer Daniels Midland Company oil tank containing soybean oil. She screamed, "Oh, my Lord, my God," and nearly drove off the side of the road, but recovered enough to continue driving.

**Impact:** She spread the word to other faithful, and the soybean tank became a popular pilgrimage site. (Since then, however, the oil tank has been repainted. Jesus is no longer visible.)

**The Sighting:** Jesus on the side of a refrigerator, Estill Springs, Tennessee
**Revelation:** When Arlene Gardner bought a new refrigerator, she had the old one dragged out onto her front porch. A few nights later, she noticed several of her neighbours were standing around staring at the old fridge. They told her that the reflection from a neighbour's porch light had created an image of Jesus on the side of the fridge. Gardner took a look and agreed.
**Impact:** Soon thousands of faithful were making pilgrimages to the site—so many, in fact, that Gardner's neighbours had their porch light disconnected, so Jesus could be seen no more. (*Note:* Not everyone agreed that Jesus had really made an appearance; as one local skeptic explained to a reporter, "When the good Lord comes, he won't come on a major appliance.")

**The Sighting:** A 900-foot Jesus at the City of Faith, Tulsa, Oklahoma
**Revelation:** This vision—one of the most publicised Jesus sightings ever—came to famed televangelist Oral Roberts on May 25, 1980…but he inexplicably kept it secret for over five months. Then one day he shared his vision and explained what he'd seen to reporters: "He reached down, put His hand under the City of Faith (a city Roberts had built), lifted it, and said to me, 'See how easy it is for me to lift it?'"

On January 4, 1987, Roberts told his followers God had appeared again, this time demanding $8 million. Roberts warned that if the money wasn't sent in by March 31, "God would call me home."
**Impact:** Roberts's followers coughed up $9.1 million.

\* \* \* \*

### Royal Gossip

Queen Elizabeth likes to do crossword puzzles. She also likes to read mysteries by Dick Francis and play games like charades.

# WHAT REALLY HAPPENED IN 1000 A.D.?

*Remember when the clock ticked down to 2000, some people began to lose control? Panicky crowds stampeded grocery stores? Isn't that what happened in the last millennium? Maybe not.*

## THE STORY

According to popular lore, Europeans in the year 999 A.D. were even more panicked about the apocalypse than people are today. As the year ticked away, they gave away or sold their possessions, set their animals loose, left their homes, and huddled in churches to pray for salvation.

## A DETAILED HISTORY

In his book *Doomsday: 1999 A.D.*, Charles Berlitz describes "the year of doom" in detail.

> "As the year 999 neared its end a sort of mass hysteria took hold of Europe. All forms of activity became affected by the specter of impending doom…Men forgave each other their debts, husbands and wives confessed suspected and unsuspected infidelities to each other…poachers proclaimed their unlawful poachings to the lords of manors…
>
> As the year rolled on toward its end, commerce dwellings were neglected and let fall into ruin…There was a wave of suicides as people sought to punish themselves in advance of Doomsday or simply could not stand the pressure of waiting for Judgement Day….
>
> As the night of December 31 approached, the general frenzy reached new heights. In Rome, the immense Basilica of St. Peter's was crowded for the midnight mass which in the belief of many might be the last mass they would ever attend on earth.

---

**37% of Canadians think Canada will become part of the U.S. in the next 50 years.**

## MEANWHILE, IN ROME...

Frederick H. Martens writes in *The Story of Human Life* that there was a dramatic New Year's Eve climax at St. Peter's:

> "Pope Sylvester II stood before the high altar. The church was overcrowded, all in it lay on their knees. The silence was so great that the rustling of the Pope's white sleeves as he moved about the altar could be heard. And there was still another sound... that seemed to measure out the last minutes of the earth's thousand years of existence between towns and cities was largely interrupted; since the coming of Christ—the door of the church sacristy stood open, and the audience heard the regular, uninterrupted tick, tick, tock of the great clock which hung within....
>
> The midnight mass had been said, and a deathly silence fell. The audience waited....Pope Sylvester said not a word....The clock kept on ticking....Like children afraid of the dark, all those in the church lay with their faces to the ground, and did not venture to look up. The sweat of terror ran from many an icy brow, and knees and feet which had fallen asleep lost all feeling. Then, suddenly—the clock stopped ticking! Among the congregation the beginning of a scream of terror began to form in many a throat. Stricken dead by fear, several bodies dropped on the stone floor.

## WHEW!

Berlitz picks up the narrative again: "Then the clock began to strike. It struck one, two, three, four. It struck twelve. The twelfth stroke echoed out, and a deathly silence still reigned! Then it was that Pope Sylvester turned around, and with the proud smile of a victor stretched out his hands in blessing over the heads of those who filled the church....Men and women fell in each other's arms, laughing and crying and exchanging the kiss of peace. Thus ended the thousandth year after the birth of Christ."

# FROG CULTURE IN OZ? FAIR DINKUM!

*What have an escaped Australian convict and a bunch of French explorers got to do with a trumpet which blows at dawn, a ballet class and a gooey chocolate pastry? Read on to find out.*

"**YA GOT BUCKLEY'S, MATE.**"
On hearing this, the un-initiated visitor may quail in fear believing he has just been diagnosed with a particularly nasty disease, or jump for joy thinking he's won his fortune. Like so many Australian slang expressions, it gives no inkling of what it means.

In fact, "ya got Buckley's," or its longer version, "you've got two chances mate, Buckley's and none," means that you have a very small chance of success in whatever it is you're undertaking, and it will be a case of pure good luck rather than talent if you manage to pull it off.

The saying comes from the exploits of the convict William Buckley, who arrived in Victoria in 1803, and was part of a group sent south to settle an open, isolated spot called Sullivan Bay, on a treacherous inlet with little drinking water or timber. The settlement was doomed from the start. By Christmas, Buckley and five other convicts had escaped in a little boat, headed for Sydney, or so they thought, until they realised they'd lost their bearings and weren't going anywhere! His companions gave themselves up, but not William Buckley.

Buckley befriended a local Aboriginal tribe, the Wathaurong people, who accepted him as one of their own and taught him how to live off the land. Meanwhile, the white settlement at Sullivan Bay was abandoned.

Thirty-two years later, a group of graziers brought their sheep to Victoria in search of pastures. One night while they were relaxing in their camp, a man dressed in animal skins and carrying a spear appeared, and addressed them in rasping, halting English. It was William Buckley.

He assisted the new settlers by acting as a guide and an interpreter in their dealings with the Aborigines. Eventually Buckley was pardoned by the governor in 1835.

## POMS VS FROGS

William Buckley never knew it, but it was thanks to a bunch of French explorers that his life turned out the way it did. What is the connection? Simply this. The English were scared stiff the French might have designs on their new colony. The settlement Buckley was sent to, Sullivan Bay, was one of several set up hastily by the English in case the French explorers got there first! Their fears were not unfounded. France undertook no less than five voyages of exploration to the southern seas between 1766 and 1840.

Captain Lapérouse arrived a week after the First Fleet in Botany Bay in January 1788. The Sydney suburb of La Pérouse was named in his honour. Commander Nicolas Baudin, sent to explore the southern land for the glory of Napoleon, came across Matthew Flinders in the wild seas south of the continent at Encounter Bay in April 1802. Captain Jules S. Dumont d'Urville made several visits to Sydney and Hobart between 1824 and 1840, and was always well received.

Tasmania's east coast is a who's who of French explorers of the time: *d'Entrecasteaux* Channel, Capes *Forestier, Baudin, Bougainville* and *Sonnerat*, and even an *Ile des Phoques* (Isle of Seals).

## THE FRENCH RESISTANCE?

The English, friendly though they were, did not want the population of their Great Southern Land wearing *berets*, eating *escargots* or producing *parfumerie très chic*, so they sent groups (one including William Buckley) scurrying over land and sea, to settle in the remotest outposts, so that the Union Jack fluttered all over the country. The French got the message.

Not a cannon was fired, but a peaceful invasion took place anyway. The ANZACS who served in France in World War I woke every morning in the stinking trenches of the Western Front to the mournful trumpet sound of the "revelly"—a mispronounced version of the French for "wake up," *réveillez*. Back at home, ninety years later, schoolboys at cadet camp and soldiers on training exercises still hear it, while littlies in ballet classes wonder what to do when the teacher utters "braba" (arms low, for the words are *bras bas*), or "pleeay" (bend, *pliez*).

## FROGS IN OZ? OH LÀ LÀ!

*L' infiltration française* continued in the 1960s, when we began to adapt what we loved most from French cuisine and make it inimitably our own. Only in Australia could you find chocolate *éclairs* filled not with the delicate *crème pâtissière* of their Parisian counterparts, but with the unmistakable white sugary goo that can also be found in the archetypal Oz delight, the cream bun. Later, genuine *croissants* appeared, slathered with thick slices of melted Australian Coon cheese and ham.

Now, in a new millennium, and a much more sophisticated Australia, we look down our collective *nez* at the shortcomings of our previous generations. We eat *cuisine minceur* in *brasseries* and spend hours at pavement *cafés*, follow the fashions of *la haute couture*, and are quite *au fait* with culinary terms such as *purée* and *coulis*. Indeed, many of our number are actually moving to *la belle France* to live, and writing best-sellers about their experiences! *Oh là là!*

If the French had not been snooping around *la Nouvelle Hollande* back in 1803, William Buckley might never have gone to Sullivan Bay, might never have escaped and survived—and we might never have been able to say, "Frog Culture in Oz? Ya got Buckley's, mate."

But then, that's not really fair dinkum—eh!

\*　　\*　　\*　　\*

## NOTABLE QUOTES

"There are no foreign lands. It is the traveller only who is foreign."

**—Robert Louis Stevenson (1850–1894)**

"Every exit is an entry somewhere else."

**—Tom Stoppard**

"It's very beautiful over there!"

**—Thomas Edison on his death**

"I am just going outside and I may be some time."

**—Captain Lawrence Oates**

# "MADAM, I'M ADAM"

*A palindrome is a word or phrase that spells the same thing backward and forward. Here are the best that BRI members have sent us. Try your own. If you come up with a good one, send it to us and we'll publish it in the next edition.*

## TWO-WORD PHRASES

No, Son.

Sue us!

Pots nonstop.

Dump mud.

Go, dog!

Stack cats.

Worm row.

Party trap.

## LONGER PHRASES

Wonder if Sununu's fired now.

Never odd or even.

Ed is on no side.

Step on no pets.

Rise to vote, sir!

Naomi, did I moan?

"Desserts," I stressed.

Spit Q-Tips.

Roy, am I mayor?

A car, a man, a maraca.

Are we not drawn onward, we few, drawn onward to new era?

A man, a plan, a canal...

Panama!

Live not on evil.

If I had a Hi-Fi...

A slut nixes sex in Tulsa.

Put Eliot's toilet up.

Pull up, Bob, pull up!

Pa's a sap.

Ma is as selfless as I am.

Poor Das is a droop.

A Toyota's a Toyota.

If I had a hi-fi...

Max, I stay away at six a.m.

Man, Oprah's sharp on a.m.

## NONSENSE PHRASES

Did mom poop? Mom did.

We panic in a pew.

Yawn a more Roman way.

Mr. Owl ate my metal worm.

A dog! A panic in a pagoda!

Cigar? Toss it in a can, it is so tragic!

Did I draw Della too tall, Edward? I did?

Gate-man sees name, garage-man sees name tag.

No, Mel Gibson is a casino's big lemon.

---

**Riding hazard:** 40% of people killed from falling off a horse are drunk.

# WHO WROTE SHAKESPEARE'S PLAYS?

*We include this to inspire you to add the Bard's writing to your bathroom reading. BRI members have a lofty image to uphold, after all.*

William Shakespeare authored 36 plays, 154 sonnets, and 2 narrative poems between 1588 and 1616. Though his works are among the most influential literature of Western civilization, little is known about the man himself—and no manuscripts written in his own hand have ever been found.
• This fact has inspired speculation by pseudoscholars, cranks, and English society snobs that Shakespeare—the commoner son of a glovemaker—couldn't have been intelligent or educated enough to write "his own" works.
• Why would the real author have given the credit to Shakespeare? One theory: Many of the plays dealt with members of the English royal family and were politically controversial. It may have been too dangerous for the real author to take credit for the radical ideas they contained.
• The *real* William Shakespeare, according to this theory, was a third-rate actor, playwright, and theatre gadfly who was more than happy to take credit for work he was not capable of producing.
• Whatever the case, more than 5,000 other authors (including Queen Elizabeth I and a Catholic pope) have been proposed as the real Shakespeare. Here are five of the more popular candidates:

**1. SIR FRANCIS BACON.** An English nobleman, trusted advisor to Queen Elizabeth I, and renowned writer, scholar, and philosopher.
**Background:** The Sir Francis Bacon-as-Shakespeare theory was popularised in 1852 by Delia Bacon (no relation), a 41-year-old Connecticut spinster who detested William Shakespeare, referring to him as "a vulgar, illiterate...deer poacher" and "stableboy."

---

Couch potato fact: 80% of people who own VCRs don't know how to program them.

- Bacon believed that Shakespeare had been buried with documents that would prove her theory. She spent much of her life struggling to get permission to open the crypt. She never succeeded and died insane in 1859.

**Evidence:** According to some theorists, a number of Shakespeare's plays demonstrate "profound legal expertise." But Shakespeare was not a lawyer—and according to one theorist, "A person of Shakespeare's known background could not have gained such knowledge." Sir Francis Bacon, on the other hand, was so gifted as a lawyer that he eventually became Lord Chancellor of England.

- Shakespeare's plays also show a strong familiarity with continental Europe, though there's no evidence the Bard himself ever left England. Bacon, an aristocrat, was well travelled.
- Bacon had a reason for hiding his authorship: In the 17th century, poetry and playwriting was considered frivolous and beneath the dignity of a nobleman. Bacon may have kept his identity a secret to protect his reputation (as well as his standing in the royal court, since a number of the plays dealt with English monarchs). So he paid William Shakespeare, a nobody, to take the credit.

**2. CHRISTOPHER MARLOWE.** An accomplished playwright of the 1500s. Author of such works as *Edward the Second* and *The Tragical History of Doctor Faustus*, Marlowe was considered as talented as Shakespeare by audiences of the day.

**Background:** Unlike most candidates for the Shakespearean crown, Marlowe was already dead by the time most of Shakespeare's plays were written; according to the official story, he was stabbed to death during a drunken brawl in a pub in 1593. Marlowe theorists disagree—they believe he *faked* his death:

- Marlowe had a reputation for rowdiness, was an alleged homosexual and atheist, and may have even been an English spy.
- His wild life and radical beliefs eventually got him into trouble, and in 1593 a warrant was put out for his arrest. Marlowe theorists believe that his alleged lover, Sir Thomas Walsingham, staged the pub fight, had someone else murdered, and then bribed the coroner to report that Marlowe was the man who'd been killed. Marlowe escaped to France to continue his writing career, and Sir Thomas hired Shakespeare to publish—under his own name— the manuscripts Marlowe sent back from France.

The phrase "It's Greek to me" first appeared in Shakespeare's *Julius Caesar*.

**Evidence:** Though the theory was first suggested by W. G. Zeigler, a California lawyer, in 1895, it wasn't until the early 1900s that an Ohio professor, Thomas C. Mendenhall, checked to see if the claims were credible. He spent months analysing more than 400,000 individual words from Shakespeare's plays and comparing them with words from Marlowe's known works.

• His stunning conclusion: The two men had similar writing styles, and for both Marlowe and the Bard, "the word of greatest frequency was the four-letter word." (One problem with the research: Mendenhall studied *contemporary* editions of Shakespeare's plays, which spelled many words differently than they had appeared in the original plays.)

• Other researchers dug up Sir Thomas's grave to see if it held any clues to whether Marlowe really was a homosexual. The search turned up nothing—not even Sir Thomas.

**3. EDWARD DE VERE, 17th Earl of Oxford.** Though none of his plays survive, de Vere was an accomplished author in his own right. He's also been described as a "hot-tempered youth, a spendthrift, and a philanderer specialising in the queen's maids-of-honour."
**Background:** J. Thomas Looney, father of the de Vere-as-Shakespeare theory, was an English schoolmaster and Bard buff in the early 1900s. Over time he came to believe that Shakespeare's descriptions of Italy in *The Merchant of Venice* could only have been made by someone who'd actually been there, and Shakespeare had not. Looney began researching the lives of other writers of Shakespeare's day to see if he could find the real author. He eventually settled on de Vere.
**Evidence:** De Vere had travelled abroad. After emitting "an unfortunate flatulence in the presence of the Queen," he was compelled to leave England and spent several years travelling in Europe. During his travels he spent a great deal of time in Italy and gained the knowledge Looney alleges he needed to write *The Merchant of Venice* and other plays.

• According to Looney, many of de Vere's relatives had names that were similar to the names of characters in Shakespeare's plays—too many relatives to be a coincidence.

**4. SIR WALTER RALEIGH.** Raleigh, an "author, adventurer, and explorer," was the founding father of the state of Virginia and, like Bacon, was popular in Queen Elizabeth's court. But he fell out of favour when James I took the throne, and was beheaded in 1618.
**Background:** George S. Caldwell, an Australian, first advanced the theory that Raleigh wrote Shakespeare's plays in 1877. The theory later became popular with U.S. Senator Albert J. Beveridge, who made speeches supporting it in the 1890s. In 1914 Henry Pemberton, Jr., a Philadelphia writer, gave the theory new life in his book *Shakespeare and Sir Walter Raleigh.*
**Evidence:** Raleigh was familiar with the traditions of the royal court and the military, which were central themes in a number of Shakespeare's plays.
• Unlike Shakespeare, who was not known for being emotional, Raleigh was a passionate man, much like the characters in Shakespeare's plays.

**5. MICHEL ANGELO FLORIO.** Florio, an Italian, was a defrocked Franciscan monk who converted to Protestantism. A Calvinist, he lived in exile in England for much of his life. His son John Florio most likely knew William Shakespeare; many historians speculate that the two men were close friends.
**Background:** In 1925 Santi Paladino, a writer, visited a fortuneteller and was told that he would someday shock the world with an amazing discovery. Within four years he had published his book *Un Italiano Autore Delle Opere Shakespeariane*, which claimed that Michel Angelo Florio was the true author of Shakespeare's works.
**Evidence:** Again, the main body of circumstantial evidence is that Florio had an intimate knowledge of Italy that Shakespeare could not have possessed. Florio-as-Shakespearists believe that the elder Florio, whose experience as an exile made him leery of publishing in his own name, wrote Shakespeare's plays in *Italian*, had his son translate them into English, and paid Shakespeare to publish them under his own name.
• Shakespeare's supporters disagree, arguing that the Bard wrote the plays himself, but got a lot of his information on Italy from the Florios, who were writers themselves and owned a large library of Italian books. Shakespeare may have even borrowed from some of the Florios' writings, they say, but there's no hard evidence anyone other than Shakespeare wrote his plays.

Benito Mussolini was a schoolteacher before he went into politics.

# CARNIVAL TRICKS

*Do the booths at carnivals and travelling circuses seem rigged to you?
According to Matthew Gryczan in his book* Carnival Secrets, *many of them are. Here are some booths to look out for—
and some tips on how to beat them.*

**The Booth:** "Ring a Bottle"
**The Object:** Throw a small ring over the neck of a soft-drink bottle from a distance of about five feet.
**How It's Rigged:** The game isn't rigged, but it doesn't have to be—it's almost impossible to win.
• In 1978 researchers stood six feet away from a grouping of 100 bottles and tossed 7,000 rings at it. They recorded 12 wins—an average of one shot in every 583 throws. What's more, the researchers found that all of the 12 winning tosses were ricochets; not a single *aimed* shot had gone over the bottles. In fact, the light, plastic rings wouldn't stay on the bottles even if dropped from a height of three inches directly over the neck of the bottle.
**How to Win:** It appears that the only way to win is to throw two rings over a bottle neck at the same time. However, carnival operators usually won't let you throw more than one ring at a time.

**The Booth:** "The Bushel Basket"
**The Object:** Toss softballs into a bushel basket from a distance of about six feet.
**How It's Rigged:** The bottom of the basket is connected to the baseboard in such a way that it has a lot of spring to it, so the ball will usually bounce out.
• In addition, carnies sometimes use balls that weigh as little as 114 grams (4 ounces), rather than the 175-gram (6-¼-ounce) minimum weight of an official softball. The lighter ball makes the game harder to win.
• Some carnies use a heavier ball when demonstrating the game or to give to players for a practice shot. Then, when play begins, they switch to a lighter ball that's harder to keep in the basket.
**How to Win:** Ask to use the same ball the carny used.

**Most earthworms like to eat ice cream.**

- The best throw is to aim high, so that the ball enters the basket from a vertical rather than a horizontal angle. The worst place to put the ball is directly on the bottom of the basket.
- Aim for the lip or the sides of the basket. If the rules prohibit these shots, the game will be tough to win.

**The Booth:** "Shoot Out the Dots"
**The Object:** Using soft graphite bullets, shoot out all the red in three to five dots printed on a paper target.
**How It's Rigged:** The bullet, called an "arcade load," is discharged from the rifle barrel in little chunks. Propelled by a low-powder charge that ranges from a .22 cap to a .22-short, the chunks barely penetrate the target.

- Even if the bullet remained intact, it would not be able to take out all of the red of the .22 calibre-sized dots, because its diameter ranges from .15 calibre to .177 calibre. Besides, the chunks of graphite *tear* the paper target instead of punching out a clean hole. So there's always some red left on the target, even with a direct hit.
**How to Win:** In many cases, winning is impossible. During a trial, one carny testified that she'd never had one winner in 365,000 plays over five and a half years—despite the fact the game was frequented by U.S. naval personnel with experience in shooting guns.

**The Booth:** "The Milk Can"
**The Object:** Toss a softball into a 45-litre (10-gallon) milk can.
**How It's Rigged:** Most carnival cans aren't ordinary dairy cans. For the midway game, a concave piece of steel is welded to the rim of the can's opening, reducing the size of the hole the ball must travel through to anything from 17 cm (6½ inches) down to 11 cm (4⅜ inches) in diameter.

- At one game played at a state fair in 1987, there were 15 wins out of a total of 1,279 tries—one win for every 86 balls thrown.
**How to Win:** Carnies say the best way to win is to give the ball a backspin and try to hit the back edge of the can.
- Another way: Toss the ball as high as you can, so that it drops straight into the hole. This isn't always easy; operators often hang prizes from the rafters of the booth to make high tosses difficult.

# PUTTING THE 'O' BACK INTO OZZIE!

*What about the great Australian "o"? Australians have managed to create an entire lexicon out of adding this unassuming letter to unsuspecting words. Check out these words!*

| | |
|---|---|
| **aggro** | aggressive |
| **ambo** | an ambulance officer, or an ambulance |
| **ammo** | ammunition |
| **arvo** | the afternoon |
| **avo** | avocado |
| **barro** | embarrassing |
| **berko** | bersek |
| **biffo** | a blow or punch |
| **bizzo** | business |
| **blotto** | completely drunk |
| **bozo** | an idiot |
| **cammo** | a military camouflage pattern |
| **chiro** | a chiropractor |
| **combo** | a combination or blend |
| **compo** | compensation for injury |
| **demo** | a demonstration |
| **doco** | a documentary |
| **drongo** | a stupid person |
| **evo** | evening |
| **exo** | excellent |
| **fabo** | great, fantastic |
| **femmo** | a feminist |
| **garbo** | someone who collects the garbage |
| **goodo** | an exclamation of pleasure |
| **gyno** | gynaecologist |
| **impro** | improvisation |
| **info** | information |
| **Jacko** | a kookaburra |
| **journo** | journalist |
| **kiddo** | a young person |

---

The first intercolonial cricket match was held in 1856—NSW v Victoria. NSW won.

| | |
|---|---|
| **lammo** | a lamington |
| **lingo** | language |
| **milko** | someone who sells milk |
| **neato** | excellent |
| **nutso** | crazy, mad |
| **osteo** | an osteopath |
| **physio** | a physiotherapist |
| **pongo** | smelly |
| **psycho** | a psychopath |
| **pubbo** | a child from a public school |
| **rego** | vehicle registration |
| **retro** | a style from a previous era |
| **righto** | indicating agreement |
| **salvos** | Salvation Army |
| **sarvo** | this afternoon |
| **sambo** | a sandwich |
| **servo** | a service station |
| **smoko** | a rest from work |
| **troppo** | mentally disturbed |
| **unco** | uncoordinated, clumsy |
| **vego** | vegetarian |
| **wacko** | eccentric |
| **wino** | someone who drinks too much wine |
| **yucko** | repulsive |
| **yobbo** | an aggressive, surly person |
| **yummo** | having a great taste, delicious |
| **zippo** | nought, nothing |

\*     \*     \*     \*

## DID YOU KNOW?

The brand name might be Speedos, but the swimming costumes worn by lifesavers and other Australian males are on the linguistic move. The latest slang term for these particularly Australian swimmers is 'budgie smugglers.'

The most watched TV program on Australian TV in 2002 was the 'National IQ Test.'

# THEY WENT THAT-A-WAY

*Malcolm Forbes wrote a fascinating book about the deaths of famous people. Here are some of the weirdest stories he found.*

## FRANCIS BACON
**Claim to Fame:** One of the great minds of the late 16th century. A statesman, philosopher, writer, and scientist. Some people believe he's the real author of Shakespeare's plays (see page 74).
**How He Died:** Stuffing snow into a chicken.
**Postmortem:** One afternoon in 1625, Bacon was watching a snowstorm. He began wondering if snow might be as good a meat preservative as salt…and decided to find out. With a friend, he rode through the storm to a nearby peasant's cottage, bought a chicken, and had it butchered. Then, standing outside in the cold, he stuffed the chicken with snow to freeze it. The chicken never froze, but Bacon did. He caught a serious chill and never recovered. He died from bronchitis a few weeks later.

## WILLIAM HENRY HARRISON
**Claim to Fame:** Ninth president of the United States; elected in 1841 at the age of 67.
**How He Died:** Pneumonia.
**Postmortem:** Harrison's advanced age had been an issue in his race against incumbent president Martin van Buren. Perhaps because of this—to demonstrate his strength—he rode on horseback in his inaugural parade without a hat, gloves, or overcoat. Then he stood outside in the snow for more than one and a half hours, delivering his inaugural address.

The experience weakened him, and a few weeks later he caught pneumonia. Within a week he was delirious, and on April 4—just one month after his inauguration—he died. He served in office long enough to keep only one campaign promise: not to run for a second term.

There are approximately 1500 peanuts in every kilogram of peanut butter.

## AESCHYLUS
**Claim to Fame:** Greek playwright in 500 B.C. Many historians consider him the father of Greek tragedies.
**How He Died:** An eagle dropped a tortoise on his head.
**Postmortem:** According to legend, an eagle was trying to crack open a tortoise by dropping it on a hard rock. It mistook Aeschylus's head (he was bald) for a rock and dropped it on him instead.

## TYCHO BRAHE
**Claim to Fame:** An important Danish astronomer of the 16th century. His groundbreaking research enabled Sir Isaac Newton to come up with the theory of gravity.
**How He Died:** Didn't get to the bathroom on time.
**Postmortem:** In the 16th century, it was considered an insult to leave a banquet table before the meal was over. Brahe, known to drink excessively, had a bladder condition—but failed to relieve himself before the feast started. He made matters worse by drinking too much at the dinner, but was too polite to ask to be excused. His bladder finally burst, killing him slowly and painfully over the next 11 days.

## JEROME IRVING RODALE
**Claim to Fame:** Founding father of the organic food movement, creator of *Organic Farming and Gardening* magazine. Founded Rodale Press, a major publishing company.
**How He Died:** On the "Dick Cavett Show," while discussing the health benefits of organic food.
**Postmortem:** Rodale, who bragged, "I'm going to live to 100 unless I'm run down by a sugar-crazed taxi-driver," was only 72 when he appeared on the "Dick Cavett Show" in January 1971. Partway through the interview, he dropped dead in his chair. Cause of death: a heart attack. The show was never aired.

## ATTILA THE HUN
**Claim to Fame:** One of the most notorious villains in history. By 450 A.D., his 500,000-man army conquered all of Asia—from Mongolia to the edge of the Russian empire—by destroying villages and pillaging the countryside.

**How He Died:** He got a nosebleed on his wedding night.
**Postmortem:** In 453 Attila married a young girl named Ildico.
Despite his reputation for ferocity on the battlefield, he tended to
eat and drink lightly during large banquets. But on his wedding
night he really cut loose, gorging himself on food and drink.
Sometime during the night he suffered a nosebleed, but was too
drunk to notice. He drowned in his own blood and was found
dead the next morning.

## JIM FIXX
**Claim to Fame:** Author of the best-selling *Complete Book of
Running*, which started the jogging craze of the 1970s.
**How He Died:** A heart attack...while jogging.
**Postmortem:** Fixx was visiting Greensboro, Vermont. He walked
out of his house and began jogging. He'd only gone a short
distance when he had a massive coronary. His autopsy revealed
that one of his coronary arteries was 99% clogged, another was
80% obstructed, and a third was 70% blocked—and that Fixx
had had three other heart attacks in the weeks prior to his death
(when he'd competed in 19-km [12-mile] and 8-km [5-mile]
races).

## HORACE WELLS
**Claim to Fame:** Pioneered the use of anaesthesia in the 1840s.
**How He Died:** Used anaesthetics to commit suicide.
**Postmortem:** While experimenting with various gases during his
anaesthesia research, Wells became addicted to chloroform. In
1848 he was arrested for splashing sulfuric acid on two women
outside his home. In a letter he wrote from jail, he blamed
chloroform for his problems, claiming he'd gotten high before
the attack. Four days later he was found dead in his cell. He'd
anaesthetised himself with chloroform, then slashed open his
thigh with a razor.

\*　　\*　　\*　　\*

### And Now for Something Completely Different
• Elvis Presley was a big Monty Python fan; he saw *Monty Python
and the Holy Grail* at least five times.
• The King's favourite board games were Monopoly and Scrabble.
Neutrogena was his favourite soap.

**Most of the villains in the Bible have red hair.**

# THE ELVIS SIDESHOW

*Hurry, hurry, step right up! See the amazing Elvis freaks!*

**R**ichard Tweddell III. Inventor of the Elvis Vegiform, a plastic garden mould that fits over young vegetables and gets them to grow into the shape of the King. He says, "[Elvis-shaped] vegetables are more weighty, and the flavour is enhanced."

**Nicholas "S&L-vis" D'Ambra.** An Elvis impersonator with a social conscience. "S&L-vis" takes on the savings and loan scandal with songs like "Tax-break Hotel." Sample lyrics: "The deal the bank board gave them; was too good to be true; for every dollar they put in there; there's 15 from you."

**"Major" Bill Smith.** Believes the King is still alive and claims to have regular phone conversations with him. Smith, a 68-year-old Texan, is a religious man; he sees Elvis as a sort of mini-messiah: "Elvis is coming back in the spirit of Elijah….Praise God, he's coming back….This thing's about to bust right open." He has devoted his life to paving the way for the Second Coming of Elvis, which he considers the Lord's work. "Like Elvis told me, 'I'm walkin' the line God has drawn for me.' It's what the Holy Spirit told me to do."

**Peter Singh.** A Sikh living in Wales, England, he croons Elvis hits, Indian-style, to customers at his pub. Favourites include "Who's Sari Now," "My Popadum Told Me," and "Singh, Singh, Singh."

**Uri Yoali.** An Israeli Arab, owner of a roadside diner called The Elvis Inn, located in the Holy Land just 11,263 km (7,000 miles) from Memphis. "It's not just for tourists," Yoali says, "Elvis is my life." The diner is decorated with 728 pictures and posters of the King. It boasts a 3.6-metre (12-foot), 227-kg (500-pound), epoxy-and-plaster likeness of Presley outside its entrance. "I've always dreamed of seeing Elvis big," Yoali says, "In my mind he is so large, bigger even than this."

**Danny Uwnawich.** Owner of Melodyland, a small, three-bedroom version of Graceland in California's San Fernando Valley. Highlight: A white wrought-iron gate. Like the gate at Graceland, it's shaped like an open music book. According to Uwnawich, "The only people who have those gates is me and Him."

Termites can't hear.

# DUBIOUS ACHIEVERS

*Here are some of the stranger people listed in*
*the* Guinness Book of World Records.

**R**andy Ober, Bentonville, Arkansas
**Achievement:** Spit a wad of tobacco 14.5 metres (47 feet,
7 inches) in 1982.

**Joe Ponder,** Love Valley, North Carolina
**Achievement:** Lifted a 275-kg (606-pound) pumpkin 46 cm
(18 inches) off the ground with his teeth in 1985.

**Neil Sullivan,** Birmingham, England
**Achievement:** Carried a large bag of "household coal" 55 km
(34 miles) on May 24, 1986. It took him 12 hours and 45 minutes.

**Travis Johnson,** Elsberry, Missouri
**Achievement:** Held nine baseballs in his hand "without any
adhesives" in 1989.

**David Beattie and Adrian Simons,** London, England
**Achievement:** Rode up and down escalators at the Top Shop in
London for 101 hours in 1989. Estimated distance of travel:
214 km (133 miles).

**Pieter van Loggerenberg,** Hoedspruit, South Africa
**Achievement:** Played the accordion for 85 hours during a wildlife
festival in 1987.

**Michel Lotito,** Grenoble, France
**Achievement:** Has been eating metal and glass since 1959;
currently he eats more than 1 kg (2.2 pounds) of metal every day.
Since 1966 he has eaten 10 bicycles, a supermarket food cart,
7 televisions, 6 chandeliers, a coffin, and a Cessna aeroplane.

**"Country" Bill White,** Killeen, Texas
**Achievement:** Buried alive in a coffin, more than 1.83 metres (6 feet)
underground, for 341 days in July 1981. Only connection to the
outside world: a 10-cm (4-inch) tube used for feeding and breathing.

**King Taufa'ahau,** Tonga
**Achievement:** World's fattest king; weighed 210 kg (462 pounds)
in 1976.

In the novel Frankenstein, the monster's name was Adam.

**Alfred West**
Achievement: Split a human hair into 17 different pieces "on eight different occasions."

**Remy Bricka,** Paris, France
Achievement: In 1988, using 4-metre (13-foot)-long floating "skis," he "walked" across the Atlantic Ocean from Tenerife, Spain, to Trinidad (a distance of 5,635 km [3,502 miles]). The trip took 60 days.

**Steve Urner,** Tehachapi, California
Achievement: Threw a dried, "100% organic" cow chip more than 81 metres (266 feet) on August 4, 1981.

**N. Ravi,** Tamil Nadu, India
Achievement: Stood on one foot for 34 hours in 1982.

**"Hercules" John Massis,** Oostakker, Belgium
Achievement: Used teeth to stop a helicopter from taking off, 1979.

**Zolilio Diaz,** Spain
Achievement: Rolled a hoop from Mieres to Madrid, Spain, and back—a distance of more than 965 km (600 miles). It took him 18 days.

**Nine employees of the Bruntsfield Bedding Centre,** Scotland
Achievement: Pushed a wheeled hospital bed 5,201 km (3,233 miles) between June 21 and July 26, 1979.

**Fred Jipp,** New York City, New York
Achievement: Most illegal marriages. Between 1949 and 1981, using over 50 aliases, married 104 women in 27 states and 14 foreign countries. Sentenced to 34 years in prison and fined $336,000.

**Octavio Guillen and Adriana Martinez,** Mexico City, Mexico
Achievement: Longest engagement: 67 years. They finally tied the knot in 1969. Both were age 82.

**Sisters Jill Bradbury and Chris Humpish,** London, England
Achievement: Made a bed (2 sheets, 1 undersheet, 1 blanket, 1 pillow, and a bedspread) in 19 seconds flat on October 8, 1985.

Seven of the 50 most popular TV broadcasts ever were episodes of "The Beverly Hillbillies."

# THE BIRDS AND THE BEES

*When people talk about "the birds and the bees," this probably isn't what they had in mind. Here are some of the weirder ways animals reproduce.*

## SQUID

The male squid's sperm are contained in 13-mm (½-inch)-long pencil-shaped "packages" called spermatophores, which are located in a pouch near his gills. When the male is ready to reproduce, he grabs some of the spermatophores with one of his tentacles and deposits them deep inside the gill chamber of a female squid. The spermatophores remain inside the female until she ovulates, when they explode into a cloud of sperm and fertilise the egg. (In some species the male's arm breaks off inside the female and remains there until it is absorbed by her body.)

## SLOTHS

Sloths are the only land animals besides humans that regularly mate face to face. One important difference: they do it while hanging from tree branches by their arms.

## SEA URCHINS

Sea urchins expel their semen directly into the surrounding seawater, doing nothing to ensure that it ever reaches an unfertilised egg. If the current is right, the semen will eventually be carried to an egg, and reproduction will take place.

## "NOSE," OR "VAQUERO," FROGS

When the female is ready to reproduce, she lays about 20 unfertilised eggs. Nearby male frogs surround the eggs, fertilise them, and then guard them for about two weeks. As soon as they can see tadpoles forming within the eggs, each frog immediately tries to "swallow" as many eggs as possible, depositing them in a large throat sac that extends from its chin to its thighs. The eggs remain there until the tadpoles metamorphosise completely into frogs, when they enter the world by crawling out of the father's mouth.

## MUD TURTLES

The female mud turtle has a pair of bladders that she uses to build a nesting pit for her eggs. When she is ready to lay her fertilised eggs, she fills the bladders with water, and then partially empties them over the patch of dirt she wants to use for her nest. Then she starts digging, emptying the rest of the water in her bladders as she digs. When the bladders are empty, she returns to the water to refill them, then returns to the nest and continues digging. When she finishes, she kicks her eggs into the hole with her feet or tail, and covers the nest with fresh mud.

## EUROPEAN CUCKOOS

Like all species of cuckoos, the European cuckoo does not build its own nest. Instead, it lays its eggs in the nests of other species of birds. Some types of cuckoos remove the original eggs from the nest, other types leave them in the nest, and the host mother raises all the young as if they were her own. But the offspring of the European cuckoo are more aggressive than most: a few hours after one is born it begins kicking, an involuntary response that lasts about four days. By that time, the fledgling has usually kicked everything out of the nest—including any other baby birds.

## SNAILS

Snails practise a form of foreplay in which they shoot chalky "love darts" at each other to determine if they are members of the same species. Because snails are hermaphrodites—they have male and female sex organs—each snail will impregnate the other.

## DUCKS

According to one study, young male ducks are often disinterested in sex—even to the point of resisting the advances of females who are "in the mood." Sometimes the ducks appear to make elaborate excuses for why they cannot have sex, such as chasing away an imaginary enemy, taking an unneeded bath, etc. But the male ducks make up for it in later life: after they select a mate.

## AFRICAN ELEPHANTS

According to at least one study, female elephants act as midwives for one another when the hour of birth draws near. One researcher reported observing three female elephants leaving their herd and approaching a thicket. One of the females went into the thicket, while the other two stood guard outside, driving away any elephant or other animal that tried to approach. After a while the sentries returned to the herd, followed shortly afterwards by the third elephant and her newborn.

## SPIDERS
Because the male spider has no sex organ, he has to squeeze sperm from his belly onto his web, which he then picks up with his antennae before going off in search of a female spider. Male spiders also have to be careful once they find a female; if they aren't careful, the female will bite their head off during sex.

## PRAYING MANTISES
As soon as the male praying mantis mounts the female, the female bites his head off. Undeterred, the male continues mating while the female eats his shoulders and upper abdomen. Unlike most other creatures, the male mantis's brain *prevents* him from releasing sperm, so the female *has* to bite his head off.

## BEES
Only one male bee in a hive has the right to mate with the Queen, a process that takes about two seconds. When the male bee pulls away, his penis breaks off and remains inside the Queen, while he falls to the bottom of the hive and bleeds to death.

## SNAKES
Female snakes mate with several male snakes during each mating cycle and can store sperm in their bodies for months. According to one theory, snakes do this in order to have a "sperm contest" inside their bodies, somehow allowing only the healthiest sperm to fertilise their eggs. This increases the number of live births per season, increasing the chance that the species will survive.

## GREAT GREY SLUGS
Grey slugs are also hermaphrodites and engage in foreplay consisting of circling one another for hours, generating lots of slime in the process. Then they mate while hanging from ropes of slime.

# PRIME CRIME TIME DOWN UNDER

*To become a recognised villain in old Australia took some serious
doing. Given the thousands of convicts transported here,
competition must have been fierce.*

**W**HO'D HAVE THOUGHT IT?
No question, Australia's bushrangers had a leg up,
perhaps because comparisons could be drawn between
their criminal ways and the legends of the American West. While
some were escaped convicts, most were born in Australia to poverty
and had real or imagined grievances with the social structure of the
period. However, a pantheon of other fortune hunters, remittance
men, louts, losers and lags managed to beat back the bushranger
opposition to take their places in the Australian Hall of Infamy.

Some of these dastardly folk arrived in Australia under
appointment of the Crown, just as they had in every other colony
of the British Empire. Such appointments were treated as a way to
"cleanse" the peerage of the British Isles. Australia's gentry didn't
see it quite that way. A resident ruling class was an important
tradition, a clear indication of civilization. Unfortunately, they
were hard pressed to attract respectable peerage to Australia. Not
only was Australia at the farthest corner of the Empire at the
time, since the late 18th century, it had become the home of
thousands of convicts transported out of the Isles. As a result, the
locals often lionised the lesser lights who alighted from the ships
of the Empire, some of whom were particularly dim.

## SIPPING IN JUDGMENT

There was, for example, Richard Atkins, the son of a baronet,
who was appointed to a judgeship in Sydney, a key position in
Australia. Atkins started his "career" in typical English remittance
fashion, being handed a substantial sum by his father and sent off
to make his fortune, preferably ne'er to be heard from again. He
blew most of it, however, bought himself a military commission,
later sold it, and then skipped out on his creditors to Australia.

---

**Australia separated from Asia and Antarctica 45 million years ago.**

His willingness to take a bribe while on the bench was exceeded only by his love of drink. Sometimes he was visibly intoxicated while sitting trials—perhaps to the point of forgetting who had bribed him for what! His susceptibility to the grog was to throw him into infamy when he inadvertently helped set the stage for the Rum Rebellion by presiding over the trial of one, John MacArthur, owed money by Atkins, who was therefore somewhat biased in his judgments—mostly from the point of view of discharging the debt by getting rid of MacArthur. Even fellow judges rose against Atkins on that occasion.

Another of the same ilk was Alexander "Dandy" Baxter. He, too, walked ashore with an appointment as a judge. He, too, had a penchant for drink, then wife beating. To his credit, the governor of the colony, a conscientious, senstive man named Macquarie, sent him packing, a remarkable occurrence in those days when peers were rare and treasured but their scandalous behaviour commonplace. The extent to which Dandy offended even the Australian sense of propriety during those times must have been profound and public.

### TRULY A CLASS ACT

Obscure scions of minor peers were not the only ones who made it to Australia by appointment, so to speak. In 1802, a genuine Knight of the Realm made it to Australia but, unfortunately for him, Sir Henry Browne Hayes arrived, by appointment of the justice system, as a convicted felon. Nevertheless, Sir Henry was treated as a cut above the common convicts. He arrived on the good ship *Atlas*. Because of space required by the captain for 9,500 litres (2,100 gallons) of bootleg rum and roomy accommodation for his Lordship, more than one-third of the cramped convicts on the ship died en route—the worst tragedy in Australia's convict transportation era.

Sir Henry had been transported for kidnapping and forcing himself (by shotgun) upon the daughter of a local banker—rather odd behaviour for a man who was already a respected "Sir" and sheriff of Ireland's County Cork at the time. Once in Australia, he remained a thorn in the side of the government for a decade, racking up five convictions for disrespect to officials, raising a riot, and other such misdemeanours.

Dutch navigator Willem Jansz was the first European to land in Australia in 1606.

## DEMON RUM

The business of rum on the *Atlas* introduced two other men, both
of whom figure influentially in Australian colonial history.
Unlikely enough, one was William Bligh, that luckless captain of
the *Bounty*. The other was John MacArthur, nemesis of Bligh, his
henchman Judge Atkins and just about anyone else who didn't
support his views.

Rum was the currency of the colony of New South Wales. John
MacArthur controlled its traffic through his role as military
paymaster and convict manager to the extent he felt he controlled
the country. Captain Bligh was appointed governor, explicitly
charged to eradicate the rum monopoly and neutralise the
military, later called the Rum Corps.

## ALL'S WELL THAT ENDS WELL

Promptly MacArthur, with assistance from military commander
George Johnston, organised the Rum Rebellion—shades of the
Boston Tea Party—and threw Bligh in jail, where he languished
for two years. Bligh went on to become vice-admiral of the Royal
Navy. MacArthur became the largest sheep farmer in Australia.
However, as MacArthur was so busy with his politics—scheming,
manipulating, pontificating and generally messing about as
political aspirants are wont to do, it was his wife, Elizabeth, who
was the actual builder of the wool empire. Put simply, MacArthur
was a lousy businessman, but he could talk a good job.

## THE FIRST GREAT WHITE SHARK

Some miscreants came in pomp and circumstance and a few came
in chains. However, most other crumbs from the British upper
crust came armed with letters of introduction from Lord This or
That. These letters were often all the cachet needed to acquire
land grants for farms and an assignment of convicts to work them.
The letters sometimes were sufficiently impressive that bearers
were offered choice government positions.

One such was Dudley Fereday, mere son of a coal magnate.
Equipped with the usual letters, he secured a position as sheriff in
Van Diemen's Land, now Tasmania. Certainly canny and
somewhat unscrupulous, Fereday distinguished himself as

Before the Eiffel Tower was built in 1889, the pyramids were the tallest construction on Earth.

Australian's most successful colonial loan shark. Being the local sheriff, he undoubtedly had some extraordinary leverage when it came time to collect from tardy debtors.

## THE BUMP IN THE NIGHT

Then came John Giles Price, whom some regard as the most villainous man in Australian history. Even today his name is invoked by harried mothers to make their children behave. The fourth son of a baronet, heir only to a blown fortune and a handful of Introductions, Price proved himself on the surface to be a straight-minded, resolute, hard-working chap, with a knack for keeping convicts in line. These talents led to an appointment as commandant of Norfolk Island—already the harshest prison in Australia. Price was to take the treatment of prisoners to new heights of cruelty.

## BOGEYMAN RULES

He believed his convicts to be the worst of the worst and treated them accordingly. During the six years he ruled Norfolk, he became legendary for his autocratic demeanour, excessive and arbitrary punishments, and his practice of appointing the worst convicts as overseers of the rabble. General brutality, torture, starvation, and capital punishment were the order of Price's days. In later years he took a post as inspector-general of prisons in Victoria. Enough was enough. A group of convicts at Williamstown, a penal quarry near Melbourne, found an opportunity and killed him.

In Australia's Hall of Infamy, John Giles Price holds a special place—that reserved for the bogeyman.

\*     \*     \*     \*

## NOTABLE AUSTRALIAN QUOTES

"Considering his environment, he (Ned Kelly) was a superior man. He possessed great natural ability and, under favourable circumstances, would probably have become a leader of men in good society."
> —**Police constable Alexander Fitzpatrick, whose complaint against Ned Kelly made him an outlaw (1911)**

# ONE NUCLEAR BOMB CAN RUIN YOUR WHOLE DAY

*We don't want to make you paranoid, but*
*all of these incidents really happened.*

**1.** In July 1956, a B-47 aircraft ploughed into a storage igloo 32 km (20 miles) outside of Cambridge, England. The plane's jet fuel burst into flames almost immediately, but for some reason didn't ignite the contents of the igloo. A lucky thing, too—it contained three Mark 6 nuclear bombs.

**2.** In 1958 a B-47E accidentally dropped a nuclear bomb into a Mars Bluff, South Carolina, family's vegetable garden. The bomb didn't explode, but it did damage five houses and a church. Air Force officials apologised.

**3.** In 1961 a B-52 dropped two 24-megaton bombs on a North Carolina farm. According to one physicist: "Only a single switch prevented the bombs from detonating."

**4.** In 1966 another B-52 carrying four 20-megaton bombs crashed in Palomares, Spain—with one of the bombs splashing into the Mediterranean Sea. It took the U.S. 6th fleet—using 33 ships and 3,000 men—several weeks to find the missing bomb.

**5.** In 1980 a repairman working on a Titan II missile in Arkansas dropped a wrench—which bounced off the floor, punctured the missile, and set off an explosion that blew the top off the silo and threw the warhead 183 metres (600 feet) into the air.

**6.** Did June 3, 1980, seem tense to you? It did to the Strategic Air Command in Omaha, Nebraska. Their computers detected a Soviet submarine missile attack in progress. Within minutes, more than 100 B-52s were in the air, but the SAC soon called off the counterattack—the computers had made a mistake. The culprit: a 46¢ computer chip. Three days later the same mistake happened again.

---

Ninety percent of all animal species in the history of the Earth are now extinct.

# MEET THE BEATLES

*The Beatles were personalities, as entertaining in interviews as they were on record. To prove it, here are excerpts from Beatle press conferences held in the mid-1960s, when the group had become popular. At the time, rock bands were still considered vacuous non-artists. It's interesting to see how the Beatles helped change that.*

**R**eporter: Ringo, why do you think you get more fan mail than anyone else in the group?
**Ringo:** I don't know. I suppose it's because more people write to me.

**Reporter:** Do you date much?
**Ringo:** What are you doing tonight?

**Reporter:** How do you like this welcome [in the U.S.]?
**Ringo:** So this is America. They all seem out of their minds.

**Reporter:** What do you do when you're cooped up in a hotel room between shows?
**George:** We ice skate.

**Reporter:** How did you find America?
**Ringo:** We went to Greenland and made a left turn.

**Reporter:** Why do teenagers stand up and scream piercingly and painfully when you appear?
**Paul:** None of us know. But we've heard that teenagers go to our shows just to scream. A lot of them don't even want to listen because they have our records. We kind of like the screaming teenagers. If they want to pay their money and sit out there and shout, that's their business. We aren't going to be like little dictators and say, "You've got to shut up." The commotion doesn't bother us anymore. It's come to be like working in a bell factory. You don't hear the bells after a while.

**Reporter:** Would you like to walk down the street without being recognised?
**John:** We used to do that with no money in our pockets. There's no point in it.

**Reporter:** Are you scared when crowds scream at you?
**John:** More so in Dallas than in other places perhaps.

**Reporter:** Is it true you can't sing?
**John (pointing to George):** Not me. Him.

**Reporter:** Why don't you smile George?
**George:** I'll hurt my lips.

**Reporter:** What's your reaction to a Seattle psychiatrist's opinion that you are a menace?
**George:** Psychiatrists are a menace.

**Reporter:** Do you plan to record any anti-war songs?
**John:** All our songs are anti-war.

**Reporter:** Does all the adulation from teenage girls affect you?
**John:** When I feel my head start to swell, I look at Ringo and know perfectly well we're not supermen.

**Reporter:** Do you resent fans ripping up your sheets for souvenirs?
**Ringo:** No I don't mind. So long as I'm not in them while the ripping is going on.

**Reporter:** Do you follow politics?
**John:** I get spasms of being intellectual. I read a bit about politics but I don't think I'd vote for anyone. No message from any of those phony politicians is coming through to me.

**Reporter:** What's the most unusual request you've had?
**John:** I wouldn't like to say.

**Reporter:** What do you plan to do next?
**John:** We're not going to fizzle out in half a day. But afterwards I'm not going to change into a tap dancing musical. I'll just develop what I'm doing at the moment, although whatever I say now I'll change my mind next week. I mean, we all know that bit about: "It won't be the same when you're twenty-five." I couldn't care less. This isn't show business. It's something else. This is different from anything that anybody imagines. You don't go on from this. You do this and then you finish.

**Reporter:** Do you like topless bathing suits?
**Ringo:** We've been wearing them for years.

When snakes are born with two heads, they fight each other for food.

**Reporter:** Girls rushed toward my car because it had press identification and they thought I met you. How do you explain this phenomenon?
**John:** You're lovely to look at.

**Reporter:** How do you add up success?
**John, Paul, George, Ringo:** Money.

**Reporter:** What will you do when Beatlemania subsides?
**John:** Count the money.

**Reporter:** What do you think of the Bomb?
**Paul:** It's disturbing that people should go around blowing us up, but if an atom bomb should explode I'd say, "Oh well, no point in saying anything else, is there." People are so crackers. I know the bomb is ethically wrong but I won't go around crying. I suppose I could do something like wearing those "ban the bomb" things, but it's something like religion that I don't think about. It doesn't fit in with my life.

**Reporter:** What do you think of space shots?
**John:** You see one, you've seen them all.

**Reporter:** What do you think about the pamphlet calling you four Communists?
**Paul:** Us, Communists? Why, we can't be Communists. We're the world's number one capitalists. Imagine us. Communists!

**Reporter:** What's your biggest fear?
**John:** The thing I'm afraid of is growing old. I hate that. You get old and you've missed it somehow. The old always resent the young and vice-versa.

**Reporter:** What about the recent criticism of your lyrics?
**Paul:** If you start reading things into them you might as well start singing hymns.

**Reporter:** You were at the Playboy Club last night. What did you think of it?
**Paul:** The Playboy and I are just good friends.

**Reporter:** George, is the place you were brought up a bit like Greenwich Village?
**George:** No. More like The Bowery.

MOOO: Most cows give more milk when they listen to music.

**Reporter:** Ringo, how do you manage to find all those parties?
**Ringo:** I don't know. I just end up at them.
**Paul:** On tour we don't go out much. Ringo's always out, though.
**John:** Ringo freelances.

**Reporter:** There's a "Stamp Out the Beatles" movement underway in Detroit. What are you going to do about it?
**Paul:** We're going to start a campaign to stamp out Detroit.

**Reporter:** Who thought up the name, Beatles?
**Paul:** I thought of it.
**Reporter:** Why?
**Paul:** Why not?

**Reporter:** Beethoven figures in one of your songs. What do you think of Beethoven?
**Ringo:** He's great. Especially his poetry.

**Reporter:** Ringo, why do you wear two rings on each hand?
**Ringo:** Because I can't fit them through my nose.

**Reporter:** When you do a new song, how do you decide who sings the lead?
**John:** We just get together and whoever knows most of the words sings the lead.

**Reporter:** Do you think it's wrong to set such a bad example to teenagers, smoking the way you do?
**Ringo:** It's better than being alcoholics.

**Reporter:** What do you think of the criticism that you are not very good?
**George:** We're not.

**Reporter:** What do you believe is the reason you are the most popular singing group today?
**John:** We've no idea. If we did, we'd get four long-haired boys, put them together and become their managers.

**Reporter:** You've admitted to being agnostics. Are you also irreverent?
**Paul:** We are agnostics...so there's no point in being irreverent.

---

There are an estimated 508,000 metric tonnes of tea in China.

# WORDPLAY

*We use these words all the time, but most of us have no idea where they came from. Fortunately, we're on the job, ready to supply their history and make your brief (?) stay in the john an educational one.*

**POTLUCK.** In the Middle Ages, cooks threw all their leftovers into a pot of water that was kept boiling most of the time. This makeshift stew was eaten by the family or fed to strangers when no other food was available. Since food was thrown in at random, its quality and taste depended entirely on luck.

**JUKEBOX.** The term "juke" was originally a New Orleans slang expression meaning "to have sex." Jukeboxes got their name because they were popular in houses of prostitution known as juke joints.

**SLUSH FUND.** "Slush" was originally the name for kitchen grease from the galleys of naval sailing ships. Most of this sludge was used to lubricate masts of the ship; the rest was sold with other garbage whenever the ship entered port. Money made from the sale was kept in a "slush fund," used to buy items for enlisted men.

**HAYWIRE.** Bales of hay are held together with tightly strung wire. If the wire snaps, it whips around wildly and can injure people standing nearby.

**BROKE.** Many banks in post-Renaissance Europe issued small, porcelain "borrower's tiles" to their creditworthy customers. Like credit cards, these tiles were imprinted with the owner's name, his credit limit, and the name of the bank. Each time the customer wanted to borrow money, he had to present the tile to the bank teller, who would compare the imprinted credit limit with how much the customer had already borrowed. If the borrower was past the limit, the teller "broke" the tile on the spot.

**BOMB.** The term "bomb," long in use as a name for explosive devices, was first used to describe a bad theatre play by Grevile Corks, theatre critic for the *New York Standard* in the 1920s.

---

Queen Elizabeth and Prince Philip of Great Britain are 2nd, 3rd, 4th, and 5th cousins.

When one particularly bad play closed after only two performances, Corks wryly observed: "Since the producers were so eager to clear the theatre, they might have tried a smoke bomb instead. It would have been quicker for the audience, and less painful." The column was so popular that Corks started the "Bomb of the Year" award for the worst play on Broadway.

**OUTSKIRTS.** As medieval English towns grew too big to fit inside town walls, houses and other buildings were built outside them. These buildings surrounded the wall the same way a woman's skirt surrounds her waist—and became known as the town's "skirts." People living on the outer fringes of even *these* buildings were considered to be living in the *outskirts* of the town.

**BANGS.** In the early 19th century, it was common for English noblemen to maintain elaborate stables for their horses. But hard times in following years made stables an expensive luxury. Many nobles were forced to reduce their staffs—which meant that the remaining grooms had less time to spend on each horse. One innovation that resulted: instead of spending hours trimming each horse's tail, grooms cut all tail hair the same length, a process they called "banging off." Eventually the "banged" look became popular as a woman's hairstyle, too.

**HUSBAND.** Comes from the German words *Hus* and *Bunda*, which mean "house" and "owner." The word originally had nothing to do with marital status, except for the fact that home ownership made husbands extremely desirable marriage partners.

**WIFE.** Comes from the Anglo-Saxon words *wifan* and *mann*, which mean "weaver" and "human." In ancient times there were no words that specifically described males or females; one way Anglo-Saxons denoted the difference was to use the word *wifmann* or "weaver-human," since weaving was a task traditionally performed by women.

**PENKNIFE.** One problem with quill pens was that their tips dulled quickly and needed constant sharpening. Knife makers of the 15th century produced special knives for that purpose; their sharp blades and compact size made them popular items.

# AUSTRALIANS DID IT FIRST!

*Maybe it's the geographical isolation. Maybe it's the way time
stretches across long, hot summers of blue skies and humid nights.
Whatever the reason, Australians have always found the time
and inclination to invent.*

**B**LACK BOX FLIGHT RECORDER: This was the
brainchild of Dr David Warren of the Aeronautical
Research Laboratory in Melbourne. In the 1950s, after a
series of unexplained air crashes, he developed the idea to build a
machine that recorded the movements and voices of flight crew.
This could then be used in the event of a crash to determine vital
information about the cause of the crash.

Following an aircraft crash in Queensland in 1960, Australia
became the first country in the world to make flight recorders
compulsory on all aircraft. Every commercial plane in the world
now has a flight recorder on board.

Although they are commonly called "black boxes," flight
recorders are actually bright orange. This makes them easier to
find in a plane crash site.

**THE OWEN SUBMACHINE GUN:** Perhaps Evelyn Owen
always wanted a gun named after him. When he first developed
the prototype for the submachine gun in 1939, nobody was
interested in it. But not for long! In 1941, the gun went into
production. About 50,000 were manufactured during World
War II.

**COCHLEAR IMPLANTS (for bionic ears):** The Bionic Man
had bionic ears, but now they are also the reality for people in
more than 60 countries around the world. The Australian
scientists at the University of Melbourne first began to research
cochlear implants in the 1960s. In 1978, Rod Saunders, a deaf
man, regained some hearing when such an implant was fitted into
his cochlea (a structure in the inner ear that looks like a snail
shell). The implant stimulates the auditory nerve electrically.

**POLYMER BANKNOTES:** It's not play money. It's for real! The world's first polymer banknote was the $10 note issued to mark the Australian Bicentenary in 1988. By 1996, polymer banknotes were being used everywhere. The advantages of these banknotes are many: they last longer, they function better in ATMs, they can be recycled and, most importantly, they can't be counterfeited.

**WINE CASK:** They've got a lot to answer for—the inventors of the wine cask. It was originally developed by a South Australian winery in the 1960s as a way to sell cheap red wine in bulk. Polyethylene bags were filled with more than 4 litres (7 pints) of wine and would collapse as the wine was tapped out, so no air could get in to spoil the wine. It was then placed into a cardboard box. The concept soon took off and Australian wine exports blazed their way into the international wine market.

**CLEAN UP AUSTRALIA DAY:** Sydney property developer Ian Kiernan came up with this idea in 1986. Shocked by the rubbish he saw in the oceans as he sailed around the world, he decided to start by cleaning up his own back yard—Australia. In 1989, he organised Clean Up the Harbour Day. Clean Up Australia Day followed a year later and is now one of the best-attended community events in the country. In 2000, more than 40 million volunteers from more than 120 different countries took part in Clean Up the World Day.

## AND SOME MORE AUSTRALIAN FIRSTS:

**Stump-jump plough** (1876)—a plough that can jump over stumps and stones.

**Stripper harvester** (1882)—a machine that strips the crop as it harvests it.

**First feature-length film** (1906)—*The Story of Ned Kelly*.

**Aspro** (1915)—a drug used to relieve headaches.

**Car radio** (1924)—the first car radio was fitted to an Australian car.

**Frozen embryo baby** (1984)—the first frozen embryo baby was born.

# ON A CAROUSEL

*Just "sitting there watchin' the wheels go 'round and 'round?" While you're there, you might as well learn a little bit about the origin of the carousel and other rides, as told by BRI member Jack Mingo.*

## THE CAROUSEL

The name *carousel* originated with a popular 12th-century Arabian horseman's game called *carosellos*, or "little wars." The rules were simple: teams rode in circles throwing perfume-filled clay balls from one rider to another. If a ball of perfume broke, the team lost. Their penalty: they carried the smell of defeat with them for days after.

The game was brought to Europe by knights returning from the Crusades, and it evolved into elaborate, colourful tourneys called *carousels*.

**Making the Rounds.** In the 17th century, the French developed a device to help young nobles train for carousels. It featured legless wooden horses attached to a centre pole. As the centre pole turned (powered by real horses, mules, or people), the nobles on their wooden steeds would try to spear hanging rings with their lances. (This later evolved into the "catching the brass ring" tradition.) The carousel device gradually evolved into a popular form of entertainment. The peasants rode on barrel-like horses; the nobles rode in elaborate chariots and boats.

**The Machine Age.** Until the 1860s, carousels, which had become popular all over Europe, were still dependent on horses and mules for power. But that changed when Frederick Savage, an English engineer, designed a portable steam engine, which could turn as many as four rows of horses on a 15-metre (48-foot) diameter wheel. Later, Savage also patented designs for the overhead camshafts and gears that moved the wooden horses up and down. This new type of carousel—called a "round-about" (later, merry-go-round)—was a huge success throughout Europe. Ads for carousels first appeared in America as early as 1800. Typically, offering fun was not enough—carousel owners also felt obliged to claim that doctors recommended the rides to improve blood circulation.

## THE FERRIS WHEEL

A 33-year-old American engineer named George Washington Ferris designed a giant "observation wheel" for Chicago's World's Columbian Exhibition in 1893, as an American counterpart to the Eiffel Tower (which had been unveiled four years earlier). At 76 metres (250 feet) in diameter, this first Ferris wheel could carry more than 2,000 passengers high above the city…and bring them smoothly back down. It was the hit of the fair; some 1.5 million people rode in it.

It was such a success, writes Tad Tuleja in *Namesakes*, that "it fostered many imitators at the turn of the century, the most notable being a 91-metre (300-foot) wheel constructed for the 1897 London Fair and a 60-metre (197-foot) one built for Vienna's Prater Park in 1896….These giants proved impractical, of course, for the many carnival midways where Ferris's invention now prospers; the average travelling wheel today is about 15 metres (50 feet) in diameter."

In 1904 Ferris's original wheel, which cost $385,000 to build, was dismantled and sold for scrap. It brought in less than $2,000.

## ROLLER COASTERS

The roller coaster was invented by an showman in Russia who built elaborate ice slides in St. Petersburg during the 15th century. Catherine the Great enjoyed the ice slides so much that she ordered tiny wheels added to the sleds so she could ride in the summer.

• The first "modern" roller coaster was built in Coney Island in 1884, more than 400 years later.

• Believe it or not, statistically, roller coasters are much safer than merry-go-rounds. One reason: People rarely decide to jump off a roller coaster while the ride is still moving. Also, the safety restraints work better. Despite that, 27 people died on roller coasters between 1973 and 1988.

• Designers purposely create the illusion that your head is in danger of being chopped by a low overhang at the bottom of a hill. Actually there's almost always a 3-metre (9-foot) clearance.

• Americans take more than an estimated 214 million roller coaster rides each year.

\* \* \* \*

"We won't make a sequel, but we may well make a second episode."
—Jon Peters, *film producer*

# OXYMORONS

*Here's a list of oxymorons sent to us by BRI member Peter McCracken. In case you don't know, an oxymoron is a common phrase made up of two words that appear to contradict each other.*

| | |
|---|---|
| Military Intelligence | Death Benefits |
| Light Heavyweight | Upside Down |
| Jumbo Shrimp | Original Copy |
| Painless Dentistry | Random Order |
| Drag Race | Irrational Logic |
| Friendly Fire | Business Ethics |
| Criminal Justice | Slightly Pregnant |
| Permanent Temporary | Holy Wars |
| Amtrack Schedule | Half Dead |
| Genuine Imitation | Supreme Court |
| Mandatory Option | Even Odds |
| Protective Custody | Baby Grand |
| Limited Nuclear War | Inside Out |
| Dear Occupant | Fresh Frozen |
| Standard Deviation | Moral Majority |
| Freezer Burn | Truth in Advertising |
| Pretty Ugly | Friendly Takeover |
| Industrial Park | Good Grief |
| Loyal Opposition | United Nations |
| Eternal Life | Baked Alaska |
| Natural Additives | Plastic Glasses |
| Student Teacher | Peacekeeping Missiles |
| Educational Television | Somewhat Addictive |
| Nonworking Mother | Science Fiction |
| Active Reserves | Open Secret |
| Full-Price Discount | Unofficial Record |
| Limited Immunity | Tax Return |

# IT'S IN THE CARDS

*Do you like to play poker?…gin rummy?…bridge…or (in the bathroom) solitaire? Then maybe we can interest you in a couple of pages on the origin of playing cards.*

## HISTORY

**Origin.** The first playing cards are believed to have come from the Mamelukes, people of mixed Turkish and Mongolian blood who ruled Egypt from 1250 to 1517. Like today's standard playing cards, the Mamelukes' deck had 52 cards and four suits (swords, polo sticks, cups, and coins), with three face cards and 10 numbered cards per suit. Mameluke decks did not include queens or jacks; they used "Deputy Kings" and "Second," or "Under Deputy Kings," instead.

**European Popularity.** In the mid-1300s, the cards were introduced to Europe, where they spawned a gaming craze similar to the Monopoly or Trivial Pursuit fads of the 20th century. Historians measure their popularity not by how many times people wrote about them (cards received little or no mention) or by the number of decks that survive (few did), but by the number of cities that *banned* them. Paris was one of the first: it outlawed card-playing among "working men" in 1377. Other cities soon followed, and by the mid-1400s, anti-card sentiments reached a fervor. During one public demonstration in Nuremburg, led by the Catholic priest and future saint John Capistran (better known by his Spanish name, Juan Capistrano), more than 40,000 decks of cards, tens of thousands of dice, and 3,000 backgammon boards were burned in a public bonfire. None of the attempts to eliminate card-playing were successful; in fact, cards are one of only a few items of the 12th century that survive almost unchanged to this day.

## THAT SUITS ME FINE

• The four modern suits—hearts, clubs, spades, and diamonds—originated in France around 1480, at a time when card makers were beginning to mass-produce decks for the first time.

• The simple single-colour designs were easier to paint using stencils and cheaper to produce than the more elaborate designs that had been popular in the past.

• Not all today's cards use diamonds, hearts, spades, and clubs as suit symbols. Traditional German cards use hearts, leaves, acorns, and bells; Swiss cards use roses, shields, acorns, and bells; and Italian cards use swords, batons, cups, and coins.

## CARD FACTS

• For more than 500 years, playing cards were much larger than today's versions and didn't have the *indices* (the numbers, letters, and suit marks on the top left corners) that let you read the cards in a tightly held hand. Card players either had to hold their cards in both hands to read them (which made them easy for other players to see), or else had to memorise them and then play with none of the cards showing. In the mid-19th century, card makers began adding the indices in decks called "squeezers" (which let you hold the cards closely together).

• It was in "squeezer" decks that the jacks became a part of the deck. Earlier they had been called knaves, which, like kings, started with the letter "K". To avoid the confusion of having two types of cards with the letter "K", card makers changed *knaves to jacks* (a slang term for the knaves already) and used the letter "J" instead.

• The first face cards were elaborately painted, full-length portraits. While beautiful, they posed a serious disadvantage: when they were dealt upside down, novice players tended to turn them right-side-up—telling experienced players how many face cards were in their hand. Card makers corrected this in the 19th century, when they began making decks with "double-ended" face cards.

• The joker is the youngest—and the only American—card in the deck. It was added in the mid-19th century, when it was the highest-value card in an American game called Euchre. From there it gained popularity as a "wild" card in poker and other games.

• In November 1742, an Englishman named Edmond Hoyle published a rule book on the popular game of Whist. The book was so successful that dozens of writers plagiarised it, even using the name "Hoyle's" in the pirate editions. Today's "Hoyle's" rule books are descendants of the *plagiarised* versions, not the original.

• The word "ace" is derived from the Latin word *as*, which means the "smallest unit of coinage."

There are no words in the English language that rhyme with purple.

# THE SECRETS OF A HARLEQUIN ROMANCE

*Romance novels account for a hefty chunk of the paperback book market. If you're looking for a few extra bucks, writing one may be a way to pick them up. So, for you aspiring "writers," here are some facts and guidelines about Harlequin Romances.*

## VITAL STATS

**History:** Harlequin Books was founded in Winnipeg, Manitoba, in 1949 to reprint romance novels put out by the British publisher Mills & Boon. In 1958 Richard and Mary Bonnycastle bought the company, rechristened it Harlequin Enterprises, and set up headquarters in Toronto. Now, with more than 10 billion romances sold, Harlequin is the McDonalds of paperback publishing. They print books in some 17 languages and ships to more than 100 different countries.

**Sales:** In 1970 Harlequin sold 3 million books. Now it sells more than 200 million a year. The company estimates that every six seconds, another Harlequin romance is sold.

**Market:** Romance is the biggest-selling area of the paperback book market—25% to 40% of all mass-market paperback sales...and Harlequin has an estimated 80% of that market. Surveys show that romance addicts will spend up to $60 a month on romances (and read them in less than two hours apiece).

**Audience:** More than 100 million people worldwide read romances regularly—mostly in the U.S., Germany, France, the U.K. and Australia. But Harlequin reports that sales are growing steadily in Asia. Company surveys indicate that 50% of its North American readers are college-educated, and a third make more than $30,000 a year.

## YOU CAN WRITE A ROMANCE

Tired of reading other people's fantasies? Think you've got what it takes to pen prose powerful enough to promote palpitations? Want to try your hand at writing a romance novel? Here are excerpts from the editorial guidelines for a basic Harlequin romance. This is the information Harlequin supplies to all prospective writers, and we provide it here as a service to you.

**Guidelines:** "What we are looking for are romances with…strong believable characters, not stereotypes; stories that centre on the development of the romance between the heroine and hero, with the emphasis on feelings and emotions."

**Style:** "Keep 'strong' language (swear words) and highly provocative, sensual language to a minimum.

"Descriptions of sex or sexual feeling should be kept to a minimum in Romances. Love scenes are fine, but the descriptions of such, which should not go on for pages, should deal with how the heroine feels (perhaps the hero, too)—her emotional responses, not just purely physical sensations. Leave a lot to the imagination. A kiss and an embrace, if well told, can be just as stimulating to the reader as pages of graphically described sensual scenes."

**Heroine:** "Generally, younger than the hero, relatively inexperienced sexually, though this fact need not be stressed. She should hold traditional (not to be equated with old-fashioned) moral standards…The heroine need not be a career woman, nor even a woman with a fascinating, different job…She may hold just an average job, earning average income; she may be unemployed. If she works in a traditional woman's job—secretarial, nursing, teaching, etc.—that's okay, too.

**Hero:** "Try to avoid excessive age difference; for instance, the 17-year-old heroine and the 37-year-old hero. He should be very attractive, worldly and successful in his field and, unlike the heroine, quite sexually experienced, and this fact may be implied."

### SEND NOW!

Want more info? Send for complete guidelines. Enclose a self-addressed, stamped envelope to Harlequin Enterprises, Ltd., 225 Duncan Mill Road, Don Mills, Ontario, Canada M3B 3K9. (Don't quit your day job: Publishers receive up to 1,000 unsolicited manuscripts every month. For the few books they do buy, they pay advances between $1,000 and $15,000, with royalties of 7% to 8%.)

# UNSUNG SUPERHEROES

*Imagine inventing one of the most popular comic characters...and getting only $130 for it. That's what happened to these guys.*

**THE HEROES:** Jerry Siegel and Joseph Shuster
**WHAT THEY DID:** Created Superman, the most popular comic book character in history.

One night in 1934, 17-year-old Jerry Siegel, an aspiring comic book writer fresh out of high school, came up with the idea for Superman. He was so excited that at dawn he ran 12 blocks to tell his friend and partner, Joseph Shuster.

The pair began drawing up cartoon panels showing their hero in action. They sent samples to newspaper comic strip editors all over the country, but no one was interested. Finally, in 1938, DC Comics agreed to print a Superman comic and paid Siegel and Shuster $130 ($10 a page for 13 pages of work) for it. In addition, the two were hired as staff artists to draw future Superman comics.

Superman made his first appearance in June 1938. He was an instant smash. Over the years he inspired a radio show, animated cartoons, a TV series, movies, and licensed products. In the 1970s alone, Superman products grossed about $1 billion.

**THE SAD FACTS:** When Siegel and Shuster sold the first comic to DC for $130 and signed on as staff artists, they effectively signed away all rights to Superman. From then on, all the money went to DC Comics.

They continued drawing the strip for DC until 1948, when the company fired them for asking for a share of the profits. Both men filed suits against DC...which they ultimately lost. By the 1970s, both were broke, living on money made by selling old comic books and other memorabilia they still owned. Shuster was unemployed, nearly blind, and living in a tiny apartment in Queens, New York.

Finally, in 1975, Warner Communications (owner of DC) voluntarily gave them pensions of $20,000 a year. In 1981 these were increased to $30,000—plus a $15,000 bonus after the first *Superman* film grossed $275 million. That was all the compensation the two men ever received for their creation.

---

You're more likely to get stung by a bee on a windy day than in any other weather.

# SHUTE ACROSS THE WORLD

*Nevil Shute told the world about Australia in novels such as*
A Town Like Alice.

## THE MYSTERIOUS OZ

In the 1950s and 1960s, few Brits knew anyone who had been to Australia and come back to tell the tale. Thousands decamped via the famous ten-pound, one-way immigration ticket but, of course, they mostly stayed put in Oz. So the great sunny continent of the Southern Hemisphere remained, to most, as remote and romantic (or out of sight and out of mind) as it had a century earlier when British judges were still cheerily dispatching convicts.

Enter the best-selling novels of Nevil Shute. They were to the 1950s and 60s what *Home and Away* and *Neighbours* were to the 1990s. They put Australia on the map. For most citizens of chilly Britain, *A Town Like Alice*, *Beyond the Black Stump* and Shute's other Australian novels were the sole source of information about everyday life in the land of the kangaroo. This was a chap who let you smell the gum trees, hear the Australian accents, feel the heat and see the dirt of the desert. And he made you think, too. *On the Beach*, a pessimistic post-nuclear war tale, is probably his most famous novel of all.

## SHUTE FOR THE STARS

But no Aussie was Mr Nevil Shute Norway. He was a Londoner and a thoroughbred Englishman. Born in 1899, he attended the famous boys' school at Shrewsbury. Then he went to Balliol College, Oxford no less. Engineering was his thing and, after graduation, Shute worked for many years in the burgeoning aircraft industry.

That was his day job. At night he was busily scribbling novels and short stories and wasn't put off by the huge heap of rejection slips that soon arrived from publishers. However, determination paid off. His first novel, *Marazan*, based on his experiences in the

---

**Men are three times more likely than women to commit suicide after an unhappy love affair.**

aviation industry, was published in 1926. After that his publishing career took off and he even sold some film rights. He used his given names Nevil and Shute as a pen name to avoid offending his bosses in the day job—and got famous!

## THE PEN IS MIGHTIER THAN THE SWORD

Then air travel began to get commonplace. It no longer seemed adventurous and Shute got bored. So he resigned and decided to live by the pen alone.

But there was a war coming, which meant there were other things to do. In 1939, he joined the Royal Naval Volunteer Reserve as a sub-lieutenant and rose to become a lieutenant commander. Experimenting with secret weapons suited this story-telling engineer down to the ground and provided plenty of fodder for his later fiction. After the war he was angry about Britain's high taxes and what he regarded as British decadence. (Has anything changed?) He also thought that Britain was forgetting to value the personal independence and freedom for which it had gone to war.

## THE LIFE OF AN EX-PATRIOT

Shute wanted out and Australia was the choice. Soon he and Mrs Norway were settled at Langwarrin in Victoria. Not long after, in 1950, there followed one of the great romantic stories of the twentieth century—*A Town Like Alice*. In it Jean Padget uses an unexpected legacy to travel from London to Alice Springs to see a place colourfully described to her several years earlier by an Australian she had met and fallen in love with during the occupation of Malaya by the Japanese. She thinks he is dead, killed by the Japanese. Read it if you don't know what happened. You've a treat in store.

Not only does *A Town Like Alice* tell anyone who doesn't know what farming in the outback was like in 1950, it is also one of those tear-jerker classics that is affectionately passed down in families through the generations. Mothers give it to their daughters and dads to their lads with fond memories of how moved they were when they first read it.

Shute, who set several of his post-war books in the adopted country he loved, died in Melbourne in 1960. All 22 of his novels are still in print somewhere in the world—quite a legacy!

# PATRON SAINTS

*The Roman Catholic Church has more than 5,000 saints, many of whom are "patron saints"—protectors of certain professions, sick people, animals, even hobbies. Here are a few of the more interesting ones.*

**Saint Matthew:** Patron Saint of Accountants. (He was a tax collector before becoming an apostle.)

**Saint Joseph of Cupertino:** Patron Saint of Air Travellers. (Nicknamed "The Flying Friar," he could levitate.)

**Saint Fiacre:** Patron Saint of Taxi Drivers, Hemorrhoid Sufferers, and Venereal Disease.

**Saint Matrona:** Patron Saint of Dysentery Sufferers.

**Saint Louis IX of France:** Patron Saint of Button Makers.

**Saint Adrian of Nicomedia:** Patron Saint of Arms Dealers.

**Saint Anne:** Patron Saint of Women in Labour. (Not to be confused with Saint John Thwing, Patron Saint of Women in *Difficult* Labour.)

**Saint Nicholas of Myra** (also known as Santa Claus): Patron Saint of Children and Pawnbrokers.

**Saint Bernardino of Siena:** Patron Saint of Advertisers and Hoarseness.

**Saint Blaise:** Patron Saint of Throats (he saved a child from choking) and Diseased Cattle (he also healed animals).

**Saint Joseph:** Patron Saint of Opposition to Atheistic Communism.

**Saint Sebastian:** Patron Saint of Neighbourhood Watch Groups.

**Saint Joseph of Arimathea:** Patron Saint of Funeral Directors.

**Saint Eligius:** Patron Saint of Petrol Station Workers. (He miraculously cured horses, the precursors to automobiles.)

**Saint Martin de Porres:** Patron Saint of Race Relations, Social Justice, and Italian Hairdressers.

**Saint Martha:** Patron Saint of Dietitians.

# ACCIDENTAL DISCOVERIES

*Not all scientific progress is the product of systematic experimentation.
A number of important modern discoveries have been a matter of
chance—which means you should keep your eyes and ears open,
even while you're just sitting there on the john. You never
know what might happen.*

**The Discovery:** Insulin
**How It Happened:** In 1889 Joseph von Mering and
Oscar Minkowski, two German scientists, were trying to
understand more about the digestive system. As part of their
experiments, they removed the pancreas from a living dog to see
what role the organ plays in digestion.

The next day a laboratory assistant noticed an extraordinary
number of flies buzzing around the dog's urine. Von Mering and
Minkowski examined the urine to see why…and were surprised
to discover that it contained a high concentration of sugar. This
indicated that the pancreas plays a role in removing sugar from
the bloodstream.

**Legacy:** Von Mering and Minkowski were never able to isolate
the chemical that produced this effect, but their discovery enabled
John J. R. MacLeod and Frederick Banting, two Canadian
researchers, to develop insulin extracts from horse and pig
pancreases and to pioneer their use as a treatment for diabetes
in 1921.

**The Discovery:** Photography
**How It Happened:** The *camera obscura*, designed by Leonardo da
Vinci in the early 1500s and perfected in 1573 by E. Danti, was a
workable camera. It was widely used in the early 1800s—but not
for taking photographs. The reason: The technology for photos
didn't exist. People used the camera for tracing images instead,
placing transparent paper over its glass plate.

In the 1830s, French artist L. J. M. Daguerre began
experimenting with ways of recording a camera's images on light-
sensitive photographic plates. By 1838 he'd made some progress;

using silver-coated sheets of copper, he found a way to capture an image.

However, the image was so faint that it was barely visible. He tried dozens of substances to see if they'd darken it…but nothing worked. Frustrated, Daguerre put the photographic plate away in a cabinet filled with chemicals and moved on to other projects. A few days later, Daguerre took the plate out. To his astonishment, the plate had mysteriously darkened; now the image was perfectly visible. One of the chemicals in the cabinet was almost certainly responsible…but which one?

He devised a method to find out. Each day he removed one chemical from the cabinet and put a fresh photographic plate in. If the plate still darkened overnight, the chemical would be disqualified. If it didn't, he'd know he'd found the chemical he was looking for. It seemed like a good idea, but even after *all* the chemicals had been removed, the plate continued to darken. Daguerre wondered why. Then, examining the cabinet closely, he noticed a few drops of mercury that had spilled from a broken thermometer onto one of the shelves.

**Legacy:** Later experiments with mercury vapour proved that this substance was responsible. The daguerrotype's worldwide popularity paved the way for the development of photography.

**The Discovery:** Safety glass
**How It Happened:** In 1903 Edouard Benedictus, a French chemist, was experimenting in his lab when he dropped an empty glass flask on the floor. It shattered, but remained in the shape of a flask. Benedictus was bewildered. When he examined the flask more closely, he discovered that the inside was coated with a film residue of cellulose nitrate, a chemical he'd been working with earlier. The film had held the glass together.

Not long afterward, Benedictus read a newspaper article about a girl who had been badly injured by flying glass in a car accident. He thought back to the glass flask in his lab and realised that coating automobile windshields, as the inside of the flask had been coated, would make them less dangerous.

**Legacy:** Variations of the safety glass he produced—a layer of plastic sandwiched by two layers of glass—are still used in automobiles today.

# BOX-OFFICE BLOOPERS II

*Here are a few more movie mistakes to look for in popular films.*

**M**ovie: *Rear Window* (1954)
**Scene:** Jimmy Stewart, in a cast and sitting in a wheelchair, argues with Grace Kelly.
**Blooper:** His cast switches from his left leg to his right.

**Movie:** *Raiders of the Lost Ark* (1982)
**Scene:** German soldiers and Gestapo agents lift the ark.
**Blooper:** Paintings of C-3PO and R2-D2, the androids from *Star Wars* (another George Lucas film), are included among the hieroglyphics on the wall.

**Movie:** *Close Encounters of the Third Kind* (1977)
**Scene:** Richard Dreyfus and Melinda Dillon smash through several road blocks as they near Devil's Tower.
**Blooper:** The licence plate on their station wagon keeps changing.

**Movie:** *Abbot and Costello Go to Mars* (1953)
**Blooper:** In the movie they actually go to Venus.

**Movie:** *Camelot* (1967)
**Scene:** King Arthur (Richard Harris) praises his medieval kingdom while speaking to some of his subjects.
**Blooper:** Harris is wearing a Band-Aid on his neck.

**Movie:** *The Fortune Cookie* (1966)
**Scene:** Walter Matthau leaves one room and enters another—and appears to lose weight in the process.
**Blooper:** Matthau suffered a heart attack while this scene was being filmed; only half was completed before he entered the hospital. He returned five months later to finish the job— 40 pounds lighter than he was in the first part of the scene.

**Movie:** *Diamonds Are Forever* (1971)
**Scene:** James Bond tips his Ford Mustang up onto two wheels and drives through a narrow alley to escape from the bad guys.
**Blooper:** The Mustang enters the alley on its two right wheels— and leaves the alley on its two *left* wheels.

Sherlock Holmes kept his tobacco in the toe of a Persian slipper.

# THE TRUTH ABOUT LEMMINGS

*You've probably heard that lemmings commit mass suicide when they experience overpopulation. It turns out that isn't true…and you can blame the myth on the Walt Disney Company.*

## THE MYTH

In 1958 Walt Disney produced *White Wilderness*, a documentary about life in the Arctic. This film gave us the first close look at the strange habits of arctic rodents called lemmings.

• "They quite literally eat themselves out of house and home," says the narrator. "With things as crowded as this, someone has to make room for somebody somehow. And so, Nature herself takes a hand….A kind of compulsion seizes each tiny rodent and, carried along by an unreasoning hysteria, each falls into step for a march that will take them to a strange destiny."

• The film shows a pack of lemmings marching to the sea, where they "dutifully toss themselves over a cliff into certain death in icy Arctic waters." "The last shot," says critic William Poundstone, "shows the sea awash with dying lemmings."

• The narrator says: "Gradually strength wanes…determination ebbs away…and the Arctic Sea is dotted with tiny bobbing bodies."

## THE TRUTH

• According to a 1983 investigation by Canadian Broadcasting Corporation producer Brian Vallee, *White Wilderness*'s lemming scene was sheer fabrication.

• Vallee says the lemmings were brought to Alberta—a landlocked province that isn't their natural habitat—where Disney folks put them on a giant turntable piled with snow to film the "migration segment."

• Then, Vallee reports, they recaptured the lemmings and took them to a cliff over a river. "When the well-adjusted lemmings wouldn't jump," writes Poundstone, "the Disney people gave Nature a hand [and tossed them off]….Lemmings don't commit mass suicide. As far as zoologists can tell, it's a myth."

# MEN OF LETTERS

*In his book* Dear Wit, *H. Jack Lang collected celebrities' humorous correspondence. Here are a few examples.*

## GIVE HIM A BRAKE

In 1872, George Westinghouse asked Cornelius Vanderbilt, multimillionaire president of the New York Central Railroad, to listen to his ideas about developing an "air brake." Vanderbilt wrote back:
*I have no time to waste on fools. —Vanderbilt*
After the brake was successfully tested on another railroad, Vanderbilt wrote to Westinghouse asking to see it. Westinghouse wrote back:
*I have no time to waste on fools. —Westinghouse*

## FIERY WRITING

The celebrated author Somerset Maugham once received a manuscript from a young writer, accompanied by a letter that said:
*Do you think I should put more fire into my stories?*
Maugham replied: *No. Vice versa.*

## GIVE HIM A SIGN

In the early 1960s, columnist Leonard Lyons complained to President John F. Kennedy that JFK's signature was only worth $65 to collectors—compared to $175 for George Washington and $75 for Franklin Roosevelt. Kennedy responded:
*Dear Leonard: In order not to depress the market any further, I will not sign this letter.*

## NO JOKE

A publisher who wanted an endorsement for a humour book sent Groucho Marx a copy and asked for Groucho's comments. Marx wrote back:
*I've been laughing ever since I picked up your book. Some day I'm going to read it. —Groucho*

---

Germans drink more beer per capita than any other nation on Earth.

## MAKING THE BREAST OF IT
At dinner, Winston Churchill asked his American hostess, "May I have a breast?" She replied: "In this country, it is customary to ask for white or dark meat." The next day, as an apology, Churchill sent her an orchid, with a card that said:
*Madam: I would be most obliged if you would pin this on your white meat. —Winston Churchill*

## ARE YOU SURE?
Playwright Eugene O'Neill received a cable from Hollywood bombshell Jean Harlow asking him to write a play for her. "Reply collect in 20 words," the cable requested. O'Neill cabled back:
*NO NO NO NO NO NO NO NO NO NO*
*NO NO NO NO NO NO NO NO NO NO*

## FANCY FOOTWORK
Jack London's publisher sent him the following letter when the famous novelist missed a publishing deadline:
*My dear Jack London: If I do not receive those stories from you by noon tomorrow, I'm going to put on my heaviest soled shoes, come down to your room, and kick you downstairs. I always keep my promises. —Editor*
London wrote back:
*Dear Sir: I, too, would always keep my promises if I could fulfill them with my feet. —Jack London*

## WHAT'S THE STORY?
After a news item reported that Rudyard Kipling was paid $5 a word for his magazine articles, an autograph collector sent him a check for $5 and a letter asking for a single word. Kipling wrote back:
*Thanks. —Rudyard Kipling*
Afterward the autograph-seeker wrote back:
*Dear Mr. Kipling: I sold the story of your one-word reply to a magazine for two hundred dollars. The enclosed cheque is your half.*

# OH, KATE!

*Katharine Hepburn was one of the greatest actors of all times. Here are some of her unscripted comments.*

"When I started out, I didn't have any desire to be an actress or to learn how to act. I just wanted to be famous."

"Sometimes I wonder if men and women really suit each other. Perhaps they should live next door and just visit now and then."

"If you give audiences half a chance they'll do half your acting for you."

"Being a housewife and a mother is the biggest job in the world, but if it doesn't interest you, don't do it....I would have made a terrible parent. The first time my child didn't do what I wanted, I'd kill him."

"I find men today less manly ...but a woman of my age is not in a position to know exactly how manly they are."

"Great performing in any field is total simplicity, the capacity to get to the essence, to eliminate all the frills and foibles."

"If you survive long enough, you're revered—rather like an old building."

"I don't care what is written about me as long as it isn't true."

"A sharp knife cuts the quickest and hurts the least."

"Life is to be lived. If you have to support yourself, you had bloody well better find some way that is going to be interesting. And you don't do that by sitting around wondering about yourself."

"What the hell—you might be right, you might be wrong... but don't just *avoid*."

"The male sex, as a sex, does not universally appeal to me."

"You can't change the music of your soul."

"Life's what's important. Walking, houses, family. Birth and pain and joy. Acting's just waiting for a custard pie."

---

Ruling class: Winston Churchill and Franklin Roosevelt were seventh cousins once removed.

# SYDNEY, SHARKS AND SWIMMING

*Sydneysiders have a healthy respect for sharks—after all it's their domain we are entering—but it hasn't always been safe to swim at Sydney beaches.*

Prior to 1900, swimming at Sydney's beaches was illegal due to the strict decency and clothing standards of the day. With the new century came new attitudes and the pastime of swimming at surf beaches increased in popularity as more and more people learnt how to swim.

### AN OFFAL STORY
Concurrent with this new fashion for beach swimming was the establishment of sewerage outfall pipes off Sydney's beaches. The Malabar sewerage pipe, off Sydney's southern beaches, handled the offal from one of Sydney's largest abattoir and the amount of meat and lard discharged untreated into the Pacific Ocean was enough to sustain not only a huge population of seabirds but also an unnaturally large population of sharks. It has been recorded that the stomach contents of a large great white shark caught off the Malabar outfall in 1940 included several legs of mutton, a hindquarter of a pig and a large amount of horseflesh.

### HUNGRY HUNTERS
The level of shark attacks at Sydney's beaches was at its greatest in the two decades between 1920 to 1940 when 18 attacks were recorded. This high level was due to a combination of factors: the increased popularity of surfing and swimming at coastal beaches; the closure of the Eden whaling station, which forced the shark population to find other food sources; the burgeoning Sydney population; and the location of the sewerage outfall pipes.

### THE NET RESULT
In 1935, a committee was set up to investigate how other parts of the world handled shark protection and in 1937, it was decided to

---

When the platypus was sent to England in 1798 it was considered a hoax.

run mesh nets off the surf beaches of Sydney. The nets were set near the bottom, so that swimmers and boats were not entangled. The nets acted not only as a barrier to keep the sharks out but also as a means of catching and killing the sharks. As most sharks produce very few young, by killing the adult sharks it was a very effective and efficient way to reduce the resident shark population in as short a time as possible.

A total of 1,500 sharks were caught in the first year of meshing off Sydney in 1939, including 900 very large sharks thought to be man killers. As time went by, fewer and fewer were caught. Less than 150 sharks of all sizes were caught in 2002 and this lower number continues today.

For over 70 years, Sydney's beaches have been meshed to protect swimmers from shark attacks. There have been only two shark attacks (one fatal in 1951) on Sydney's beaches since meshing started.

\*　　\*　　\*　　\*

## GENTLE GIANTS

In the shark world, being the biggest doesn't necessarily mean being the most dangerous.

Often confused with whales because of their size and tendency to swim close to the surface, the whale shark, with its distinctive skin pattern of white spots and stripes, can grow up to lengths of 20 metres (66 feet), and takes the prize for being the largest fish on Earth. However, with a diet of plankton and small fish, the whale shark is harmless to humans and extremely docile in nature.

Ningaloo Reef, off the coast of northern Western Australia, draws scientists and tourists each year as it plays host to an annual visit by countless numbers of these sharks. During the months of March through to May, the corals on the reef have a mass spawning and it is this which attracts great numbers of these plankton-eating whale sharks—a spectacle not repeated anywhere else in the world.

The most common weed in Australia is alligator weed. Lantana is number ten.

# MORE CARNIVAL TRICKS

*Here's more information about carnival booths to look out for—and some tips on how to beat them.*

**T**he Booth: "Plate pitch"
**The Object:** Players toss coins onto plates sitting on the heads of large stuffed animals. If a coin remains on the plate, the player wins the animal.
**How It's Rigged:** Some carnival suppliers put their glass plates in a furnace for 48 hours. The heat makes the sides of the plates droop, so the surface of the plate is significantly flatter than that of the same style of plate found in stores. This makes it easier for the coins to slip off the plates.
• Some operators polish the dishes with furniture wax to make them slippery, or set them on an angle so the coins slide off.
**How to Win:** It helps to practise at home for this one.
• The best pitches are thrown softly, in a low arc. According to one manufacturer, if the coin lands flat against the back edge of the plate in Plate Pitch, it will rebound back into the centre.
• Toss the coin so it travels in a line to other plates if it skips off the first plate.

**The Booth:** "Spill the Milk"
**The Object:** Throw a ball and knock down a pyramid of three aluminum bottles shaped like old-fashioned milk bottles. Knocking all three pins completely off their stand wins you a prize.
**How It's Rigged:** The bottles look identical, but they don't weigh the same amount. Some carnies set a heavier bottle on the bottom row. That way, the ball will hit the lighter two bottles first, and won't have enough energy to knock the heavy bottle off.
• Some unscrupulous operators fill the bottles with molten lead, so they're too heavy to be knocked over with a softball. Other operators cast lead in the *side* of the bottle so it can be knocked down, but not off the stand.
• If the player is allowed two shots, there may be a different setup. One bottle may be unweighted, while the remaining two

---

According to astronaut Neil Armstrong, the moon's surface is "fine and powdery."

are different weights. The carny sets the unweighted bottle on top and gives the player a heavier softball. If the player strikes the centre of the pyramid, the top bottle flies off, the lighter lower bottle is knocked over, and the heavier bottle remains standing. Then the player is given an ultralight ball that can't be thrown hard enough to knock over the heaviest bottle.

**How to Win:** Make sure the game isn't rigged. Ask about the weights of the bottles and the ball and don't play until you get a satisfactory answer. Ask to examine the bottles. Check whether they're the same weight or if the weight is distributed unevenly.

• Carnies say the best way to win at Spill the Milk is a direct hit in the triangular area where the three bottles meet.

**The Booth:** "High Striker"

**The Object:** Using an oversized mallet, hit a cast-iron striker to the top of a 6.5-metre (21-foot)-high tower to ring the bell.

**How It's Rigged:** Most High Strikers in use today are honest, but, according to one manufacturer, some early models used several "guy wires" that held up the tower. Unknown to players, one of the guy wires led from a stake directly down the front of the tower. The striker travelled along this wire.

• The unscrupulous agent would lean up against the phony guy wire and keep it taut enough so a player could ring the bell on the first and second tries. But on the player's third swing (the one that could win the prize), the agent would stop leaning on the wire. With the wire slack, the striker brushed against the tower as it travelled skyward, and friction prevented it from reaching the top. The player had no chance to win the grand prize for three rings.

**How to Win:** "The trade secret is to hit the pad squarely, just as if you were splitting wood," according to the manufacturer.

**The Booth:** "Basketball"

**The Object:** Toss the basketball into a hoop while standing behind a designated foul line.

**How It's Rigged:** Some operators overinflate the balls, so they have more bounce and are tougher to get through the hoop. Others don't attach the hoops securely to the backboard, so the rims vibrate when struck by the ball. This keeps rim shots from going in.

# THE STORY OF LAS VEGAS

*Have you ever wondered how Las Vegas became the gambling capital of the world? Here's the story.*

**N**AME
"Las Vegas" means "the meadows" or "the fertile plains" in Spanish. The city acquired this name in the early 1800s, when it was a peaceful rest stop on the Old Spanish Trail.

**HISTORY.** Ironically, the Mormons were the first to settle Las Vegas, in 1855. They built the first church, first fort, and first school in Nevada, only to abandon them three years later. Pioneers were still using the site as a watering hole and, as one missionary noted, few could be induced to attend the church. "Only one man attended," he wrote. "The rest of them were gambling and swearing at their camps."

Las Vegas didn't become a real town until almost 50 years later. Because of its central location and ample water supply, the railroad decided it would make an ideal stop on the transcontinental train line. They bought the land and, one scorching hot day in 1905, auctioned it off to 1,200 eager settlers. A few days later, the town appeared: a haphazard assortment of canvas tent saloons, gambling clubs, and drinking parlours that quickly established the city's character and reputation. Despite prohibitionist protests, Las Vegas maintained its early emphasis on nightlife and continued to flourish throughout the 1920s. "Such places as the Red Rooster, the Blue Goose, the Owl, and Pair-o-Dice were temporarily inconvenienced from time to time by raids from federal agents," writes one local historian. "But they were, of course, as safe as a church from local interference."

In 1931 the Nevada state legislature enacted two well-publicised "reforms": They liberalised divorce laws, changing residency requirements from six months to six weeks, and officially legalised gambling. Now Las Vegas had two unique attractions. While the rest of the country was suffering through the Great Depression, Las Vegas casinos made a killing catering to the workers constructing nearby Boulder Dam, as well as the 230,000 tourists who came to see it. (Las Vegas also became a significant divorce centre after movie star Clark Gable's wife, Rhea, chose it as the place to divorce him.)

The first full-fledged resort, the plush El Rancho Vegas, was built in 1940. Another (the New Frontier) followed, and the notorious Vegas "strip" was established. A military base and a magnesium plant were installed nearby in the early 1940s, and both brought more people to the area and kept the town prosperous through World War II. By 1970 more than half of Nevada's entire population lived in Las Vegas.

**MAIN INDUSTRY.** Las Vegas as we know it today might never have been born if it weren't for gangster Ben "Bugsy" Siegel. Wanted for murder in New York, Siegel was sent out West to set up a booking service for the mob and became obsessed with the idea of creating a "glittering gambling mecca in the desert." He borrowed $6 million in mob money and constructed the Flamingo Hotel, a lavish olive-green castle surrounded by a 16-hectare (40-acre) garden that was planted literally overnight in imported soil brought in by truck.

Unfortunately for Bugsy, the Flamingo was initially a bust. To top it off, the mob found out he'd been skimming profits. They had him killed in 1947. But business at the Flamingo picked up, and over the next few years Mafia-owned resort casinos sprang up all along Highway 91, the Las Vegas strip.

According to *The Encyclopedia of American Crime*, for example:
- Meyer Lansky put up much of the money for the Thunderbird.
- The Desert Inn was owned by the head of the Cleveland mob.
- The Dunes "was a goldmine" for the New England mob.
- The Sahara "was launched by the Chicago mob."

"Despite the huge profits," the *Encyclopedia* adds, "by the mid-'50s the mob had started selling off its properties to individuals and corporations. In the 1960s billionaire Howard Hughes started buying one casino after another. In the early 1970s the mob's interest in Vegas was reportedly at a low point, but by the close of the decade, many observers concluded, mobsters were returning to the scene."

# MORE EPITAPHS

*More unusual epitaphs and tombstone rhymes from
our wandering BRI tombstoneologists.*

*Seen in Oxfordshire, England:*
**Here lies the body of
John Eldred,**
At least he will be here when
he is dead.
But now at this time, he is
alive,
The 14th of August, 1765.

*Seen in Plymouth, USA:*
**Richard Lawton**
Here lie the bones of Richard
Lawton,
Whose death, alas! was
strangely brought on.
Trying his corns one day to
mow off,
His razor slipped and cut his
toe off.
His toe, or rather, what it grew
to,
An inflammation quickly flew
to.
Which took, Alas! to
mortifying,
And was the cause of Richard's
dying.

*Seen in Luton, England:*
**Thomas Proctor**
Here lies the body of Thomas
Proctor,
Who lived and died without
a doctor.

*Seen in Shrewsbury, England:*
**Here lies the body of Martha
Dias,**
Who was always uneasy, and
not over-pious;
She lived to the age of three
score and ten,
And gave to the worms what
she refused to the men.

*Seen in Marshfield, USA:*
**Here lies the body of William
Jay,**
Who died maintaining his right
of way;
He was right, dead right, as he
sped along,
But he's just as dead as if he'd
been wrong.

*Seen in Lee, USA:*
**In Memory of Mrs. Alpha
White, Weight 309 lbs.**
Open wide ye heavenly gates
That lead to the heavenly
shore;
Our father suffered in passing
through
And Mother weighs much
more.

*Seen in Putman, USA:*
**Phineas G. Wright**
Going, But Know Not Where

# FAMILIAR MELODIES

*Some tunes are so familiar that it seems like they've just always
been around. Of course, every song has its beginning. Here
are the stories of how some old favourites were written.*

**D**IXIE
Written in 1859 by Daniel Decatur Emmett for a
blackface minstrel show. Ironically, though his song
became the anthem of the South, Emmett was a northerner who
detested the Confederacy. When he found out the song was going
to be sung at Confederate President Jefferson Davis's inauguration,
he told friends, "If I had known to what use they were going to
put my song, I'll be damned if I'd have written it."

**HERE COMES THE BRIDE**
Composer Richard Wagner wrote the "Bridal Chorus" in 1848 for
his opera *Lohengrin*. He used it to score a scene in which the hero
and his new bride undress on their wedding night and prepare to
consummate their marriage. It was first used as a bridal march in
1858, when Princess Victoria (daughter of England's Queen
Victoria) married Prince Frederick William of Prussia.
Interestingly, because of the sexual nature of the original opera
scene, some religions object to using the song in wedding
ceremonies.

**CHOPSTICKS**
In 1877, 16-year-old Euphemia Allen, a British girl, published
"Chopsticks" under the pseudonym Arthur de Lulli. Included with
the sheet music were instructions telling the pianist to play the
song "with both hands turned sideways, the little fingers lowest,
so that the movement of the hands imitates the chopping from
which this waltz gets its name." Allen never wrote another song.

**TAPS**
As late as 1862, the U.S. military used a song called "Extinguish
Lights" to officially end the day. General Daniel Butterfield
disliked the song…so he decided to compose a new one to replace
it. He couldn't play the bugle, so he composed by whistling notes
to his butler, who'd play them back for Butterfield to evaluate.
They went through dozens of tunes before he got one he liked.

---

Aztec emperor Montezuma had a nephew, Cuitlahac, whose name meant "plenty of excrement."

# MEET DR. SEUSS

*Say hello to Dr. Seuss, a rhymer of rhymes both tight and loose.*
*A BRI favourite he really is; the following story is really his.*

**V**ITAL STATS
**Born:** March 2, 1904
**Died:** September 25, 1991, age 87
• Although married twice, he never had any children. His slogan: "You have 'em, I'll amuse 'em."
**Real Name:** Theodore Seuss Geisel
• He adopted "Seuss" as his writing name during Prohibition, while attending Dartmouth College. The reason: He was caught with a half-pint of gin in his room and was told to resign as editor of the college humour magazine as punishment. Instead, he just stopped using Geisel as a byline.
• Years later, he added "Dr." to his name "to sound more scientific." He didn't officially become a doctor until 1956, when Dartmouth gave him an honorary doctorate.

## CAREER STATS
**Accomplishments:** He wrote 48 books, selling more than 100 million copies in 20 languages. (Including four of the top 10 best-selling hardcover children's books of all time: *The Cat in the Hat, Green Eggs and Ham, Hop on Pop,* and *One Fish, Two Fish, Red Fish, Blue Fish.*)
• As a filmmaker, he won three Oscars—two for documentaries made in the 1940s (*Hitler Lives,* about Americans troops, and *Design for Death,* about Japanese warlords), and one in 1951 for animation (*Gerald McBoing-Boing*). By that time, he had written four kids' books and turned down Hollywood screenplay offers in order to keep writing them.
• In 1984 he won the Pulitzer Prize for his contribution to children's literature.
**Flops:** Only one—a novel called *The Seven Lady Godivas,* an "utterly ridiculous retelling of the story of Lady Godiva" that was first published in 1937 and republished 40 years later. He always wanted to write "The Great American Novel"…but the book bombed in 1977, too.

A typical eggshell takes up 12% of an egg's weight.

**How He Got Started:** He was working as a cartoonist in the late 1920s for *Judge* magazine. One of his cartoons "showed a knight using Flit insecticide to kill dragons." Someone associated with Flit's ad agency (McCann-Erikson) saw the cartoon and hired Geisel. For the next 10 years he created ads for Flit and other Standard Oil products. His greatest claim to fame at the time: a well-known ad phrase, "Quick Henry, the Flit!"

His contract with McCann-Erikson allowed him to write and publish books for kids, so he wrote *To Think That I Saw It on Mulberry Street*. It was turned down by 27 publishers. Said Seuss: "The excuse I got for all those rejections was that there was nothing on the market quite like it, so they didn't know whether it would sell." Vanguard Press finally picked it up in 1937, and it was an immediate success. So he quit the ad agency and began writing kids' books full-time.

## HOW HE GOT HIS IDEAS

"The most asked question of any successful author," Seuss said in 1989, "is 'How do you get your ideas for books?' " Over the years he did reveal a number of his inspirations:

### Horton Hatches the Egg

"Sometimes you have luck when you are doodling. I did one day when I was drawing some trees. Then I began drawing elephants. I had a window that was open, and the wind blew the elephant on top of the tree; I looked at it and said, 'What do you suppose that elephant is doing there?' The answer was: 'He is hatching an egg.' Then all I had to do was write a book about it. I've left that window open ever since, but it's never happened again."

### Green Eggs and Ham

• Bennett Cerf, the founder and publisher of Random House, bet Geisel $50 that he couldn't write a book using just 50 words.
• Geisel won the bet. "It's the only book I ever wrote that still makes me laugh," he said 25 years later. He added: "Bennett never paid!"

### Marvin K. Mooney, Will You Please Go Now?

"The puppy-like creature constantly asked to 'go' is ex-President Richard M. Nixon."

### The Lorax

Dr. Seuss's favourite book, he said, "is about people who raise hell in the environment and leave nothing behind." He wrote the story on a laundry list as he sat at a hotel pool in Kenya, watching a herd of elephants with his wife. "I wrote it as a piece of propaganda and disguised the fact," he told a reporter. "I was on the soapbox. I wasn't afraid of preaching—but I was afraid of being dull."

### Yertle the Turtle

"Yertle the turtle is Adolf Hitler."

### The 500 Hats of Bartholomew Cubbins

In 1937 Geisel was on a commuter train in Connecticut. "There was a very stiff broker sitting in front of me. I wondered what his reaction would be if I took his hat off and threw it out the window. I decided that he was so stuffy he would grow a new one."

### The Cat in the Hat

• In the early 1950s, novelist John Hersey was on a panel that analysed how reading was taught in a Connecticut school system. In May 1954, *Life* magazine published excerpts of the panel's report (called "Why Do Students Bog Down on the First R?"). In it, Hersey wrote that one of the major impediments to learning was the dull "Dick and Jane" material students were given— especially the illustrations. Kids, he said, should be inspired with "drawings like those wonderfully imaginative geniuses among children's illustrators, Tenniel, Howard Pyle, Dr. Seuss."

• A textbook publisher read the article and agreed. He contacted Dr. Seuss and asked him to create a reading book. The publisher sent Seuss a list of 400 words and told him to pick 220 to use in the book. The reason: People felt this was the maximum that "kids could absorb at one time."

• "Geisel went through the list once, twice and got nowhere," reports *Parents* magazine. "He decided to give it one more shot; if he could find two words that rhymed, they'd form the title and theme of the book. Within moments, *cat* and *hat* leaped off the page. But then it took him nine months to write the entire book."

# IT'S AUSTRALIAN, THAT'S WHAT!

*From red-back spiders to turquoise beaches and lifesavers, Australia is a land of icons. Here are just some of them—past and present.*

**H**ills **Hoist Clothes Line.** In 1945, Lance Hill conceived the idea for a rotary clothes line fitted with a hoist that allowed the frame to be raised and lowered. Rows of Hills Hoists soon lined suburban backyards, while crisp, white washing flew uniformly in the breeze. Thanks to inner-city living and smaller backyards, Hills Hoists are no longer such a familiar sight, but they are still sold throughout Australia, Asia, Europe and North America.

**Holden Cars.** If you think of an Australian car, you think of a Holden. It was the brainchild of General Motors Holden, a car-making company with roots dating back to the early 1900s. The first Holden that came off the assembly line, the FX model, was christened by Prime Minister Ben Chiefly in 1948. A sedan, it was priced at $1,466. The FB Holden hit the road in 1960. Modelled on the classic 1950 Chevy shape, this stylish vehicle soon became an automotive benchmark in luxury, design and engineering.

**Ute.** Victoria's Ford Motor Company came up with the idea of the multi-purpose "utility truck" in 1934. The "ute" was a farm truck that could also double as the family car on the weekends. The ute soon became synonymous with the Australian way of life: it was rugged and hard working, but also versatile, practical and, with a good dose of water, clean and presentable!

**Akubra.** Initially it was a stockman's hat, but now the Akubra sits comfortably on all kinds of heads—from film and sporting personalities to the average Australian man or woman. Benjamin Dunkerley first started to make the hats that would eventually be called "Akubras" in the early 1870s. Little did he know that in the 21st century, his 100 percent rabbit-crushed fur hat would be

---

Only two spiders in Australia are potentially fatal—the funnel web and red-back spider.

available in all kinds of styles from Aussie Gold and Banjo Patterson (for the more patriotic wearers) to Top Hat and Sombrero (for a touch of the exotic!). And if you're in any doubt as to whether your Akubra makes the top ten of the most popular Akubras, here's a ready reckoner (in descending order of popularity):

- Cattleman
- Snowy River
- Coober Pedy
- Bronco
- Arena
- Territory
- Pastoralist
- Plainsman
- Coolabah
- Leisure Time

**Hint**: Here's a typically Australian tip for cleaning your Akubra: use eucalyptus oil, or eucalyptus wash!

**Boomerang.** Australian Aborigines have used boomerangs to hunt and fight for thousands of years. Heavy boomerangs, or "throwing sticks," are thrown straight along the ground for distances of up to 200 metres (656 feet). They can easily kill a small animal, such as a rabbit, or stun a bigger animal, such as a kangaroo or a dingo.

Lighter boomerangs that return to the owner are thrown with a flick of the wrist. The boomerang then sweeps in a wide circle to scare animals out into open areas, before swinging back to the thrower.

**Victa Lawnmower.** Don't you hate it when the peace of Saturday mornings is shattered by the drone of a lawnmower? It was out with the old push mowers and in with a new petrol-powered lawnmower when Mervyn Victor Richardson developed the Victa in 1952. With enough power in its rotary-action blades to cut thick long grass, huge areas of rough grass were now turned into manageable lawn. By 1992, Victa had sold more than five million lawnmowers.

# CONDOM SENSE

*Condoms used to be an embarrassing subject. Now they're advertised in the magazines that BRI members often stash in the bathroom. Here's some condom trivia.*

**O**RIGIN
Condoms were invented in the mid-1500s by Gabriel Fallopius, an Italian doctor. (He was also the first person to describe fallopian tubes in medical literature.) His creation was made of linen and soon earned the nickname "overcoat". Fallopius believed that they prevented syphilis. They didn't.

## NAME
Legend has it that condoms were named after the Earl of Condom, personal physician to King Charles II of England in the mid-1600s. The king feared catching syphilis from his dozens of mistresses and ordered the earl to devise a solution.
• Condom's invention, a sheath made of oiled sheep intestine, became popular among the king's noblemen (who were also looking for protection against venereal disease). It was the noblemen, not Condom, who called the prophylactics "condoms." Condom hated having his name associated with them.
• Condoms became known as "rubbers" in the 1850s, when they actually *were* made of vulcanised rubber. These were thick, expensive, and uncomfortable. Owners were supposed to wash them out and reuse them until they cracked or tore. Disposable, thin latex condoms did not become widely available until the 1930s.

## MISCELLANY
• Four billion condoms are sold worldwide every year—enough to circle the globe 16 times.
• How does the U.S. Food and Drug Administration test the strength of condoms? By filling them with air until they pop. The average condom swells to the size of a watermelon before it bursts. Government regulators also cut condoms into rubberband-like pieces and stretch them until they snap.
• Most Muslim countries forbid the sale of green condoms, because green is a sacred colour in Islam.

# CONTROVERSIAL CHARACTERS

*Even cartoon characters and dolls can be accused of being a bad influence on children. Here are a few who have caused major controversy.*

**T**he Character: Mighty Mouse
**The Controversy:** Did Mighty Mouse take cocaine on April 23, 1988, in the TV cartoon show, *Mighty Mouse: The New Adventures?*
**The Fight:** In 1988 a Tupelo, Mississippi, watchdog group called the American Family Association (AFA) complained to CBS about a scene in a *Mighty Mouse: The New Adventure* cartoon. Reverend Donald Wildmon, head of the AFA, described the scene as follows: "Mighty Mouse is down in the dumps, and he reaches in his cape, pulls out a substance and sniffs it through his nostrils, and from that point on in the cartoon he is his normal self." Wildmon charged that the substance Mighty Mouse "snorted" was cocaine.
**The Reaction:** CBS producer Ralph Bakshi, who was responsible for the cartoon, angrily rejected the accusation: "This is Nazism and McCarthyism all over again. I don't advocate drugs—that's death. I'm a cartoonist, an artist, not a pornographer. Who are these people anyway? Why does anybody listen to them?" According to Bakshi, Mighty Mouse was actually sniffing crushed flowers he had placed in his pocket during an earlier scene. According to the CBS version of the story, Mighty Mouse was sad because the female character he was attracted to did not love him. So he took out the flowers she'd given him in the earlier scene and sniffed them.

**The Characters:** Popeye the Sailor and Olive Oyl
**The Controversy:** Should Popeye and Olive take a pro-choice stand on abortion?
**The Fight:** In July 1992, Bobby London, the artist who wrote and drew the syndicated *Popeye* comic strip for King Features, decided

---

"to show these old cartoon characters coping with the modern world." He submitted a strip with the following plot:
- Olive Oyl receives a baby Bluto doll in the mail and doesn't want to keep it.
- She and Popeye get into an argument about what to do with it. Olive Oyl tells Popeye that she wants to "send the baby back to its maker."
- Two priests happen to be walking by and hear the argument. They mistakenly assume that Olive Oyl is talking about having an abortion and try to persuade her not to do it. When that fails, the priests try to get passers-by to help. Olive Oyl tells them that "she can do what she wants to do, because it's her life."

**The Reaction:** King Features fired London and withdrew the strip before it was published.

**The Character:** Mattel's Barbie doll
**The Controversy:** Does Barbie promote the "radical agenda" of environmentalism?
**The Fight:** In the wake of Earth Day 1990, Mattel decided to promote its new line of Barbie dolls with the "Barbie Summit," an all-expenses-paid gathering of children who had submitted winning suggestions on how to improve the world. In the commercial announcing the contest, Barbie asked viewers how they would help make the world a better place—and offered a seemingly innocuous suggestion: "We could keep the trees from falling, keep the eagles soaring," she said.

But the Oregon Lands Commission, an anti-environmentalist lobbying group, was outraged with the ad. They claimed it was exposing children to "the preservationist's radical agenda." "We want to wake up corporate American to the fact that powerful, monied groups are at work shutting down the engines of this country and they are doing it in the name of environmentalism," the commission's spokesperson claimed. The commission organised a boycott, telling its 61,000 members that buying Barbie dolls "would help stop timber harvesting."

**The Reaction:** Mattel went ahead with the promotion, which was a success. "We kind of thought," explained a Mattel spokesperson, "how can anybody criticise a program that is designed to give children a voice in a world they are going to inherit?"

# INSIDE CITIZEN KANE

*Recently, Citizen Kane was voted the #1 movie of the century. Here's some info on America's most celebrated feature film, provided by BRI member Ross Owens.*

**B**ACKGROUND
On October 30, 1938, the Mercury Theatre of the Air broadcast a radio dramatisation of H. G. Wells's *War of the Worlds*, in which Martians invade the Earth (*Ed. note:* See "Mars Invasion," *Bathroom Reader #3*). The plot was implausible, but the performance was so realistic that thousands of Americans believed it—and actually fled their homes or prepared for a full-scale Martian war.

The man behind the radio play was 23-year-old Orson Welles (who produced and directed the broadcast). The publicity he received made him a national celebrity, and two years later RKO studios hired him to direct *Citizen Kane*, a film about a newspaper mogul who destroys his life in an endless pursuit of power.

## WILLIAM RANDOLPH HEARST

• In many ways, it's amazing that *Citizen Kane* was ever made. Though its characters were supposedly fictional, the film was actually a scathing biography of real-life press baron William Randolph Hearst—head of the Hearst Newspaper chain and one of the most powerful people in America. Naturally, he wanted the movie stopped.

• When he learned that RKO was making the movie, Hearst tried to have the film destroyed. Working through the head of MGM studios, he tried to bribe RKO president George Schaefer with $800,000 (the amount *Citizen Kane* cost to make) to destroy the film's negative. Schaefer refused.

• When that attempt failed, Hearst threatened to sue the studio for libel. RKO took the threat seriously; it delayed the film's release for two months until its lawyers were convinced that the suit wouldn't stand up in court.

• Hearst kept the heat on. Before the film hit the theatres, rumors began spreading that Hearst was planning to attack the entire film industry—not just RKO—in newspaper editorials. This frightened the major Hollywood studios (which also owned or

controlled most U.S. moviehouses), so they refused to show
*Citizen Kane* in their theatres. It had to premiere in smaller,
independent theatres.

## THE OUTCOME
• The film premiered in 1939. It was a commercial flop, due in
large part to Hearst's attacks…plus the fact that his papers
wouldn't accept advertising for it.
• Hearst's influence was felt even at the Academy Awards—
where Hearst supporters in the audience booed loudly every time
the picture was mentioned. Nominated in 8 different categories
(including Best Picture), *Kane* won only one award—for Best
Original Screenplay. It lost Best Picture to a film called *How
Green Was My Valley*.
• Orson Welles never recovered from the disaster. RKO refused
to give him the level of artistic freedom he had making *Kane*, and
most of his later film projects either failed or were never finished.

## THE SECRET WORD
**The Idea.** The first scene of the movie shows Charles Foster Kane
crying out the mysterious name "Rosebud" on his deathbed. The
name remains a secret until the last scene, when it's revealed that
Rosebud was the name of Kane's childhood sled. The idea of
giving Charles Foster Kane a sled was first suggested by Herman J.
Mankiewicz, the film's screenwriter. As a boy, Mankiewicz had
had his favourite bicycle stolen, an experience he never forgot. He
thought a similar story would be useful in the film.
**The Name.** No one knows exactly how the sled got the name
"Rosebud." Some suggestions:
• Orson Welles sometimes told interviewers that Rosebud was
the pet name Hearst had given mistress Marion Davies's
nose…but in other interviews, he claimed it was the nickname
Hearst had given to Davies's private parts.
• Welles's biographer, Charles Higham, points out that the 1914
Kentucky Derby winner was Old Rosebud—and that a reporter in
the movie suggests that Rosebud may have been a racehorse.
• Rosebud may actually have been the nickname of one of the
staff's ex-girlfriends. In 1942 a woman threatened to sue Herman
Mankiewicz, claiming she'd been the writer's mistress in the 1920s
and that Rosebud was a nickname he'd given *her*.

# ORDER IN THE COURT!

*Disorderly Conduct and Disorder in the Court are two books featuring amusing selections from court transcripts. They make great bathroom reading material—especially for lawyers. These quotes are taken directly from court records. People really said this stuff.*

**B**ORED IN COURT
**Defendant:** "Judge, I want you to appoint me another lawyer."
**Judge:** "And why is that?"
**Defendant:** "Because the public defender isn't interested in my case."
**Judge (to Public Defender):** "Do you have any comments on your defendant's motion?"
**Public Defender:** "I'm sorry, Your Honor, I wasn't listening."

## JUDGE & JURY

**Judge:** "Is there any reason you could not serve as a juror in this case?"
**Potential juror:** "I don't want to be away from my job for that long."
**Judge:** "Can't they do without you at work?"
**Potential juror:** "Yes, but I don't want them to know it."

**Judge to Defendant:** "You have a right to a trial by jury, but you may waive that right. What do you wish to do?"
**Defendant:** (Hesitates.)
**Lawyer to Defendant:** "Waive."
**Defendant:** (Waves at the judge.)

## UNTIL PROVEN GUILTY

**Lawyer:** "Have you ever been convicted of a felony?"
**Defendant:** "Yes."
**Lawyer:** "How many?"
**Defendant:** "One, so far."

**Judge:** "The charge here is theft of frozen chickens. Are you the defendant, sir?"
**Defendant:** "No, sir, I'm the guy who stole the chickens."

**10% of Americans read the Bible every day.**

**Defence Attorney:** "Are you sure you did not enter the Seven-Eleven and hold up the cashier on June 17 of this year?"
**Defendant:** "I'm pretty sure."

## ALICE IN LAWYERLAND
**Lawyer:** "Could you briefly describe the type of construction equipment used in your business?"
**Witness:** "Four tractors."
**Lawyer:** "What kind of tractors are they?"
**Witness:** "Fords."
**Lawyer:** "Did you say 'four?' "
**Witness:** "Ford. Ford. Like the Ford. It is a Ford tractor."
**Lawyer:** "You didn't say 'four,' you just said 'Ford?' "
**Witness:** "Yes, Ford. That is what you asked me, what kind of tractors."
**Lawyer:** "Are there four Ford tractors? Is that what there is?"
**Witness:** "No, no. You asked me what kind of a tractor it was and I said Ford tractors."
**Lawyer:** "How many tractors are there?"
**Witness:** "Four."

## GOOD CALL
**Judge:** "It is the judgment of this court that you be sentenced to the state prison...for a term of ten years, the maximum penalty."
**District Attorney:** "Will that be dangerous or non-dangerous offender, Your Honour?"
**Judge:** "Well, considering the flagrant nature of his offense, the court finds that he's a dangerous offender."
**Defendant:** "How in the hell can you find me a dangerous offender? There's nothing in there showing any violent crime. What's wrong with anybody anyway? You take that son-of-a-bitch and—"
**Judge:** "That will be it; you're remanded to the custody of the sheriff."
**Defendant:** "You son-of-a-bitch. You bald-headed son-of-a-bitch, when I get out of there, I'll blow your f——g head away. You no-good bald-headed son-of-a-bitch."
**Judge:** "Get that down in the record, he's threatened to blow the judge's head off."

In 1955 a book was returned to the Cambridge University library that was 288 years overdue.

## MISTAKEN IDENTITY?

**Prosecutor:** "Could you point to someone in this courtroom, or maybe yourself, to indicate exactly how close to a hair colour you are referring to?"

**Witness:** "Well, something like hers (points at the defence attorney) except for more—the woman right here in front (points at defence attorney again). Except for more cheap bleached-blond hair."

**Prosecutor:** "May the record reflect, Your Honour, the witness has identified Defence Counsel as the cheap blonde."

## HOT WITNESS

**Prosecutor:** "Did you observe anything?"

**Witness:** "Yes, we did. When we found the vehicle, we saw several unusual items in the car on the right front floorboard of the vehicle. There was what appeared to be a Molotov cocktail, a green bottle—"

**Defence lawyer:** "Objection. I'm going to object to that word, Molotov cocktail."

**Judge:** "What is your legal objection, Counsel?"

**Defence lawyer:** "It's inflammatory, Your Honour."

## SPEAK OF THE DEVIL

**Judge:** "Mr. E., you're charged here with driving a motor vehicle under the influence of alcohol. How do you plead, guilty or not guilty?"

**Defendant:** "I'm guilty as hell."

**Judge:** "Let the record reflect the defendant is guilty as hell."

\*   \*   \*   \*

## LIFE'S LIKE THAT

Two professors were sitting on a balcony at a nudist colony. "Have you read Marx?" the philosopher said to the historian. "Yes," the historian replied. "They're from the wicker chairs."

# THAT MAGNIFICENT MAN IN HIS FLYING MACHINE

*It was a time of daredevil flights, madcap aerial manoeuvres, and daring flights across uncharted territories. And one man wanted to claim the skies as his own.*

## VERSATILE SMITHY

Sir Charles Kingsford Smith was an aviation pioneer who set world records. And for his accomplishments he has an enduring presence in Australian history—a Sydney suburb is named after him as is the Sydney International airport; a street in Brisbane bears his name; and his plane, the *Southern Cross*, is featured on our $20 note.

Born in 1897, Smithy always knew that he wanted to fly. He signed up for World War I as soon as he could. On one mission, his plane was riddled with bullets—Smithy was shot in the foot and as a result had to have three toes amputated.

At the age of 20, Charles Kingsford Smith was presented with the Military Cross for bravery as a pilot by King George V. But that was where the war ended for Smithy.

When he returned to Australia, he became a pilot for West Australian Airways and delivered mail throughout the outback. Next he spent some time in Hollywood as a stuntman, sometimes dangling by his legs from the belly of a plane.

## FLYING INTO HISTORY

In 1927, he and his co-copilot, Charles Ulm, broke the round-Australia record by flying 12, 070 kilometres (7,500 miles) in 10 days and 5.5 hours—halving the previous record. This was just the beginning. Smithy began to ignite the world's imagination by a series of long-distance flights that criss-crossed the globe.

• On May 31, 1928, he and Ulm made the first air crossing of the Pacific when they set off from San Francisco, via Honolulu and Suva, in the wood-and-fabric plane that would become

Queen bees don't use their stingers—except to kill other queen bees.

synonymous with Smithy—the *Southern Cross*. In an open cockpit and with limited navigational equipment, they successfully flew across the featureless ocean. Eighty-three hours and 11,736 km (7,294 miles) later, they arrived in Brisbane. Crowds of more than 300,000 people greeted them when they flew into Sydney.

• On August 8, 1928, Smithy and Ulm made the first non-stop flight across Australia from Melbourne to Perth, a distance of 1,754 kilometres (1,090 miles).

• On September 10, 1928, Smithy made the first trans-Tasman flight from Sydney to New Zealand. Even fierce storms over the Tasman Sea weren't enough to stop him from reaching Christchurch after 14 hours in the air. People began to call him the "Columbus of the Skies."

• On June 25, 1929, he and Ulm really made history when they flew the *Southern Cross* from Australia to England in a record-breaking time of 12 days and 18 hours.

• In 1930, Smithy made the first successful east-west crossing of the North Atlantic when he flew the *Southern Cross* from London to New York.

• In 1930, he flew to Oakland Airport, California, and became the first pilot to circumnavigate the world.

• In 1930, Smithy flew 16,000 km (9, 944 miles) solo in the *Southern Cross Junior* and broke the England to Australia record by flying from London to Darwin in 9 days 22 hours and 15 minutes.

• In 1933, he broke the record for the solo flight from England to Australia by flying from London to Darwin in 7 days 4 hours and 44 minutes.

• In 1934, he made the first flight from Sydney to San Francisco—a more difficult route than his previous journey from San Francisco to Brisbane.

Smithy soon held more long-distance flying records than anyone else in the world. But there were always new records to set in the fiercely competitive world of aviation.

## OVER AND OUT

In November 1935, Smithy and his co-pilot, Tommy Pethybridge, took off from Croydon airport in London in the *Lady Southern Cross*. They were attempting to break the England to Australia record of 52 hours. A month later, however, came the news that nobody could believe—Smithy's plane had disappeared. He was 38 years old.

The plane had last been seen near the island of Aye, off the coast of Burma. Did the plane crash into the island or, as more recent investigations suggest, does the wreckage of the *Lady Southern Cross* lie beyond Burma in unknown seas? The final resting place of Australia's greatest aviator remains a mystery.

\*    \*    \*    \*

## BURNING BRIGHT!

**Background:** Midnight Oil rocked Australian airwaves for more than two decades. They were a truly Australian band with a completely Australian sound.

**The Band:** For 25 years the rock band Midnight Oil sang about being Australian. Their songs dealt with Aboriginal land rights, the environment, and what it was like to live in a land down under.

The band was spearheaded by high-profile activist Peter Garrett, President of the Australian Conservation Foundation and former member of Greenpeace International. The intensity of their songs was matched by the intensity of their live performances and the compelling figure of Peter Garrett, who seemed to embody the "power and the passion" of their words.

It was the political stage that ultimately interested Midnight Oil. In 1990, they performed on the streets of New York outside the offices of Exxon to protest against the effects of the Exxon Valdexzoil spill off the coast of Alaska. In the closing ceremony of the 2000 Sydney Olympic Games, the band performed *Beds are Burning* while wearing black clothes covered with the word "sorry."

In 2002, the members of the band left the spotlight and went their separate ways. Their music, however, burns on.

# A BREED APART

*Ever wonder why a Dachsund is so long and skinny—or why Great Danes are so tall? The answer: They were bred with a specific purpose in mind. Here are the stories behind the names and appearances of some of the world's most popular dog breeds.*

**B**ASSET HOUNDS. The name comes from the French adjective *bas*, which means "low thing." Originally bred to hunt rabbits, raccoons, and other small mammals. Their short legs make them relatively slow runners, but they're especially adept at chasing prey through thickets.

**BULLDOGS.** According to legend, in 1209 A.D. Lord William Earl Warren of Stamford, England, was looking out onto his meadow and saw two dogs fighting a bull. He so admired their courage that he gave the meadow to the townspeople—on the condition that they begin holding annual dog-bull fights. Over the next 600 years, bull baiting became a popular sport, and the bulldog breed evolved along with it. Like pit-bulls, bulldogs were originally bred to be fearless and vicious. But in 1835, bull baiting was banned in England. Bulldog lovers used breeding techniques to eliminate their viciousness, making them acceptable house pets.

**COCKER SPANIELS.** A member of the spaniel family of dogs that dates back to the 14th century. Their small size made them ideal for hunting woodcocks, earning them the name cockers, which eventually became cocking spaniels, then cocker spaniels.

**FRENCH POODLES.** Actually bred in 15th-century Germany as hunting dogs. The name "poodle" comes from the German word *pudeln*, which means "to splash." The reason: they're good swimmers and were often used to retrieve game from ponds, etc.

**GREAT DANES.** Got their name from the French, who thought they were Danish. They weren't: they were actually from Germany, where they were bred large enough to tackle and kill wild boars.

**ROTTWEILERS.** When soldiers of ancient Rome went into battle, they had no way of bringing enough fresh meat with them to last the entire campaign. So they brought cattle—and Rottweiler dogs to herd them. In 700 A.D., the local duke in an area of Germany the Romans had once occupied commissioned a Catholic church to be built near the ruins of some Roman baths. Because the baths had red tile roofs, the Duke issued instructions to build at "*das Rote Wil,*"—the red tiles. Later the area became known as the town of Rottweil, and the breed of dogs the Romans had left behind were called Rottweilers.

**GREYHOUNDS.** One of the oldest breeds of dogs; dating back as far as ancient Egypt (where they were a favourite pet of the pharoahs). Tomb paintings nearly 5,000 years old depict them hunting wild goats, deer, and other animals. According to one theory, they're actually named after the Greeks, taking their name from the word *Graius*, which means Grecian or Greek.

**DACHSHUNDS.** Although the name is derived from the German words *Dachs* (badger) and *Hund* (dog), dachshunds have been used to hunt animals as large as wild boars. Their long bodies make them ideal for chasing badgers and rabbits through their tunnels.

**BLOODHOUNDS.** The bloodhound's unrivalled sense of smell has made it one of the most popular hunting dogs in history. Dog experts believe it dates back several hundred years B.C. and was first used as a hunting dog in and around Constantinople. Its skills were so valuable that it became known as a royal, or "blooded," hound and was a favourite pet of aristocrats.

**PEKINGESE.** Came from imperial China, where the purest breeds were reserved for members of the royal family. The dogs were so precious that when British troops sacked the Imperial Palace in 1860, most of the pets were destroyed by their owners…who preferred killing them to surrendering them to the enemy. However one woman—the Emperor's aunt—committed suicide before she killed her dogs, and the British found five of them hiding behind a curtain in her quarters. The dogs were brought back to England, and one was presented to Queen Victoria. She fell in love with it, and the breed immediately became popular.

# ON THE LINE

*Odds & ends of telephone trivia and lore, from
the fabulous* Bathroom Reader *library.*

**ORIGIN OF THE PHONE NUMBER**
"The early phone exchanges listed only the names of
'subscribers' to the service, and the operators had to
memorise all of them in order to connect one to the other. The
idea of a telephone number was vigorously resisted by customers as
an indignity and loss of personal identification. However, during
an epidemic of measles in Lowell, Massachusetts in 1880, a
respected physician named Dr. Parker recommended the use of
numbers because he feared paralysis of the town's telephone
system if the four operators succumbed. He felt numbers would
make it easier for substitute operators to be trained. Surprisingly,
no one complained...and the new system proved so practical that
by 1895, official instructions to operators specified, 'Number
Please?' as the proper response to a customer."
—*The Telephone Book,* **by H. M. Boettinger**

**MESSAGE FROM A VISIONARY**
*The following was sent in a letter to "the organisers of the New Electric
Telephone Company" by Alexander Graham Bell on March 25, 1878.*
"At the present time we have a perfect network of gas pipes and
water pipes throughout our large cities. We have main pipes laid
under the streets [connected to] various dwellings, enabling people
to draw their supplies of gas and water from a common source.
  "In a similar manner it is conceivable that cables of telephone
wires could be laid under ground, or suspended overhead,
communicating by branch wires with private dwellings, counting
houses, shops, manufactories, etc., uniting them through the main
cable with a central office where the wire could be connected as
desired, establishing direct communication between any two
places in the city. Such a plan as this, though impracticable at
the present moment, will, I firmly believe, be the outcome of the
introduction of the telephone to the public....I [also] believe that
in the future, wires will unite the head offices of telephone

companies in different cities, and a man in one part of the country may communicate by word of mouth with another in a distant place."

## THE PRESIDENT AND THE TELEPHONE

"After the invention of the telephone in 1876, one might think that the president…would be one of the first persons to have one of the new instruments. Actually, a telephone was installed in the White House in 1877, during the administration of Rutherford B. Hayes. But that doesn't mean that the president had a phone. The phone was not even in his office, and it was used mainly by staff members and news reporters.

"Until 1898 chief executives rarely used the telephone, and none had an instrument in his office. When the president wanted to make a phone call, he had to leave his desk and go down the hall to the phone, just like everyone else. That changed abruptly in 1898 when war broke out with Spain. With action on two fronts, in Cuba and the Philippines, the president was suddenly faced with the need for more rapid communications than could be effected by the old methods.

"Accordingly, [a technician] was brought to the White House to install a communications centre…[which] provided President McKinley with private telephone lines to the War and Navy departments…There was also a direct line to Tampa, Florida, the primary staging area for the invasion of Cuba." That was the first time the telephone was deemed absolutely essential at 1600 Pennsylvanian Avenue.

—*The Telephone and Its Several Inventors,* by Lewis Coe

## EARLY TELEPHONE ETIQUETTE

"The subscriber has the right to expect the first word from the operator to be always 'Number?' to which the word 'Please' had better be added, but is not absolutely required.

"The subscriber has the right to expect the operator, if necessary, to say, 'That line is busy'; simply 'Busy' won't do.

"The operator has a right to expect that the subscriber will have the number ready when the operator answers, and that the operator will not be compelled to wait while the subscriber looks it up in the directory.

The average jellyfish is 95% water.

"Also that the subscriber will give the number in a a clear and distinct voice, and if the operator misunderstands a number, that she will be corrected, without evidence of anger in the tone of the subscriber."

—*Telephone Etiquette,* **published in 1905**

## OLDIES BUT GOODIES

• "New York City's first phone directory was issued in 1878. It was a small card with a printed list of 271 names. Almost a century later, 44 of the businesses listed in that first directory were still in operation, four of them at the very same address."

• Early rural telephone wires were strung across just about anything that was standing—not only telephone pulse, but windmills, silos, and even fence posts. In fact, it was fairly common for phone conversations to sputter and die out as a result of cattle rubbing against the fence lines."

• "Back in 1909, when 18,000 calls were placed daily between New York and Chicago (earning Bell $22,000, seven times a week), a special long distance salon was opened in Manhattan. To entice paying customers and get them into the 'long-distance habit', the New York Telephone company sent taxis to pick them up and bring them to the salon, whereupon they were escorted over oriental carpets to a gilded booth draped with silk curtains."

—*The What to Do While You're Holding the Phone Book,*
**by Gary Owens**

## THE BIRTH OF THE PAY PHONE

"It started at home, where families subscribed to telephone service and paid a monthly bill to lease the company's instrument. This phone was off-limits to non-subscribers, however. And early on, there were plenty of these. How, then, to summon the doctor? The police? The fire department? What would happen if a phoneless neighbour used another's phone? Who paid? How? How much? And what if it was three in the morning?

"With problems ranging from bookkeeping to friend keeping, it was essential that telephones be made accessible to all. Thus the first public pay station in the world went into service on June 1, 1880, in the office of the Connecticut Telephone Company in

**Thomas Edison was afraid of the dark.**

New Haven....For ten cents, paid to a uniformed attendant, anyone could talk to anyone.

"Soon, however, the coin-operated telephone was invented by William Gray. According to legend, Mr. Gray had been turned away by cold-hearted neighbours when he sought to use their telephone to call a doctor during a family emergency. Determined not to let it happen again—to himself or other 'phoneless people'—he patented and built 'the first coin-controlled apparatus for telephones.' It was installed in the Hartford Bank in 1889."

*—Once Upon a Telephone,*
**by Ellen Stern and Emily Gwathmey**

## LEARNING TO DEAL WITH THE TELEPHONE

**1917:** "Another hall abomination is a telephone. Unless we want our guests to know the price of their roast, or the family to listen aghast while we tell a white lie for society's sake, or the cook to hear us asking for a new one's references, don't put your telephone in the hall closet it, or keep it upstairs, where the family alone are the bored 'listeners in.'"

*—Interior Decoration for Modern Needs,*
**by Agnes Foster Wright**

**1927:** "...Then the telephone. Children usually love to use it and they should be taught to speak courteously on the pain of not being allowed to answer it. Children commit all sorts of discourtesies over the telephone if not checked and one often hears the casual 'Yep' and 'What?' and 'Wait.'"

*—Good Manners for Children,*
**by Elsie C. Mead and Theordora Mead Abel**

**The 1940s:** "When you have finished your telephone visit, and courteously said 'good-bye' or 'thank you,' replace the receiver gently. Slamming the receiver might cause a sharp crack in the ear of the person with whom you have been talking. Since you would not 'slam the door' after an actual visit, be just as careful in closing you telephone door.

*—You and Your Telephone,*
**distributed by the New York Telephone Company**

---

Janis Joplin was nominated "Ugliest Man on Campus" while in college.

## SOUNDS PHONY

"When the Bell system introduced push-button phone service, it could hardly have anticipated that the push-button phone would become America's most popular new musical instrument.

"Each of the buttons produces a different musical tone. If you punch out 33363213, you'll get a respectable rendition of "Raindrops Keep Fallin' On My Head"; 005883 plays the first bars of "Beethoven's Fifth Symphony"; and 1199009 gives you "Twinkle, Twinkle Little Star." It's unwise to try it, however, unless you call a friend first for the recital, because otherwise you might find yourself inadvertently serenading someone expensively by long distance."

—*The What to Do While You're Holding the Phone Book*,
by Gary Owens

## THE HISTORY OF "DIAL-A-PRAYER"

"Around 1955 (long before answering machines were available), a number of churches—notably the Hitchcock Memorial Presbyterian church in Scarsdale, New York—began broadcasting brief recorded prayers continuously by phone; after the Hitchcock's service had been publicised in a local newspaper, there was such a backlog of calls that the Scarsdale telephone system became temporarily jammed. By 1956 so many Dial-A-Prayer services were being offered by churches around the nation that *Time* magazine said they had become 'almost a characteristic feature of U.S. religion.'

"Later, in the 1960s and 1970s there would be many variations, most of them live rather than recorded: Dial-A-Shoulder, in New York, offering a sympathetic listener to any problem; Medicall in Chicago, offering quick medical consultation for a small fee; Operation Venus in Philadelphia, a free venereal-disease information service; Hot Line in Los Angeles, offering advice on personal problems to teenagers; and Dial-A-Joke, in New York, designed to make callers laugh at a recorded routine by a professional comedian.

"Today, these seem routine…but at the time they were a revolution—a whole new way to use the telephone."

—*Telephone: The First Hundred Years*,
by John Brooks

According to zoologists, elephants love to eat licorice.

# CRIKEY!

*Wrestling crocs and picking up hissing, venomous snakes, is all
in a day's work for this croc hunter.*

A star was "hatched" when the Discovery Channel's new
documentary, *The Crocodile Hunter*, showed off the unique
talents of Steve Irwin. Phones went red-hot, wanting
to know more about Steve, the Director of the Australia Zoo
in Queensland.

## CROCS RULE!
Steve first made his name in the Queensland government's rogue
crocodile relocation programme. Often catching the crocs single-
handedly, he became their most successful hunter, safely
relocating dozens of troublesome crocodiles without harm to them
or to him!

## HE'S A LITTLE RIPPER
Steve had ideal training for it. He learnt all about reptiles from his
dad, Bob. Bob and Steve's mum, Lyn, ran the Queensland Reptile
and Fauna Park (now called Australia Zoo), a centre for animals,
wildlife conservation and rehabilitation. Steve has spent his entire
life living and working with animals—he was in the thick of it
from the word go! For his sixth birthday, Steve was given a
4 metre (13 foot) scrub python and by the age of nine, he was
jumping into North Queensland rivers at night and catching
crocodiles. As a father-and-son team, Bob and Steve have caught,
or bred and then raised, every crocodile at the zoo.

Bob and Lyn retired in 1992 and Steve took over the reins of
the zoo. He married Terri Raines, an American whom he met
when she visited the zoo. Terri stars with Steve in *The Crocodile
Hunter*. Their daughter Bindi and dog Sui make up this dynamic
family.

## DANGER, DANGER, DANGER
The scar tissue on Steve's hands attests to the dangers of his job.
He has had a few bites from non-venomous reptiles, but never by

---

The highest point on the Australian continent is Mount Kosciuszko. The lowest is Lake Eyre.

a venomous snake. His handling technique with venomous snakes is one of respect and caution. However, wrestling crocs over the years has taken its toll physically on Steve. He has had surgery on his knees three times and more recently, shoulder surgery.

## FLAT OUT LIKE A LIZARD DRINKIN'

Through a chance encounter with a friend who was producing a TV commercial at the zoo in 1990, a punt was taken to show off Steve's diverse and entertaining talents. Since his TV debut in 1992, Steve has made 50 episodes of *The Crocodile Hunter*, 52 episodes of *Croc Files*, published a book, *The Crocodile Hunter: The Incredible Life and Adventures of Steve and Terri Irwin* and released his first movie, *The Crocodile Hunter Collision Course*. Around 500 million people in 136 countries have seen *The Crocodile Hunter* documentaries. The strong conservation message of these documentaries reflects Steve's passion to educate and enlighten people on our magnificent wildlife, particularly misunderstood and feared animals.

## CRIKEY THAT WAS DANGEROUS

Steve has a number of favourite sayings. These include:
*She's a little ripper*
*Beaut' bonza, mate*
*Crocs' rule*
*Danger, danger, danger*
*G'Day, mate*
*Good on ya'*
*Have a look at this beauty*
*We're flat out like lizards drinkin'*
*Holy smokes that was close*
*I'll give you the drum*
*She's fine as frog hair, mate*
*I'm shaking like a leaf*
*No worries, mate*
*See ya round like a rissole*
*She'll be right, mate*
*We're grinnin' like a flathead*
and the best of all…*Crikey that was dangerous!*

Australia's first Olympic gold medallist was Edwin Flack in 1896.

# DR. WHO?

*"Dr. Who" was the longest running sci-fi show in television history, and one of the longest running dramatic programs. Here's the story of how the good Doctor came to be.*

**B**ACKGROUND. Before "Dr. Who" debuted, there had never been a family-oriented science fiction show in Britain. There had been a few radio shows, but on TV they'd all been strictly adult or strictly for children. There was no precedent for "Dr. Who." No one had any idea it would become an overnight success. But it did—literally.

**How It Started.** It was 1962. The BBC was expanding its line of TV programs and wanted to offer a new Saturday evening family show that would be educational as well as entertaining. They called in two people—Sydney Newman (creator of "The Avengers") and Donald Wilson (later creator of "The Forsythe Saga") to come up with it. Newman wanted to make the program science fiction. Wilson wanted history, so they compromised and came up with a time traveller.

OK. Now what was he going to travel in? They wanted 1) a space ship that didn't look like a space ship and 2) something cheap. It was originally planned for the device to have "chameleon circuits" that would enable it to blend in with its surroundings (in Greece it would like a column, in a field it would like a rock, etc.). Since the first story took place in London, the time machine started off looking like a telephone booth. An immediate problem: the budget didn't allow them to keep changing it. So the time machine remained a telephone booth.

"Dr. Who" was an immediate sensation. For six years the writers got away without saying anything specific about the doctor's origin. There were vague hints that he was fleeing from something, but that was it. Finally the producers needed an explanation. So they finally "revealed" that Dr. Who was a time lord from the planet Gallifrey.

## INSIDE FACTS

**In The Beginning.** H.G. Wells' *The Time Machine* was the source that inspired Sydney Newman, "Dr.Who's" co-creator, to come up with his time-traveller.

**Bad Timing.** The first episode of "Dr. Who" was aired in England on Nov. 23, 1963, the day after John F. Kennedy's assassination. Because of the assassination, the BBC figured a lot of people had missed the first show (good guess), so the following week they showed the first episode again, right before the second one.

**It Seemed Like a Good Idea.** The original idea behind "Dr. Who" was serious. By having contemporary characters travel back in time and witness important historical events, the show could make the past seem alive to its young audience. Ratings of the historical episodes were poor, while the fantastic adventures in outer space attracted huge numbers of viewers.

**Calling Dr. Who.** The Doctor's time machine, which looks like a police telephone booth, is called a TARDIS. The name is an acronym invented by Dr. Who's companion, Susan. It stands for Time and Relative Dimension in Space.

**Successful Transplant.** "Dr. Who" was first sold to American TV in 1973. It never really caught on and it wasn't until Lionheart Television syndicated it through PBS in the early 1980s with a different star, that the show really took off. All the PBS channels started carrying it. Then they started ordering newer episodes, with yet *another* star. That led to the resyndication of the earlier series.

## DR. WHO'S ENEMIES

**The Daleks.** Mutated organisms living in mobile war machines, they have a "dislike for the unlike." Anything that isn't a Dalek shouldn't be allowed to exist, so they kill everything in sight.

**The Cybermen.** Were human once, but all their bodies have been replaced by mechanical parts. Have no emotions and believe that, logically, they should control the universe.

**The Yeti.** Robots controlled by the Great Intelligence, an extradimensional entity attempting to enter our universe.

**The Sontarans.** Cloned warriors who live for combat. They're fighting "an interminable war against the Rutans."

**The Ice Warriors.** The only villains in "Dr. Who" who ever reformed. They're Martians who left home and have returned.

---

It takes 12 bees their entire lifetime to make a tablespoon of honey.

# SPACED OUT

*Some people who claim to have seen UFOs seem completely off their rockers. Others seem more credible. Here are five real-life "sightings." Did they really see UFOs...or are they just making it up? You decide.*

**The Place:** Gulf Breeze, Florida, November 1987
**The Sighting:** "Four-foot-tall grey aliens who sometimes speak Spanish."
**Background:** Ed Walters (a Gulf Breeze developer) and his wife, Frances (president of the local PTA), claim to have had repeated encounters with the Spanish-speaking space aliens over several months in 1987. In March 1990, the couple wrote a book, *The Gulf Breeze Sightings*, that chronicles their experiences.

**The Place:** Greece, 1979
**The Sighting:** Space aliens that "looked like foetuses wearing wrap-around sunglasses."
**Background:** Joseph Ostrom, an advertising executive, was honeymooning with his wife in Greece. One evening, he says, their hotel room "filled with an orangish-red light," and a large alien (wearing a silver suit) led him to the roof of the hotel. His wife stayed behind. Suddenly, a turquoise ray-beam pulled him into the space ship that was hovering overhead. The aliens on the ship examined him, but he didn't mind. "When they did their exam, I felt love and support. It was as if we knew each other." The aliens hypnotised Ostrom to forget the experience, and he did. But several years later he visited an Earthling hypnotist, and the memories came flooding back, changing his life forever. After a second hypnosis, Ostrom quit his job and moved to Colorado. Today he makes his living conducting New Age workshops and writing. He is the author of the book *You and Your Aura*.

**The Place:** Mundrabilla, Australia, 1988
**The Sighting:** A "huge bright glowing object."
**Background:** Fay Knowles and her three sons were driving along Eyre Highway when their car was sucked into the air. One of the sons told reporters, "we were doing about 110 km (68 miles) per

hour when it came over us and suddenly lifted the car off the road. We felt the thump on the roof and then it started lifting us. We were frightened and began to yell, but our voices had changed." Then the car was violently dropped back to earth. The shock of the landing blew out one of the rear tires; police officers who later inspected the car said the roof had been damaged and that the car was covered inside and out with "a thick layer of black ash." Several other UFO sightings were reported the same night—some more than 160 km (100 miles) away. An aeroplane flying overhead saw a bright light hovering nearby; a truck driver on the same highway also reported being followed; and a fishing trawler spotted a UFO from offshore. Police officials told reporters they were taking the multiple sightings "seriously."

**The Place:** Somewhere near the Martian moon Phobos, 1989
**The Sighting:** A "mysterious…long, faintly aerodynamic shaped pencil-like object with round ends."
**Background:** On March 25, 1989, the unmanned Soviet space probe Phobos transmitted a photograph to Earth of a strange object that appeared to have darted into the range of the probe's camera. According to news reports, immediately after transmitting the photograph, the Soviet probe stopped transmitting signals back to Earth and "inexplicably disappeared." It has been missing ever since. Marina Popovich, a top Soviet test pilot, displayed the photograph at a UFO convention and explained that the probe's "encounter" and last photograph could be explained either as a legitimate UFO sighting, or the last, faulty transmission of a malfunctioning camera system.

**The Place:** Mount Vernon, Missouri, 1984
**The Sighting:** Aliens kidnapping cows.
**Background:** One morning Paula Watson, a Mount Vernon resident, witnessed space aliens kidnapping cows near her house. Later in the day while canning vegetables in her basement, she noticed a "silvery alien with large eyes" peeking at her through the basement window. She tried to speak to the alien, but it backed away and she fell asleep. The next thing Watson knew she was inside the alien's spaceship being examined. "I was standing up on a white table and the…alien was running his hands down my body, scanning my body." Watson was later returned to Earth unharmed.

# THE SYDNEY TO HOBART YACHT RACE

*The Sydney to Hobart Yacht Race is one of the world's most challenging ocean races, notorious for its uncertain weather and for the short, steep seas of Bass Strait. It has been the scene of controversy, triumph and tragedy.*

## A COLOURFUL START

The "Hobart" as it is colloquially known, is 630 nautical miles long and starts in Sydney every year on Boxing Day, 26 December. Crowds turn out in their thousands to send off the fleet, which travels down the east coast of Australia, across Bass Strait, down the east coast of Tasmania, around Tasman Island, across Storm Bay, then up the Derwent River to the finishing line off historic Battery Point in Hobart.

## AN OFFICER AND SOME GENTLEMEN

The first race was held in 1945, when British naval officer, John Illingworth, convinced a group of friends to turn their Christmas cruise into a race. Nine yachts entered. *Rani*, skippered by Illingworth, was the winner and reached Hobart in 6 days, 14 hours and 22 minutes. The last boat to reach Hobart was *Wayfarer*, taking 11 days, 6 hours and 20 minutes. The race was declared a success and became an annual event.

A handicap system—designed to take into account the advantage bigger and faster designs have over the smaller, slower yachts—was soon introduced to ensure that the winner was based on the skill and performance of the crew.

But it's certainly not new yachts or young crew that only compete. In 1994, among the largest fleet to set off (391 yachts) were two yachts that started in the inaugural race (*Archina* and *Winston Churchill*) and in their crews were two yachtsmen in there 70s who had sailed in the inaugural race in 1945. *Archina* came 13th in its division and *Winston Churchill* 19th in its division.

## WAYWARD WIND

The unpredictability of the wind and the sea has always been the race's biggest challenge. In recent years, the worst races have been in 1984, 1993 and 1998. In 1984, 150 yachts set out and 104 retired in strong- to gale-force southerly winds. In 1993, only 38 yachts finished out of 110 starters. They were confronted with south-westerly and southerly fronts with gusts of up to 70 knots. Tragedy hit in 1998 when winds of up to 80 knots and waves as big as 15–20 metres (50–66 feet) persisted for 36 hours. Of the 115 yachts entered, 71 retired, 7 boats were abandoned and 5 boats sank. During the gale-force winds, 55 yachtsmen were rescued and 6 yachtsmen died at sea.

## GETTING THE LOW DOWN

There have been many highlights in the race's 58-year history including the fastest race, the closest race, the most controversial race and notable achievements in line and handicap honours.

• The fastest yacht to date is *Nokia* (Denmark) in 1999. It took 1 day, 19 hours, 48 minutes, 2 seconds.

• In 1990, the race ended in a controversial disqualification. The maxi *Rothmans* crossed the line first, but was disqualified for using a sail with illegal advertising on it. The Race Media Director claimed that the sail was used only because all the other sails were damaged.

• The 1982 race saw the closest finish in the event's history. *Condor* (Bermuda) crossed the line just seven seconds ahead of the Sydney maxi *Apollo*.

• Only five yachts have taken the double line and handicap honours: *Rani* (1945), *American Eagle* (1972), *Kialoa* (1977), *New Zealand* (1980) and *Sovereign* (1987).

• The cutter *Morna*, later named *Kurrewa IV*, took line honours seven times, the first in 1946.

• Only one yacht, *Freya*, has won the race three times on overall corrected time (handicap), the first in 1963. Designed, built and sailed by brothers Trygve and Magnus Halvorsen, the yacht won the race five times.

---

The name of the town Coober Pedy means "white fella down a hole."

# THE SEARCH FOR AMELIA EARHART

*Was she the victim of a fuel shortage, a bad navigator, or the Japanese military? America's most famous aviatrix vanished on July 2, 1937. Now, over 60 years later, we may be close to finding out what really happened to her.*

**BACKGROUND**

She was the best-known—and perhaps the greatest—female aviator in American history...which is all the more remarkable because of the age in which she lived. Born in 1897, Amelia Mary Earhart began her flying career in 1921, at a time when few women had careers of any kind and had only won the right to vote a few years earlier.

She took her first flying lessons at the age of 24, and, after 2½ hours of instruction, told her teacher, "Life will be incomplete unless I own my own plane." By her 25th birthday she'd saved enough money working at her father's law firm, as a telephone company clerk, and hauling gravel, to buy one. Within another year she set her first world record, becoming the first pilot to fly at 4,267 metres (14,000 feet).

In 1928 Earhart became the first woman to fly across the Atlantic Ocean when she flew with pilot Wilmer Stultz. Ironically, she was asked to make the flight merely because she was a woman, not because of her flying talent. Charles Lindbergh had already made the first solo transatlantic flight in 1927, and Stultz was looking for a way of attracting attention to his flight. So he brought Earhart along...as a passenger.

That was the first—and last—frivolous flying record she would ever set. In 1930 she set the speed record for women at 291 km (181 mph); in 1932 she became the first woman to fly solo across the Atlantic; on another flight became the first woman to fly solo across the continental United States; and in 1935 became the first pilot of either gender to fly from Hawaii to the U.S. mainland. (She also set several speed and distance records during her career.) By the mid-1930s, "Lady Lindy" was as famous as Charles

Lindbergh. But her greatest flying attempt lay ahead of her. In 1937 she tried to circumnavigate the globe along the equator. She never made it.

## THE FINAL FLIGHT

Earhart described her round-the-world flight as "the one last big trip in her." Taking off from Oakland, California, on May 21, 1937, she and her navigator, Frederick Noonan, flew more than three-quarters of the way around the world, making stops in South America, Africa, the Middle East, Asia, and the South Pacific. But when they landed in New Guinea on June 28, the most difficult part of the journey lay ahead: the 4,113-km (2,556-mile) flight from New Guinea to Howland Island, a "tiny speck" of an island in the middle of the Pacific. It would be difficult to find even in the best conditions.

Monitoring the flight from Howland Island was the Coast Guard cutter *Itasca*. The *Lady Lindy*, Amelia's aeroplane, rolled off the runway at 10:22 a.m. on July 2. She remained in contact with the radio operator in New Guinea for seven hours, then was out of contact until well after midnight.

• Finally, at 2:45 a.m., the Itasca picked up her first radio transmission. Another short message was picked up at 3:45 a.m.: "Earhart. Overcast."

• At 4:00 a.m., the *Itasca* radioed back: "What is your position? Please acknowledge." There was no response.

• At 4:43 a.m., she radioed in again, but her voice was too faint to pick up anything other than "partly cloudy."

• The next signal was heard at 6:14 a.m., 15 minutes before the plane's scheduled landing at Howland. She asked the *Itasca* to take a bearing on the signal, so that Noonan could plot their position. The signal was too short and faint to take a bearing. At 6:45 a.m., Earhart radioed a second time to ask for a bearing, but the signal again was too short.

• A more ominous message was received at 7:42 a.m.: "We must be on you but cannot see you but gas is running low. Been unable to reach you by radio. We are flying at altitude one thousand feet. Only one half hour gas left." One radio operator described Earhart's voice as "a quick drawl like from a rain barrel." She was lost, panicking, and nearly out of fuel. She would radio two more

times before 8:00 a.m. asking the *Itasca* to take a bearing, but each time her signals were too weak.
• Her next message was received at 8:44 a.m., a half hour past the time she predicted her fuel would run out: "We are on the line of position 156–157. Will repeat message…We are running north and south." Operators described her voice as "shrill and breathless, her words tumbling over one another." That was the last confirmed message she would broadcast. Then Amelia Earhart vanished.

## UNANSWERED QUESTION: WHAT WENT WRONG?
**Theory #1:** Noonan's erratic behaviour and faulty navigation sent the plane off course, dooming it.
**Suspicious Facts**
• Noonan was an alcoholic. A former Pan Am pilot, he'd been fired from the airline because of his drinking problem. He claimed to have his drinking under control, but during a stopover in Hawaii he'd gotten drunk in his hotel room. According to one reporter in Hawaii, Earhart didn't want him to continue with the flight.
• The episode in Hawaii may not have been the only one. During a stopover in Calcutta, Earhart reported to her husband that she was "starting to have personnel trouble," but that she could "handle the situation." Paul Collins, a friend of Earhart's, overheard the conversation. He took this to mean that Noonan had gotten drunk again. Whatever it meant, Earhart was still having "personnel trouble" when she phoned from New Guinea, the last stopover before she disappeared.
• Why would Earhart have used Noonan as her navigator in the first place? According to one theory, the reason was financial: unlike other navigators, "the reputed alcoholic would work for very little money."

**Theory #2:** Earhart herself was to blame. Despite her fame as America's premier aviatrix, according to many pilots who knew her, she was actually a poor pilot—and an even worse navigator—who was unfamiliar with the plane she was flying.
**Suspicious Facts**
• Earhart had very little experience flying the Lockheed Electra she used on the trip. It was her first twin-engine plane, "a powerful, complicated aircraft loaded with special equipment" that was different from any other plane she had owned. Even so,

in the eyes of the pilots who trained her to fly it, she didn't spend enough time getting to know it.

• In fact, her round-the-world flight was delayed after she crashed the plane during takeoff on March 20. Paul Mantz, her mentor and trainer, blamed the accident on her, claiming she had "jockeyed" the throttle. Paul Capp, another pilot who knew her, described her as "an inept pilot who would not take the advice of experts."

• Earhart's skills as a Morse code operator were atrocious—even though Morse code, which could be transmitted in the worst of conditions, was the most reliable form of communication. Earhart preferred to transmit by voice, which required a much more powerful signal and was harder to intercept. (In fact, she preferred voice communication so much that partway through the flight she abandoned some of her Morse code radios and flew the rest of the trip without them. She also dumped a 76-metre (250-foot)-long antenna, which made the remaining radios far less powerful.)

• Earhart was also a poor navigator. During the flight to the African coast her miscalculations set her 262 km (163 miles) off course—a mistake that would have been deadly if the plane had been low on fuel. Some theorists speculate that if her navigation and Morse code skills had been better, she might have survived.

## UNANSWERED QUESTION: WHAT HAPPENED?

**Theory #1:** Earhart ran out of fuel before sighting land, ditched her plane in the sea, and drowned.

**Suspicious Facts**

• This is the most popular theory...and it's supported by the fact that no conclusive proof has ever been found indicating what really happened. According to one newspaper report, "nothing has been found that can be traced irrefutably to the plane or its crew: nothing bearing a serial number, for example, such as the plane's engines or propellers, nor any numbered equipment known to belong to the aviators."

• However, the islands in many areas of the South Pacific are scattered with the wreckage of 1930s-era planes. A lot of the major sea battles of World War II were fought in the Pacific; many fighter pilots ditched on nearby islands. This makes it next to impossible to confirm that any given piece of wreckage belonged to Earhart's plane, unless it contains a serial number or includes a personal effect of some kind.

**Theory #2:** Earhart was captured by the Japanese.

• According to this theory, Earhart and Noonan were using their flight as a cover for a number of reconnaissance flights over Japanese-held islands in the South Pacific. The Roosevelt administration believed that war with Japan was inevitable and may have asked Earhart to help gather intelligence information. Some theorists suggest that after one such flight over the Truck Islands, they got lost in a storm, ran out of fuel, and were forced to land on an atoll in the Marshall Islands (which at the time were controlled by Japan). Earhart and Noonan were captured, imprisoned, and eventually died in captivity.

**Suspicious Facts**

• In 1967 CBS reporter Fred Goerner met a California woman who claimed to have seen two captured Americans—one man and one woman, matching the descriptions of Noonan and Earhart—on the Japanese island of Saipan in 1937. Acting on the tip, Groener went to Saipan, where he found more than a dozen island natives who told similar stories about "American fliers who had been captured as spies," including one man who claimed to have been imprisoned in a cell next to an "American woman flyer."

• Fleet Admiral Chester W. Nimitz, commander of U.S. naval forces in the Pacific during the war, reportedly also believed that Earhart and Noonan had been captured and killed by the Japanese; in one statement in 1966 he said, "I want to tell you Earhart and her navigator did go down in the Marshalls and were picked up by the Japanese." The Japanese government denies the charge.

• Goerner believes that when the Marines recaptured Saipan in 1944, they unearthed Earhart and Noonan's bones and returned them to the United States. He thinks the bones were secretly turned over to the National Archives, which has kept them hidden away ever since. Why? The reason is as mysterious as the disappearance.

• Alternate theory: Joe Klass, author of *Amelia Earhart Lives*, also believes that Earhart was captured by the Japanese. But he argues that Earhart survived the war and may have even returned to the United States to live under an assumed name. According to his theory, the Japanese cut a deal with the United States to return Earhart safely after the war if the U.S. promised not to try Emperor Hirohito as a war criminal. The U.S. kept its promise, and Earhart was allowed to return home. She may have lived as long as the 1970s, protecting her privacy by living under an assumed name.

**Theory #3:** Earhart and Noonan crash-landed on a deserted island in the South Pacific, hundreds of kilometres off course from their original destination, where they died from exposure and thirst a few days later.

**Suspicious Facts**

• For three days after Earhart and Noonan disappeared, mysterious radio signals were picked up by ships looking for Earhart's plane. The signals were transmitted in English in a female voice; some radio operators familiar with Earhart's voice recognised it as hers. They were misunderstood at the time, but if they were indeed broadcast by Earhart, they gave several clues to her whereabouts.

• One signal said, "We are on the line of position 156–157"; another said, "Don't hold—with us—much longer—above water—shut off." Others had similar messages. At the end of the three days, the signals abruptly stopped.

• If those signals were indeed sent by Earhart, she must have landed *somewhere* to have been able to broadcast them. Nikumaroro Island, 563 km (350 miles) north of Howland Island, is a likely candidate for the crash site. The mysterious broadcasts offer several clues:

– Nikumaroro is one of the few islands within range of Earhart's plane—and it was in their "line of position 156–157."
– One of the last transmissions described a "ship on a reef south of equator." For years afterward researchers assumed that the "ship" being described in the transmission was Earhart's plane. But perhaps it wasn't: one of Nikumaroro's most prominent landmarks is a large shipwreck off the south shore of the island—four degrees south of the equator.
– Why were those final broadcasts separated by hours of silence? For more than 40 years it was assumed that they were broadcast at random intervals. But in the late 1980s, Thomas Gannon and Thomas Willi, two retired military navigators,

proposed a theory: Nearly out of fuel, Earhart and Noonan landed on a part of the island's coral reef that was above sea level only during low tide. This meant that they could only broadcast during low tide, when the radio's batteries weren't flooded and the plane's engine could be used to recharge them.
– To test their theory, Gannon and Willi compared the times the signals were broadcast to a chart listing high and low tides on Nikumaroro Island on the week of the disappearance. All but one of the signals were broadcast during Nikumaroro's low tide.

**Other Evidence**
• In 1960 Floyd Kilts, a retired Coast Guard carpenter, told the *San Diego Tribune* that while assigned to the island in 1946, one of the island's natives told him about a female skeleton that had been found on the island in the late 1930s. According to the story, the skeleton was found alongside a pair of American shoes and a bottle of cognac—at a time when no Americans lived on the island.

When the island's magistrate learned of the skeleton, he remembered the story about Earhart and decided to turn the bones over to U.S. authorities. So he put the bones in a gunnysack and set sail with a group of native islanders for Fiji. But he died mysteriously en route—and the natives, fearing the bones, threw them overboard.

• Many aspects of this story were later confirmed; in 1938 Gerald Gallagher, the island's magistrate, *did* fall ill while en route to Fiji and died shortly after landing. But it is not known whether or not he had any bones with him when he died.

**UPDATE**
To date, Nikumaroro Island and nearby McKean Island (thought to be another possible crash site) have been searched extensively. In March 1992, a search team on Nikumaroro found a sheet of aircraft aluminum that they believed was from Earhart's plane…but that theory was later disproved. Other artifacts recovered include a cigarette lighter manufactured in the 1930s (Noonan was a smoker) and pieces from a size-9 shoe (Earhart wore size 9). But no conclusive evidence has been found. The search continues.

# YOU'RE MY INSPIRATION

*It's fascinating to see how many pop characters—real and fictional—are inspired by other characters. Here's a handful of examples.*

**TINKER BELL.** Walt Disney's animators reputedly gave her Marilyn Monroe's measurements. (Some say it was Betty Grable's.)

**JAFAR, the Grand Vizier.** The villain in the 1993 animated film *Aladdin*—described by the director as a "treacherous vizier…who seeks the power of the enchanted lamp to claim the throne for his own greedy purposes"—was inspired by Nancy Reagan. The Sultan, a doddering, kindly leader, was inspired by Nancy's husband.

**THE EMPEROR in the *Star Wars* movies.** In early drafts of the *Star Wars* scripts, George Lucas portrayed the emperor as "an elected official who is corrupted by power and subverts the democratic process." Lucas modelled him after Richard Nixon.

**MICK JAGGER.** Studied the way Marilyn Monroe moved, and learned to mimic her onstage.

**THE STATUE OF LIBERTY.** The face of Miss Liberty, sculpted by Frederic Auguste Bartholdi, was inspired by his mother. Ironically, although the statue has welcomed immigrants to New York City since 1886, Madame Bartholdi was "a domineering bigot."

**DR. STRANGELOVE.** Dr. Kissinger, I presume? According to Penny Stallings in *Flesh & Fantasy*, "[Director] Stanley Kubrick…made a special trip to Harvard to meet Dr. Henry Kissinger while researching the title role for his screen adaptation of *Dr. Strangelove*."

**DR. JEKYL & MR. HYDE.** Inspired by Dr. Horace Wells, celebrated inventor of modern anaesthetics. He got hooked on ether and went mad; he was jailed for throwing acid in a woman's face while under its effects.

# RED DOG

*A true story of a truly remarkable Aussie dog.*

**T**ALLY HO
From the vast, inhospitable region of the Pilbara in northern Western Australia, in an area defined by blistering hot temperatures and where the only signs of life can be the large termite mounds that erupt out of the red earth, comes a true story of a truly remarkable dog.

Locals called him Red Dog, though his real name was originally Tally Ho. He was a red cloud Kelpie, a working dog, bred to withstand the rigours and harshness of the Australian outback.

Like most working dogs, Red Dog's life was supposed to follow a time-honoured routine. Dawn to dusk mustering stock with the odd dip in the too-few water troughs to slay the thirst. Trips to town in the back of the ute were the highlight of the week, so too the rare pat from the master. It was a hard life, and if you survived the heat, the snakebites, the tick infestations and the odd cattle kick, there was no guarantee that you would escape a bullet once you began to slow down.

For the first few years of Red Dog's life, his lot was just that. His owner, John, was better than most and Red Dog was a loyal and enthusiastic companion and worker. But John died suddenly and Red Dog's world fell apart.

## DOG DAY AFTERNOONS

Red Dog started to visit all the places that John had taken him in the hope that his master was there. He was often seen hanging around their old haunts for days at a time, intently watching the arrival of each person or car in the vain hope that John had returned and they could resume their life together.

Months went by and Red Dog managed to avoid all attempts by well-wishers to give him another home. He began to look further afield and started to hitch lifts in cars and trucks to other towns.

Red Dog would sit by the side of the road until locals driving by would stop and open the door for him to jump in. He was happy

---

The first Australian Aboriginal word was "kangaroo" and was spelt "kanguroo."

to sit there and enjoy the ride and would bark when he wanted to be let out.

When car travel didn't get him far enough, Red Dog extended his travel options to buses and trains. The bus drivers got so used to Red Dog hitching a lift on their buses that they started to leave a seat empty just for him, and woe betide anyone who sat there. Not only would the drivers and other passengers get irritated if someone had the temerity to sit in Red's seat, but Red himself would sit and glare at the offending passenger until his seat was rightfully vacated.

Although often covered with ticks and frequently sporting cuts and grazes (not to mention his bouts of chronic flatulence), Red Dog was not the most prepossessing of dogs, but he had a roguish charm and sweet nature that besotted everyone whose path he crossed. He had an uncanny knack of turning up at a barbecue just as the sausages were being dished up; he invariably made friends long enough to secure a free lunch before he headed off on another one of his adventures.

### GONE TO THE DOGS
For nine years Red Dog was a much-loved character of the nor'-west. He died in 1979 from eating poisoned bait.

Today if you visit Dampier in Western Australia, you will see a statue to Red Dog at the entrance to the town. It was erected by the townspeople in loving memory of their dear friend.

\*  \*  \*  \*

### DOG DAYS
The days when Rover was a typical dog name are over. These days, people are naming their dogs as they would their children. Check out this list of the top ten dog names in Australia, ranked from one to ten, to see how your pooch rates.

**Male dogs:** Max, Sam, Jack, Toby, Jake, Oscar, Charlie, Jess, Zac, Monty

**Female dogs:** Jessie, Molly, Cloe, Bonnie, Lucy, Sasha, Sally, Tess, Daisy, Zoe

Australia's dingo fence is over twice as long as the Great Wall of China.

# FAMILIAR PHRASES

*Here are the origins of some well-known sayings.*

## A LOOSE CANNON
**Meaning:** Dangerously out of control.
**Origin:** On old-time warships, cannons were mounted on "wheeled carriages." When they weren't being used, they were tied down. "Now imagine a warship rolling and pitching in a violent gale." A gun breaks loose and starts rolling around the ship— "a ton or so of metal on wheels rolling unpredictably about the deck, crippling or killing any sailor unlucky enough to get in the way and perhaps smashing through the ship's side. Human loose cannons are equally dangerous to their associates and to bystanders." (From *Loose Cannons and Red Herrings*, by Robert Claiborne)

## DYED IN THE WOOL
**Meaning:** Dedicated, committed, uncompromising.
**Origin:** From the textile trade. "It was discovered that yarn that's dyed 'in the wool'—before being woven—retained its colour better than yarn that was dyed 'in the piece,' i.e. after being woven." So if something's dyed-in-the-wool, it's unlikely to change. (From *Getting to the Roots*, by Martin Manser)

## GET YOUR DUCKS LINED UP IN A ROW
**Meaning:** Get organised, ready for action.
**Origin:** Refers to setting up bowling pins—which were called *duckpins* in early America, because people thought they looked like ducks.

## FIRST RATE
**Meaning:** The very best.
**Origin:** "In the 1600s a system for rating British naval ships according to their size and strength was developed. There were six different ratings, with a warship of the first rate being the largest and most heavily armed and one of the sixth rate being considerably smaller and having far fewer guns." The general public picked up the phrase right away, using it for anything topnotch. (From *Why You Say It*, by Webb Garrison)

---

**The average American spends less than two hours a day with his or her family.**

# START YOUR OWN COUNTRY

*Ever wondered what it'd be like to be king—or president—*
*of your own country? Here are some people who found out.*

**A**TLANTIS
**Founding Father:** J. L. Mott, a Danish sea captain
**History:** In 930 A.D., Leif Ericson, a Viking explorer,
discovered some Caribbean islands he mistook for remnants of the
lost continent of Atlantis. In 1934, claiming to be Ericson's
descendant, Mott declared himself the rightful heir to the islands,
which he could not locate but believed "were somewhere near
Panama." He drafted a one-page constitution and began issuing
passports and triangle-shaped postage stamps.
**What Happened:** The International Postal Union refused to
recognise Mott's postage stamps. Then, in 1936, Mott was almost
arrested for trying to enter the United States using an Atlantis
passport. By 1954 the elusive country had been renamed the
Empire of Atlantis and Lemuria. Despite the country's fancy new
name, however, all attempts to actually *locate* it have failed.

### GRANBIA
**Founding Father:** Andrew Richardson, a Liverpool postal worker
**History:** In the 1970s, Richardson declared his semi-detached flat
to be the independent nation of Granbia (the rest of the building
remained a part of the United Kingdom).
**What Happened:** He lost interest, and the apartment reverted to
England by default.

### NEW ATLANTIS
**Founding Father:** Leicester Hemingway, little brother of author
Ernest Hemingway
**History:** In 1964 he built a 2.5-by-9-metre (8-by-30-foot) floating
bamboo platform 11 kms (7 miles) off the coast of Jamaica,
anchoring it to the ocean floor with a Ford engine block. "I can
stand on the platform, walk around on it, and salute the flag, all of

---

which I do periodically," Hemingway bragged to reporters. "There are no taxes here, because taxes are for people not smart enough to start their own countries."

**What Happened:** Part of the country was destroyed by fishermen in search of scrap wood; the rest sank in a storm.

## HUTT RIVER PROVINCE PRINCIPALITY

**Founding Father:** "Prince" Leonard George Casely, an Australian wheat farmer

**History:** When the Western Australia Wheat Quota Board limited the amount of wheat he could grow in 1969, Casely and his 7,485-hectare (18,500-acre) farm seceded. He designed his own national flag and motto, printed his own money, and set up his own parliament.

**What Happened:** Australia refused to recognise his sovereignty, so in 1977 he declared war. Nothing came of it—he backed down two days later and re-established diplomatic relations. Casely claims he pays no Australian taxes, but admits he makes payments to the Australian government as an "international courtesy."

## ISLE OF THE ROSES

**Founding Father:** Giorgio Rosa, an Italian engineering professor

**History:** Rosa built a tower in the Adriatic Sea large enough to contain a bar, restaurant, and post office, and declared independence from Italy.

**What Happened:** The Italian government ignored him at first— but after a while they invaded the tower and blew it up.

## SOLAR ATLANTIC EMPIRE

**Founding Father:** David Owen, a writer for the *Atlantic Monthly*

**History:** Owen wanted to form his own country but couldn't find any available land. So he took possession of the sun, one of the last unclaimed territories in the solar system. He backed up his claim by writing a letter to the U.S. State Department asking for official recognition. "The sun should now be referred to as the Solar Atlantic Empire," he wrote, "and I, henceforth, will be known as Lord High Suzerain of Outer Space."

**What Happened:** The State Department wrote back saying that it was unable to consider his application.

# FAMOUS
# FOR 15 MINUTES

*Here it is again—our feature based on Andy Warhol's prophetic comment chat "in the future, everyone will be famous for 15 minutes." Here's how a few people are using up their allotted quarter-hour.*

**T**HE STAR: Angelyne (she won't tell anyone her real name)
**THE HEADLINE:** *Blonde Bimbo's Billboards Bring Big Bonus*
**WHAT HAPPENED:** In 1981 Angelyne—an out-of-work busty blonde—began posting billboards of herself all over L.A. (they simply said *Angelyne*, and listed a phone number) and distributing hot-pink press releases (describing her as "a living icon, Hollywood billboard queen, the new Love Goddess of the Future!" from her pink Corvette. Later she had a 26-metre (85-foot)-high likeness of herself painted on the side of a building at Hollywood and Vine.

The result: She made more than 250 media appearances, including bit parts in films like *Earth Girls Are Easy* and *L.A. Story*. Her billboard appeared in the opening montage of "Moonlighting" and in an issue of *National Geographic*.
**THE AFTERMATH:** She never made it as a sex symbol, but has come to represent, as one writer put it, "raw fame, unsullied by any known talent, charm, or accomplishments." She doesn't mind. "I'm the first person in the history of Hollywood to be famous for doing nothing," she says, and adds: "I really don't want to be famous for being an actress. I just want to be famous for the magic I possess."

**THE STAR:** Larry Villella
**THE HEADLINE:** *14-Year-Old Chips in to Cut Deficit*
**WHAT HAPPENED:** In February 1993, President Clinton was trying to drum up support for his "deficit-reduction plan." So Larry Villella, a 14-year-old from Fargo, North Dakota, sent the White House $1,000 (money he earned watering trees) to help pay it off.

Somehow, the media found out about Larry's cheque *before* it got to Washington—and every U.S. news service reported it as a major story. Larry was an instant celebrity. He was invited to appear on network TV talk shows, where he told interviewers his story—and got a chance to plug a tree-watering gizmo he'd invented.

**THE AFTERMATH:** He inspired people all over the U.S. One San Francisco man even sent the White House 170 kgs (375 lbs) of coins (about $500) he'd been saving. As for Larry's cheque: Clinton sent it back with a note that said: "I am very impressed with your concern…but I cannot accept your money." (Bonus: Bill Cosby sent Larry $2,000 as "a thank-you on behalf of the American people.")

**THE STAR:** Keron Thomas, a 16-year-old New York student
**THE HEADLINE:** *New York Youth Takes A-Train on Joyride*
**WHAT HAPPENED:** On May 8, 1993, a man carrying a set of motorman's tools and a Transit Authority identification signed in at New York City's subway trainyard. "I'm the substitute man," he said. "Got anything for me?" They did—an A train.
The only problem: he wasn't the substitute man—and wasn't even a transit employee. He was Keron Thomas, a high school student. Thomas drove his train the length of Manhattan and all the way to Queens, carrying an estimated 2,000 passengers and making 85 stops along the way (he was even on *schedule*). The trip was so uneventful that he probably would have gotten away with it…until he took a turn too fast and set off the emergency brakes. He escaped before they learned his true identity, but investigators arrested him two days later.
**THE AFTERMATH:** He pled guilty to three misdemeanours and was sentenced to three years' probation. Why such a light sentence? As *The New York Times* said, authorities were "wary of punishing a folk hero." As he left the courtroom, he declared: "I'm going to be a train engineer."

**THE STAR:** Don Calhoun
**THE HEADLINE:** *Lucky Fan Hits $1 Million Shot in Chicago*
**WHAT HAPPENED:** On April 14, 1993, a 23-year-old office supply salesman named Don Calhoun got a free ticket to an NBA game between the Miami Heat and the Chicago Bulls.
As Calhoun headed for his seat at the game, someone told him he'd been picked to take the "Million Dollar Shot" (a promotion

sponsored by Coca-Cola and a local restaurant chain). He'd get to shoot a basket. The prize: $1 million. Eighteen people had already tried and failed. (Why was he picked? *His shoes:* the Bulls marketing representative loved his yellow suede hiking boots.) At first he didn't want to do it—he even suggested that his friend make the shot instead. But the Bulls representative insisted. "I thought she was crazy," Calhoun told reporters. "But she ran after me, so I shrugged and said 'Okay.'" During a time-out early in the third period, he was brought to the floor. He took one dribble, launched the ball, and…basket!

**THE AFTERMATH:** Just about every sportscaster in the country carried Calhoun's Cinderella story on the news that night. He also did radio interviews, TV shows, even NBC's "Today" show. But a few days later, the bubble burst: it turned out Calhoun had played 11 games of college basketball, and the rules stipulated that no one who'd played in college could participate. But the ensuing publicity was so bad that Coke, the owner of the Bulls, and the restaurant all assured him he'd get his money anyway.

**THE STAR:** Holden Hollom
**THE HEADLINE:** *Frisco Cabbie Nabs Runaway Crook*
**WHAT HAPPENED:** On a June night in 1989, Hollom, a 51-year-old San Francisco cabbie (and former stunt driver) was driving a fare up Market Street, when he saw someone knock down a woman and steal her purse. He gave chase, yelling to his surprised passenger, "You're riding for free!"

He cornered the purse snatcher (a 96-kg [212-lb] ex-criminal) in an alley. To keep him from running away, he pinned him to the wall with his cab bumper. Newspapers all over the country reported the citizen's arrest as an example of what's *right* about America, and lauded Hollom for getting involved. He appeared on every major talk show, including "Larry King" and "Donahue."

**AFTERMATH:** The crook had to undergo three operations on his legs, and in 1992 sued Hollom for using excessive force. When he won, and was awarded $24,500 by a jury, the verdict got as much attention as the original incident. It generated more than $100,000 from outraged sympathisers who felt the cabbie had been shafted. (The verdict was later overturned.) Fleeting fame: Hollom later ran for the S.F. Board of Supervisors, but came in 19th in a field of 26 candidates.

The average person sheds a complete layer of skin every 28 days.

# WHAT DOES IT SAY?

*Here's a game where the position of words and letters is part of
the sentence. See if you can figure out what these say. If you need
a sample answer, check out the Hints at the end of the last column.
Answers on page 484.*

1. A letter was addressed to:
WOOD
JOHN
MASS
*Who got it; where did they live?*

2. I thought I heard a noise
outside, but it was
ALL 0

3. Let's have STANDING
AN

4.        LOOK
LOOK U LOOK
LOOK

5. "Remember," she said to the
group,
WE WESTAND FALL

6. "Why'd he do that?" Jesse
asked. "Well, son," I said, he's
a DKI

7. Texas? I love
S P A C E S

8. "Drat! My watch broke."
Time to get it RE-RE

9. "I remember the 1960s," she
said, GNIKOOL

10. No, we're not living
together anymore. It's a
L E G A L

11. Haven't seen him in a
while. He's
FAR          HOME

12. Careful, I warned my
sister. He's a WOWOLFOL

13. "How do I get out of
here?" he asked. I said, "Just
calm down and put the
RAC

14. I tried to teach her, but no
luck. I guess she's a
DLIHC

15. When it's raining...
AN UMBRELLA
SHEME

**HINTS (if you need them):**
The answer to #1 is John
Underwood, Andover Mass
(JOHN under WOOD and
over MASS)
Answer to #14: I guess she's a
*backward child.* (DLIHC is child
spelled backward.)

---

Three Australians die each year testing if a 9V battery works on their tongue.

# ACCORDING TO SHAW...

*A few thoughts from George Bernard Shaw, the curmudgeon who was considered the greatest English playwright since Shakespeare.*

"I often quote myself; it adds spice to my conversation."

"Youth is a wonderful thing. What a crime to waste it on children."

"When a stupid man is doing something he is ashamed of, he always declares that it is his duty."

"A perpetual holiday is a good working definition of hell."

"A government which robs Peter to pay Paul can always count on the support of Paul."

"I am a gentleman; I live by robbing the poor."

"England and America are two countries separated by the same language."

"If all economists were laid end to end they would not reach a conclusion."

"Life does not cease to be funny when people die any more than it ceases to be serious when people laugh."

"No man can be a pure specialist without being, in a strict sense, an idiot."

"There may be some doubt as to who are the best people to have in charge of children, but there can be no doubt that parents are the worst."

"We should all be obliged to appear before a board every five years and justify our existence...on pain of liquidation."

"The fickleness of the women whom I love is only equalled by the infernal constancy of the women who love me."

"The power of accurate observation is commonly called cynicism by those who have not got it."

"The trouble with her is that she lacks the power of conversation but not the power of speech."

"There is no satisfaction in hanging a man who does not object to it."

# BOTTOMS UP FOR THIS AUSSIE BATTLER!

*You don't hear about this kind of turtle every day. In fact, this rare Australian turtle brings a whole new technique to underwater breathing.*

## THE INS AND OUTS

At first glance, you might think that the Fitzroy River turtle is just like any other turtle. When it is out of water, for example, it breathes with its lungs, just like other turtles. But unlike many freshwater turtles, the Fitzroy River turtle can also breathe underwater—for up to eight hours, and maybe even longer. How? It can breathe through its bottom!

The Fitzroy River turtle is the size of a dinner plate and is found in only a few freshwater rivers near Rockhampton, north of Brisbane. It sucks water into its two abdominal chambers through a small opening called a cloaca (which it also uses to excrete). The two chambers are lined with thousands of tiny projections (papillae) that can absorb oxygen from the water.

Lying very still on the riverbed breathing through your bottom is a very good way to avoid predators and danger.

## A BUM DEAL

Unfortunately, despite its unusual breathing technique, the Fitzroy River turtle is recognised as one of the most threatened species of freshwater turtle in eastern Australia. What a bummer!

\* \* \* \*

## LIFE'S LIKE THAT

**Q:** What's the difference between a fish and a piano?
**A:** You can't tuna fish.

**Q:** What do you call a fish with no eyes?
**A:** Fsh!

Tornadoes can last as long as nine hours.

# APRIL FOOLS!

*Why is April 1 a "fools' day"? The most plausible explanation is one
we wrote in the first* Bathroom Reader: *"Until 1564 it was a tradition
to begin the New Year with a week of celebration, ending with a big
party. But the calendar was different then; the New Year began on
March 25, and the biggest party fell on April 1. In 1564 a new
calendar made January 1 the New Year. People who forgot—
or didn't realise—what had happened, and still showed up to
celebrate on April 1, were called 'April fools.'" These days, most
of the memorable April Fools' jokes are played by radio and
TV stations. Here are a few recent classics.*

## PASTA FARMING

On April 1, 1966, the BBC broadcast a TV documentary
on spaghetti-growing in Italy. Among the film's highlights:
footage of Italian farmers picking market-ready spaghetti from
"spaghetti plants." To the BBC's astonishment, British viewers
accepted the news that Italy's "pasta farmers" had been able to
fight off the "spaghetti weevil, which has been especially
destructive recently."

## HE'S BA-A-ACK

In 1992 National Public Radio's "Talk of the Nation" news show
announced on April 1 that Richard Nixon had entered the race
for president. They actually interviewed the "former president"
(played by impressionist Rich Little) on the air. "I never did
anything wrong," he announced, "and I won't ever do it again."
Listeners actually called the show to comment. "Nixon is more
trustworthy than Clinton," one remarked. "Nixon never screwed
around with anyone's wife except his own. And according to some
accounts, not even with her."

## GRAVITATIONAL PULL

On April 1, 1976, a famous British astronomer told BBC radio
audiences that since the planet Pluto would be passing close to
Jupiter on April 1, the Earth's gravitational pull would decrease
slightly for about 24 hours. He explained that listeners would feel
the effect most if they jumped into the air at precisely 9:47 a.m.

that morning. The BBC switchboard was jammed with listeners calling to say that the experiment had worked.

## COLOURFUL BROADCAST
In the 1970s, Britain's Radio Norwich announced on April 1 that it was experimenting with "colour radio," and that the tests would affect the brilliance of tuning lights on radios at home. Some listeners actually reported seeing results: one complained that the experiment had affected the traffic lights in his area; another asked the station managers how much longer the bright colours he saw would be streaming out of his radio.

## ICEBERGS ON THE MOVE
On April 1, 1978, Dick Smith made world headlines when he towed an "iceberg" into Sydney Harbour. He reported that an overseas company was considering a feasibility study into towing icebergs from Antarctica to Saudi Arabia to provide fresh water. The towing barge was actually piled high with fire-fighting foam and covered in clear plastic.

## DRIVING PRANK
One year a Paris radio station announced that from April 1 on, all Europe would begin driving on the left. Some drivers actually started driving on the left side of the road. A number of accidents resulted (no fatalities, though).

## NEEDLING PEOPLE
In 1989 a Seattle TV station interrupted its regular April 1 broadcast with a report that the city's famous Space Needle had collapsed, destroying nearby buildings in the fall. The report included fake eyewitness accounts from the scene, which were punctuated with bogus updates from the studio newsroom. The "live" footage was so realistic that viewers jammed emergency lines trying to find out if their loved ones were safe. The station later apologised.

## THE JOKE IS RED
Even the media of the former Soviet Union celebrates April Fools' Day. In 1992 the Moscow press printed stories claiming that gay rights activists had crossed the Atlantic Ocean in condoms, and that the Moscow City Council was planning a second subway system "in the interest of competition."

# Q & A:
# ASK THE EXPERTS

*Everyone's got a question or two they'd like answered—basic stuff, like "Why is the sky blue" Here are a few of those questions, with answers from books by some of the world's top trivia experts.*

**H**OLY QUESTION
**Q:** *Why are manhole covers round?*
**A:** "So they can't be dropped *through* the manhole itself. Squares, rectangles, ovals, and other shapes could be positioned so they'd slip into the manhole. Round manhole covers rest on a lip that's smaller than the cover. So the size and shape keeps the manhole cover from falling in." (From *The Book of Answers*, by Barbara Berliner)

**SHOE TIME**
**Q:** *How and why did people start shining their shoes?*
**A:** "A high polish on shoes is a tradition passed down from the Spanish caballero (gentleman on horseback), whose shiny boots served notice that he rode his own horse and didn't walk along dusty roads with lesser men." (From *Do Elephants Swim?*, compiled by Robert M. Jones)

**NIPPED IN THE BUD**
**Q:** *Why do men have nipples?*
**A:** "Males actually have the anatomical equipment in place to provide milk, but it lies dormant unless stimulated by estrogen, the female hormone. Might men have suckled babies in the distant past? No one knows." (From *Why Do Men Have Nipples*, by Katherine Dunn)

**PRUNY SKIN**
**Q:** *Why does your skin get wrinkled when you soak for a long time in water?*
**A:** Normally, skin is water-resistant because of a "protective barrier of keratin," a protein made by the epidermis to keep

---

*The Great Salt Lake is only 4 metres (13 feet) deep.*

moisture, bacteria, and other unwanted stuff out. But if skin is immersed in water for a long time, moisture gets through and "the cells in the epidermal layer…absorb water and swell. The enlarged cells cause the skin to pucker and wrinkle."

Luckily, they don't stay that way. "Several minutes after towelling off, the water in the skin cells evaporates, and the cells return to their normal shape and size. Otherwise, we would all be walking around looking like the raisins." (From *The Book of Totally Useless Information*, by Don Voorhees)

### EGGS-ACTLY!

Q: *Why don't people ever eat turkey eggs?*
A: "They don't taste good. More precisely, they don't have as much water in them as chicken eggs. The next time you eat a couple of chicken eggs, think about how wet they are. But a turkey egg, if exposed to high heat, turns rubbery." (From *Why Things Are, Volume II*, by Joel Achenbach)

### HALF-WIT?

Q: *Is the old saying true that "we only use 10% of our brains?"*
A: "No—you use every part of your brain. Not every area at the same time, of course; they all do different things at different times. At any given moment, only about 5% of your brain cells are actually firing—that is, working. So in one sense this is actually true. But as far as we know, there are no parts that never do *anything.*" (From *Know It All!*, by Ed Zotti)

### EAT LIKE A BIRD

Q: *How do birds find worms underground?*
A: "When a bird stands on the ground near a worm that is crawling underneath, it can feel the earth's vibrations with its very sensitive feet. It will also cock its head to put into operation the low-frequency apparatus of its ears. Then, when it zeroes in on the victim, it pierces the earth with a sudden stab of its beak, grabs the worm, and pulls it out." (From *How Do Flies Walk Upside Down?*, by Martin M. Goldwyn)

# PEOPLE-WATCHING

*It's scary what behaviour experts can predict about us. All it takes is a few studies...and they know more about what we'll do in a situation than we do. Following are the results from a few of those studies, including some from* The Book of You *by Bernard Asbell. Here's lookin' at you, kid!*

O N NONVERBAL COMMUNICATION...
*A variety of factors affect the way we silently communicate with each other.*

• For instance, one study shows that if you've been told that a person you're about to meet has a lot in common with you, you'll actually position yourself physically closer to that person than if you've been informed you're "opposites."

• According to another study, your nationality plays a role in how "touchy-feely" you are. For instance, over an hour long coffee break in a cafe...

– American friends will touch each other in conversation about twice.

– British friends generally won't touch each other at all.

– By comparison, the French can't keep their hands off each other; they average about 110 touches an hour.

– But Puerto Ricans were the most tactile in the study, with about 180 "touches" in the same period.

• Something else to remember, next time you find yourself chatting with someone you don't know: According to Asbell...

– "If you're a man, the farther you sit from the other person, (within a range of .6–3 metres [2–10 feet]), the more willing you are to talk intimately about yourself."

– "If you're a woman, the closer you sit together (within a range of .6–3 metres [2–10 feet]) the more willing you are to tell intimate details about yourself."

– "Within that same range (whether you're a man or a woman), you'll talk with a stranger longer and volunteer the most about intimate topics at a distance of 1.5 metres (5 feet)."

## ON GIVING & LIVING...

- Want long life? A recent study of about 2,700 individuals found lower death rates among those who volunteered their time to a favourite charity or cause.
- Another interesting study in behaviour had students watch a movie on Mother Teresa. The film depicted her administering to the needy and sick, bringing comfort and solace. Immediately following the film, researchers found in the students, a significant increase in immunoglobulin, an antibody that helps the body fight respiratory infections.

## ON ROMANCE & DATING...

- The most common thing we all do when we want to be romantic is say "I love you" to our partner. Sweet...but not as effective as you might think. When people were asked "How you'd want your lover to treat you to romance" in a study, the most common answer was "lying around in front of a fire."
- Other choices included: "Taking a shower together" and "Walking on the beach." Ironically, hearing "I love you" came in twelfth.

*Other people-watching facts:*
- If you're a man and you get anxious about dating, chances are that male friendships are also cause for anxiety.
- First-date anxiety for a guy almost never centres around sex. It's usually worry about what to talk about, how to behave, and what to expect.
- First dates are tough for everyone, but if you're a guy, you're probably going to be a lot more uptight about the situation than the woman is.
- If it's any consolation, however, the chances are that if you're a man—even if you're uptight about an encounter—you probably like your body more than your date does hers. Studies show that men are generally more likely to see their bodies as attractive to women than woman are to see their bodies as attractive to men.

# COLOURS

*Colours have a lot more impact on our daily lives than you might think. Here are some things researchers have found out about people and colour.*

**BLUE**
• Blue has a tranquillising effect. Bridges are often painted blue to discourage suicide attempts. And according to one report: "When schoolroom walls were changed from orange and white to blue, students' blood pressure levels dropped and their behaviour and learning comprehension soared."
• Researchers say blue is the #1 colour for women's jumpers, because women think men like it. (They're right; it's men's favourite colour.)

**RED**
• Red is a stimulant that can cause "restlessness and insomnia" if it's used in bedrooms.
• According to marketing studies, red makes people oblivious to how much time is passing. That's why it's "the colour of choice for bars and casinos."
• Women tend to prefer blue-toned reds, while men like yellowish reds. Businesses keep this in mind. For example: the

Ford Mustang, which is targeted to men, is orange-red (called "Arrest-me" red at Ford); the Probe, targeted to women, is offered in more blue-red shades.

**GREEN**
• Because it reminds people of fields and foliage, green makes us feel secure. Researchers say it's a good colour for bedrooms; and green kitchens reportedly make cooks more creative.
• Studies show that "people working in green environments get less stomach aches than people in areas where other colours predominate."

**YELLOW**
• It's the colour most likely to stop traffic...or sell a house.
• But yellow also represents "caution or temporariness— so car rental agencies and taxis use it, but not banks."
• Too much yellow makes people anxious. "Babies cry more and temperamental people explode more in yellow rooms."

# FRED HOLLOWS—THE SEEING-EYE DOCTOR

*Fred Hollows was truly a man with vision.*

Every five seconds someone in the world goes blind. Of all of these, a staggering eighty percent could have been avoided. Why then did these people lose their sight? The answer is, in most cases, because the necessary care was not in place. That is when someone like Fred Hollows comes in and does something about it.

## A MAN WITH A MISSION
Fred Hollows was a man with a great heart and an even greater need to help people. In his youth, he wanted to become a missionary but after working in a mental hospital, he changed his mind. Born in New Zealand on 9 April, 1929, he graduated from the University of Otago as a doctor in 1956 and then specialised in eye surgery.

## BUSH SURGERY
In 1965, after spending some years in Britain, he landed a job in Sydney and, five years later, was the head of the Eye Department at one of Sydney's leading hospitals. On a visit to the Northern Territory in the late 1960s, he was appalled to realise that all the children in the camp had trachoma—a curable eye disease caused by an infection, which can lead to blindness if not treated quickly. Aboriginal children were becoming blind by factors that could, in many instances, be remedied easily. With the backing of the Royal Australian College of Ophthalmologists, Fred Hollows went to work setting up a national program to fight eye diseases in Australian Aboriginals. He launched the program in 1976 and took a mobile medical team to the outback. With Fred Hollows as a constant inspiration, other doctors and volunteers gave their time to the program. In three years, the team examined over 100,000 people, prescribed thousands of pairs of glasses, and performed over 1,000 operations. With this program, Fred

---

**Australia has the lowest population density in the world—2 people per square kilometre.**

Hollows and his team halved curable blindness amongst Australian Aboriginals.

## THE CALL OF THE WORLD

In the late 1980s, Fred Hollows answered the "call" from the Third World and took his work overseas. He had discovered that some 20 million people in developing countries were blind because of cataracts. This problem in the eye's lens can often be cured by inserting a new, synthetic lens in an operation that lasts about 15 minutes. Fred Hollows also learned that Eritrea, one of the poorest countries in the world, had a great number of blind people and no money or eye doctors to help them. Always a believer that the best way to help people is to teach them how to help themselves, he decided to raise money to build a factory to make cheap lenses and train local doctors to perform the operation to insert the lenses. He asked Australians to help him in his dream and so passionate was his plea that he raised more than six million dollars. In doing so, Fred Hollows gave back vision to thousands of people.

## A FOUNDATION FOR THE FUTURE

Fred Hollows carried on working even after, in 1989, he knew that he was dying of cancer. He was determined that his program would survive and his wife, Gabi Hollows, was equally determined to see his work continue. In 1992, the Fred Hollows Foundation was launched.

Fred Hollows died on 10 February, 1993, and, to this day, his work continues. By 1998, the Foundation had helped restore the sight to one-quarter of a million people and had trained over 500 eye surgeons. Today the Foundation works in a number of different countries including Australia, Eritrea, Bangladesh, Vietnam, Botswana, Ethiopia, Malawi, Tanzania, India, Nepal, China and Pakistan to name just a few; has built lens factories in Nepal, Vietnam and Eritrea; and has helped restore the sight to more than one million people.

To some Fred Hollows was a saint while to others he was a wild colonial boy. Perhaps his friend Peter Corris defined him best when he said that he was "a common man doing uncommon things."

# MISS PIGGY

*Porcine words of wisdom from one of the world's favourite pigs.*

## DIET TIPS
"Never eat anything at one sitting that you can't lift."
"Always use one of the new—and far more reliable—elastic measuring tapes to check on your waistline."

## ARTICHOKES
"These things are just plain annoying…after all the trouble you go to, you get about as much actual 'food' out of eating an artichoke as you would from licking thirty or forty postage stamps. Have the shrimp cocktail instead."

## PERFUME
"Perfume is a subject dear to my heart. I have so many favourites: Arome de Grenouille, Okéfénokée, Eau Contraire, Fume de Ma Tante, Blast du Past, Kermes, Je suis Swell, and Attention S'il Vous Plait, to name but a few."

## TIPPING
"There are several ways of calculating the tip after a meal. I find that the best is to divide the bill by the height of the waiter. Thus, a bill of $12.00 brought by a 6 foot (1.82 m) waiter calls for a $2.00 tip."

## TRAVEL TIPS
"If you're travelling alone, beware of seatmates who, by way of starting a conversation, make remarks like, 'I just have to talk to someone—my teeth are spying on me' or 'Did you know that squirrels are the devil's oven mitts?' "
"Public telephones in Europe are like our pinball machines. They are primarily a form of entertainment and a test of skill rather than a means of communication."

## HOTELS
"Generally speaking, the length and grandness of a hotel's name are an exact opposite reflection of its quality. Thus the Hotel Central will prove to be a clean, pleasant place in a good part of town, and the Hotel Royal Majestic-Fantastic will be a fleabag next to a topless bowling alley."

## HATS
"Someone you like is wearing an ugly hat, and she asks you to give her your honest opinion of it: 'What a lovely chapeau! But if I may make one teensy suggestion? If it blows off, don't chase it.' "

**Pigs killed off the dodo bird.**

# STRANGE LAWSUITS

*These days, it seems that people will sue each other over practically anything. Here are a few real-life examples of unusual legal battles.*

**THE PLAINTIFF:** Frank Zaffere, a 44-year-old Chicago lawyer

**THE DEFENDANT:** Maria Dillon, his 21-year-old ex-fiance

**THE LAWSUIT:** In June 1992—about two months before they were supposed to get married—Dillon broke off the engagement. Zaffere responded by suing her for $40,310.48 to cover his "lost courting expenses." In a letter sent to Dillon, he wrote, "I am still willing to marry you on the conditions herein below set forth: 1) We proceed with our marriage within 45 days of the date of this letter; 2) You confirm [that you]…will forever be faithful to me; 3) You promise…that you will never lie to me again about anything." He closed with: "Please feel free to call me if you have any questions or would like to discuss any of the matters discussed herein. Sincerely, Frank."

"He's trying to…make me say, 'OK Frank, I'll marry you,'" said Dillon. "But…I can't imagine telling my children as a bedtime story that Mummy and Daddy got married because of a lawsuit."

**THE VERDICT:** The case was dismissed.

**THE PLAINTIFF:** 27-year-old Scott Abrams

**THE DEFENDANTS:** The owners and managers of his apartment building

**THE LAWSUIT:** During an electrical storm in 1991, Abrams was sitting on the ledge of the apartment-building roof with his feet in a puddle of water. He was hit by lightning and suffered a cardiac arrest; fortunately, he was revived by a rescue squad. But in 1993 he filed a $2 million lawsuit charging the defendants with negligence. His reason: "They should have provided signs and brighter paint."

**THE VERDICT:** Pending.

In New Orleans, the soil is too wet for regular burials—so the dead are buried above ground.

**THE PLAINTIFF:** Ronald Askew, a 50-year-old banker from Santa Ana, California
**THE DEFENDANT:** His ex-wife, Bonnette
**THE LAWSUIT:** In 1991, after more than a decade of marriage, Bonnette admitted to her husband that although she loved him, she'd never really found him sexually attractive. He sued her for fraud, saying he "wouldn't have married her had he known her feelings."
**THE VERDICT:** Incredibly, he won. The jury awarded him $242,000 in damages.

**THE PLAINTIFF:** The family of 89-year-old Mimi Goldberg, a Jewish woman who died in 1991
**THE DEFENDANT:** The Associated Memorial Group, a Hawaiian firm that ran nine funeral homes
**THE LAWSUIT:** In 1993 Goldberg's body was shipped from the Nuuanu Mortuary in Hawaii to California. When the casket was opened at an Oakland synagogue, "the remains of a dissected foetal pig in a plastic bag" were found resting next to the body. A mortuary representative said the pig had been put there accidentally by an employee "whose wife was taking a class requiring the dissection of foetal pigs." The woman's family, horrified because Jewish religious law specifically bans pork, sued.
**THE VERDICT:** The family won $750,000. In addition, the funeral home was ordered to make a donation to the U.S. Holocaust Memorial, and print an apology in leading West Coast newspapers.

**THE PLAINTIFF:** Dimitri K. Sleem, a 38-year-old Yale graduate
**THE DEFENDANT:** Yale University
**THE LAWSUIT:** In April 1993, an old college friend called Sleem to read him the entry listed under his name in the 1993 Yale alumni directory. It said: "I have come to terms with my homosexuality and the reality of AIDS in my life. I am at peace." Sleem—who didn't have AIDS, wasn't gay, and was married with four children—filed a $5 million libel suit against Yale.
**THE VERDICT:** Still pending. Meanwhile, Yale hired a handwriting expert to find out who submitted the false statement.

# THE CURSE OF KING TUT

*After Tutankhamen's tomb was unearthed in 1922, a number of people associated with the discovery died mysterious deaths. Was it coincidence…or was it a curse?*

**BACKGROUND** King Tutankhamen reigned from about 1334 to 1325 B.C., at the height of ancient Egypt's glory. The "boy king" was only about 9 when he was crowned, and died mysteriously at the age of 18 or 19. He was buried beside other pharaohs in the Valley of the Kings, near the Nile River at Luxor, the capital of ancient Egypt.

## THE DISCOVERY

King Tutankhamen's tomb remained undisturbed for more than 3,000 years until it was unearthed in November 1922 by Howard Carter, an amateur archaeologist commissioned by the English nobleman Lord Carnarvon to find it. Carter's discovery was due largely to luck; having exhausted a number of other leads, he finally decided to dig in a rocky patch of ground between the tombs of three other pharaohs. Nearly 1 metre (3 feet) under the soil he found the first of a series of 16 steps, which led down to a sealed stone door. Markings on the door confirmed that it was a royal tomb. Realising what he had discovered, Carter ordered the steps buried again, and wired Lord Carnarvon in London to join him.

Three weeks later, Carnarvon arrived and digging resumed. The first stone door was opened, revealing a 9-metre (30-foot)-long passageway leading to a second stone door. Carter opened the second door and, peeking into the darkness with the light of a single candle, was greeted by an amazing sight—two entire rooms stuffed with priceless gold artifacts that had not seen the light of day for more than 30 centuries. The room was so crammed with statues, chariots, furniture, and other objects that it took two full months to catalogue and remove items in the first room alone. Tutankhamen's body lay in a solid gold coffin in the next room;

the gold coffin was itself encased inside three other coffins, which rested inside a huge golden shrine that took up nearly the entire room.

The discovery of the site was hailed as "the greatest find in the annals of archaeology." Unlike other tombs, Tutankhamen's was almost completely undisturbed by graverobbers; its hundreds of artifacts provided a glimpse of ancient Egyptian cultural life that had never been seen before.

## THE CURSE

But unearthing the treasures may have been a dangerous move— soon after the Tut discovery was announced, rumours about a curse on his tomb's defilers began to circulate. They weren't taken seriously—until Lord Carnarvon came down with a mysterious fever and died.

The curse gained credibility when word came from Lord Carnarvon's home in England at 1:50 a.m.—the exact moment of Lord Carnarvon's death—that his favourite dog had suddenly collapsed and died. And at *precisely* the same moment, Cairo was plunged into darkness, due to an unexplainable power failure.

**Other Deaths:** Over the next several years, a series of people associated with the Tut excavation died unexpectedly, often under mysterious circumstances. The dead in 1923 alone included Lord Carnarvon's brother, Col. Aubrey Herbert; Cairo archaeologist Achmed Kamal, and American Egyptologist William Henry Goodyear.

• The following year, British radiologist Archibald Reed died on his way to Luxor, where he planned to X-ray Tut's still-unopened coffin. Oxford archaeologist Hugh Eveyln-White, who had dug in the necropolis at Thebes, also died in 1924.

• Edouard Neville, Carter's teacher, as well as George Jay-Gould, Carnarvon's friend, papyrus expert Bernard Greenfell, American Egyptologist Aaron Ember, and the nurse who attended to Lord Carnarvon all died in 1926. Ember's death was particularly spooky—he was attempting to rescue from his burning house a manuscript he had worked on for years: *The Egyptian Book of the Dead*.

• In 1929 Lord Carnarvon's wife, Lady Almina, died, as did John Maxwell, the Earl's friend and executor, and Carter's secretary,

If you keep your goldfish in a dark room, they'll turn white.

Richard Bethell, who was found dead in bed, apparently from circulatory failure, at the age of 35.

## THE AFTERMATH

Fallout from the rumours of the curse continued for years, as did the string of mysterious deaths.

• As accounts of the deaths circulated, hysteria spread. In England, hundreds of people shipped everything they had that was even remotely Egyptian to the British Museum—including an arm from a mummy.

• The popularity of the curse legend led to a series of classic horror films: *The Mummy* (1932), starring Boris Karloff, and *The Mummy's Hand* (1940) and three sequels starring Lon Chaney, Jr.—*The Mummy's Tomb* (1942), *The Mummy's Ghost* and *The Mummy's Curse* (both 1944).

## LAST WORDS

• Was the curse for real? Many prominent people insisted that it wasn't. They argued that the mortality rates of people associated with the Tutankhamen discovery and other finds were no higher than that of the general public. Dr. Gamal Mehrez, Director-General of the Egyptian Museum in Cairo, disputed the curse in an interview made several years after the discovery of Tut's tomb. "All my life," he said, "I have had to deal with pharaonic tombs and mummies. I am surely the best proof that it is all coincidence." Four weeks later he dropped dead of circulatory failure, as workers were moving Tutankhamen's gold mask for transport to London.

• For what it's worth, Lord Carnarvon's son, the sixth Earl of Carnarvon, accepts the curse at face value. Shortly after the fifth earl's burial, a woman claiming psychic powers appeared at Highclere Castle and warned the sixth earl, "Don't go near your father's grave! It will bring you bad luck!" The wary earl heeded her advice and never visited the grave. In 1977 he told an NBC interviewer that he "neither believed nor disbelieved" the curse— but added that he would "not accept a million pounds to enter the tomb of Tutankhamen."

*  *  *  *

**Profound thought:** "It's a question of whether we're going to go forward with the future, or past to the back." —*Dan Quayle*

# THE GODZILLA QUIZ

*Here's a multiple-choice quiz to find out how much you really know
about filmdom's most famous dinosaur. Answers are on page 484.*

**1.** Godzilla first lumbered out of the ocean in a 1954 film titled
*Gojira*. The dino-monster was awakened from a million-year
slumber by A-bomb testing underseas and went on a rampage,
destroying Tokyo, wreaking havoc with his radioactive breath. In
1956, the movie was brought to the U.S. as *Godzilla, King of
Monsters* ("Makes King Kong Look Like a Midget!"). How did
they adapt it for American audiences?
**a)** They made it seem as though Godzilla was fighting for the
U.S. during World War II.
**b)** They inserted footage of Godzilla destroying New York City
and Washington, D.C. as well.
**c)** They added Raymond Burr, casting him as a hospitalised
reporter who remembers the whole incident as a flashback.

**2.** The first Japanese sequel to *Gojira* was made in 1955. But
when this flick finally made it to the U.S. in 1959, it didn't
mention Godzilla in the title. What was it called, and why?
**a)** *The Monster vs. the Maiden*; the studio tried to make it sexier.
**b)** *The Rockin' Monster*; rock 'n' roll movies were hot.
**c)** *Gigantis*; it was illegal to use the name Godzilla.

**3.** In the 1964 flick, *Godzilla vs. Megalon*, Godzilla saves the
world from the Seatopians, an evil alien race that plans to take
over using two secret weapons—Gaigan and Megalon. How would
you describe this evil pair?
**a)** A King Kong-like ape and a giant poisonous frog.
**b)** A giant cockroach and a robot with a buzz saw in his stomach.
**c)** A giant pickle and a Richard Nixon look-alike.

**4.** *Godzilla vs. the Thing* was released in 1964. What Thing did
Godzilla fight?
**a)** A giant rabbit.
**b)** A giant moth.
**c)** A giant spider.

---

Bathroom news: Franklin Roosevelt thought up the name "United Nations" in the shower.

**5.** How did Godzilla celebrate his 20th anniversary in 1974?
**a)** He fought a Godzilla robot from outer space.
**b)** He saved the world from a giant alien grasshopper.
**c)** He made an appearance on the "The Tonight Show."

**6.** *Godzilla on Monster Island* was released in 1971. The plot: Earth is invaded again. This time it's giant cockroaches from outer space, using monsters to do their dirty work. They've got Gaigan (the monster in *Godzilla vs. Megalon*) and Ghidrah. Who's Ghidrah?
**a)** Godzilla's mother-in-law.
**b)** A giant anteater.
**c)** A three-headed dragon.

**7.** In 1972 a scientist discovers a growing mass in a polluted lake. He wonders if it's a giant tadpole…but no! It's a new monster named Hedora. What will Godzilla be fighting this time?
**a)** The Smog Monster—an 122-metre (400-foot) blob of garbage.
**b)** The Phlegm Monster—a 2 tonne (2-ton) ball of mucus.
**c)** The Sludge Monster—an 18-metre (60-foot) wide hunk of waste.

**8.** In *Godzilla's Revenge*, released in 1969, Godzilla returns for what purpose?
**a)** To settle a score with another monster named Gorgo.
**b)** To show a little kid how to fight bullies.
**c)** To get revenge on Raymond Burr.

**9.** In the 1966 epic, *Godzilla vs. the Sea Monster*, Godzilla fights for the Free World against Red Bamboo, an evil totalitarian group. Their secret weapon is Ebirah. Who is he?
**a)** A hypnotist who can brainwash Godzilla.
**b)** A mechanical jellyfish.
**c)** A giant lobster.

**10.** In 1969 Godzilla reappeared with Minya. What was special about this new monster?
**a)** It was Godzilla's mother.
**b)** It was Godzilla's cousin.
**c)** It was Godzilla's son.

# THE BIRDSVILLE RACES

*Forget the Melbourne Cup. It might be the horse race that stops an entire nation every November but, for a total Aussie outback experience, the Birdsville Races are the place to be.*

## CELEBRATING BIRDSVILLE STYLE

There are a few differences between the Melbourne Cup and the Birdsville Races. You won't see fancy hats and champagne cocktails at the Birdsville Races and you won't be fashion spotting either, or getting a crash course in a "who's who" of the racing world. But the Birdsville Races will definitely offer you a unique glimpse of an outback way of life with heat, dust, flies, parched stretches of land, and the warmth of the local people and their total enthusiasm for a good time. Birdsville people may live in one of the most remote Australian towns, but this is the biggest event of the outback year, and they're determined to enjoy it!

## A BIRD'S EYE VIEW

The small town of Birdsville lies on the edge of the Simpson Desert, the Strezleckie and the Great Stony Desert (which is a bit of a giveaway to the type of country around here). It's 1,161 km (722 miles) from Adelaide and 1,850 km (1,150 miles) from Brisbane. All the roads that lead to Birdsville are unsealed—it's a long, dusty journey through some of Australia's harshest and driest country. But distances are nothing to Australians who live in the outback. They'll drive 100 km (62 miles) or more to see a movie, go to a bush dance or have a barbecue. These people love a party!

## BIRDS IN THE DESERT

Birdsville first came into being in the late 1880s as a stop-off point for drovers moving their cattle along the Diamantina River. In fact, the town was originally called Diamantina Crossing. It was supposedly changed to "Birdsville" because of the enormous numbers of birds in the area. And the name "Birdsville" does seems to suit this little desert oasis.

## AND NOW...THE MAIN EVENT

Today, the population of Birdsville hovers around 120 people. The township consists of the famous Birdsville Pub, a caravan park, a general store, a museum and an art gallery. For most of the year, there's a quiet, unhurried feeling about the town. But for two days every year in September, the town becomes a bustling hub. It's time for the Birdsville Races.

Thousands of visitors from all over Australia, and the world, stream into the town. Dust-caked four-wheel drives line the streets and light aircraft taxi around the temporary airport, which soon doubles as a carpark. There are tents and sleeping bodies everywhere.

The Birdsville Cup was first run in 1882, and the cup distance has been 1,600 metres ever since. Today, the race is held to raise funds for the Royal Flying Doctor Service and Birdsville Hospital. The racecourse is about 3 km (1.9 miles) south of Birdsville, on a claypan alongside the sand dunes. The two-day race meeting includes a 12-race program and prize money that is more than $110,000. The Birdsville Cup is a much-valued trophy. And when the excitement of the races is over, there's some serious drinking to be done. The amount of alcohol drunk during the Birdsville Races is as famous as the races themselves. It sure is a thirsty business—race watching!

\*　　\*　　\*　　\*

## LIFE'S LIKE THAT

The father of five children wins a toy at the Royal Easter Show. He calls his kids together to ask which one should have the present.

"Who is the most obedient?" he asks.
"Who never talks back to mother?"
"Who does everything she says?"
Five small voices answer in unison.
"Okay Dad. You get the toy."

# SILLY BRITISH VILLAGE NAMES

*People often ask how we find the material for our Bathroom Readers. This one was easy—Uncle John was doing some leisurely bathroom reading one morning, checking out the six newspapers he gets, when he found himself laughing at an article in the* Wall Street Journal. *That led to more research…and now we've got enough silly English names to last a lifetime—or at least a sitting! Here are a few dozen of our favourites.*

## ROADMAP AS COMIC BOOK

"New York has Flushing. Maryland has Boring. Pennsylvania, of course, has Intercourse," the *Wall Street Journal* reports. "But probably no territory in the English-speaking world can match Britain's wealth of ludicrous place names: Crackpot, Dorking, Fattahead, Goonbell, Giggleswick, Nether Poppleton, Wormelow Tump, Yornder Bognie. The litany, which swells with each page of the atlas, sounds like a Monty Python gag."

For example: According to Chris Longhurst, in *Daft Place Names*, you might already have visited…

- Foulbog
- Dull
- Muck
- Mold
- Moss of Barmuckity
- Belchford
- Burpham
- Lickey End
- Spital in the Street
- Bug's Bottom
- Pratts Bottom
- Slack Bottom
- Iron's Bottom
- Horsey

- Bunny
- Corney
- Swine Sty
- Pig Street
- Dog Village
- Donkey Town
- Toad's Mouth
- Maggots End
- Ufton Nervet
- Crazies Hill
- Shootup Hill
- Bat and Ball
- Pity Me
- No Place
- Haltwhistle
- Slaggyford

- Nether Wallop
- Weeford
- Limpley Stoke
- Nempnett
- Thrubwell
- Butcombe
- Bell End
- Great Bulging
- Eggborough
- Ham
- Pill
- Christmas Pie
- Furzedown
- World's End

---

The word "checkmate" comes from the Persian *shah mat*, which means "the king is dead".

## UPPER AND LOWER

"Over time," the *Wall Street Journal* continues, "many villages also have subdivided, with silly consequences: Great Snoring and Little Snoring, Middle Wallop and Nether Wallop, Helions Bumpstead and Steeple Bumpstead, Sheepy Magna (Latin for 'big') and Sheepy Parva (Latin for 'small'). Then there is the English habit of designating 'upper' and 'lower' ends of villages, which may grow into communities of their own. Optimists, for instance, will feel at home in the hamlet of Upperup—which is reached, appropriately, via High Street.

" 'If the hamlet grows any more, we'll have to call one end of it Upper Upperup,' jokes Charles Hadfield, a local historian."

### Other pairs:
- Fetcham and Bookham (too bad there's no Jail'am)
- Downham and Turnham Green (in West London)
- "Piddles and Puddles, leading to Poole. (Or away from Poole, depending which side you start)," writes Longhurst
- Upper and Lower Peover

### HERE AND THERE...

- There's a river in the south somewhere (Dorset) called the River Piddle," Longhurst notes in *Daft Place Names*. "Around it are placed called 'Puddletown' and 'Piddlehampton.' Don't know why they get puddle from piddle." He adds: "And there's a village by the name of Nasty, to the southeast 272 of Leighton Buzzard. I've only been past it (never to it) but the idea of the Nasty Village Pub, Nasty Inn, Nasty Bakery, etc. somehow appeal to me."
- "Goon" is Cornish for "pasture." As a result, there are plenty of Goons dotting the English countryside. For example: Goonbell, Goongumpus, Goonearl, Goonown and Gooninnis. "It's true we have a lot of goons here," says one resident. "but I've never thought of that as funny.
- Regarding the village of Piddle: A funny name? "Not if you live there," writes the *WSJ*. "Ian Curthoy's, a pig farmer in North Piddle, gripes that passersby often pose for snapshots beside signs for the village—usually while piddling. Other travelers steal the signs, a common nuisance in villages with silly names. Asked about the origin of Piddle's name, Mr. Curthoys replies: 'It's a wet

place, isn't it?' Sloshing through the mud to feed his sows, he smiles, adding: 'There was a South Piddle once, but it dried up.' "
• And finally, the town called Ugley. Its most famous civic group: The Ugley Women's Institute, "a group that meets every month in the Ugley Village Hall and "holds scholarly lectures and afternoon teas." Members have tried to rename it the Women's Institute of Ugley, but no one pays attention. When the members have to identify their affiliation at conventions, they wind up announcing: "We're Ugley."

\*　　\*　　\*　　\*

### SILLY NAMES AROUND THE WORLD
From *Daft Name Places*:

• In Newfoundland, Canada, you can find: Heart's Content, Heart's Desire, Heart's Delight, Tickle Harbour, Come By Chance, Goobies, Little Heart's Ease, Seldom, St. Jones Within, Sop's Arm, Sheshatsheits and Toogood Arm.
• "There is a village about half an hour's train ride north of Tromsoe, Norway, on the way to Bodo, called Hell."
• In Germany, there are two towns near Munich called Grub and Poing.
• There's a Bavarian mountain (near Garmisch-Partenkirchen to be precise) known as the Wank. You can even take the Wankbahn to the top.
• In Texas, there's apparently a place called Myass.
• Reportedly, there's a road near Tucson, Arizona called the Superchicken Highway.

\*　　\*　　\*　　\*

*...And two useful phrases to learn for your next trip to France:*

1. "Excuse me, waiter, but there's a German Shepherd in my soup."
*Pardon, garçon, mais il y a un berger allemand dans mon potage*

2. "May I have a manicure with my toast, please?"
*Est-ce que je peux faire une manicure avec mon pain grillé, s'il vous plaît*

# THE WORLD'S MOST POPULAR TWINS

*To most people, all twins are fascinating but the original
Siamese twins would have to be the most fascinating of all.*

**C**HANG AND ENG BUNKER
**Claim to Fame:** The original "Siamese twins."
**Background:** Chang and Eng—"left" and "right" in
Thai—were born at Meklong, Siam (Thailand) on May 11, 1811,
permanently attached at the chest by a band of skin. They were
discovered by an American sea captain who put them on display
in Europe and America—where P. T. Barnum bought out their
contract.

The Bunkers became world-famous as "Siamese twins." They
managed to live relatively normal lives, becoming American
citizens, marrying (unattached) sisters Adelaide and Sarah Yates
in 1864, and somehow fathering 22 children between them.
They spent their entire lives looking for a doctor who'd guarantee
they'd both survive an operation to separate them, but never
found one. They died hours apart in 1874.

**Gossip:** Chang and Eng hated each other—and fought constantly.
According to an 1874 article in the *Philadelphia Medical Times*,
"Eng was very good-natured, Chang cross and irritable….Chang
drank pretty heavily—at times getting drunk; but Eng never
drank. They often quarrelled; and, of course, under the
circumstances their quarrels were bitter. They sometimes came
to blows, and on one occasion came under the jurisdiction of
the courts."

\*     \*     \*     \*

## REAL BOOKS . . . UNREAL TITLES!
*Leadership Secrets of Atilla the Hun* (1995)
*Three Weeks in Wet Sheets* (1856)
*Who's Who in Barbed Wire* (1970)
*Build Your Own Hindenburg* (1983)

Sotheby's auction house sold a 200-year-old piece of Tibetan cheese for $1,513 in 1993.

# FAMILIAR NAMES

*Some people become famous because their names become commonly associated with an item or activity. You know the names, now here are the people.*

**Marie Ann Smith.** An Australian market gardener and grandmother. In the mid 1800's she first cultivated a variety of green apple at Eastwood in Sydney. The Granny Smith apple is now one of Australia's favourite varieties.

**Andre Marie Ampere.** A 19th-century French physicist. His work on electricity and magnetism "laid the groundwork for modern electrodynamics." The standard unit of electrical current—the *ampere*, or *amp*—was named after him.

**Fitzherbert Batty.** A Jamaican lawyer. "In 1839," writes an English etymologist, "he was certified as insane, which attracted considerable interest in London." His surname became "an affectionate euphemism to describe someone who is harmlessly insane."

**William Beukel.** A 14th-century Dutchman. Invented the process "by which we shrink and sour cucumbers." The result was originally called a *beckel* or *pekel*, after him. It eventually became known as a *pickle*.

**Mr. Doily (or Doyley).** A 17th-century London merchant whose first name has been forgotten. "He became prosperous," says *Webster's Dictionary*, "by selling various summer fabrics trimmed with embroidery or crochet work, and, being a good businessman, used up the remnants by making ornamental mats for the table called *doilies*."

**Hans Geiger.** German physicist. In 1920 he perfected a device for measuring radioactivity—the *Geiger counter*.

**Col. E. G. Booz (or Booze).** An 18th-century Philadelphia distiller who sold his Booz Whiskey in log cabin-shaped bottles. His product helped make the Old English term *booze* (from *bouse*, "to drink") slang for alcohol.

**Archibald Campbell, the third Duke of Argyll.** Powerful Scottish noble in the early 1700s. Had the Campbell clan tartan woven into his *argyle* socks.

---

The Tyrannosaurus rex's razor-sharp teeth were about 15 cm (6 inches) long.

**Enoch Bartlett.** A 19th-century businessman. Distributed a new kind of pear developed by a Massachusetts farmer. Eventually bought the farm and named the pear after himself.

**Brandley, Voorhis, and Day.** Owners of an underwear manufacturing company. Known by their initials: BVD's.

**Robert Wilhelm Bunsen.** German chemist in the mid-1800s. Invented the gas burner used in chemistry labs.

**Lambert de Begue.** A monk whose 12th-century followers were wandering mendicants. His name—pronounced *beg*—became synonymous with his followers' activities.

**Rudolph Boysen.** California botanist. In 1923, he successfully crossed blackberries and raspberries to create *boysenberries*.

**Charles F. Richter.** A 20th-century American seismologist. In 1935 he came up with a scale for measuring the "amplitude of the seismic waves radiating from the epicentre of an earthquake." The *Richter scale* is now used worldwide to understand the magnitude of shock waves.

**Thomas "Jim Crow" Rice.** A white "blackface" comedian. In 1835 he came up with a typically racist song-and-dance routine that went: "Wheel about, turn about/Do just so/Every time I wheel about/I jump 'Jim Crow.' " For some reason, this phrase came to refer to all discrimination by whites against blacks.

\*       \*       \*       \*

## TOTALLY IRRELEVANT FACTS

Barbie's full name is Barbara Millicent Roberts.

Rats and horses can't vomit.

It is impossible to lick your elbow.

A prawn's heart is in its head.

In the course of an average life, you will, while asleep, swallow 70 assorted insects and 10 spiders.

A quarter of all photocopier faults are caused by people sitting on them and photocopying their bottom!

Most lipstick contains fish scales.

More than 50% of the people in the world have never made or received a telephone call.

---

The distance between a Boeing 747's wingtips is longer than the Wright Brothers' first flight.

# THE GOODYEAR BLIMP

*No major sporting event is complete without it. In fact,*
*it's probably the best-known lighter-than-air ship ever*
*(except maybe the Hindenburg, which is famous for blowing up).*
*Here's the story of the Goodyear blimp.*

In 1809 Charles Goodyear, a hardware merchant from
Connecticut, saw that rubber had tremendous commercial
potential—but only if it could be made less sticky and would
hold a shape better than it already did.

So he obtained a large quantity of latex, and tried mixing it
with everything in his desk, cellar, and pantry—including witch
hazel, ink, and cream cheese—with no luck. One day he tried
mixing rubber with sulfur. Then, while working on something
else, he accidentally knocked the sulfurised rubber mixture onto
a hot stove. He found that the rubber had changed form: it was
no longer sticky and it snapped back to its original shape when
stretched. He named the process *Vulcanizing* after Vulcan, the
Roman god of fire.

## THE GOODYEAR COMPANY

Goodyear didn't get rich from his discovery—he died penniless in
1860. But when Frank A. Seiberling started a rubber company in
Akron, Ohio, in 1898, he decided to name it after the inventor.
It's likely he hoped to profit from the confusion created by having
a name similar to another Akron rubber company, B.F. Goodrich.

Goodyear's first products were bicycle and horse carriage tyres,
rubber pads for horseshoes, rubber bands, and poker chips. The
company produced its first auto tyres in 1901, aeroplane tyres in
1909, and, using a Scottish process for rubberised fabric, the skins
for aeroplanes in 1910. (This was back when aeroplanes were
based on kite designs and made mostly of wood and cloth.)

The same rubberised fabric turned out to be useful for lighter-
than-air craft, and Goodyear flew its first dirigible in 1922.

## THE MILITARY CONNECTION

The military used Goodyear blimps for observation and
reconnaissance during World War I and World War II. After
World War II, Goodyear bought five of its blimps back from the

---

Most popular sheet-music song of all time: "Yes, We Have No Bananas".

armed forces. It painted them and began using them for promotional purposes. But the company's executives didn't see the value of having blimps. In 1958 they tried to ground the airships permanently, to save the operating and maintenance expenses.

The plan was stalled at the last minute by a plea from Goodyear's publicity director, Robert Lane. To demonstrate the blimps' worth to the company, he scheduled a six-month marathon tour that sent the airship *Mayflower* barnstorming the Eastern Seaboard. It generated so much favorable press that the executives were convinced to keep it.

The blimps' first TV coverage was an Orange Bowl game in the mid-1960s. Now they're used in about 90 televised events a year. Goodyear doesn't charge TV networks; the publicity generated makes the free service worthwhile.

## BLIMP FACTS

• Each blimp is equipped with a crew of 23, consisting of 5 pilots, 17 support members who work on rotating schedules, and 1 public relations representative. The blimps cruise at a speed of 72–80 km (45–50 mph) with a maximum of 105 km (65 mph) unless there's a really good wind.

• Each blimp can carry 9 passengers along with the crew. The seats have no seatbelts.

• The camera operator shoots from the passenger compartment through an open window from about 360 metres (1,200 feet) up, from which you can see everything, read a scoreboard, and hear the roar of a crowd. The hardest sport to film is golf, because the pilots have to be careful not to disturb a golfer's shot with engine noise or by casting a sudden shadow over the green.

• If punctured, the worst that will happen is that the blimp will slowly lose altitude. Good thing, too, since the company reports that a blimp is shot at about 20 times a year.

• Each blimp is 58 metres (192 feet) long, 18 metres (59 feet) high, and holds 5,676 cubic metres (202,700 cubic feet) of helium. The helium does leak out, like a balloon's air, and has to be "topped off" every four months or so.

• The word *blimp* is credited to Lt. A. D. Cunningham of Britain's Royal Navy Air Service. In 1915 he whimsically flicked his thumb against the inflated wall of an airship and imitated the sound it made: "Blimp!"

# AUSTRALIANISMS!

*Have you always wanted to know where some of our distinctive
Australian words came from? You might be very surprised at
their origins. Read on...*

## DRONGO

**Meaning:** A noun used by Australians to mean "an idiotic
person or fool"

**Origin:** A drongo is a species of bird found in northern Australia,
which, unlike every other migratory bird in the world, heads to
colder climates in winter not warmer ones. It might very well have
its own reasons for doing this but on the face of it, its behaviour
looks utterly stupid.

## CARK

**Meaning:** Used by Aussies across the land to indicate something
has died, as in "the computer has carked it"

**Origin:** There are two schools of thought on the origin of this
word. One is that it is similar to the sound a crow makes as it feeds
on a dead carcass, the other is that it is derived from a medieval
English word meaning "load" or "burden." To be "carked" was
therefore to be loaded down or burdened, ultimately to death.

## COBBER

**Meaning:** Used interchangeably with "mate" to indicate friend
or acquaintance

**Origin:** Far more popular in usage in the first half of the 20th
century, the word cobber is rarely heard these days. Derived from
the English word "cob" which means "to take a liking to."

## OCKER

**Meaning:** Refers to a rough and uncultivated Australian person

**Origin:** During the 1960s there was an Australian television show
called the *Mavis Bramston Show*. One of the characters on this
show was a man called "Ocker." He was always portrayed in
shorts, singlet and thongs, leaning on a bar, sinking a glass of beer
and talking in a broad Australian accent. Thereafter the word

---

A snowstorm becomes a blizzard when the temp drops below –7°C and wind speed hits 56 km.

"ocker" came to represent everything that was associated with an exaggerated portrayal of anything Australian in a rough and down-to-earth way.

## BUNG
**Meaning:** Broken or dead
**Origin:** Comes from the Aboriginal word for dead. It found its way into the Australian language where the phrase "to go bung" meant "to die."

## TRUE BLUE
**Meaning:** Used affectionately to refer to anything that is 100% Australian born and bred
**Origin:** The expression was used as far back as the middle ages, when Chaucer used it in a 14th century poem. The colour blue has always been associated with loyalty and constancy so the term "true blue" originally meant to be faithful, staunch and unwavering in one's faith and principles. The phrase came to Australia with the first settlers in the 18th century and came to be associated with the working classes and unions, especially the Shearers' union.

## DINKUM (ALSO FAIR DINKUM OR DINKY-DI)
**Meaning:** Something that is true, honest or genuine
**Origin:** This icon of Australian speech actually comes from the English word "dinkum," which means work.

## BONZER
**Meaning:** Excellent, very good
**Origin:** First recorded usage of this word was in the early 20th century and its derivation is either from the French word "bon" meaning good or the English word "bouncer" meaning "anything very large of its kind."

## BODGIE
**Meaning:** Something that is worthless, fake, shoddy
**Origin:** Derived from the old English word of "bodge" which meant "to work clumsily."

## BLUDGER

**Meaning:** A worthless idler; one who exploits unemployment benefits by avoiding gainful employment

**Origin:** Derived from the English word "bludgeoner" which meant someone who carried a bludgeon, short stick or club, and was usually involved with petty crime for which he used the bludgeon as a weapon. Thus they lived off the earnings of others.

## BOGEY/BOGEY-HOLE

**Meaning:** To bathe or swim; swimming hole

**Origin:** Comes from the Aboriginal word for "swim." Early settlers to Sydney heard the local aboriginal people use this word in reference to bathing or swimming and started to use it and incorporate it into the Australian language.

## YAKKA

**Meaning:** Hard work

**Origin:** Derived from the Aboriginal word "yaga" meaning "work." Yakka found its way into the Australian lexicon by the middle of the 19th century and is now firmly entrenched.

## CHUCK

**Meaning:** To throw as in "I chucked the rubbish out in the garbage bin"

**Origin:** Although this word seems very Australian, chuck is an English word dating back to the 16th century. However, Australians have added their own special touch to this word and also use it to mean vomiting.

## COOEE

**Meaning:** A call to another person or party to indicate your whereabouts in the bush

**Origin:** Derived from the Aboriginal word "cuwe" meaning to "come here."

---

Australian men participate more in sport than Australian women (53% compared with 43%).

# GO ASK ALICE

*Alice in Wonderland and Through the Looking Glass aren't just for kids. They're great reading for grown-ups, too. Especially in the bathroom. Here are some sample quotes.*

"Dear, dear! How queer everything is today! I wonder if I've been changed in the night? Let me think: was I the same when I got up this morning? I almost think I can remember feeling a little different. But if I'm not the same, the next questions is, '*Who am* I' Ah, that's the puzzle!"

—**Alice, *Alice in Wonderland***

"Cheshire Puss," began Alice, "would you tell me, please, which way I ought to go from here?"

"That depends a good deal on where you want to get to," said the Cat.

"I don't much care where—" said Alice.

"Then it doesn't matter which way you go," said the Cat.

"—so long as I get *somewhere*," Alice added as an explanation.

"Oh, you're sure to do that," said the Cat, "if only you walk long enough."

—***Alice in Wonderland***

Alice laughed. "There's no use in trying," she said. "One can't believe impossible things."

"I daresay you haven't had much practice," said the Queen. "When I was your age, I always did it for half-an-hour a day. Why, sometimes I've believed as many as six impossible things before breakfast."

—***Through the Looking Glass***

"You should say what you mean," said the March Hare.

"I do," Alice hastily replied; "at least—I mean what I say— that's the same thing, you know."

"Not the same thing a bit!" said the Hatter. "Why, you might just as well say that 'I see what I eat' is the same as 'I eat what I see'!"

"You might as well say," added the March Hare, "that 'I like what I get' is the same thing as 'I get what I like'!"

"You might just as well say," added the Dormouse, "that

'I breathe when I sleep' is the same thing as 'I sleep when I breathe'!"

"It *is* the same thing with you," said the Hatter.

—*Alice in Wonderland*

"It's no use going back to yesterday, because I was a different person then."

—*Alice, Alice in Wonderland*

"Be what you would seem to be—or, if you would like it put more simply—never imagine yourself not to be otherwise than what it might appear to others that what you were or might have been was not otherwise than what you had been would have appeared to them to be otherwise."

—**The Duchess,** *Alice in Wonderland*

"Take some more tea," the March Hare said to Alice, very earnestly.

"I've had nothing yet," Alice replied in an offended tone: "So I can't take more."

"You mean you can't take less," said the hatter: "It's very easy to take *more* than nothing."

—*Alice in Wonderland*

"If everybody minded their own business," the Duchess said in a hoarse growl, "the world would go round a deal faster than it does."

"Which would not be an advantage," said Alice. "Just think what work it would make with the day and night! You see, the earth takes twenty-four hours to turn round on its axis—"

"Talking of axes," said the Duchess, "chop off her head!"

—*Alice in Wonderland*

\*     \*     \*     \*

## NOTABLE AUSTRALIAN QUOTES

"I grew up thinking there was one unpardonable sin—to be boring."

—**Germaine Greer**

"Never take any notice of anonymous letters, unless you get a few thousand on the same subject."

—**Sir Robert Menzies**

# WEDDING SUPERSTITIONS

*If this book was Modern Bride, we'd probably call these "wedding traditions" rather than superstitions. But think about it—most of them were started by people who believed in evil spirits and witches and talismans.*

**B**RIDAL VEIL. The veil has served a number of purposes throughout history, including: 1) protecting the bride from the "evil eye" 2) protecting her from jealous spinsters (who might also be witches); and 3) protecting the groom, his family, and other wedding guests from the bride's psychic powers—just in case she has any.

**WEDDING KISS.** A toned-down but direct throwback to the days when the couple was required to consummate their marriage in the presence of several witnesses, to insure that the consummation actually took place.

**BRIDE'S GARTER AND BOUQUET OF FLOWERS.** Originally the groomsmen fought with each other to see who would get the bride's garter, which was supposed to bring good luck to the person who possessed it. But the Catholic Church frowned on the rowdy practice, and it was eventually replaced by a milder custom: the bride throwing a bouquet of flowers to her bridesmaids. Today the customs exist side-by-side.

**WEDDING RINGS.** One of the oldest wedding practices. Ancient Egyptians, Romans, and Greeks all exchanged rings during their wedding ceremonies. Because a circle is a round, unending shape, it came to symbolise the ideal love that was supposed to come from marriage: it flowed from one person to the other and back again, forever. The ring has always been worn on the left hand—and was originally worn on the thumb. It was later moved to the index finger and then to the middle finger, and eventually ended up on the third, or "medical," finger. Reason: The third finger was believed to lead straight to the heart, via a single nerve.

---

**Experts say: Humans and elephants are the only animals that can stand on their heads.**

**HONEYMOON.** This European tradition dates back hundreds of years and gets its name from the fact that newlyweds were expected to drink honey (believed to be an aphrodisiac) during the period of one full cycle of the moon (about a month).

**THROWING RICE OR CONFETTI.** Originally a fertility ritual. Wedding guests threw wheat at the bride only, in the hope that she would bear children the same way that wheat produced bread.

**WEDDING CAKE.** Guests originally gave "bride-cakes" to a just-married woman to encourage fertility.

**JUNE WEDDING.** It was customary for Romans to marry in June to honour the queen of the gods, Juno—who was also the goddess of women. They hoped to win her favour to make the marriage last, and make childbirth easier.

**CARRYING THE BRIDE OVER THE THRESHOLD.** Romans thought good and evil spirits hung around the entrance of a home. They also believed that if you walked into your house left foot first, the evil spirits won. So to be sure the bride—whom Romans figured was "in a highly enotional state and very apt to be careless"—didn't accidentally step into her new home with the wrong foot, the groom just picked her up and carried her.

**RECEPTION SPEECH.** In pre-Christian Rome, newlyweds hired an "official joker" to tell dirty stories to guests during the reception. The Romans believed that "unclean" thoughts in the minds of guests turned the attention of vengeful gods away from the newly-weds, which helped protect them from evil.

**DECORATING THE WEDDING CAR.** In medieval France, when a couple was unpopular, people derided them publicly by banging on pots, kettles, etc. This was a *charivari*, or "rough serenade." In America it became a *shivaree*, and people got the treatment from friends. This gave way to a new custom—trying to keep a couple from consummating their marriage by making noise at their window. When newlyweds began leaving weddings by car, the only way to harass them was to deface the vehicle.

# LIMERICKS

*Limericks have been around since the 1700s. Here are
some that readers have sent us over the years.*

There once was a spinster from
Wheeling,
Endowed with such
delicate feeling,
That she thought any chair
Should not have its legs bare,
So, she kept her eyes fixed
on the ceiling.

There was a young lady
of Kent,
Who always said just what she
meant;
People said, "she's a dear—So
unique—so sincere—"
But they shunned her by
common consent.

There once was a pious
young priest,
Who lived almost wholly
on yeast;
"For," he said, "it is plain
We must all rise again,
And I want to get started
at least."

I sat next to the Duchess
at tea,
Distressed as a person
could be.
Her rumblings abdominal
Were simply phenomenal—
And everyone thought
it was me!

A rocket explorer
named Wright
Once travelled much faster
than light.
He set out one day
In a relative way,
And returned
on the previous night.

There once was an old man
of Boolong
Who frightened the birds
with his song.
It wasn't the words
Which astonished the birds
But the horrible
*dooble ontong.*

A classical scholar
from Flint
Developed a
curious squint.
With her left-handed eye
She could scan the whole sky
While the other was reading
small print.

There was a young girl
from Detroit
Who at kissing was
very adroit;
She could pucker her lips
Into total eclipse,
Or open them out
like a quoit.

---

Q. Who invented swim flippers? A. Benjamin Franklin.

# FAMILIAR PHRASES

*Here are the origins of a few common phrases.*

**T**O CLOSE RANKS
**Meaning:** To present a united front.
**Origin:** "In the old-time European armies, the soldiers were aligned side-by-side, in neat rows, or ranks, on the battlefield. When the enemy attacked, officers would order the troops to close ranks; that is, to move the rows close together, so that the enemy faced a seemingly impregnable mass of men." (From *Fighting Words*, by Christine Ammer)

**FOR THE BIRDS**
**Meaning:** Worthless.
**Origin:** According to Robert Claiborne in *Loose Cannons and Red Herrrings*, it refers to city streets before cars. "When I was a youngster on the streets of New York, one could both see and smell the emissions of horse-drawn wagons. Since there was no way of controlling these emissions, they, or the undigested oats in them, served to nourish a large population of English sparrows. If you say something's for the birds, you're politely saying that it's horseshit."

**BEYOND THE PALE**
**Meaning:** Socially unacceptable.
**Origin:** "The pale in this expression has nothing to do with the whitish colour, but comes originally from Latin *palus*, meaning a pole or stake. Since stakes are used to mark boundaries, a pale was a particular area within certain limits." The pale that inspired this expression was the area around Dublin in Ireland. Until the 1500s, that area was subject to British law. "Those who lived beyond the pale were outside English jurisdiction and were thought to be uncivilized." (From *Getting to the Roots*, by Martin Manser)

Malaysians wash their babies in beer to protect them from disease.

## I'VE GOT A FROG IN MY THROAT
**Meaning:** I'm hoarse from a cold.
**Origin:** Surprisingly, this wasn't inspired by the croaking sound of a cold-sufferer's voice, but a weird medical practice. "In the Middle Ages," says Christine Ammer in *It's Raining Cats and Dogs*, "throat infections such as thrush were sometimes treated by putting a live frog head first into the patient's mouth; by inhaling, the frog was believed to draw out the patient's infection into its own body. The treatment is happily obsolete, but its memory survives in the 19th-century term *frog in one's throat*."

## KEEPING UP WITH THE JONESES
**Meaning:** Trying to do as well as your neighbours.
**Origin:** "Keeping Up with the Joneses" was the name of a comic strip by Arthur R. "Pop" Momand that ran in the *New York Globe* from 1913 to 1931. At first, Momand planned to call it "Keeping Up with the Smiths," but his real-life neighbours were named Smith, and a lot of his material came from observing them. So he picked another common surname. (From *Why Do We Say It?*, by Nigel Rees)

## XXX
**Meaning:** A kiss, at the end of a letter.
**Origin:** In medieval times, when most people were illiterate, "contracts were not considered legal until each signer included St. Andrew's cross after his name." (Or instead of a signature, if the signer couldn't write.) To prove his sincerity, the signer was then required to kiss the X. "Through the centuries this custom faded out, but the letter X [became associated] with a kiss." This is also probably where the phrase "sealed with a kiss" comes from. (From *I've Got Goose Pimples*, by Martin Vanoni)

## TO READ BETWEEN THE LINES
**Meaning:** To perceive or understand a hidden meaning.
**Origin:** In the 16th century, it became common for politicians, soldiers, and businessmen to write in code. "To a person ignorant of the code, a secret paper was meaningless. Ordinary folk fascinated with this mystery concluded that the meaning was not in lines of gibberish, but in the space between them." (From *Why You Say It*, by Webb Garrison)

---

# HEROES IN THE WATER—OUR SURF-LIFESAVERS

*The sun is bright and the waves are powerful. The "nippers" are in action and the rubber duckies are patrolling. It's just another Sunday morning in Australia.*

You don't have to be an Adonis to be involved in Surf Life Saving Australia. Membership is open to both males and females from the age of seven upwards. It is one of the largest volunteer organisations in the world with over 77,000 members in more than 260 clubs. They protect thousands of kilometres of Australian coastline and since 1907, more than 400,000 rescues by surf-lifesavers have been recorded. Their mission is "to provide a safe beach and aquatic environment throughout Australia".

## DEFYING THE LAW

Australian surf-lifesaving clubs were the first in the world and we have William Gocher to thank for that. In 1902, he defied the current law that prohibited swimming in sunlight hours. Men and women were allowed to "bathe" in the early morning and late evening only, and at separate times. Gocher entered the water at Manly Beach at noon. He was apprehended, but no charges were laid. As the sport of "surf bathing" grew, the obvious dangers associated with it spurred more proficient swimmers to protect others from the dangers of the ocean.

## HUMBLE BEGINNINGS

The first surf club was formed by a group of swimmers at Bronte in 1903. The rescue equipment was a surf belt that was a modified ship's life jacket packed with cork with a rope attached. The rope was coiled on a pole stuck in the sand in the centre of the beach. A lifesaver wearing the surf belt would swim out to a distressed swimmer and the beach crew would reel them back to the safety of the shore. Legend has it that the first person to be saved was an eight-year-old boy Charles Kingsford-Smith, who later became a famous aviator and the first person to fly across the Pacific from the United States to Australia (see pages 143–145). Surf clubs grew in size and number and by 1907, the New South Wales Surf Bathing Association, later to be changed to Surf Life Saving Australia, was formed.

## BLACK SUNDAY

A reminder of the real worth of Surf Life Saving Australia occurred on Sunday 6 February, 1938. A series of freak waves pounded Bondi Beach. Forty people were knocked unconscious, and five of these drowned. Lifesavers eventually rescued 300 people on the day now known as "Black Sunday."

\*    \*    \*    \*

## GREEN AND GOLD

The chant "Aussie Aussie Aussie Oi Oi Oi" deafens the crowd and fills Aussie hearts with pride as a blur of green and gold flashes pass. But why the colours green and gold?

The green and gold colours come from our national floral emblem—the golden wattle, Acacia pycnantha. The desire for a national identity began with Federation in 1901, which spurred the adoption of national symbols, including floral emblems.

The golden wattle is a small tree that grows in the understorey of open forest, woodland and in open scrub in South Australia, Victoria, New South Wales and the Australian Capital Territory. In 1912, wattle was included as a decoration surrounding the Commonwealth Coat of Arms. Even though wattle was accepted as our national flower, it took 87 years for it to be officially recognised. A debate raged throughout the early 1900s as to whether it should be the wattle or the waratah (*Telopea speciosissima*). Unlike waratah, wattle is not unique to Australia. In 1962, the waratah was declared the floral emblem for NSW and in 1988, the golden wattle was proclaimed our national floral emblem. Since 1992, the first day of spring (1 September) is now observed as National Wattle Day.

# CAFFEINE FACTS

*What's our favourite drug? You guessed it—caffeine. We use more caffeine than all other drugs—legal or illegal—combined. Want to know what the stuff is doing to you? Here's a quick overview.*

## BACKGROUND

If you start the day with a strong cup of coffee or tea, you're not alone. Americans alone ingest the caffeine equivalent of 530 million cups of coffee *every day*. Caffeine is the world's most popular mood-altering drug. It's also one of the oldest: according to archaeologists, man has been brewing beverages from caffeine-based plants since the Stone Age.

## HOW IT PICKS YOU UP

*Caffeine doesn't keep you awake by supplying extra energy; rather, it fools your body into thinking it isn't tired.*
• When your brain is tired and wants to slow down, it releases a chemical called *adenosine*.
• Adenosine travels to special cells called *receptors*, where it goes to work counteracting the chemicals that stimulate your brain.
• Caffeine mimics adenosine; so it can "plug up" your receptors and prevent adenosine from getting through. Result: Your brain never gets the signal to slow down, and keeps building up stimulants.

## JAVA JUNKIES

After a while, your brain figures out what's going on, and increases the number of receptor cells so it has enough for both caffeine *and* adenosine.

When that happens, caffeine can't keep you awake anymore… unless you *increase* the amount you drink so it can "plug up" the new receptor cells as well.
• This whole process only takes about a week. In that time, you essentially become a caffeine addict. Your brain is literally restructuring itself to run on caffeine; take the caffeine away and your brain has too many receptor cells to operate properly.
• If you quit ingesting caffeine "cold turkey," your brain begins to reduce the number of receptors right away. But the process takes

The big chill: The South Pole is colder than the North Pole.

about two weeks, and during that time your body sends out mild "distress signals" in the form of headaches, lethargy, fatigue, muscle pain, nausea, and sometimes even stiffness and flu-like symptoms. As a result, most doctors recommend cutting out caffeine gradually.

## CAFFEINE'S EFFECTS

• **Good:** Caffeine has been scientifically proven to temporarily increase alertness, comprehension, memory, reflexes, and even the rate of learning. It also helps increase clarity of thought.
• **Bad:** Too much caffeine can cause hand tremors, loss of coordination or appetite, insomnia, and in extreme cases, trembling, nausea, heart palpitations and diarrhoea.
• Widely varying the amount of caffeine you ingest can put a strain on your liver, pancreas, heart, and nervous system. And if you're prone to ulcers, caffeine can make your situation worse.
• If you manage to consume the equivalent of 70–100 cups of coffee in one sitting, you'll experience convulsions, and may even die.

## CAFFEINE FACTS

• The average Australian drinks 210 milligrams of caffeine a day. That's equal to 2–3 cups of coffee, depending on how strong it is.
• How you make your coffee has a lot to do with how much caffeine you get. Instant coffee contains 65 milligrams of caffeine per serving; coffee brewed in a percolator has 80 milligrams; and coffee made using the "drip method" has 155 milligrams.
• Top four sources of caffeine in the Australian diet: coffee, soft drinks, tea, and chocolate, in that order. The average Australian gets 75% of their caffeine from coffee. Other sources include over-the-counter painkillers, appetite suppressants, cold remedies, and some prescription drugs.
• What happens to the caffeine that's removed from decaf coffee? Most of it is sold to soft drink companies and put into soft drinks. (Cola contains some caffeine naturally, but they like to add even more.)
• Do you drink more caffeine than your kids do? If you correct for body weight, probably not. Kilogram for kilogram, kids often get as much caffeine from chocolate and soft drinks as their parents get from coffee, tea, and other sources.

# ENGLISH/JAPANESE WORDS

*Purists in the Land of the Rising Sun don't like it, but the Japanese language is becoming more Westernised. A number of words that commonly appear in Japanese pop culture have been loosely adapted from English. Here are some of them, written phonetically. See if you can tell what they mean. Answers are at the bottom of the page.*

1. Biiru
2. Terebi
3. Nyusu
4. Supotsu
5. Basu
6. Rajio
7. Gasu
8. Hoteru
9. Resutoran
10. Sabisu
11. Memba
12. Peii
13. Kappu
14. Bata
15. Sekkusu
16. Bitami
17. Dezain
18. Pantsu
19. Supu
20. Dorama
21. Sosu
22. Burausu
23. Sutecchi
24. Bonasu
25. Kado
26. Pointo
27. Makudonarudo
28. Sungurasu
29. Sunobbari
30. Caresu
31. Weta
32. Tawa
33. Sumato
34. Boru
35. Gorufu
36. Sumoggu

## ANSWERS

1. beer; 2. TV; 3. news; 4. sports; 5. bus; 6. radio; 7. gas; 8. hotel; 9. restaurant; 10. service; 11. member; 12. page; 13. cup; 14. butter; 15. sex; 16. vitamin; 17. design; 18. pants; 19. soup; 20. drama; 21. sauce; 22. blouse; 23. stitch; 24. bonus; 25. card; 26. point; 27. McDonald's; 28. sunglasses; 29. snobbery; 30. caress; 31. waiter; 32. tower; 33. smart; 34. ball; 35. golf; 36. smog

# OOPS !

*Everyone's amused by tales of outrageous blunders—probably because
it's comforting to know that someone's screwing up even worse
that we are. So here's an ego-building page from the BRI.
Go ahead and feel superior for a few minutes.*

## PUBLISHING BOMB

"In 1978 Random House issued a cookbook that
contained a potentially lethal mistake. *Woman's Day
Crockery Cuisine* offered a recipe for caramel slices that
inadvertently left out one simple ingredient—water. It was soon
discovered that if the recipe was followed exactly, a can of
condensed milk called for in the book could explode. Random
House had to recall 10,000 copies of the book" to correct the
potentially lethal recipe.

**—From The Blunder Book, by M. L. Ginsberg**

## TAKE THAT!

"In 1941 the British warship *Trinidad* sighted a German destroyer
and fired a torpedo at it. The icy Arctic waters apparently affected
the torpedo's steering mechanism—it began to curve in a slow are.
As the crew watched in horror, it continued curving slowly
around until it was speeding right back at them at forty knots.
The *Trinidad*'s torpedo slammed into the *Trinidad* and caused so
much damage that it put the warship out of action for the rest of
the war."

**—From The Emperor Who Ate the Bible, by Scott Morris**

## SOLID PLANNING

"In 1974 the Nigerian government decided to initiate a 'Third
National Nigerian Development Plan,' intended to bring the
country in a single leap into line with most developed Western
nations.

"The planners calculated that to build the new roads, airfields,
and military buildings which the plan required would call for
some 20 million tonnes of cement. This was duly ordered and
shipped by freighters from all over the world, to be unloaded at
Lagos docks.

"Unfortunately, the Nigerian planners had not considered the fact that the docks were only capable of handling two thousand tonnes a day. Working every day, it would have taken 27 years to unload just the ships that were at one point waiting at sea off Lagos. These contained a third of the world's supply of cement— much of it showing its fine quality by setting in the hold of the freighters."

—From *David Frost's Book of the World's Worst Decisions*

## CALLING ALL CARS

In 1977 American carmakers actually recalled more vehicles than they produced: 9.3 million cars were made in the United States that year; 10.4 million were recalled.

## RAISING THE DEAD

"A mixup at a company that makes compact disks resulted in rock music with lines like 'God told me to skin you alive' being shipped to radio stations labelled as religious music.

"The Southern Baptist Radio-TV Commission, which markets a weekly religious radio program called 'Powerline,' is calling more than 1,200 radio stations across the country to warn them that some CDs it sent out for religious broadcasts are mislabelled.

"The CDs are supposed to contain inspirational talks and music. They are actually the alternative rock band Dead Kennedys' album, 'Fresh Fruit for Rotting Vegetables.' "

—Reported in the *Chicago Tribune*, June 22, 1993

## HAPPY BIRTHDAY

"Festivities marking the centennial of organised soccer in Hereford, England, were cancelled abruptly when officials discovered the league was only 90 years old."

—From *News of the Weird*

## USING HIS HEAD

"On May 26, 1993, Texas Rangers outfielder Jose Canseco went back for a fly ball hit by Carlos Martinez of the Cleveland Indians. It missed his glove, bounced off his head, and ricocheted into the stands for a home run. 'I thought I had it,' Canseco explained later. 'Now I'll be on ESPN for a month.' "

—From the *San Francisco Chronicle*

# FABULOUS FLOPS

*Next time you see the hype for some amazing "can't miss"*
*phenomenon, hold on to a healthy sense of skepticism*
*by remembering these duds.*

**E**SPERANTO
**Glorious Prediction:** "Where will Esperanto be tomorrow
as a world language? 1) Everyone will *learn* Esperanto;
2) Everyone will *use* Esperanto; 3) It will be the international
*neutral* language; and 4) It will be a major step toward *world peace*
*and prosperity.*

**Background:** Esperanto was created in 1887 by Lazarus Ludwig
Zamenhof, an idealistic 28-year-old Polish ophthalmologist.
According to one account, "Zamenhof's neighbours—Poles,
Russians, Estonians, Latvians, and Germans—profoundly
misunderstood and mistrusted each other in a multitude of
tongues. It was his dream to fashion a new language they could
share, and through which they could learn to coexist." Drawing
on nearly all the romance languages, Zamenhof created a
simplified, hybrid version with only 16 rules of grammar, no
irregular verbs (English has 728), and words that could be changed
from nouns to adjectives, adverbs, or verbs by changing the vowel
at the end of the word. He published his language under the
pseudonym. Dr. Esperanto, which translates as "one who hopes."

**What Happened:** Despite more than 100 years of lobbying by
Esperanto devotees, the language has never taken hold. Still,
today there are thousands of Esperanto speakers organised into
clubs in 100 countries around the world—including special-
interest chapters for vegetarians and nudists.

## THE COMET KAHOUTEK
**Glorious Prediction:** "Kahoutek will be the greatest sky show of
the century, with a brilliance fifty times that of Halley's comet
and a tail extending across a sixth of the sky." One Harvard
astronomer even predicted that the comet's tail length "might
reach 36 times the apparent diametre of the full moon."

---

**"The more outrageous a subject can get, the more I like it."—Alfred Hitchcock**

**Background:** The comet, "a grimy lump of chemical ice some three miles in diameter" was discovered by German astronomer Lubos Kahoutek in 1973.

**What Happened:** Nothing. On January 15, 1974, the comet came as close to the earth as it would get in 80,000 years—and no one on Earth could see it. One astronomer described the spectacle as "a thrown egg, that missed." Where was Dr. Kahoutek? He and 1,692 other passengers were on the Queen Elizabeth 2, which had been specially chartered for the event. As *Newssweek* magazine put it, "The weather turned out rough and overcast, and Dr. Kahoutek spent much of the voyage too seasick to leave his cabin." Two weeks later the comet did emit a burst of explosive colour—but by then it was so close to the sun that only three people saw it—the astronauts aboard Skylab.

\* \* \* \*

## HOLLYWOOD-ISMS
Some funny observations taken from *Star Speak: Hollywood on Everything* by Doug McClelland.

"In Hollywood, the executives have Picassos and Chagalls on their walls and would kill to have lunch with Chuck Norris. That's why you have movies like *Howard the Duck*."
> —*David Steinberg*

"It is not true I was born a monster. Hollywood made me one."
> —*Boris Karloff*

"The best time I ever had with Joan Crawford was when I pushed her down the stairs in *Whatever Happened to Baby Jane?*"
> —*Bette Davis*

"I had a dog named Duke. Every fireman in town knew that hound, because he chased all the firewagons. They knew the dog's name, but not mine, so the next thing I was Duke, too. I was named for a damn dog!"
> —*John Wayne*

"If the scripts were as great as the sets, what a town Hollywood would be!"
> —*W. Somerset Maugham*

Australian bartenders say they hear more complaints about work than any other subject.

# BARNUM'S HISTORY LESSON

*P. T. Barnum said, "There's a sucker born every minute"...then he proved it with his sideshows and circuses. He also wrote about it. In a book called* Humbugs of the World, *published in 1866, he delightedly catalogued some of the great hoaxes in history. This excerpt was one of his favourites. It took place in 1667 in France, when an ambassador from Persia arrived at the pampered court of Louis XIV.*

**THE AMBASSADOR ARRIVES**

It was announced formally, one morning, to Louis XIV, that His Most Serene Excellency, Riza Bey, with an interminable tail of titles, hangers-on and equipages, had reached the port of Marseilles to lay before the great "King of the Franks" brotherly congratulations and gorgeous presents from his own illustrious master, the Shah of Persia.

The ambassador and his suite were lodged in sumptuous apartments in the Tuileries, under the care and guidance of King Louis's own assistant majordomo and a guard of courtiers and regiments of Royal Swiss. Banqueting and music filled the first evening; and the next day His Majesty sent the Duc de Richelieu to announce that he would receive them on the third evening at Versailles.

**THE AMBASSADOR IS WELCOMED**

Meanwhile the most extensive preparations were made for the audience; when the time arrived, the entire Gallery of Mirrors was crowded with the beauty, the chivalry, the wit, taste, and intellect of France at that dazzling period. Louis the Great himself never appeared to finer advantage. His royal countenance was lighted up with pride and satisfaction as the Envoy of the haughty Oriental king approached the splendid throne on which he sat. As he descended a step to meet him, the Persian envoy bent the knee, and with uncovered head presented the credentials of his mission. A grand ball and supper concluded this night of splendour, and Riza Bey was launched at the French court; every member of the illustrious court tried to outdo his peers with the value of the books,

---

World record: In 1993, Japan became the first country with 1/5 of its population age 65 or older.

pictures, gems, etc. which they heaped upon the illustrious Persian.

The latter gentleman very quietly smoked his pipe and lounged on his divan before company—and diligently packed up the goods when he and his jolly companions were left alone. The presents of the Shah had not yet arrived, but were daily expected, and from time to time the olive-coloured suite was diminished by the departure of one of the number with his chest on a special mission to England, Austria, or other European powers. In the meantime, the Bey was feted in all directions…and it was whispered that the fair ones of the court were, from the first, eager to bestow their favours.

## THE AMBASSADOR'S PLANS

The King favoured his Persian pet with numerous personal interviews, at which, in broken French, the Envoy unfolded the most imposing of schemes of conquest and commerce that his master was willing to share with his great brother of France. At one of these, tête-à-têtes, the magnificent Riza Bey, upon whom the King had already conferred his own portrait set in diamonds, and other gifts worth several millions of francs, placed in the Royal hand several fragments of opal and turquoise said to have been found near the Caspian sea, which teemed with limitless treasures of the same kind, and which the Shah of Persia proposed to divide with France for the honour of her alliance. The King was enchanted.

## THE AMBASSADOR DISAPPEARS

At length, word was sent to Versailles that the gifts from the Shah had come, and a day was appointed for their presentation. The day arrived, and the Hall of Audience was again thrown open. All was jubilee; the King and the court waited, but no Persian—no Riza Bey—and no presents from the Shah!

That morning three men had left the Tuileries at daylight with a bag and a bundle, never to return. They were Riza Bey and his last bodyguards; the bag and the bundle were the smallest in bulk but the most precious in value of a month's plunder. The turquoises and opals bestowed upon the King turned out, on close inspection, to be a new and very ingenious variety of coloured glass.

Of course, a hue and cry was raised—but totally in vain. It was afterward believed that a noted barber and suspected bandit, who had once really travelled in Persia, was the perpetrator of this pretty joke. But no one was sure—no one ever heard from him again.

The Danish flag, used since the 13th century, is the oldest unchanged national flag in existence.

# AUSTRALIA'S RABBIT-PROOF FENCE

*Australia is just one large paddock, really. Perhaps that's what the early colonists thought when they came up with the idea of erecting a rabbit-proof fence along the states' borders.*

## WRASCALLY WRABBITS

It all started in 1859. Without wanting to point the historical finger, that was when Englishman Thomas Austin released rabbits on his property near Geelong in Victoria so that he could continue to enjoy the English custom of "hunting." Other landowners adopted this practice and soon rabbits were running riot on properties all over Victoria and New South Wales.

## RABBITS, RABBITS, EVERYWHERE

Because the expression "breeding like rabbits" is not just a turn of phrase, it wasn't long before rabbits were popping up everywhere. In fact, it took just 37 years for them to find their way to Queensland, go over to South Australia and across the continent to Western Australia. And in a continent the size of Australia, these are massive distances!

By the turn of the twentieth century, Australia was overrun with rabbits. In 1901, the Government Surveyor surveyed a route for a rabbit-proof fence and construction began later that year. After seven years and many hours of hard labour, the largest continuous fence in the world stood proudly in its isolation. It ran from the top of Australia to the bottom.

## THE LAST LAUGH

The rabbit-proof fence, however, was not successful. It was myxomatosis that eventually reduced the rabbit population (but that's another story!). Inspecting and maintaining the rabbit-proof fence was a huge job. Rabbits found their way through holes in the fence, and burrowed under it. They were unstoppable.

Australia was the third country after the US and Russia to launch a satellite into orbit.

According to Henry Lawson, Australia's bush poet, the last laugh definitely belongs to the rabbits. In his short story *Hungerford*, which appeared in *While the Billy Boils* (published in 1896), Lawson had this to say about the rabbit-proof fence:

> …we found Hungerford and camped there for a day. The town is right on the Queensland border, and an interprovincial rabbit-proof fence—with rabbits on both sides of it—runs across the main street.
>
> This fence is a standing joke with Australian rabbits—about the only joke they have out there, except for the memory of Pasteur and poison and inoculation. It is amusing to go a little way out of town, about sunset, and watch them crack Noah's Ark rabbit jokes about that fence, and burrow under and play leap-frog over it till they get tired.

## DON'T FENCE ME IN

Parts of the rabbit-proof fence still stand today. The height varies depending on the size of the animal being kept at bay.
• In parts of Western Australia, the fence keeps emus out of the wheat belt.
• In South Australia, the fence keeps kangaroos away from the crops.
• In Queensland, the fence keeps rabbits and dingoes out of crop and grain areas.

## DID YOU KNOW?

In the 1930s, three young Aboriginal girls called Molly, Gracie and Daisy were removed from their families by the government of the day and placed in a home where they were to be trained as servants for a white family. The girls escaped and walked for hundreds of kilometres, using the rabbit-proof fence as their guide, all the way back to their families.

Australian director Phillip Noyce's movie, *Rabbit-Proof Fence*, depicts the girls' journey and their incredible tenacity. It is based on the book *Follow the Rabbit-Proof Fence* by Doris Pilkington and Nugi Garimara.

**Australia has a larger area covered by snow in winter than Switzerland.**

# WORD ORIGINS

*We use them, and we understand them. But where do familiar words come from? Probably not where you'd guess. Here are a few examples.*

**Debonair**
French for "of good air." In the Middle Ages, people's health was judged partly by how they smelled. A person who gave off "good air" was presumed healthier and happier.

**Gymnasium**
Meant "to train naked" in ancient Greece, where athletes wore little or nothing.

**Carnival**
Literal meaning: "Flesh, farewell." Refers to traditional pre-Lenten feast (like Mardi Gras) after which people usually fasted.

**Daisy**
Comes from "day's eye." When the sun comes out, it opens its yellow eye.

**Ukelele**
In the 1800s, an English sailor gave such enthusiastic performances with this instrument that he was nicknamed *Ukelele*—"little jumping flea" in Hawaiian. He went on to popularise it around the world.

**Gung Ho**
Means "work together" in Chinese. After a group called Carlson's Raiders used it as their motto in WWII, it became a term to describe an enthusiastic soldier.

**Ballot**
Italian term for "small ball or pebble." Origin: Italian citizens once voted by casting a small pebble or ball into one of several boxes.

**Jiggle**
Refers to the jig (a dance).

**Genuine**
Originally meant "placed on the knees." In ancient Rome, a father legally claimed his newborn child by sitting in front of his family and placing the child on his knee.

**Cab**
Old Italian term for goat. The first carriages for public hire bounced so much they reminded people of goats romping on a hillside.

**Alibi means "elsewhere" in Latin.**

# THE WHOLE TOOTH

*Some info to give you a little historical perspective
when you're brushing your teeth.*

**TOOTHBRUSHES.** People have been cleaning their teeth for thousands of years, but the implements they used weren't much like toothbrushes. Many cultures used "chew sticks," pencil-sized twigs with one end frayed into soft bristles; they've been found in Egyptian tombs dating back to 3000 B.C.

The first toothbrush to resemble modern ones originated in China around 1498. The bristles were plucked from hogs and set into handles of bone or bamboo. But animal hair is porous and water-absorbent, which makes it a breeding ground for bacteria; so brushing often did more harm than good. Nevertheless, by the 19th century, hogs-hair brushes were the standard for people who brushed.

Toothbrushing didn't become widely popular in the U.S. until the late 1930s. Two reasons for its spread: with the invention of nylon bristles by DuPont chemists in 1938, Americans finally had a hygienic substitute for hogs-hair; and every soldier who fought in World War II was instructed in oral hygiene and issued a brush—when the war ended they brought the habit home to their families.

**TOOTHPASTE.** History's first recorded toothpaste was an Egyptian mixture of ground pumice and strong wine. But the early Romans brushed their teeth with human urine…and also used it as a mouthwash. Actually, urine was an active component in tooth-pastes and mouthwashes until well into the 18th century—the ammonia it contains gave them strong cleansing power.

*Fluoridated* toothpaste came about as the result of a discovery made in Naples, Italy, in 1802, when local dentists noticed yellowish-brown spots on their patients' teeth—but no cavities. Subsequent examination revealed that high levels of fluoride in the water caused the spots *and* prevented tooth decay, and that less fluoride protected teeth without causing the spots. It took a while for the discovery to be implemented; the first U.S. fluoridated water tests didn't take place until 1915, and Crest, the first toothpaste with fluoride in it ("Look, Ma…") didn't hit stores until 1956.

Poll results: 59% of married men and 61% of married women say sex gets better after marriage.

# GIVE YOURSELF SOME CREDIT

*Did you use a credit card to buy this book? Credit cards are a way of life to most people. In fact, you could argue that those little pieces of plastic are actually the backbone of the Australian economy. How's that for a scary thought?...And they haven't even been around that long. Here is a brief history.*

**B**ACKGROUND By the 1950s, petrol companies, department stores, and major hotels had developed their own credit cards—small pieces of cardboard or metal plates they gave their best customers to use instead of cash (allowing holders to pay for purchases at the end of the month). But these early cards were different than the ones we use today—they were only accepted at the business that had issued them.

### THE FIRST SUPPER

According to legend, that all changed in one night in 1950, when businessman Robert X. McNamara finished his dinner in a posh New York restaurant—and realised that he didn't have enough cash to pay for the meal. His wife had to drive across town to pay for it, which embarrassed him deeply. But it also gave him an idea: why not issue a "diners card" that people could use to pay for meals when they were short of cash?

McNamara proposed his idea to a number of restaurants around town. In exchange for honouring his new "Diners Club" card, he would pay for the meal of anyone who presented the card. Diners Club would absorb the risk of non-payment; the restaurant got the money even if the cardholder was a deadbeat. How the card made its money: it paid the restaurants 90¢ to 95¢ on the dollar, billed the cardholder $1.00, and kept the difference in the form of a "discount." The restaurants balked at this arrangement at first, but McNamara convinced them that people with cards would spend more money—and more often—than people without them. By the end of the year, he had signed up 27 New York restaurants and 200 cardholders. The age of the credit card as we know it had begun.

## CREDIT CARD FACTS

- The average Australian holds 2.9 credit cards. In America, credit card companies send out more than 1 billion new credit card offers every year.
- Why do merchants like credit cards? On average, consumers spend 23% more money when they pay with credit cards than when they pay cash.
- It's illegal now, but credit card companies used to mail credit cards to people who hadn't even applied for them. It wasn't always good business: In 1966, five Chicago banks banded together and mailed five million credit cards to people who hadn't asked for them. But "the banks had been less than cautious in assembling their mailing lists. Some families received 15 cards. Dead people and babies got cards. A dachshund named Alice was sent not one but four cards, one of which arrived with the promise that Alice would be welcomed as a 'preferred customer' at many of Chicago's finest restaurants."
- In 1972 Walter Cavanagh and a friend bet a dinner to see who could accumulate the most credit cards. Eight years later he won the bet—and broke the world record—by applying for and getting 1,003 credit cards, weighing 15 kg (34 pounds) and entitling him to $1.25 million in credit. He's still applying for credit cards, and has set a goal of 10,000 cards.
- In 1987 aspiring moviemaker Robert Townsend paid for his first film, *Hollywood Shuffle*, by charging $100,000 on his 15 personal credit cards. Luckily, the movie made enough money for him to pay back the money.

\*     \*     \*     \*

An Afghanistan diplomat visiting the US for the first time was being wined and dined by the State Department. The diplomat was not used to the salt in American foods (French fries, salami, anchovies etc) and was constantly sending his manservant Abdul to fetch him a glass of water.

Time and time again Abdul would scamper off and return with a glass of water, but then came the time when he returned empty handed.

"Abdul, you son of an ugly camel, where is my water?" demanded the diplomat.

---

**What's an ermine? A weasel whose coat has turned white for the winter.**

# SCRATCH 'N' SNIFF

*No, this is not a scratch 'n' sniff page—it's about
the scratch 'n' sniff phenomenon.*

**B**ACKGROUND
For years advertisers understood that scents help sell
products, but they couldn't find a way to include smells in
printed advertisements. The first attempt came in the 1950s,
when newspaper companies tried printing with scented ink. The
experiment flopped—either the smells dissipated rapidly, or they
mixed with the newspaper's smell, spoiling the effect.

In 1969 the 3M Corp. and National Cash Register Co. (NCR)
each developed a way to impregnate printed advertisements with
fragrances. They called the technique "microencapsulation,"
because it literally sealed the smells in the surface of the ad until
the consumer released them by scratching the page. For the first
time in history, products as diverse as bananas, bourbon, shaving
cream, dill pickles, pine trees—and, of course, perfume, could be
advertised using their scents.

## HOW IT WORKS

• The printing company takes a product like perfume or food,
and extracts its aromatic oils.
• The oils are mixed with water, which breaks them up into tiny
droplets—an average of one million drops per six square
centimetres (one square inch).
• The droplets are sprayed onto paper or some other surface, and
are covered with a layer of plastic resin or gum arabic.
• The scent remains fresh beneath the resin until someone
scratches the surface. This bursts the layer of resin or gum that
holds the droplets, and the smell escapes.

## SCRATCH 'N' SNIFF FACTS

• Scratch 'n' sniff pages and scented pages aren't just novelties;
they're big business. According to a study commissioned by Ralph
Lauren Fragrances, 76% of women who buy new perfumes are
introduced to the fragrances through scented inserts in magazines.
• On average, scented pages cost twice as much as scent-free ads.

---

Five most persuasive words in the English language: discover, easy, guarantee, health, and results.

- A lot of people hate perfume strips, despite their popularity with perfume and ad companies. In fact, they can actually make sensitive people ill. In June 1991, a man wrote to *The New Yorker* complaining that "A very noxious and pervacious [sic] odor invaded this house with the mail today. Much to our surprise, it came from the arriving copy of *The New Yorker*....I am an elderly asthmatic, allergic to perfume, and although I have retched occasionally at some material in *The New Yorker*, I have never vomited on it before." As a result of his and other complaints, many magazines now offer scented and unscented editions.
- Another problem was that magazines were running more and more ads with perfume strips. Magazines got so smelly that perfume companies had to limit the number that could appear— and the post office itself began regulating scented inserts.

## WEIRD USES

- In 1989 the English National Opera produced a scratch 'n' sniff version of Prokofiev's "Love for Three Oranges." Audience members received a special "fragrance panel" at the beginning of the play, along with instructions telling them when to sniff. The card even contained a scent for an unpleasant character named Farfarello, who has "bad breath and emits gasses." His smell was supposed to be "a cross between bad eggs and body odor," but the stench was so overpowering that it made the entire fragrance panel stink. In later performances of the play, his scent was left out.
- In 1990 the rock group Swamp Zombies released *Scratch and Sniff Car Crash*, an album whose cover smelled like burnt rubber. Weird inspiration: The band members got the idea after two of them narrowly escaped serious injury in automobile accidents.
- In 1989 the RJ Reynolds Tobacco company test-marketed Chelsea cigarettes, a brand targeted at women. Its major selling point: the smokes were rolled in a paper that gave off a sweet smell when it burned. They promoted the brand with scratch 'n' sniff newspaper ads showing off the scented papers. The ads smelled great—but cigarette sales stank, and the brand was dropped.
- In 1989 BEI Defense Systems, a Dallas missile manufacturer, ran a scratch 'n' sniff ad in *Armed Forces Journal* touting the company's "extraordinarily lethal" Flechette rocket. The ad smelled like cordite (the explosive contained in the warhead), an aroma the company called "the smell of victory".

# WHERE THE SURF'S ALWAYS UP

*Australia may have its share of couch potatoes but when they get stirred up, they do more than replace the batteries in their remotes—they go surfing!*

**B**ONDING AT BONDI
Among medical people, a mini-mal might be misconstrued as a scaled-down epileptic seizure. To compulsives shoppers, a mini-mal may be a short string of retail shops. To Australians along the coast, a mini-mal is a surfboard less than 3 metres ( 9 feet) long. It's really a mini-malibu, a Californian creation for fun in the surf and sun when the waves don't crest too high and the reefs aren't too sharp. For these Australians, Saturday morning is the time to pull on the cossie, load the esky with beer, grab the mini-mal and head for Bondi, Curl Curl or Dee Why, where the tubes are like gun barrels and the waves break onto the shore like rolling thunder.

More than mini-mals are paddled out to wait for a wave. Fishes, squishes, squashes and other short boards are also there, along with a smattering of longboards and other strange shapes. So are ten thousand surfers strung along the front and jockeying for position. The beaches are covered with bodies, from the shoreline to the tidal reaches. The air above the towels and sun umbrellas is so redolent with sunscreen the fumes should be bottled.

## BREAKS ARE WHERE YOU FIND THEM
Around Sydney isn't the only place Australians can surf. National pastimes can't be held to one locale, not in a country where surf is the siren and certainly not in a country with a longer seacoast than any other island in the world—reef, point and beach breaks abound.

Surfing the Queensland coast, for example, can offer more challenges than the famed Banzai pipeline of Oahu. South, near the New South Wales border, is much favoured. Further north, survivors say, nasty poisonous box jellyfish like to school up and body surf—anybody's body—and sharks have been known to occasionally chow down on fibreglass surfboards and any succulents that may be on them. But these hazards can seem trivial to some intrepid surfers. West of Ceduna in South Australia offers fantastic surfing breaks, provided the local great white sharks, those of *Jaws* fame, choose not to live up to their reputation for ill-tempered and indiscriminate voracity.

Off some shores, there's more to meet the eye than a shark fin slicing the water. Two Mile Reef, up the road from Port Campbell, generates waves that could intimidate a pro-surfer if sanity is factored in. Then, just past there is Massacres, where the faint of heart never venture and fools only once.

## SO WHAT'S THE BIG DEAL?
What possible attraction does this sport hold for Australians? They've been at it since before beach bunnies and California girls were created on a Hollywood back lot. It may not be as popular as barbies and footy; however, cricket, lawn bowling, even hiking up Mount Kosciuszko can't make the same list for camaraderie, dedication and excitement. Surfing is rash, brash and aggressive. With all of that, even a beginner riding shoreward on a soft lazy swell can exude enough charisma to catch the eye of the opposite sex, that other compelling allure of Australian beaches.

## WIPE OUT
The Americans actually got first crack at importing the sport more than fifty years before Australians knew it existed. The illustrious Mark Twain gave it a try while visiting Hawaii. He wiped out, described his misfortune to the American public, and America's loss became Australia's gain.

## THE FIRST WAX HEADS
Surfing finally made it to Australia in 1915 on the hand-carved surfboard of the Olympic gold-medal swimmer from Hawaii, Duke Kahanamoku. When Duke saw the irresistible surf, he promptly carved a board from some local lumber and paddled out to catch a wave and create some history.

Following his example that same day was the first Australian to ride a surfboard—a woman as it happened. Her name was Isabel Letham. Sixteen-year-old Isabel was already a regular on the northern beaches of Sydney, well-known as a surf aquaplanist, a cousin to surfing but not quite in the same league. The sport involved riding, or more often lying, on a wide board to crest into

The first life-saving club in the world was formed in Bondi in 1906.

shore on a wave, skimming along rather like a car on a rain-slicked highway. After watching the Duke, Isabel persuaded her father to construct a 25-kg (56-lb) redwood surfboard and the rest is history. Later, Isabel spent several years in California trying to make it as a stuntwoman in the movies, but the waves beckoned. For a brief period in San Francisco she taught water ballet and remedial swimming, then returned to Australia where she conducted classes into her seventies. In 1978, the Australian Women's Board Riders Association named Isabel a Life Member.

Before long, often unkempt and somewhat suspect bronzed surfers replaced Australia's famed lifeguards as resident beach icons. Whereas the lifeguards politely strutted about most of the time, intermittently exhibiting feats of derring-do, the surfers were a continuous show. Plus, many of them had attitude. No surprise, the first world champion surfing competition was held in Australia. Nor should it be a surprise, that many of the great surfing legends have been Australians.

## TALK THE TALK
The sport is now so popular hardly a soul who goes to an Australian beach doesn't get lost in a conversation about tail rockers, rails, vees, concaves and flats. Even the beach-bound know a popout from a composite, and most can instantly spot a custom board from as far away as the other end of the beach. These Lamborghinis of the surf tend to stand out, especially if it's a sleek progressive longboard.

## WALK THE WALK
Finally, of course, the sport has its fanatics—surfers truly stoked with their boards. Sometimes they can be found on the beach, distanced from non-waxheads, as the pecking order dictates. They usually have a wistful, patient look in their eye as they watch the water, knowing that soon a potent line-up will begin, knowing that soon they'll be paddling out, catching the wave, swerving, ducking, and speeding to outrace the curl poised to come down on them from four metres above. And, if it's an off day, their look will be more inner-directed, dreaming the dreams of remote juice like no other in its profound, heart-stopping power and majesty.

# FAMILIAR PHRASES

*Here are more origins of common phrases.*

**B**ORN WITH A SILVER SPOON IN ONE'S MOUTH
**Meaning:** Pampered; lucky; born into wealth or prosperous circumstances.
**Origin:** At one time, it was customary for godparents to give their godchild a silver spoon at the baby's christening. These people were usually well-off, so the spoon came to represent the child's good fortune.

**BITE THE BULLET**
**Meaning:** Get on with a difficult or unpleasant task.
**Origin:** "Although one can find other explanations, it seems most plausible that the term originated in battlefield surgery before the days of anaesthesia. A surgeon about to operate on a wounded soldier would urge him to bite on a bullet of soft lead to distract him from the pain; at least it would minimise his ability to scream and thus divert the surgeon." (From *The Dictionay of Clichés*, by James Rogers)

**SOMETHING FITS TO A "T"**
**Meaning:** It fits perfectly.
**Origin:** Commonly thought of as a reference to the T-square, which is used to draw parallel lines and angles. But this phrase was used in the 1600s, before anyone called the tool a T-square.
"A more likely explanation is that the expression was originally 'to a tittle.' A tittle was the dot over the 'i', so the phrase meant 'to a dot' or 'fine point.'" (From *Why Do We Say It*, by Nigel Rees)

**THINGS WILL PAN OUT/ HAVEN'T PANNED OUT**
**Meaning:** Optimistic view that things will work out/things haven't worked out.
**Origin:** When prospectors look for gold, they kneel by a river or stream and wash dirt from the bed in a shallow pan. This is called *panning.* Traditionally, when prospectors were sure they'd find gold, they said things "would pan out." When they didn't find it, they said things "didn't pan out." (From *Gold!*, by Gordon Javna)

## YOU'RE NO SPRING CHICKEN
**Meaning:** You're not young anymore; you're past your prime.
**Origin:** "Until recent generations, there were no incubators and few warm hen houses. That meant chicks couldn't be raised during winter. New England growers found that those born in the spring brought premium prices in the summer market places. When these Yankee traders tried to pass off old birds as part of the spring crop, smart buyers would protest that the bird was 'no spring chicken.'" (From *Why You Say It*, by Webb Garrison)

## CLEAR THE DECKS
**Meaning:** Prepare for action; take care of minor matters, so you can focus on important ones.
**Origin:** A battle order in the days of sailing ships. "A crew prepared for battle by removing or fastening down all loose objects on deck that might otherwise get in the way of the guns or be knocked down and injure a sailor." (From *Fighting Words*, by Christine Ammer)

## TRYING TO MAKE BOTH ENDS MEET
**Meaning:** Trying to stretch your income to live within your means.
**Origin:** On sailing ships of the 1400s and 1500s, sails "were raised and lowered separately, and the rigging involved hundreds of ropes. Some were permanently fixed. When such a rope broke, most preferred to replace it rather than attempt a repair job." But ship owners who were low on cash often told their captains "to pull broken rope ends together and splice them." So "a piece of rigging was stretched to the limit in order for both ends to meet." Gradually, the term moved from ship to shore, and came to mean stretching things to the limit because of a shortage of funds. (From *I've Got Goose Pimples*, by Martin Vanoni)

\*    \*    \*    \*

**Important thought:** "If you're killed, you've lost a very important part of your life."

—*Brooke Shields*

Owls are the only birds that can see the colour blue.

# FAMOUS TRIALS: THE WITCHES OF SALEM

*Here's a bit of American history we're all familiar with…but know almost nothing about. The BRI wants to change that, because we don't want witch trials—or witch hunts—in our era. After all, someone just might decide that reading in the bathroom is a sign of demonic possession!*

**B**ACKGROUND The trouble at Salem, Massachusetts, began with two young girls acting oddly. It exploded into one of the strangest cases of mass hysteria in American history. In the six-month period between March and September 1692, 27 people were convicted on witchcraft charges; 20 were executed, and more than 100 other people were in prison awaiting trial.

## CHILD'S PLAY

In March 1692, nine-year-old Betty Parris and her cousin Abigail Williams, 12, were experimenting with a fortune-telling trick they'd learned from Tituba, the Parris family's West Indian slave. To find out what kind of men they'd marry when they grew up, they put an egg white in a glass…and then studied the shape it made in the glass.

But instead of glimpsing their future husbands, the girls saw an image that appeared to be "in the likeness of a coffin." The apparition shocked them…and over the next few days they exhibited behaviour that witnesses described as "foolish, ridiculous speeches," "odd postures," "distempers," and "fits."

Reverend Samuel Parris was startled by his daughter's condition and took her to see William Griggs, the family doctor. Griggs couldn't find out what was wrong with the girl, but he suspected the problem had supernatural origins. He told Rev. Parris that he thought the girl had fallen victim to "the Evil Hand"—witchcraft. The family tried to keep Betty's condition a secret, but rumours began spreading almost immediately—and within two months at least eight other girls began exhibiting similar forms of bizarre behaviour.

## THE PARANOIA GROWS

The citizens of Salem Village demanded that the authorities take action. The local officials subjected the young girls to intense questioning, and soon the girls began naming names. The first three women they accused of witchcraft were Tituba and two other women from Salem Village, Sarah Good and Sarah Osborne.

The three women were arrested and held for questioning. A few weeks later two more suspects, Martha Cory and Rebecca Nurse, were arrested on similar charges. And at the end of April a sixth person—the Reverend George Burroughs, a minister that Abigail Williams identified as the leader of the witches—was arrested and imprisoned. The girls continued to name names. By the middle of May, more than 100 people had been arrested for witchcraft.

## THE TRIALS

On May 14, 1692, the newly appointed governor, Sir William Phips, arrived from England. He immediately set up a special court, the Court of Oyer and Terminer, to hear the witchcraft trials that were clogging the colonial legal system.

• The first case heard was that against Bridget Bishop. She was quickly found guilty of witchcraft, sentenced to death, and then hung on June 10.

• On June 19 the court met a second time, and in a single day heard the cases of five accused women, found them all guilty, and sentenced them to death. They were hung on July 19.

• On August 5 the court heard six more cases, and sentenced all six women to death. One woman, Elizabeth Proctor, was spared because she was pregnant—and the authorities didn't want to kill an innocent life along with a guilty one. The remaining five women were executed on August 19.

• Six more people were sentenced to death in early September. (Only four were executed: one person was reprieved, and another woman managed to escape from prison with the help of friends.) The remaining sentences were carried out on September 22.

• On September 17, the court handed down nine more death sentences. (This time five of the accused "confessed" in exchange for a commutation of the death sentence and were not hung.) The remaining four were hung on September 22.

• Two days later, the trials claimed their last victim when Giles Cory, an accused wizard, was executed by "pressing" (he was slowly crushed to death under heavy weights) after he refused to enter a plea.

## REVERSAL OF FORTUNE
By now the hysteria surrounding the witch trials was at its peak: 19 accused "witches" had been hung, about 50 had "confessed" in exchange for lenient treatment, more than 100 people accused of witchcraft were under arrest and awaiting trial—and another 200 people had been accused of witchcraft but had not yet been arrested. Despite all this, the afflicted girls were still exhibiting bizarre behaviour. But public opinion began to turn against the trials. Community leaders began to publicly question the methods that the courts used to convict suspected witches. The accused were denied access to defense counsel, and were tried in chains before jurors who had been chosen from church membership lists.

The integrity of the girls then came under question. Some of the adults even charged that they were faking their illnesses and accusing innocent people for the fun of it. One colonist even testified later that one of the bewitched girls had bragged to him that "she did it for sport."

As the number of accused persons grew into the hundreds, fears of falling victim to witchcraft were replaced by an even greater fear: that of being falsely accused of witchcraft. The growing opposition to the proceedings came from all segments of society: common people, ministers—even from the court itself.

## THE AFTERMATH
Once the tide had turned against the Salem witchcraft trials, many of the participants themselves began having second thoughts. Many of the jurors admitted their errors, witnesses recanted their testimony, and one judge on the Court of Oyer and Terminer, Samuel Sewall, publicly admitted his error on the steps of the Old South Church in 1697. The Massachusetts legislature made amends as well: in 1711 it reversed all of the convictions issued by the Court of Oyer and Terminer (and did it a second time in 1957), and it made financial restitution to the relatives of the executed, "the whole amounting unto five hundred seventy eight pounds and twelve shillings."

# THE COOLEST MOVIE LINES EVER

*Here's an entry inspired by the Captain of Cool, Gene Sculatti, and his book* Too Cool.

**THE WILD ONE**
**Girl to Brando:** "Hey Johnny, what are you rebelling against?"
**Brando:** "Whaddaya got?"

**THE KILLERS**
**Claude Akens:** "You said Johnny North died. How'd he die?"
**Clu Gulager:** "Questions... he asked one too many."

**HIGH SCHOOL CONFIDENTIAL**
(*Teenage interpretation of Queen Isabella's reaction to Columbus*)
"Christy, what is this jazz you puttin' down 'bout our planet being round? Everybody's hip that it's square!"

**THE COURT JESTER**
**Mildred Natwick:** "The pellet with the poison's in the flagon with the dragon. The chalice from the palace holds the brew that is true."
**Danny Kaye:** "What about the vessel with the pestle?"

**OCEANS 11** (*to doc examining X-rays*) "So tell me, doc. Is it the big casino?"

**I WAS A TEENAGE FRANKENSTEIN**
"I know you have a civil tongue in your head. I sewed it there myself."

**THE BIG CARNIVAL**
"I've met some hard-boiled eggs in my time, but you— you're 20 minutes."

**MIDNIGHT RUN**
**Dennis Farina** (*to henchman*): "I want this guy taken out and I want him taken out fast. You and that other dummy better start gettin' more personally involved in your work, or I'm gonna stab you through the heart with a f——pencil. You understand?"
**Henchman:** "You got it, Jimmy."

**THE SWEET SMELL OF SUCCESS**
(*Hustler Tony Curtis, about to go into action*) "Watch me make a hundred-yard run with no legs."

**GOODFELLAS**
"I'm an average nobody. I get to live the rest of my life like a schnook."

# THREE MEMORABLE SALES PROMOTIONS

*Companies are always trying to get our attention—and our money—
with catchy slogans, free stuff, discounts, and so on.
But occasionally a promotion stands out for ineptitude...
or cleverness. Here are three examples.*

**A PENNY SAVED**
**The Company:** *Reader's Digest*
**The Promotion:** For years the *Digest* solicited
subscriptions with a letter that began, "An ancient Persian poet
once said, 'If thou hast two pennies, spend one for bread and the
other to buy hyacinths for the soul...'" In 1956 someone decided
to give it a new twist by including two pennies with each letter.
The point: People could keep one, and send the other back with
their subscription order to get the "soul-satisfying" *Digest*.
**What Happened:** The magazine planned to send out 50 million
letters, which meant they needed 100 million coins—enough to
deplete the entire New York area of pennies. The U.S. Mint
intervened, forcing *Reader's Digest* to make quick arrangements to
ship in 60 million more pennies from all over the country. Then,
when the company finally got all the pennies it needed, it stored
them all in one room—and the floor collapsed under the weight.
In the end, though, it was worth the effort—the promo drew a
record number of responses.

**HOOVERGATE**
**The Company:** Hoover Europe, England's most prestigious
manufacturer of vacuum cleaners
**The Promotion:** In 1992 Hoover tried to put a little life into
the British vacuum market by offering an incredible deal: Any
customer who bought at least 100 British pounds' (about $300)
worth of Hoover merchandise got two free round-trip plane tickets
to a European destination. Customers who bought 250 pounds'
worth ($750) qualified for two tickets to either New York or
Orlando, Florida.

**What Happened:** It was one of the biggest marketing fiascos in history. Customers realised the obvious—vacuum cleaners are cheaper than airline tickets—and snapped up every available Hoover. An estimated 200,000 customers—roughly 1 in every 300 people in Great Britain and Ireland—claimed they qualified for free flights.

The company sold so many vacuums that the factory switched to a seven-day work week to meet the demand—which made it, as one observer noted, "a classic case of mispricing a promotion so that the more products the company sold, the more money it lost." The promotion caused such a run on airline tickets that Hoover had to charter entire planes to meet the demand.

The promotion cost the company $48.8 million more than it expected—and cost 3 top executives their jobs. The parent company, Maytag, had to take a $10.5 million loss in the first quarter of 1993.

## NORTH TO ALASKA
**The Company:** Quaker Oats

**The Promotion:** Quaker was the long-time sponsor of "Sergeant Preston of the Yukon," a popular kids' TV series. In 1955 they decided to create a tie-in between the show and some cereals that weren't selling too well—Quaker Puffed Rice and Quaker Puffed Wheat. Their ad agency came up with an unusual plan: Buy up a parcel of land on the Yukon River in Alaska, then subdivide it into 21 million six square-centimetre (one square-inch) parcels and give away a real deed to one of the parcels in each box of cereal.

**What Happened:** According to *Getting It Right the Second Time*, "[Quaker's ad exec] and a company lawyer flew to Dawson, Alaska, selected a 8-hectare (19.11-acre) plot of ice on the Yukon River from the air, and bought it for $10,000. [The ad man] wanted to go home, but the Quaker lawyer insisted on investigating the land close up by boat. As it turned out, the boat developed a leak in the middle of the half-frozen river, and the passengers were forced to jump overboard. They paddled back to shore, only to find they'd missed their dogsled connection back to the airstrip. As darkness fell, the Quaker contingent was forced to walk 10 km (6 miles) in subzero weather to meet the aircraft and go home."

Was it worth the aggravation? Quaker thought so. They sold more than 21 million boxes of Puffed Rice/Wheat; it has been cited as one of the three most successful cereal promotions ever.

---

The world's first "motor-hotel", or motel opened in California in 1925.

# FACING FACTS

*Facts can be reassuring, surprising or even scary. We may be unique, but we are still a part of a large group. See where you stand with these Australian statistics.*

## POPULATION DYNAMICS

- There is one birth in Australia every 2 minutes and 5 seconds.
- There is one death every 3 minutes and 48 seconds.
- The life expectancy for males born in 2001 is 77.2 years; for females it is 82.6 years.
- There is a net gain of one international migrant every 5 minutes and 50 seconds, which leads to an overall total population increase through migration of one person every 2 minutes and 35 seconds.

## GROWING UP

- Pocket money is received by 54 percent of children aged 10–17. Seven percent of this group receive $30 a week or more.
- Australians who left high school before Year 12 and say they are satisfied with their life is 73 percent; those who finished Year 12 and say the same is 90 percent.
- Women account for 55 percent of new university graduates.

## TILL DEATH DO US PART

- In 1981, 38 percent of marriages were performed by civil celebrants; in 2001 it was 53 percent.
- Divorced people have an 80 percent chance of remarrying, particularly between the ages of 25–29 years.
- The proportion of marriages in 2001 that involved a bride or groom who had been married before was one in three.

## OUR HOUSE

- Eighty percent of all dwellings are separate houses.
- Fifty eight percent of owner-occupiers have done renovations in the last ten years. The most common renovations are kitchen and bathroom upgrades.

**Australia Day was first celebrated in 1818.**

• Ninety nine percent of households have a television, 60 percent have computers and 49 percent have air conditioners.
• The average number of plastic bags used by Australian shoppers each year is 360 while the total number of plastic bags used in Australia each year is 6.9 billion.

## HEALTH AND WELLBEING

• The average number of times Australians have sex each year is 84 and the average duration is 20.7 minutes.
• In 2001, 32 percent of people did no exercise compared to 38 percent in 1990.
• Regular breast examinations are done by 78 percent of women; regular Pap tests by 60 percent.
• In 2001, 12 percent of Australians (2.2 million) had asthma.
• The number of people in Australia with hepatitis C infection is 16,000 with 210,000 new cases each year.
• Diabetes is the seventh highest cause of death in Australia, with 55,000 new cases diagnosed each year.
• The proportion of Australians who believe it is the government's role to care for the needy is 57 percent; of Britons, 46 per cent; of Americans, 25 percent.

\*     \*     \*     \*

### DID YOU KNOW?

**Australia was...**
• The first country to introduce a pre-paid postage system (1838).
• The first country in the world to have a secret ballot in elections (1856).
• The first country to develop a refrigeration plant (1858).
• The first country to take up skiing as a sport (1863).
• The first country in the world to give women the vote (1894).
• The first country in the world to beat America in the America's Cup (1983).
• The only country in the world to have participated in every modern Olympic Games.
• The first country to introduce swimming freestyle with the head in the water (called the Australian Crawl).
• The first country to hold a bathing beauty contest (1920).
• The first country to introduce a regular "around the world" airline service (1958).

# LEFT-HANDED FACTS

*We've considered doing something about left-handedness for
several years, but the question always comes up—are there enough
left-handed bathroom readers to make it worthwhile? After six years,
we finally don't care; we just want to use the information.
So here's a section for lefties.*

A re you left-handed? If so, you're not alone—but you're
definitely outnumbered; lefties make up only 5% to 15%
of the general population. If you're a female leftie, you're
even more unusual—there are roughly 50% more left-handed
males than females. For centuries scientists have tried to figure out
what makes people left- or right-handed, and they still aren't sure
why. (They're not even sure if all lefties are that way for the same
reason.) Here are some theories:

## WHAT MAKES A LEFTIE?

• Scientists used to think that left- and right-handedness was
purely a genetic trait, but now they have doubts. Reason: in 20%
of all sets of identical twins, one sibling is left-handed, and the
other is right-handed.

• Some scientists think the hand you prefer is determined by
whether you're a "right-brained" person or a "left-brained" person.
The right half of the brain controls the left side of the body, as
well as spatial / musical / aesthetic judgement and perception; the
left half controls the right side of the body, plus communication
skills. Lefties are generally right-brained.

• Support for this theory: most children begin demonstrating a
preference for one hand over the other at the same time their
central nervous system is growing and maturing. This leads some
scientists to believe the two processes are linked.

• According to another theory, before birth all babies are right-
handed—which means that the left side of their brain is
dominant. But during a stressful or difficult birth, oxygen
deficiency can cause damage to the left side of the brain, making
it weaker and enabling the right side to compete against it for
dominance. If the right side wins out, the baby will become
left-handed.

**See for yourself:** Sitcom characters on TV rarely say goodbye when they hang up the phone.

250

- This theory also explains, researchers claim, why twins, any child born to a smoker, or children born to a mother more than 30 years old are more likely to be left-handed: they are more prone to stressful births. Children of stressful births are also more likely to stammer and suffer dyslexia, traits that are more common in lefties.

## LEFT-HANDED HISTORY

- No matter what makes lefties what they are, they've been discriminated against for thousands of years—in nearly every culture on Earth. Some examples:
- The artwork found in ancient Egyptian tombs portrays most Egyptians as right-handed. But their enemies are portrayed as left-handers, a sign they saw left-handedness as an undesirable trait.
- Ancient Greeks never crossed their left leg over their right, and believed a person's sex was determined by their position in the womb—with the female, or "lesser sex," sitting on the left side of the womb.
- The Romans placed special significance on right-handedness as well. Custom dictated that they enter friends' homes "with the right foot forward"…and turn their heads to the right to sneeze. Their language showed the same bias: the Latin word for left was *sinister* (which also meant "evil" or "ominous"), the word for right was *dexter* (which came to mean "skillful," or "adroit"). Even the word ambidextrous literally means "right-handed with both hands."
- The Ango-Saxon root for left is *lyft*, which means "weak," "broken," or "worthless." *Riht* means "straight," "just," or "erect."

## BIBLICAL BIAS

- The Bible is biased in favour of right-handed people. Both the Old and New Testament refer to "the right hand of God." One Old Testament town, Nineveh, is so wicked that its citizens "cannot discern between their right hand and their left hand."
- The saints also followed the right-hand rule; according to early Christian legend, they were so pious even as infants that they refused to nurse from their mother's left breast.
- The distinction is made even in religious art: Jesus and God are nearly always drawn giving blessings with their right hand, and the Devil is usually portrayed doing evil with his left hand.

---

**In case you were wondering: The little flap in the back of your throat is called uvula.**

# MTV FACTS

*MTV has been with us since the early 1980s. These pages were
contributed by Larry Kelp, an American music writer.*

**I WANT MY MTV!**
In 1981 Robert Pittman, a 27-year-old vice president in
charge of new programming at Warner-Amex, came up with
an idea for Music Television, an all-music channel that would
play almost nothing but rock videos. The gimmick: free
programming—the videos would be supplied by record companies
at no charge. "The explicit aim," explains one critic, "was to
deliver the notoriously difficult-to-reach 14 to 34 demographic
segment to the record companies, beer manufacturers, and pimple
cream makers."

Based on that appeal, Pittman talked Warner into investing
$30 million in the idea. Four years later, Warner-Amex sold MTV
to Viacom for $550 million. In 1992 its estimated worth was
$2 billion. Today it broadcasts in more than 50 different countries.

**GETTING STARTED**
• Pittman planned to call the channel TV-1, but immediately ran
into a problem: "Our legal department found another business
with that name. The best we could get was TV-M...and TV-M it
was, until our head of music programming said, "Don't you think
MTV sounds a little better than TV-M?"
• The design for the logo was another fluke. "Originally,"
Pittman recalls, "We thought MTV would be three equal-size
letters like ABC, NBC and CBS. But...three 'kids' in a loft
downtown, Manhattan Design, came up with the idea for a big M,
with TV spray-painted over it. We just cut the paint drips off the
TV, and that's the logo. We paid about $1,000 for one of the
decade's best-known logos."
• MTV originally planned to use astronaut Neil Armstrong's
words, "One small step for man, one giant leap for mankind," with
its now-famous "Moon Man" station identification. "But a few
days before we launched," Pittman says, "an executive came flying
into my office. We had just received a letter from Armstrong's
lawyer threatening to sue us if we used his client's voice. We had

no time and, worse, no money to redo this on-air ID. So we took his voice off and used the ID with just music. Not at all what we had envisioned, yet, fortunately, it worked fine."

## MTV DATA
• MTV went on air at midnight, August 1, 1981. Its first video was the Buggies' prophetic "Video Killed the Radio Star."
• The average MTV viewer tunes in for 16 minutes at a time.
• MTV's VJs have a short shelf life. Once they start looking old, they're retired.
• Not all of the music channel's fans are teenagers. One unusual audience: medical offices. *Prevention* magazine says MTV in the doctor's office helps relieve women's tension before medical exams.
• MTV reaches 75% of those households inhabited by people 18 to 34 years old and 85% of the households with one teenager.
• While many countries served by MTV Europe have local programming with their own VJs, most are in English, the global language of rock. In Holland, a Flemish language show was dropped because viewers complained that it wasn't in English.

## YO, MTV!
It took constant badgering by 25-year-old former intern Ted Demme (nephew of film director Jonathan) to get MTV to air a rap show, "Yo! MTV Raps," in 1989. He argued that white suburban kids wanted rap. The execs gave him one shot at it. "Yo!" was aired on a Saturday. By Monday the ratings and calls were so impressive that "Yo!" got a daily slot, and quickly became MTV's top-rated show.

## UNPLUGGED
In 1990 MTV first aired "Unplugged," which went against everything music videos had stood for. Instead of stars lip-synching to prerecorded tracks, "Unplugged" taped them live in front of a studio audience, and forced them to use acoustic instruments, making music and talent the focus. What could have been a gimmick turned into a trend when Paul McCartney released his "Unplugged" appearance as an album, and it became one of his best-selling albums. Two years later, Eric Clapton did the same, which made "Layla" a hit song all over again and earned him Grammy Awards as well as platinum records.

# AUNT LENNA'S PUZZLES

*Some adventures with my favourite aunt. Answers are on p. 486.*

**M**URDER AT THE BIG HOTEL
My Aunt Lenna loves puzzles. Not complicated ones—just the kind people call *brain teasers*. "I don't like those puzzles where you have to be a genius at maths," she often says. "I want simple puzzles of logic."

One day she was reading a mystery, and she began musing out loud: "It was a very large, fancy hotel. The hotel detective was making his rounds, walking in the hallway…when suddenly he heard a woman cry, 'Please! Don't shoot me, Steve!' And a shot rang out!"

"Sounds original, Aunt Lenna."

"Well now, hold on, Nephew. The detective ran as fast as he could to the room the shot came from, and pushed his way in. The body of a woman who'd been shot lay in a corner of the room; the gun that had been used to kill her was on the floor near her. On the opposite side of the room stood a postman, an accountant, and a lawyer. For a moment, the detective hesitated as he looked at them. Then he strode up to the postman and said—'You're under arrest for murder.'"

"A little hasty, wasn't he? Or was there some evidence you're not mentioning?"

"He wasn't hasty, and there was no other evidence…and the detective made the right choice."

"Well, how did he know?"

*How did he?*

Aunt Lenna likes word games, too. Some are real groaners. Like she once asked me, "What word is it that when you take away the whole, you still have some left?" Another time she asked, "Can you make one word out of the letters D R E N O O W?"

*Got the answers?*

---

Our experts say: In your lifetime, you'll sleep about 220,000 hours.

# SHAKESPEARE SAYETH...

*Here's the "high culture" section of the* Bathroom Reader.

"The first thing we do, let's kill all the lawyers."

"Neither a borrower, nor a lender be; For oft loses both itself and friend."

"He is well paid that is well satisfied."

"What's in a name? That which we call a rose / By any other name would smell as sweet."

"Some are born great, some achieve greatness, and some have greatness thrust upon them."

"Though this be madness, yet there is method in it."

"When Fortune means to men most good, she looks upon them with a threatening eye."

"Remuneration! O! that's the Latin word for three farthings."

"Words pay no debts."

"You taught me language; and my profit on't is, I know how to curse."

"Talkers are not good doers."

"The saying is true, the empty vessel makes the loudest sound."

"My words fly up, my thoughts remain below: Words without thoughts never to heaven go."

"If all the year were playing holidays / To sport would be as tedious as to work."

"The fault, dear Brutus, is not in our stars / But in ourselves."

"A politician...One that would circumvent God."

"When my love swears that she is made of truth / I do believe her, though I know she lies."

"Let me have no lying; it becomes none but tradesmen."

"If it be a sin to covet honour, I am the most offending soul."

"One may smile, and smile, and be a villan."

'Time is come round, and where I did begin, there shall I end."

# EVERYDAY ORIGINS

*Some quick stories about the origins of everyday objects.*

**S**COTCH TAPE. Believe it or not, the sticky stuff gets its name from an ethnic slur. When two-toned paint jobs became popular in the 1920s, Detroit carmakers asked the 3M Company for an alternative to masking tape that would provide a smooth, sharp edge where the two colours met. 3M came up with 5-cm (2-inch) wide cellophane tape, but auto companies said it was too expensive. So 3M lowered the price by only applying adhesive along the sides of the strip. That caused a problem: the new tape didn't stick—and company painters complained to the 3M salesman, "Take this tape back to your stingy 'Scotch' bosses and tell them to put more adhesive on it!" The name—and the new tape—stuck.

**BRASSIERES.** Mary Phelps Jacob, a teenage debutante in 1913, wanted to wear a rose-garlanded dress to a party one evening. But, as she later explained, her corset cover "kept peeping through the roses around my bosom." So she took it off, pinned two handkerchiefs together, and tied them behind her back with some ribbon. "The result was delicious," she later recalled. "I could move much more freely, a nearly naked feeling." The contraption eventually became known as a *brassière*—a name borrowed from the corset cover it replaced. (Jacob later became famous for riding naked through the streets of Paris on an elephant.)

**DINNER KNIVES.** Regular knives first had their points rounded and their sharp edges dulled for use at the dinner table in 1669. According to Margaret Visser, author of *The Rituals of Dinner*, this was done "apparently to prevent their use as 'toothpicks,' but probably also to discourage assassinations at meals."

**WRISTWATCHES.** Several Swiss watchmakers began attaching small watches to bracelets in 1790. Those early watches weren't considered serious timepieces, and they remained strictly a women's item until World War I, when armies recognised their usefulness in battle and began issuing them to servicemen instead of the traditional pocket watch.

---

Red is rarely used on ice cream packages because it reminds people of heat.

**FORKS.** Before forks became popular, the difference between refined and common people was the number of fingers they ate with. The upper classes used three; everyone else used five. This began to change in the 11th century, when tiny, two-pronged forks became fashionable in Italian high society. But they didn't catch on; the Catholic Church opposed them as unnatural (it was an insult to imply that the fingers God gave us weren't good enough for food), and people who used them were ridiculed as effeminate or pretentious. Forks weren't generally considered polite until the 18th century—some 800 years after they were first introduced.

**PULL-TOP BEER CANS.** In 1959 a mechanical engineer named Ermal Cleon Fraze was at a picnic when he realised he'd forgotten a can opener. No one else had one either, so he had to use the bumper guard of his car to open a can of soft drink. It took half an hour, and he vowed he'd never get stuck like that again. He patented the world's first practical pull-top can later that year, and three years later, the Pittsburgh Brewing Company tried using it on its Iron City Beer. Now every beer company does.

**REFRIGERATOR MAGNETS.** Mass-produced magnets designed for refrigerators didn't appear until 1964. They were invented by John Arnasto and his wife Arlene, who sold a line of decorative wall hooks. Arlene thought it would be cute to have a hook for refrigerator doors, so John made one with a magnet backing. The first one had a small bell and was shaped like a tea kettle. It sold well, so the Arnastos added dozens of other versions to their lines. Believe it or not, some of the rare originals are worth more than $100.

**TOOTHPASTE TUBES.** Toothpaste wasn't packaged in collapsible tubes until 1892, when Dr. Washington Wentworth Sheffield, a Connecticut dentist, copied the idea from a tube of oil-based paint. Increasing interest in sanitation and hygiene made the new invention more popular than jars of toothpaste, which mingled germs from different brushes. Toothpaste tubes became the standard almost overnight.

# THE DICKENS YOU WILL!

*Charles Dickens never set foot in Oz, but that didn't stop him from using it in his novels.*

**A**USTRALIA OR OUTER SPACE?
Australia was to Charles Dickens (1812-1870) what Mars or Venus is to us now. It was a jolly long way away and neither Charlie Dickens nor his fans knew much about it. What a convenient place to dispatch your characters to when you want them out of the way for a few hundred pages.

Take one Abel Magwitch in *Great Expectations*. He is dispatched to Botany Bay aboard a rotting hulk and is condemned to a remote and miserable life in the Southern Hemisphere for over three hundred pages and about fifteen years. And what about Mr Micawber in *David Copperfield*? Dickens decides that Mr M., his long-suffering wife and innumerable children have to be sent somewhere to start a new life. The obvious choice? You've guessed it.

## A DICKENSIAN CHILDHOOD

Dickens was born at Portsmouth, England, into a Micawber-esque family, basically respectable but penniless. At one point the whole family moved into the Marshalsea prison in London where their dad was detained for debt. By the time he was 12 years old, Charles was working in a boot-blacking factory for a pittance. Hardly the fine education you'd expect for the chap who developed into one of the most accomplished novelists who has ever written in the English language. However, it explains all those colourful low-life characters he includes in all his books. Eventually Dickens took to journalism and then to fiction and those Australian imaginings.

## A TRAVELLING MAN

Dickens was a great European traveller and he journeyed to America twice to give theatrical readings of his work. So why not

---

The dingo was the first non-native animal to be introduced into Australia.

Australia, since he wasn't averse to using it in his stories? In 1862, he was invited to visit Australia and £10,000 was raised to pay for the trip. But 24-hour budget flights with a stopover in L.A. or Singapore lay a hundred years or more into the future. For a mid-Victorian like Dickens, London to Sydney would have meant at least six weeks at sea, although it would have been somewhat more comfortable than the leg irons and privations of Magwitch's hulk.

The aging novelist was 50 by then and for some reason he decided against visiting Australia. He couldn't go to America either because of the Civil War, so he settled down to write *A Tale of Two Cities* instead.


## DICKENS DOWN UNDER
Dickens—who was also an enthusiastic womaniser—and his weary wife Catherine, produced seven children. Two of them—Edward and Alfred Dickens—eventually immigrated to Australia. Edward arrived in 1868 and became mayor of Wilcannia. He worked for the Lands Department in Moree until his death in 1902, and was buried in Greenbah Road Cemetery, Moree.

Alfred became a stock and station manager in Western Australia but a tragedy in 1879, involving a bolting horse, killed his wife and young daughter. He moved to Melbourne in 1882 and lived there until going to New York in 1912 to advise on his father's birth centennial celebrations. He died there suddenly of a heart attack and was buried in Trinity cemetery in North Manhattan.


## OZ OBSCURITY
Were the Dickens children trying to escape from the oppression of their father's fame in insular Britain, seeking a bit of the obscurity that Dickens senior just fantasised about? The sunny, vibrant reality of the developing country they found must have been poles away from the sterile fictional convenience their father made of it.

# Q & A:
# ASK THE EXPERTS

*More random questions and answers from the world's trivia experts.*

## ON THE SPOT

**Q:** *What causes freckles?*
**A:** "Except in the case of albinos, every person's skin has cells called *melanocytes*, which produce a certain amount of melanin, a dark pigment that absorbs ultraviolet light. These cells produce melanin at increasing rates when the skin is exposed to sunlight—hence the sunbather's tan. Some melanocytes are more active than others. Thus when groups of active melanocytes are surrounded by groups of less active melanocytes, the results are islands of pigment known as freckles." (From *Do Elephants Swim?* compiled by Robert M. Jones)

## INFLATED WITH PRIDE

**Q:** *Why is Chicago called the Windy City?*
**A:** Chicago is pretty windy (with a 17-km [10.3-mph] wind average), but that's not where the nickname comes from. It comes from the 1893 Chicago World's Columbia Exposition—which was supposed to commemorate the 400th anniversary of Columbus's discovery of the New World, but ended up being used by city politicos to hype Chicago. "So boastful and overblown were the local politicians' claims about the exposition and the city that a New York City newspaper editor, Charles A. Dana, nicknamed Chicago 'the windy city.' " (From *The Book of Totally Useless Information*, by Don Voorhees)

## EVERYTHING'S RELATIVE

**Q:** *Is it true that Einstein's parents once thought he was retarded?*
**A:** Believe it or not, yes. "It took Einstein so long to learn to speak (he didn't become fluent in his mother tongue of German until age nine) that his parents suspected he was 'subnormal.' His teachers agreed: according to legend, when Einstein's father asked his school-master which profession young Albert should

---

adopt, the schoolmaster replied, 'It doesn't matter; he'll never make a success of anything.' Actually, though, historians don't know all that much about his childhood. The reason: Einstein's memory for personal things was so bad that even *he* couldn't remember what happened to him as a kid. 'You are quite right,' he said when a friend commented this was hard to believe. 'My bad memory for personal things [is] really quite astounding.'

"Interesting note: Even as an adult, Einstein's genius was not immediately recognised. As late as 1910, more than five years after he published his famous papers on statistical mechanics, quantum mechanics, and the special theory of relativity, he was still only an associate professor at the University of Zurich earning just 4,500 francs a year. The meagre salary wasn't enough to live on; he was forced to supplement his income with lecture fees and by taking in student boarders. He once told a colleague: 'In my relativity theory, I set up a clock at every point in space, but in reality I find it difficult to provide even one clock in my room.' " (From *Late Night Entertainment*, by John Dollison)

## HAIRY THOUGHTS

**Q:** *Why do people get goose bumps?*
**A:** "Goose bumps are a vestige from the days when humans were covered with hair. When it got cold, the hairs stood on end, creating a trap for air and providing insulation. The hairs have long since disappeared, but in the places where they used to be, the skin still bristles, trying to get warm." (From *The Book of Answers*, by Barbara Berliner)

## SLICK QUESTION

**Q:** *Why is ice so slippery?*
**A:** "Ice has several unusual properties, one of them being that it melts when subjected to pressure. Your foot on ice is such pressure, and a film of melted ice—water—reduces the amount of friction and thus sliding can occur." (From *Science Trivia*, by Charles Cazeau)

\*     \*     \*     \*

**Believable Quote:** "I was not lying. I said things that later on seemed to be untrue."

—*Richard Nixon*

---

21,203 Japanese citizens were arrested for "the illegal sale or abuse of paint thinner" in 1993.

# FIRST REPORTS

*Over the years, we've collected "First Reports," newspaper articles that gave readers their first glimpse of something that eventually became important in some way. Here are a few examples.*

## SPACED OUT

*Most people don't know it was one incident—and one short newspaper story—that started the UFO craze. Here's the story, sent out over the AP wire from the* Pendleton East Oregonian *on June 25, 1947.*

**Pendleton, USA June 25 (AP)**—"Nine bright saucer-like objects flying at 'incredible speed' at 3,048 metres (10,000 feet) altitude were reported here today by Kenneth Arnold, a Boise, Idaho, pilot who said he could not hazard a guess as to what they were.

"Arnold, a United States Forest Service employee engaged in searching for a missing plane, said he sighted the mysterious objects yesterday at three p.m. They were flying between Mount Rainier and Mount Adams, in Washington State, he said, and appeared to weave in and out of formation. Arnold said that he clocked and estimated their speed at 1,931 km (1,200 miles) an hour.

"Enquiries at Yakima last night brought only blank stares, he said, but he added he talked today with an unidentified man from Ukiah, south of here, who said he had seen similar objects over the mountains near Ukiah yesterday.

" 'It seems impossible,' Arnold said, 'but there it is.' "

*This story was picked up by papers all over the world. At that moment, according to the* UFO Encyclopedia, *"the age of flying saucers began."*

## THE XEROX MACHINE

*When this article appeared in 1948, Xerox was still known as the Haloid Company.*

**New York, USA Oct. 23**—"A revolutionary process of inkless printing has been developed that might completely change all the operations of the printing and publishing industry. This was announced yesterday by Joseph C. Wilson, president of the Haloid Company of Rochester, New York.

"Known as 'Xerography,' this basic addition to the graphic arts reproduces pictures and text at the speed of 366 metres (1,200 feet) a minute, on any kind of surface.

---

**Male moths can smell female moths from as far as 11 km (7 miles) away.**

"Although there is no immediate prospect of applying the method to general photography, the process will be available within about six months for copying uses. Wilson said it will be in the form of a compact Xerocopying machine for reproducing letters, documents, and line work…

"Looking farther ahead, he said he foresaw incorporating the entire process in a portable Xerocamera. 'With such a camera, the picture taker can snap the shutter and within a few seconds pull out a finished Xeroprint. If he doesn't like the picture, he can discard it and try again, using the same Xero-plate.' "

## DEAR ABBY

*Dear Abby's first column appeared in the* San Francisco Chronicle *on January 9, 1956. She answered four letters. Here's one of them.*

**"Dear Abby:** Maybe you can suggest something to help my sister. She is married to a real heel. He is 1.92 m (6'3") and weighs 109 kg (240 lbs) and she is 1.52 m (5') and weighs 48 kg (106 lbs). He has a terrible temper and frequently knocks the daylights out of her.—L.L.

**"Dear L.L.:** I admit your sister is no physical match for her heavyweight husband, but I've seen smaller gals flatten out bigger guys than this with just one look. If your sister has been letting this walrus slap her around frequently, maybe she likes it. Stay out of their family battles, Chum."

## INTRODUCING THE CD

*This article appeared in the* New York Times, *March 18, 1983.*

"Five years ago, the electronics industry brought out the video-disk, heralded as the future of home entertainment systems. This month, the digital compact disk audio system will make its way into American homes, making similar promises. But marketers of the audiodisk play down the kinship, with good cause; sales of videodisks have been dismal. The compact audiodisk system, meanwhile, is expected to replace stereo turntables and albums as the industry standard within the decade.

"Some question whether the audiodisk will succeed. Players now cost $800-$900, and disks are $16-20 each, far too expensive for a popular market. "Even if prices come down…some analysts doubt whether consumers will be willing to sacrifice substantial investments in turntables and stacks of traditional recordings."

---

**Heavy thought: Your skin accounts for 16% of your body weight.**

# FAMOUS TRIALS:
# THE CADAVER SYNOD

*Here's the story of a trial that's stranger than anything
you'll ever see on television.*

**B**ACKGROUND. The late ninth century was a difficult
period in the history of the Catholic Church. The Holy
Roman Empire was disintegrating and as the empire's
power slipped away, so did the authority of the Church; not
strong enough militarily to survive on its own, it had to depend
on powerful European nobles for protection.

### HERE COMES GUIDO
In 891, Pope Stephen V turned to Duke Guido III of Spoleto for
protection. To cement the relationship, Stephen adopted him as
his son and crowned him Holy Roman Emperor.

### ...AND POPE FORMOSUS
That relationship didn't last long. Pope Stephen V died a few
months later and a new pope, Formosus I, was elected to head the
Church. Guido was suspicious of the new pope's loyalty. So in
892, he forced Formosus to crown him emperor a second time. He
also insisted that Formosus name his son Lambert "heir apparent."
   When Guido died in 894, Formosus backed out of the deal.
Rather than crown Lambert emperor, he called on King Arnulf
of the East Franks to liberate Rome from Guido's family.

### ...AND ARNULF
A year later Arnulf conquered Rome...and Formosus made him
emperor. This relationship didn't last long either: within a few
months, Arnulf had suffered paralysis and had to be carried back
to Germany; a few months after *that*, Pope Formosus died.

### ...AND LAMBERT AGAIN
Lambert, who had retreated back to Spoleto, used the crisis to
rally his troops and march on Rome. He reconquered the city
in 897.
   The new pope, Stephen VI, quickly switched sides and crowned
Lambert emperor.

---

The average Australian child aged 5–17 has three cavities—down from 11 during the 1940s.

## THE TRIAL

What followed was one of the most peculiar episodes in the history of the Catholic Church. Eager to prove his loyalty to the Spoletos, Pope Stephen convened the "cadaver synod," in which he literally had Pope Formosus's nine-month-old, rotting corpse put on trial for perjury, "coveting the papacy," and a variety of other crimes. On Stephen's orders the cadaver was disinterred, dressed in papal robes, and propped up on a throne for the trial. Since the body was in no condition to answer the charges made against it, a deacon was appointed to stand next to it during the proceedings and answer questions on its behalf.

Not surprisingly, the cadaver was found guilty on all counts. As punishment, all of Formosus's papal acts were declared null and void. The corpse itself was also desecrated: The three fingers on the right hand used to confer blessings were hacked off, and the body was stripped naked and dumped in a cemetery for foreigners. Shortly afterwards it was tossed in Tiber River, where a hermit fished it out and gave it a proper burial.

## WHAT GOES AROUND...

Stephen VI himself survived the cadaver synod by only a few months. While the gruesome synod was still in session, a strong earthquake struck Rome and destroyed the papal basilica. Taking this as a sign of God's anger with the upstart pope, and encouraged by rumours that Formosus's corpse had begun performing miracles, Formosus's supporters arrested Stephen and threw him into the papal prison, where he was later strangled.

\*       \*       \*       \*

## TIME FLIES

*According to recent studies, in a lifetime the average Australian spends...*

- 8 months opening mail
- 5 years waiting on line
- 2 years returning phone calls
- 1 year looking for misplaced items

Not yet, Mum: 23% of men between 35 and 39 live with their parents.

# BUSH TUCKER

*Short of ideas for dinner tonight? Why not try one of these recipes using genuine bush tucker?*

## WITCHETTY GRUBS

Witchetty grubs are large, edible, wood-boring grubs that are the larvae of certain Australian moths and beetles. They feed on the bark of eucalyptus trees, nestled between the bark and the trunk. Fat, cream-coloured and about 5 cm (2 inches) long, these little fellows crawl about on stumpy legs. They have been eaten raw by Aboriginal Australians for thousands of years. But if your palate is unaccustomed to this outback delicacy, perhaps the following recipe will complement that chilled bottle of Margaret River sauvignon blanc you're bound to have at hand next time you find yourself up the creek without a paddle (or the chicken you'd hope to grill that night).

### Ingredients
- witchetty grubs (as many as you can find)
- yams
- salt, pepper
- cooking oil (optional)

### Other materials
- a piece of metal (scrubbed clean)

### Method
Build a large, open fire. When ready, place the yams in coals to the side of the fire. Lay the piece of metal over the fire and let it heat up. When the metal is hot, drop some oil on it before placing the witchetty grubs on the metal plate. Move the grubs back and forth with a stick until they are brown all over. Add salt and pepper to taste. Remove the yams from the coals; break and serve with the grubs.

Great grub, mate!

---

Thirty-two percent of people who join health clubs do so between August and September.

# BARBECUE KANGAROO LOIN ON WARM VEGETABLE SALAD

Kangaroo meat is tender, richly flavoured and is delicious when roasted or barbecued. It needs to be cooked quickly and has the lowest cholesterol levels of all red meats.

**Ingredients**
- 2 kangaroo fillets
- 1 red capsicum
- 1 zucchini
- 1 clove garlic
- 1 Spanish onion
- 1 small eggplant
- 6 mushrooms
- olive oil
- balsamic vinegar
- salt, pepper

**Method**
1. Salt, pepper and lightly oil the fillets.
2. Dice the onion and garlic.
3. Chop the capsicum, zucchini, eggplant and mushrooms.
4. Beginning with the onion and garlic, place all the vegetables on a barbecue hotplate (or in a frying pan).
5. Drizzle with 2 tablespoons of olive oil, turning them often until they are brown.
6. Remove from the hotplate and drizzle with a little more olive oil and balsamic vinegar. Lightly salt and pepper.
7. Place the fillets on the hotplate, cooking each side for three minutes.
8. Remove from the hotplate and slice on an angle into long strips.
9. Mix with vegetables and serve.

Serves 2.

# COLOURS

*Here are some more fascinating things researchers have
found out about people and colour.*

## PINK

- Studies show that people almost always believe "pastries from a pink box taste better than from any other colour box."
- People are willing to pay more for personal services (e.g., haircuts) performed by people wearing pink.
- Men believe pink products do the best job, but don't want to be seen buying them. If they think someone's watching, they'll choose something brown or blue.

## ORANGE

- A quick attention-getter, it communicates informality.
- When it's used on a product, it "loudly proclaims that the product is for everyone."

## PALE BLUE

- Pale blue can actually make people feel cooler. Designers often use it in places where men work, "because men feel 5° warmer than a woman in the same room temperature."
- Blue inhibits the desire to eat; in fact, researchers say "people tend to eat less from blue plates."

- Because blue is associated with eating less, marketers use it to sell products like soda water, skim milk, and cottage cheese.

## BROWN

- Researchers say a brown suit is "a symbol of informality that invites people to open up." It's recommended for reporters and marriage counsellors.

## GREY

- Your eye processes grey more easily than any other colour.
- Even so, people often become prejudiced against it, especially in areas with a bleak climate.

## BRONZE

- This metallic hue gets a negative response. Researchers say it's "useful when rejection is desired."

## GREEN

- It's used to sell vegetables and chewing gum. But people avoid using it to sell meat, because it reminds consumers of mould.

---

Crowd control: Purse-snatching is punishable by death in Haiti.

# FIRST FILMS

*Stars like Madonna would probably just as soon forget about
what they were doing before they hit it big. You'd
never guess they started out this way.*

**T**OM SELLECK
**First Film:** *Myra Breckinridge* (1970)
**The Role:** In his 17 seconds onscreen, Selleck plays
an unnamed talent agent (listed as "The Stud" in the credits)
opposite Mae West, the star of the film, who wants to help him
find "a position." West discovered Selleck in a Pepsi commercial
and had him cast in the bit part.

**HARRISON FORD**
**First Film:** *Dead Heat on a Merry-Go-Round* (1966)
**The Role:** The 24-year-old Ford plays an unnamed bellhop who
appears in only one scene, in which con man James Coburn gets
some information from him and then refuses to give him a tip.
The part is so small that Ford is not even listed in the credits.
**Memorable Line:** "Paging Mr. Ellis…"

**MADONNA**
**First Film:** *A Certain Sacrifice* (1979)
**The Role:** In this Super 8 student film, Madonna plays a minor
character named Bruna, who shows her breasts, has "simulated"
group sex, and gets smeared with a dead man's blood. The film
is so bad that the home video version opens with a disclaimer
warning the viewer of the film's "technical inconsistancies."
**Memorable Line:** "I'm a do-do girl, and I'm looking for my do-do
boy."

**JEFF GOLDBLUM**
**First Film:** *Death Wish* (1974)
**The Role:** Goldblum plays "Freak #1," one of three unnamed
punks who break into Charles Bronson's house, kill his wife, and
rapes his daughter. Bronson spends the rest of the film (and three
sequels) gunning down punks on the streets of New York.
**Memorable Line:** "Don't jive, mother, you know what we want!"

## KEVIN COSTNER

**First Film:** *Sizzle Beach, USA* (1974)

**The Role:** Costner is John Logan, a wealthy rancher, in this film about three big-breasted women who share a house in Malibu. The girls exercise and perform household chores while topless, and one of them, Dit, falls in love with Costner's character. (Incidentally, Costner also played a corpse in *The Big Chill*, but all of his scenes were cut out.)

**Memorable Line:** "L.A. women seem to be very impressed with money."

## TOM CRUISE

**First Film:** *Endless Love* (1981)

**The Role:** Cruise plays Billy, a teen arsonist who gives the film's costar, Martin Hewitt, the idea of burning down Brooke Shields's house in order to act as a hero and win the respect of her parents.

**Memorable Line:** "When I was eight years old I was into arson."

## SYLVESTER STALLONE

**First Film:** *A Party at Kitty and Stud's,* (1970). Later renamed "The Italian Stallion" to cash in on Stallone's fame.

**The Role:** In this pre-*Rocky* soft-core porno flick, Stallone plays Stud, a frisky playboy with big hair (and small muscles) who spends much of the film entirely nude except for a medallion around his neck and a wristwatch…though he never actually engages in intercourse.

**Memorable Line:** "Mmmmm."

\*     \*     \*     \*

### CAN'T GET NO RESPECT

Stallone never lived his blue movie down. According to *Esquire* magazine, "Even when *Rocky* won the Oscar for best picture of 1976…the [only] Stallone movie in demand for the private screening rooms of Bel Air and Beverly Hills was the soft-core porn film he'd made when it was the only work he could get."

# MYTH-PRONUNCIATION

*It's surprising how many of our words are references to gods that we've never heard of. Here are some of the characters in Greek and Roman mythology we refer to daily.*

**Cereal:** Named after Ceres, the Roman goddess of grain and agriculture.

**Atlas:** One of the Greek Titans banished by Zeus when they sided with his son against him. Atlas was condemned to carry the world on his shoulders. That scene was popular with early mapmakers, who regularly put it on the covers of their books of maps. The books themselves eventually became known as atlases.

**Panic:** Named after the Greek god Pan, who was believed to howl and shriek in the middle of the night. Greeks who heard these noises often *panicked*.

**Hygiene:** Inspired by Hygeia, the Greek goddess who brings good health.

**Panacea:** The Roman goddess who cures diseases.

**Tantalise:** Tantalus was a Greek king who was punished by the other gods for trying to deceive them. He was forced to stand in a pool of water up to his chin, but when he lowered his head to drink, the water receded just out of reach. The same was true with food: whenever he reached to pick a piece of fruit from a tree, the wind blew it just out of his reach. The *tantalising* food filled him with desire, but was completely unobtainable.

**Siren:** The Greeks believed the Sirens were women who called to passing sailors with their beautiful singing voices. Sailors couldn't resist them; in fact, men were driven mad by the songs and dashed their ships on the nearby rocks in their frenzy to get closer.

**Helium:** This element, found in the gaseous atmosphere of the sun, is named after Helios, the Greek god of the sun.

**Iridescent:** Named after Iris, the Greek goddess of the rainbow.

The bald eagle's nest can weigh as much as a tonne.

**Erotic:** Named after Eros, the Greek god of…you guessed it: love.

**Brownie:** These cousins of the Girl Scouts are named after the Celtic *brownies*, small, brown-cloaked fairies that perform household chores while the family sleeps.

**Aphrodisiac:** Named after Aphrodite, the Greek goddess of love. Her specialty: stirring up feelings of desire among the other gods.

**Ghouls:** From the Arabic word *ghul*, which was an evil spirit that robbed tombs and ate corpses. Today the name is given to anyone with an unhealthy interest in the deceased.

**Lethargy:** Named after the mythical Greek river of forgetfulness, *Lethe*.

**Aegis:** Originally the name of the shield of Zeus; today anything that's protected by something else is said to be under its aegis.

**Money:** Named after Juno Moneta, the Roman goddess of money.

\*    \*    \*    \*

## MONEY FACTS
• Ancient Sparta had a creative way of preventing capital flight: They made their coins so large and heavy that it was almost impossible to take them out of the country.
• The British Pound Sterling, originally composed of 240 silver pennies, really did weigh a pound.
• The Greek word *drachma* originally meant "handful."
• Why were gold and silver so widely used in coins? They were rare, valuable, and didn't deteriorate or rust. They were also pretty to look at—which historians say was no small consideration.
• U.S. law requires that the words "liberty," "United States of America," "E Pluribus Unum," and "In God We Trust" be inscribed on all coins.
• Biggest and smallest coins in history: the 1644 Swedish *ten-daler* coin, which weighed 20 kg (43.4 lbs), and the 1740 Nepalese silver *quarter-dam* which weighed less than one gram (1/14,000 of an ounce).
• Biggest and smallest bills in history: the 14th-century Chinese *one-kwan* note which measured 23 × 33 cm (9 × 13 inches) and the 1917 Rumanian *ten-bani* note which measured 9.7 square cm (1½ square inches).

There are three colours of blood: red, blue (lobsters), and yellow (insects).

# THREE WEIRD MEDICAL CONDITIONS

*You never know what's going to happen to you, right? Like, you might
get stuck on that seat, have to call 000 and wind up in the next
edition of the* Bathroom Reader*...or you might find you've got one
of these conditions. Don't laugh—it could happen to YOU!*

## FOREIGN ACCENT SYNDROME
**When:** April 1993
**Where:** Massachusetts, USA
**Headline:** *Car Wreck Leaves American Speaking Like a Frenchman*
**News Report:** "A 46-year-old Massachusetts man walked away
from a car accident with an unexpected problem: he spoke with
a French accent.

"'At first it bothered me very much because I can't make
myself well understood,' said the man, who asked not to be
identified, in a phone interview. He said he had no experience
with a foreign language and had never even travelled farther than
New Jersey from his home in Worcester."

## MARY HART DISEASE
**When:** July 11, 1992
**Where:** New York City
**Headline:** *TV Co-Host's Voice Triggers Seizures*
**News Report:** "A neurologist reports in today's *New England
Journal of Medicine* that a woman got epileptic seizures by hearing
the voice of 'Entertainment Tonight' co-host Mary Hart.

"Symptoms included an upset feeling in the pit of her stomach,
a sense of pressure in her head, and mental confusion. 'It was very
dramatic,' said her doctor, who studied the seizures. 'She would
rub her stomach, hold her head, and then she would look
confused and out of it.'

"The woman has not had any major seizures of this type since
she stopped watching the syndicated TV show."

## VGE—VIDEO GAME EPILEPSY

**When:** April 1991

**Where:** America and Japan

**Headline:** *A Case of Nintendo Epilepsy*

**News Report:** "On screen the aliens get zapped and enemy helicopters crash and burn. But people playing video games do not expect to get hurt. Most do not, but a few wind up with a case of video game epilepsy (VGE).

"A team of Japanese neurologists recently described the problem in an issue of *Developmental Medicine and Child Neurology*. They looked at five boys and two girls, ages 4 to 13, who suffered from headaches, convulsions and blurred vision while playing games. The convulsive responses lasted only a few minutes and, in some cases, happened only during a particular scene in a particular game.

"Parents can prevent VGE. A letter in the *New England Journal of Medicine* reports a similar incident of 'Nintendo epilepsy' in a 13-year-old girl. The doctor discussed the options with her and the parents: abstention from Nintendo or anti-convulsion drugs. "The family chose the drugs, since they felt she would not be able to resist Nintendo's lure."

## ...AND NOW FOR SOME "STRANGE DEATHS"

**February 30.** When Augustus Caesar became emperor, February had 29 days in regular years and 30 days in leap years. Though the calendar had 365 days, leap years came every three years—which gradually threw the calendar out of sync with the movement of the sun. Augustus fixed this, ordering that leap years come every four years instead. While he was at it, he decided to add a day to August, the month named after him. So he shortened February to 28 days, and lengthened August to 31 days.

**Mauch Chunk, Pennsylvania.** Jim Thorpe was one of the world's most famous athletes. But he was penniless when he died in 1953. His estate couldn't pay for the memorial his widow felt he deserved, so she asked his home state, Oklahoma, to foot the bill. When they refused, she offered to bury him in any U.S. town that would change its name to Jim Thorpe. The people of Mauch Chunk accepted the offer, and the town became Jim Thorpe.

---

What a kisser: A full-grown hippo's lips are over half a metre (2 feet) wide.

# THE GREATEST LUMP OF SANDSTONE

*Is it a bird? Is it a plane? No, it's a great big rock smack bang in the middle of the Australian outback that gets hundreds of thousands of visitors a year. Why? Because it's red, that's why.*

### AN OLD LUMP OF ROCK

- Uluru, also known as Ayers Rock, is the world's biggest rock or monolith.
- It's supposed to be 600 million years old (give or take a few years) and was once part of an enormous mountain range.
- It's made of arkose, a type of sandstone that contains feldspar which changes colour according to the sun—it glows a fiery red when viewed at sunrise or sunset.
- It's 9.4 km (5.8 miles) if you walk around it and about 345 metres (1,132 feet) if you climb it.
- It was named Ayers Rock in 1872 after the then South Australian Premier, Sir Henry Ayers.
- It can be found about 450 km (280 miles) south-west of Alice Springs in the Northern Territory.

### GREAT PEBBLE

In 1985, Ayers Rock was re-named Uluru, which means "great pebble" and returned to the ownership and care of the local Aboriginal people, the Pitjantjatjara and Yankunytjatjara. They consider the site sacred and cave paintings on Uluru reflect how long Aborigines have been in the area. The Uluru-Kata Tjuta National Park, in which Uluru stands, is criss-crossed with tracks that mark mythical journeys and connect Uluru with other features in the park. The aboriginal custodians discourage people from climbing the rock due to its importance in their dreamtime. People, however, continue to climb the rock and several people have died due to the steep and dangerous terrain.

Uluru is now classified as a World Heritage site.

---

The three best-known western names in China: Jesus Christ, Richard Nixon, Elvis Presley.

# EAT YOUR VITAMINS!

*You've heard about vitamins since you were a little kid—but how much do you really know about them (besides the fact that they come in little pills)? Here's some food for thought, from BRI member John Dollison.*

**B**ACKGROUND: The cells in your body are constantly converting digested fats, proteins, and carbohydrates into energy, new tissue, and bone cells. Unfortunately, they can't perform this task alone—they need help from certain catalyst chemicals that your body can't produce (or can't produce in sufficient quantities). You have to get these chemicals—called *vitamins*—from food.

## VITAMIN HISTORY

• Long before scientists unlocked the chemical code of vitamins, it was generally understood that eating certain foods would prevent specific diseases. One example: In the 18th century people discovered that adding citrus fruits to their diet could prevent scurvy, a disease whose symptoms included internal haemorrhaging and extreme weakness. In the 19th century, it was proven that substituting unpolished rice for polished rice would prevent beriberi, whose symptoms include paralysis and anaemia.

• No one understood the relationship between these foods and the diseases they prevented until 1906, when the British biochemist Frederick Hopkins proved that in addition to proteins, carbohydrates, fats, minerals, and water, foods also contained what he called "accessory factors"—substances that the body needed to convert food into chemical forms that the body could use.

• In 1911 Casimir Funk, a Polish chemist, discovered that the beriberi-preventing substance in unpolished rice was an *amine*, a type of nitrogen-containing compound. Funk understood that the amine was vital to proper body function, so he named it "vitamine" (for "vital amine").

• A year later he and Hopkins proposed the Vitamin Hypothesis of Deficiency, which theorised that the absence of a particular vitamin in the diet could lead to certain diseases. By depriving animals of different types of foods in strictly controlled experiments, scientists identified a number of these substances.

Casanova spent the last 13 years of his life working as a librarian.

• But they still didn't understand their chemical makeup, so they couldn't give them proper scientific names. Instead, they just called them all "vitamines", and kept them separate by assigning a different letter of the alphabet to each new substance they discovered. They soon realised that many of the vitamins weren't amines at all—but by that time, the word "vitamine" had become so popular that they couldn't change it. So they just dropped the "e."

## VITAMIN BASICS
• Scientists divide vitamins into two different types: water-soluble (the B-complex vitamins and vitamin C), and fat-soluble (A, D, E, and K).

• Your body can't store water-soluble vitamins very well, so if you eat more than your RDA, or Recommended Dietary Allowance, most of them pass out of your body in your urine. That's why it's important to eat them every day.

• Fat-soluble vitamins are more easily stored: Your liver tissue can store large amounts of vitamins A and D, and vitamin E is stored in body fat and reproductive organs.

## KNOW YOUR VITAMINS
**Vitamin A (retinol).**
**Sources:** Animal fats and dairy products, green leafy vegetables, and carrots.
**Why it's needed:** Because it is a component of the pigment in the retinas of your eyes, vitamin A is necessary for good vision. It also helps keep the immune system healthy, and is necessary for the proper functioning of most organs.

**Vitamin B complex** (B1 [thiamine], B2 [riboflavin], B3 [niacin and niacinamide], B5 [pantothenic acid], biotin, folacin, and B12 [cobalamin]).
**Sources:** All meats, cereals, grains, green vegetables, dairy products, and brewer's yeast.
**Why they're needed:** B vitamins are necessary for healthy skin and for the normal operation of a number of cell processes, including digestion, respiration, blood cell and bone marrow production, and metabolism. They're also needed by the nervous system.

**Vitamin C (ascorbic acid).**
**Sources:** Fresh fruit and vegetables, especially citrus fruit and tomatoes.
**Why it's needed:** Vitamin C helps your body heal wounds and bone fractures, build tendons and other tissues, and absorb iron. It's also needed for healthy teeth, gums, and blood.

**Vitamin D.**
**Sources:** Your skin produces it when exposed to sunlight; also found in eggs, butter, and fish that have fat distributed through their tissue (salmon, tuna, sardines, oysters, etc).
**Why it's needed:** Your body uses Vitamin D to regulate its absorption of calcium and phosphorus, which makes it essential for proper bone and cartilage formation.

**Vitamin E.**
**Sources:** Green, leafy vegetables, wheat germ oil, margarine, rice.
**Why it's needed:** Vitamin E is one of the least understood vitamins, but it is known to be necessary for proper reproduction and prevention of muscular dystrophy in laboratory rats. It may also affect neuromuscular functions.

**Vitamin K.**
**Sources:** This vitamin is not made by the body itself, but by organisms that live in your intestinal tract. Also found in yoghurt, egg yolks, leafy green vegetables, and fish liver oils.
**Why it's needed:** It enables your body to synthesise the proteins required for the proper clotting of blood. Also helps reduce excessive menstrual flow in women.

## HEALTHY HINTS

It's a good idea to wash your vegetables before you eat them—but don't soak them. You'll lose a lot of the water-soluble vitamins (B and C) if you do.

If you don't eat fresh vegetables within a week of buying them, you're better off buying frozen vegetables. Fresh vegetables lose their vitamins over time, and after about a week in your refrigerator they have fewer vitamins than frozen ones. And frozen veggies almost always have more vitamins than canned vegetables.

**According to recent estimates, 99% of the universe is nothing.**

# SIBLING RIVALRY

*Brothers who go into business together don't always stay close.*
*In fact, going into business with a relative might be the best*
*way to lose a family. Here are four classic cases.*

**A**DIDAS/Adolf & Rudolf Dassler
**Background:** According to *Everybody's Business*, "Adolf and Rudolf Dassler were the sons of a poor laundress who grew up in the tiny Bavarian milltown of Herzogenerauch, near Nuremburg. Before World War II, they started a factory there to make house slippers, then branched to track shoes and soccer boots."
**Rivalry:** "They had a violent falling out and after the war went their separate ways. Rudolf left Adidas and started a rival athletic shoe company, Puma. Before long Adidas and Puma—both head-quartered in Herzogenerauch—were battling head-to-head all over the world. When Adolf died in 1978, the two brothers hadn't spoken to each other in 29 years."

## GALLO WINE/ERNEST, JULIO & JOSEPH GALLO
**Background:** Ernest, Julio, and Joseph Gallo inherited the family vineyard in 1933 when their father murdered their mother and then committed suicide. Twenty-four-year-old Ernest and 23-year-old Julio used their inheritance to start the Gallo Winery. At the same time, they raised their teenage brother, Joseph, who went to work for them as a vineyard manager when he was old enough. After toiling for his brothers for 18 years, Joseph bought a nearby ranch. He grew grapes (which he sold to the Gallo Winery) and raised cattle.
**Rivalry:** In 1983, Joseph expanded his dairy operation to include Gallo cheese...but his brothers said he was infringing on their trademark, and in 1986 they sued him. Joseph retaliated with a countersuit, claiming that his one-third share of his father's inheritance entitled him to one-third of the winery. The fight was nasty. During the trial, the winemakers accused Joseph of "running a rat-infested cheese plant"; Joseph shot back that his brothers specialised in making cheap wine for drunks. Ernest and Julio won both suits.

## REVLON/CHARLES, JOSEPH & MARTIN REVSON
**Background:** According to *Everybody's Business*, "The cosmetics giant was founded in 1932 by Charles Revson, his older brother Joseph, and Charles Lachman. A younger brother, Martin, joined the firm later. But it was Charles who led the company's drive to the top."

**Rivalry:** "Joseph left the company in 1955 because he didn't agree with Charles that Revlon should go public. He sold all his stock to the company for $2.5 million. (If he'd waited four years, the stock would have been worth $35 million.) Martin left in 1959 after bitter fights with his older brother. He sued the company, charging that his brother Charles 'engaged in a practice of mistreating executives and abusing them personally.' The brothers didn't speak to each other for 13 years. 'What brother?' Charles once said. 'I don't have a brother.'"

## KELLOGG'S/JOHN & WILLIAM KELLOGG
**Background:** In 1876, 25-year-old Dr. John Harvey Kellogg became head of the Battle Creek Sanitarium. His first official act was to hire his younger brother, William, as "chief clerk." To make the institution's vegetarian food more palatable, the brothers invented a number of foods—including Corn Flakes. Then they set up a company on the side, manufacturing and distributing their cereal around the country.

**Rivalry:** John, a world-famous doctor by 1900, insisted that Kellogg's cereals be "health foods." So he forbade the use of white sugar. William just wanted something that would sell…and when he added sugar to the flakes while John was out of the country, the partnership fell apart. "Will set out on his own…in 1906," writes William Poundstone in *Bigger Secrets*. "By 1909 the brothers weren't on speaking terms. Both spent much of the next decade suing each other. These legal actions resulted in the ruling that only Will's company could market cereal under the Kellogg's name, and in lifelong mutual enmity for the two brothers." When John Harvey died in 1942, the two hadn't spoken in 33 years.

**Quickie:** Robert, James, and Edward Mead Johnson started *Johnson & Johnson* in an old wallpaper factory. Edward left and started Mead Johnson, which now competes with Johnson & Johnson.

# Q & A:
# ASK THE EXPERTS

*More random questions and answers from leading trivia experts.*

## CRACKING THE CODE

**Q:** *How did phone companies assign area codes in the US?*
**A:** It seems strange that 212 is for New York City, and 213 is for Los Angeles, across the country. But in 1948, assigning area codes had nothing to do with geography; it had to do with how fast people could dial them (not punch them on a touchtone phone, but *dial* them on a rotary phone). The faster numbers—1, 2, and 3—were called "low dial-pull" numbers. They were given to large cities for one simple reason: it saved the phone company money.

"Millions of people called those cities every day. The faster each caller was able to dial his number, the less time the phone company's switching machines would be tied up making the connection…[and] the fewer machines the phone company had to buy.

"Today, the only concern when assigning new area codes is to make them as different as possible form neighbouring codes, so people won't confuse the numbers." (From *Know It All!*, by Ed Zotti)

## BUG OFF!

**Q:** *How do flies walk upside down?*
**A:** A fly has six legs. On each leg there are two little claws that look sort of like a lobster's claws. "Underneath the claws [are] a pair of small weblike fuzzy pads called *pulvilli*. These are functional suction pads which the fly presses to the surface to squeeze out the air and create enough suction to hold itself up. Thus, with its claws and suction pads, the little pest can walk majestically upside down." (From *How Do Flies Walk Upside Down?*, by Martin M. Goldwyn)

## STUMPED

**Q:** *Can you tell a tree's age by counting the rings on a stump?*
**A:** Not necessarily. "In temperate climates, a single ring of light and dark wood is usually added each year—but sometimes more

than one ring is produced in a growing season, or sometimes no ring at all. If a tree loses most of its leaves from a severe insect attack or drought, it begins producing dense wood and thus completes a ring. Then if a new crop of leaves grows again that same season, another ring will be formed. In a very dry year the tree might not grow at all, and no ring would be added that year." (From *Do Elephants Swim?*, compiled by Robert M. Jones)

## LOVE MATCH
**Q:** *Why is zero called Love in tennis?*
**A:** It has nothing to do with affairs of the heart. "Love is really a distortion of the French word *oeuf*, which means egg, as in goose egg." (From *The Book of Totally Useless Information*, by Don Voorhees)

## ILLOGICAL
**Q:** *Where did the people who created "Star Trek" come up with the name of Spock's home planet, Vulcan?*
**A:** Believe it or not, astronomers were sure there actually *was* a planet called Vulcan somewhere between the planet Mercury and the sun. "Its existence—first proposed by French astronomer Urbain Jean Joseph Leverrier in 1845—was hypothesised to explain a discrepancy in Mercury's orbit. Vulcan was even reported to have been observed once, but the observation was never confirmed. Einstein's general theory of relativity explained Mercury's odd orbit, and the existence of Vulcan was discredited." (From *The Book of Answers*, by Barbara Berliner)

## DARK SECRETS
**Q:** *What is espresso?*
**A:** "Espresso is Italian for 'quick,' and it refers to a particular way of brewing coffee. Various espresso machines have been devised, but the basic idea always is to heat water under pressure above the boiling point and then force it rapidly through the ground coffee. The hotter the water, the more flavour is extracted from the coffee. The shorter the brewing time, the less bitter the coffee." Espresso also refers to dark-roasted types of coffee that make the best espresso brew. (From *Why Do Men Have Nipples*, by Katherine Dunn)

The world population increases by the equivalent of the population of Mexico every year.

# A WEATHER MACHINE

*El Niño is a word that is often bandied about. But do you really know what it means? Here is a simple explanation and the impact it has on Australia.*

Australia has been at the mercy of El Niño, on and off, for several years. However, this isn't a recent phenomenon. Peruvian fishermen first recognised the appearance of unusually warm weather in the Pacific Ocean in the late 1800s. Because of its tendency to arrive around Christmas, this phenomenon was called "El Niño", which means "Christ child" in Spanish.

## WEST BECOMES EAST
El Niño is caused when warm waters, which have been held by the winds just above sea level in the western Pacific, begin to surge back across the sea to the eastern Pacific. The heated water, now in the east, generates the rain that would normally happen in the west. The cooler waters, now in the west, prevent the formation of rain that would normally fall on northern and eastern Australia.

## AS DRY AS A PUB WITH NO BEER
The dry, hot conditions created by El Niño have a wide-ranging impact on Australia, both locally and internationally. Widespread drought causes havoc across the nation:
• Livestock and wildlife compete for reduced food supplies.
• Large-scale bushfires sweep through the countryside, destroying bush, killing animals, threatening homes and claiming lives. In January 2003, 520 homes in Canberra were destroyed in just one day and four people were killed.
• Some Australian wildlife, such as the green turtle, becomes endangered because of lack of water for breeding.
• Reduce rainfall lowers export sales of agricultural goods.
• Valuable dry topsoil on inland farms is dumped hundreds of kilometres away by strong winds.

Elvis collected statuettes of Joan of Arc and Venus de Milo.

## ON AND OFF

El Niño events seem to occur about every four to seven years and normally lasts around 12 to 18 months. The degree of impact it has on Australia depends on the El Niño's strength. The stronger it is, the more intense and extensive the Australian droughts. The El Niño in 2002–03 was devastating. It was drier, hotter and created more evaporation than any other dry period. Mercifully, El Niño began to weaken between January and March 2003 and brought much needed rain to the seriously drought-affected areas of Australia.

\*     \*     \*     \*

## SUMMER SONG

It's unmistakable. The unrelenting drone of cicadas shrilling furiously in the trees. At first, it might be just a few cicadas. Then, it might be scores. Soon, it is hundreds of cicadas joining together to create this distinctive sound of summer.

The song of the cicada is a mating call that is only made by the males. Cicadas are the only insects that have developed such an effective and specialised way to produce sound. More than 180 species of cicada have been recorded in Australia. Some of the common names given to cicadas by children include: green Mondays, greengrocers, yellow Monday, black princes, mottled greys, red eyes and double drummers.

Some of the large species, such as the double drummer (well, with a name like that!), produce a loud and intense noise that is almost too painful to hear. The songs of some small species, however, are pitched so high we can't hear them at all.

Some cicadas sing only at dusk, while others sing during the heat of the day. The cicada din repels attacks from birds because the noise is too painful to the birds' ears. They have to look for dinner elsewhere!

\*     \*     \*     \*

A businessman on a trip to Germany picks up a hooker for the night. In the morning he gives her $100.00.

"I'd prefer marks," says the Fraulein.

"OK," says the businessman. "Eight out of ten!"

According to one survey, Danes spent $116 million on prostitutes in 1993.

# AUNT LENNA'S PUZZLES

*More conversations with my puzzle-loving auntie.*
*Answers are on page 486.*

**M**y Aunt Lenna is quite talkative. One day she took a cab and chattered to the driver incessantly. Finally, the man apologetically explained that his hearing aid was off, and without it he wasn't able to make out a word she said. She stopped talking for the rest of the trip, but when she got to her destination, she realised she'd been tricked.

*How did she realise this?*

Aunt Lenna was chuckling.
   "What's so funny?" I asked her.
   "Just a silly little puzzle," she said.
   "Tell me."
   "Okay. See if you can write the number *one hundred* using six 9's."
   "You mean, 9-9-9-9-9-9?"
   "That's not how you do it, but those are the numbers."

*How can I do it?*

"Such a pity," said Aunt Lenna.
   "What?" I asked.
   "Oh, my friend's wife passed away. It was quite sudden. He kissed her before he left for work, shut the apartment door, walked to the lift and pressed the ground-floor button. He immediately knew his wife had died. Very sad."
   "Wait a minute," I stopped her. "How did he know she was dead? Is he psychic?"
   Aunt Lenna shook her head.
   "Well, then what happened?"

*What did happen?*

Australia has roughly 0.3% of the world's population.

Physics isn't my strong suit, so I was stumped when Aunt Lenna asked me this question: "Suppose there are three men on one side of a river, and someone fires a gun on the other side. One man sees the smoke from the gun; another hears the gunfire; and the third sees the bullet hit the water by his feet. Which of them knows the gun was fired first?"

*Do you know the answer?*

Aunt Lenna went for a walk by the water, and came back quite upset.

"What's the matter?" I asked.

"Oh, it was terrible! There was a woman standing on the pier. There were tears in her eyes. She was very angry, and she seemed indignant over some injury that had been inflicted upon her.

"I heard her cry, 'You monster of cruelty! I've stayed with you too long. You've hurt the very foundations of my being! I've endured your tortures day after day. The first time we met, your ease and polish attracted me to you... and when you became my own, my friends were quite envious. But now...take a look at what I've suffered for your sake! You keep me from advancing myself! My standing in society has been ruined by you! If we'd never met, I might have walked in peace...but now...now we part forever!'

"And I declare, nephew, she threw something in the water. I rushed over and ..."

"Aunt Lenna! Did you call the police?!"

"Don't be silly."

"But I don't understand. Who...or what did she throw off the pier?"

*Do you know?*

"I went to a family reunion the other day," Aunt Lenna told me. There were 2 grandfathers, 2 grandmothers, 3 mothers, 3 fathers, 3 daughters, 3 sons, 2 mothers-in-law, 2 fathers-in-law, 1 son-in-law, 1 daughter-in-law, 2 brothers, and 2 sisters. Can you guess how many people there were?"

I thought for a moment. "Mm-m-m...I'd say, 10."

"That's right!" Lenna said, amazed. "How did you know?"

*How did I get that number?*

# FAMILIAR PHRASES

*More origins of common phrases.*

## TO UNDERMINE

**Meaning:** To weaken, usually secretly and gradually.
**Origin:** "The term dates from the 14th century, when it was common practice for besiegers to tunnel under the foundations of a castle, either to enter it or to weaken the walls." The tunnels were called "mines," and the damaged walls were considered "undermined." By the 15th century, any underhanded method used to defeat an enemy had become known as "undermining." (From *Fighting Words*, by Christine Ammer)

## TO THROW SOMEONE TO THE WOLVES

**Meaning:** Abandon someone; sacrifice someone to save yourself.
**Origin:** The term comes from the Victorian age, when it was popular for printmakers to depict sleighs, drawn by horses at full gallop, being chased by packs of wolves. "Traditionally, if the wolves got too close, one of the passengers was thrown out to lighten the sleigh, in hopes that the rest of the company could escape while the animals were devouring the victim." No one's sure if this really happened, but it resulted in a "durable metaphor." (From *Loose Cannons and Red Herrings*, by Robert Claiborne)

## TO TURN OVER A NEW LEAF

**Meaning:** Get a fresh start; change your ways.
**Origin:** Believe it or not, the expression has nothing to do with leaves from a plant; it refers to the "leaves" (pages) in a *book*— "the turning to a blank page in a [journal or] exercise book where one can start one's work anew. Figuratively, such a fresh start gives the possibility of learning a new lesson in the book of life's principles: a chance to begin again and mend one's ways." (From *Getting to the Roots*, by Martin Manser)

Teenage boys use more shampoo—and less deodorant—than teenage girls.

# FUN WITH ELVIS

*Imagine what a kick it would have been to hang out with the
King at Graceland. Well, it's too late now—but here
are some of the exciting moments you missed.*

**A**T THE POOL
Want to go for a dip? According to David Adler in
*The Life and Cuisine of Elvis Presley*, "Elvis enjoyed sitting
around the pool eating watermelon hearts. For entertainment
while he ate, he would float flashbulbs in the pool. Then he would
take out a .22 and shoot at them. When the flashbulbs were hit,
they would flash, and then sink to the bottom."

## ON THE FOURTH OF JULY
Every Independence Day at Graceland, Elvis had a "fireworks
display." His Memphis Mafia split into two teams, put on gloves
and football helmets, and shot fireworks at one another. "They
would level arsenals of rockets and Roman candles at each other
and blast away at point-blank range for hours," says Steve
Dunleavy in *Elvis: What Happened.*

It was all laughs: "I've backed into burning rockets and had my
ass burned half off," laughs Elvis aide Red West. "I've seen Elvis
bending over a giant rocket and watched the thing go off while he
is leaning over it, nearly blowing his fool head off. [My brother]
Sonny carries a scar on his chest to this day where one of us tried
to blow a rocket through him. Roman candles would blow up in
our hands. The house caught fire twice."

## DEMOLITION DERBY
You never knew what might happen when the King was bored.
There was a beautiful little cottage in the corner of the Graceland
property. One day, Elvis decided to demolish it...so he put on a
football helmet and revved up his bulldozer. The only problem:
his father, Vernon Presley, was sitting on the cottage porch.

According to Red West, "[He yelled] 'You better move, Daddy.'
Vernon asks why and Elvis says, 'Because I'm gonna knock the
goddamn house down.' ...Vernon gives one of those looks like

---

**Prune juice is the sixth most popular juice in the Austalia.**

'Oh, Lordie,' but he doesn't say anything…he just gets up and Elvis starts roaring away." To make it more interesting, Elvis and Red set the house on fire while they battered it with heavy machinery.

## AT THE MOVIES
The King couldn't just go out to the movies whenever he felt like it—he would have been mobbed. So he rented the whole theatre instead. "Elvis had private midnight screenings at the Memphian Theatre," writes David Adler. "They were attended by about a hundred of his friends. Admission was free, and so was the popcorn, but you had to watch the movie on Elvis's terms. Elvis made the projectionist repeat his favourite scenes. If the action got slow, such as during a love scene, the projectionist would have to skip to the next good part. Elvis once saw *Dr. Strangelove* three times straight, with a number of scenes repeated so he could figure out exactly what was going on."

"Elvis liked James Bond and *Patton*, and any movie with Peter Sellers. His favourite movie of all time was *The Party*."

## WATCHING TV
And, of course, you could always stay home and spend a quiet evening watching TV…as long as Elvis liked the programs. If not, there was a good chance he'd pull out a gun and shoot out the screen. "Honestly," Red West says, "I can't tell you how many television sets went to their death at the hands of Elvis….He would shoot out television sets in hotel rooms and in any one of the houses he had. He shot out a great big one at Graceland, in Memphis, the one he had in his bedroom."

A classic example: One afternoon in 1974, the TV was blaring while Elvis was eating his breakfast. His least favourite singer, Robert Goulet, came on. As Red related: "Very slowly, Elvis finishes what he has in his mouth, puts down his knife and fork, picks up this big mother of a .22 and—boom—blasts old Robert clean off the screen and the television set to pieces….He then puts down the .22, picks up his knife and fork and says, 'That will be enough of that s—,' and then he goes on eating."

**Elvis Trivia:** On his way to meet the U.S. President Richard Nixon in 1970 (to pose for the famous photo), the King suddenly had a food craving. He insisted that his driver pull over to buy a dozen honey-glazed donuts; then the King polished them off in one sitting as they drove to the White House.

\* \* \* \*

## CATTLE CALL

• In about 2000 B.C., man began trading bronze ingots shaped like cows (which had about the same value as a real cow). The value of these "coins" was measured by weighing them—which meant that any time a transaction was made, someone had to get out a scale to measure the value of the money.

• Around 800 B.C., the Lydians of Anatolia—who traded bean-shaped ingots made of a gold-silver alloy called *electrum*—began stamping the ingot's value onto its face. This eliminated the need for a scale and made transactions much easier.

• But switching to countable coins from weighed ones increased the chances of fraud—precious metals could be chipped or shaved off the edges of the coins. One of the techniques designed to prevent this is still evident on modern coins today, even though they no longer contain precious metals. What is it? Feel the edges of a coin. Those grooves were originally a way to tell if any metal had been shaved off.

## ANTI-COUNTERFEITING

Here are some anti-counterfeit features of paper currency you probably didn't know about:

• The currency paper is fluorescent under ultraviolet light.

• The ink is slightly magnetic—not enough for household magnets to detect, but enough for special machines to notice.

• The paper has thousands of tiny microscopic holes "drilled" into it. Reason: when the money is examined under a microscope, tiny points of light shine through.

# OOPS!

*More blunders to make you feel superior.*

**A SLIGHT MISUNDERSTANDING**
"At the end of World War II, the Allies issued the Potsdam telegram demanding that the Imperial Japanese armies surrender forthwith. The Japanese government responded with an announcement that it was withholding immediate comment on the ultimatum, pending 'deliberations' by the Imperial government.

"Unfortunately, the official Japanese government news agency, in the heat of issuing this critical statement in English, decided to translate the Japanese word that means 'withholding comment for the time being' as 'deliberately ignore.'

"A number of scholars have suggested that if the ultimatum had not been so decisively rejected, President Truman might never have authorised the A-bomb attacks on Hiroshima and Nagasaki."
**—From *David Frost's Book of the World's Worst Decisions***

**CONTROL FREAKS**
"The March 21, 1983, issue of *Time* magazine featured Lee Iacocca on the cover, along with a tease for Henry Kissinger's 'New Plan for Arms Contol.' After two hundred thousand of the covers had been printed, someone noticed a typographical error—the 'r' had been left out of 'Control.' It was printed as *Contol*.

"There had never been a misspelling on a *Time* cover in the history of the magazine. They stopped the presses, corrected the error, and withdrew all the *Contol* covers. The goof cost *Time* $100,000, and 40% of the newsstand copies went on sale a day late."
**—From *The Emperor Who Ate the Bible,* by Scott Morris**

**THE WICKED BIBLE**
In 1631, two London printers left one word out of an official edition of the Bible. The mistake cost them 3,000 pounds and nearly led to their imprisonment. The word was "not;" they left it out of the Seventh Commandment, which then told readers,

"Thou shalt commit adultery." The book became known as "the Wicked Bible."

## TRICK-OR-TREAT
"Two Illinois skydivers, Brian Voss, 30, and Alfred McInturff, 50, were tossing a pumpkin back and forth on their 1987 Halloween skydive when they accidentally dropped it from 670 metres (2,200 feet). It crashed through the roof of Becky Farrar's home, leaving orange goo all over her kitchen walls and breaking the kichen table. Said Farrar, 'If this had happened an hour earlier, we would have been sitting at the table having lunch.'"

—From *News of the Weird*

## NAKED TRUTH
PORTLAND, USA. "Amtrak apologised and issued refunds to dozens of junior high students who took a train trip with a group of rowdy grown-ups playing strip poker.

"About half the 93 members of Portland's Robert Gray Middle School band and choir said they had to ride in a car with a smoking section and were subjected to rude comments from adults who took their clothes off in a poker game. The students were returning from a music competition in San Jose, California. Amtrak has promised to send the group a refund cheque for $4,830."

—AP, June 23, 1993

## BACKFIRE
On August 7, 1979, a jet plane in the Spanish Air Force shot itself down when its own gunfire ricocheted off a hillside target, flew back, and hit the plane during field manoeuvres.

## GOOD LUCK?
"At a dinner party in the late 19th century, French playwright Victolen Sardou spilled a glass of wine. The woman sitting next to him poured salt on the stain, and Sardou picked up some of the salt and threw it over his shoulder for luck. The salt went into the eye of a waiter about to serve him some chicken. The waiter dropped the platter, and the family dog pounced on the chicken. A bone lodged in the dog's throat, and when the son of the host tried to pull it out, the dog bit him. His finger had to be amputated."

—John Berendt, *Esquire* magazine

# THE LATEST THING

*Nothing is sacred in the bathroom—go ahead and admit that you owned a pet rock or a mood ring…we understand…confession is good for the soul. And while you're pondering your follies, we'll tell you where they came from.*

**P**AC-MAN. A Japanese import that hit American shores in late 1980, Pac-Man got its name from the word *paku*, which means "eat" in Japanese. The video game was so popular that Pac-Man was named *Time* magazine's "man" of the year in 1982. That year, Americans pumped $6 *billion* in quarters into Pac-Man's mouth, more than they spent in Las Vegas casinos and movie theatres combined.

**MOOD RINGS.** The temperature-sensitive jewellery that supposedly read your emotions, Mood Rings were the brainchild of Joshua Reynolds, a New Age heir to the R.J. Reynolds tobacco fortune. Reynolds envisioned them as "portable biofeedback aids" and managed to sell $1 million worth of them in a three-month period in 1975. Even so, the company went bankrupt—but not before it inspired a hoard of imitators, including "mood panties" (underwear studded with temperature-sensitive plastic hearts).

**PET ROCKS.** One night in 1975, an out-of-work advertising executive named Gary Dahl was hanging out in a bar listening to his friends complain about their pets. It gave him an idea for the perfect "pet": a rock. He spent the next two weeks writing the *Pet Rock Training Manual*, which included instructions for house-training the rock. ("Place it on some old newspapers. The rock will know what the paper is for and will require no further instructions.") He had a friend design a box shaped like a pet carrying case—complete with air holes and a bed of straw—and then filled them with rocks he bought from a builder's supply store for a penny apiece. The rock debuted in August 1975 and sold for $3.95; by the end of October Dahl was shipping 10,000 a day. The fad encouraged a host of imitations as well as an entire Pet Rock "service industry," including dude ranches, "hair-care" products, and burials-at-sea. The fad died out in 1976.

---

Q. What do you call the eye in the end of a lariat? A. A honda.

**EARTH SHOES.** Earth Shoes were one of the best-selling shoes of the 1970s. Invented by a Danish shoe designer named Anne Kalsø, they were brought to the United States in 1969 by a woman who discovered them on a trip to Europe. She claimed they cured her back pains, but foot experts argued that the shoes—which forced wearers to walk on the backs of their feet— were actually pretty bad for you. One study found that most wearers suffered "severe pain and cramping for the first two weeks of wear"; another expert predicted that the shoes would "cripple everyone who wears them." Still, they were a counterculture hit and sold thousands of pairs a year in their peak. The original Earth Shoes company went bankrupt in 1977, the victim of cheap knockoffs and changing times.

**COATS OF ARMS.** In the '60s, anyone with $20 could send away for a crest corresponding to their last name. At the fad's peak in 1969, status-seeking Americans spent $5 million a year displaying them on sport coats, ashtrays, bank cheques, etc. Elitists were outraged. "People of good taste," one blueblood sniffed, "don't use a coat of arms they're not entitled to." But by the early 1970s, just about everyone had a crest—which defeated the purpose of having one in the first place. The fad died out soon afterwards.

**SMILEY FACES.** Introduced in 1969 by N.G. Slater, a New York button manufacturer. At first sales were slow, but by the spring of 1971 more than 20 million buttons had been sold— enough for one in every 10 Americans—making it a craze as popular as the Hula Hoop of the 1950s. Pop-culture pundits called it the "peace symbol of the seventies," and presidential candidate George McGovern adopted it as his campaign logo. The fad died out after about a year, but in the mid-1970s made a comeback— this time coloured yellow and bearing the cheerful message, "Have a Happy Day!" By the late 1970s, however, Americans were completely sick of it.

### Smiley Face Update
"Attorneys for a convicted killer asked yesterday that his death sentence be overturned because a judge signed the July 15, 1993 execution order with a 'happy face' sketch….The judge has said that he always signs his name that way as a symbol of his faith in God and that he does not plan to change it."

—*The Associated Press*

# MUTINOUS DEEDS

*Imagine a tragedy at sea—a scene of mutiny, murder and treasure.*
*It may sound like the latest Hollywood action movie, but this was*
*for real. The setting was on islands without fresh water, off the*
*coast of Western Australia in 1629.*

## A MOTLEY CREW

On its maiden voyage, the trading vessel *Batavia* set sail from Amsterdam for Java in October 1628. This flagship symbolised the wealth and power of its owner, the Dutch East India Company. She left in a flourish, heavily laden with 316 passengers, merchandise, gold, silver and gems. However, her crew was not in such a splendid state. In command was Francesco Pelsaert, a senior merchant. This annoyed the ship's skipper, Ariaen Jacobsz, as the two men were enemies from a previous voyage. Another crew member was the bankrupt undermerchant, Jeronimus Cornelisz, who had an overbearing and controlling personality. His thoughts were on the mutiny he planned in order to steal the treasure. After Jacobsz was publicly dressed down by Pelsaert after a night of wild drinking with Cornelisz, Jacobsz quickly sided with Cornelisz. However, their mutinous plans were thwarted when, in the early hours of 4 June, 1629, the *Batavia* rammed into a coral atoll off Houtman Abrolhos, a chain of islands 64 kilometres (40 miles) off the coast of Western Australian.

## ABANDON SHIP!

While 40 people drowned trying to reach the islands, another 48—Pelsaert, all the senior officers including Jacobsz, some crew and passengers—managed to secure a lifeboat and land on a small island. The rest of the passengers made it to a larger island close by and managed to salvage sufficient provisions from the *Batavia* before it broke into pieces a week later. But there was a shortage of fresh water.

Pelsaert and Jacobsz knew they were all in dire straits. They decided to sail the lifeboat to Java with a handful of crew, to obtain help. They left a note for the remaining survivors who, in horror, named the smaller island "Traitor's Island"—a name it still bears.

Thirty-three days later, they arrived safely in Java where

---

The lyre bird can mimic the call of 15 other species of birds.

Pelsaert was determined to address the cause of the shipwreck. He accused the high boatswain of outrageous behaviour before the loss of the ship and Jacobsz for negligence. The boatswain was executed and Jacobsz arrested. Two days later, Pelsaert sailed from Java on the *Sardam* to rescue the survivors on both islands. After a long, tough voyage and manoeuvring through treacherous reefs, *Sardam* sighted the islands.

## TRUE INTENTIONS
During Pelsaert's absence, Cornelisz, now the most senior company man, sent a group of soldiers to a distant island in search of water, hoping they would never survive. He now made his true intentions clear; plundering the treasure and capturing the rescue ship. With a small group of mutineers he started on a killing frenzy. Any man, woman or child that offered resistance or was a burden, became a victim.

## A HERO EMERGES
Miraculously, the group of soldiers, led by Wiebbe Hayes, had found food and water on another island that could be reached at low tide. When smoke was spied rising from this island, Cornelisz prepared to attack. Hayes was warned by survivors who had escaped from Cornelisz and organised weapons to be made from wrecked timbers and barrel hoop iron washed up on the island. Several attacks followed, but Hayes and his men were formidable opponents. An attack was in full swing when the rescue ship was sighted. Taking a small boat they had made, Hayes and some of his men warned Pelsaert of the mutiny and murders.

## THE TRAGIC TALLY
Pelsaert had the mutineers tried by the *Sardam* officers. Seven, including Cornelisz whose hands were cut off, were hanged on the islands. Another two were marooned on the mainland, while others were flogged and executed on their arrival at Java. The *Sardam* carried back 74 survivors. The total number of people who were drowned, murdered, executed or died from illness, was one hundred and eighty-five. Wiebbe Hayes was promoted to standard-bearer and others, who fought under his command, were given monetary rewards. Pelsaert died the following year, leaving behind his journal of these tragic events.

# THE AVENGERS

*If there was ever one television show that could be described as
both "stylish" and "English," it would be "The Avengers."
This secret agent send-up of the mid-'60s gave us a taste of
"swinging England"—the team of the veddy British Steed
(played by Patrick Macnee), and one of the coolest, sexiest
women ever to star on the small screen—Emma Peel
(played by Shakespearian actress Diana Rigg).*

## HOW IT STARTED

"The Avengers" immediate inspiration was a show called
*Police Surgeon*. It wasn't popular with British viewers, but
its star, Ian Hendry, was. So Sydney Newman, the head of
programming at ABC-TV in England, decided to feature him on a
new show in 1961.

Newman's plan: team Hendry with a secret-agent character in a
crusade against crime. Hendry would still play a surgeon, but he
wouldn't practice medicine. His fiancé would be killed by a gang
of criminals, and he'd become obsessed with vengeance! He would
make it his life's work, as he and Steed (the agent) formed
"The Avengers." That's how they came up with the name of the
show. "Also," admitted Newman, "it's a great title."

The "cult" Avengers—featuring Steed, played by Patrick
Macnee, and a macho female partner—evolved a little later.
During the first season, an actors' strike forced a layoff in the
show; Hendry, with a film career in mind, walked out. The
producer decided to replace him with a woman. She'd be a new
kind of heroine. Beautiful, but tough; a fighter...but a fashion
plate. After a 6-month search for the "right woman," Honor
Blackman was selected to play Cathy Gale...and the approach
worked so well that the co-ed team became an instant cult
phenomenon, one of Europe's most popular series. When
Blackman left for films three years later, Diana Rigg stepped ably
into her boots as Emma Peel and kept the show a favourite.

The show first aired in England in 1961. It debuted in America
in 1966 and ran until 1969. It was resurrected again 1976 as
*The New Avengers*.

---

## MILESTONES
"The Avengers" was the first British show ever to air in a U.S. networks autumn TV schedule. It was also the groundbreaker in portraying women as tough, capable fighters—predating today's female cops by 20 years.

## KUNG FU FIGHTING
Diana Rigg was the first person ever to do Kung Fu on the small screen. In 1965, stuntman Ray Austin went to his producers and said, "Listen, I want to do this thing called Kung Fu." They said, "Kung *what?*" and insisted that Emma, like her predecessor, stick to judo. Instead, Austin secretly taught Diana Kung Fu.

If the fight scenes look choreographed…well, they are. Every move in them was created by Austin.

## NAME GAME
Emma Peel's name was taken from the British film industry expression "M-Appeal," or "Man Appeal," which is what the show's producers were looking for in her character.

## THE LEATHER LOOK
The show helped create the "mod" fashion boom in the '60s. But the most famous of Cathy Gale's clothing, the "kinky" leather look, was created by accident when she split her pants doing karate. Clearly, something more durable was needed, and Patrick Macnee suggested a leather outfit. It became a fad—and "The Avengers" became instant fashion trendsetters.

## MERRIE OLDE ENGLAND
If you think about it while you're watching, you'll notice how "veddy English" everything is in *The Avengers*, from the scenery to the slang (they don't say "truck," they say "lorry"). Quaint? Not quite. It was an international ploy. The producers figured their only shot at selling the show in America was to offer something that Hollywood couldn't—England. So they hammered it up with the British stuff.

## THE STARS
### Patrick Macnee
- Was an assistant producer in English TV when he was offered the lead role in the new adventure series, "The Avengers." He saw his future in production, not acting, so he asked for a ridiculously high salary to discourage the offer. To his shock, they accepted.
- "They told me to make up a character, so I did," he explained later. Inspired by Leslie Howard in *The Scarlet Pimpernel*, his father, and his C.O. in the navy, Macnee made Steed very British—a cool, upper-class dandy dressed in Edwardian clothes. Predating "Swinging London" by three years, Steed was a major influence on international fashion.
- "Steed is pretty much me," he said. "I feel I'm satirising my own class—hunting, shooting, fishing, and Eton."

### Honor Blackman
Played Steed's first sidekick, and TV's first "superwoman—an anthropologist and judo expert—from 1962 to 1965. She quit to become a movie star when she was offered the role of Pussy Galore in *Goldfinger*.

### Diana Rigg
- By the time she appeared as Emma in 1965, she was already a 5-year veteran of the Royal Shakespeare Company. She'd toured Europe and America in a 1964 production of *King Lear* and appeared on United States. TV in *A Comedy of Errors*. However, she had decided to take more commercial roles to avoid being typecast as "a lady actress."
- Meanwhile, "The Avengers" producers were having a rough time replacing Honor Blackman. They'd already hired and fired one actress (Elizabeth Shepard) and had tested dozens more. Then the casting director suggested an actress she'd recently used in a TV drama—Diana Rigg.
- A screen test followed, and Diana was awarded the most coveted female TV role in Britain. The only other regular role she had on a TV series (besides emceeing *Mystery* for PBS) was a short-lived sitcom called "Diana," which aired in 1973. It bombed.

---

Ants stretch—and possibly even yawn—after resting.

# GREETINGS FROM THE WIZARD OF OZ

*The Wizard of Oz, by Frank Baum, is on the BRI's list of recommended bathroom reading for adults. Here are a few random quotes taken from it.*

## ON COURAGE

O"There is no living thing that is not afraid when it faces danger. True courage is in facing danger when you are afraid."

—**The Wizard**

## ON MONEY

"Money in Oz!...Did you suppose we are so vulgar as to use money here? If we used money to buy things, instead of love and kindness and the desires to please one another, then we should be no better than the rest of the world....Fortunately, money is not known in the Land of Oz at all. We have no rich, no poor: for what one wishes, the others all try to give him in order to make him happy, and no one in all of Oz cares to have more than he can use."

—**The Tin Woodsman**

## ON EXPERIENCE

"Can't you give me brains?" asked the Scarecrow.

"You don't need them. You are learning something every day. A baby has brains, but it doesn't know much. Experience is the only thing that brings knowledge, and the longer you are on Earth, the more experience you are sure to get."

## ON THE VALUE OF BRAINS

"I realise at present that I'm only an imitation of a man, and I assure you that it is an uncomfortable feeling to know that one is a fool. It seems to me that a body is only a machine for brains to direct, and those who have no brains themselves are liable to be directed by the brains of others."

---

The U.S. government spends $79 million a day on "intelligence."

## THE BEST THING IN THE WORLD

"Brains are not the best thing in the world," said the Tin Woods-man.

"Have you any?" enquired the Scarecrow.

"No, my head is quite empty," answered the Tin Woodsman. "But once I had brains, and a heart also; so, having tried them both, I should much rather have a heart...for brains do not make one happy, and happiness is the best thing in the world."

\*　　\*　　\*　　\*

### ...And Now, Back to the World of Facts & Stats

• There are an estimated 5,000 foreign languages spoken throughout the world today—and nearly all of them have a dictionary translating them into English.

• The largest encyclopedia of all time was a 16th-century Chinese encyclopedia; it was 22,937 volumes.

• Do you know what "unabridged" means when it refers to English dictionaries? It doesn't mean the work contains all the words in the English language; it just means that it contains all the words listed in earlier editions.

• The world's first Mongolian-English dictionary was published in 1953.

• What language has the most words? Mandarin Chinese, which has an estimated 800,000 words. English is believed to rank second.

• In English dictionaries, the letter "T" has the most entries.

• Few English dictionaries agree on which word is the longest in the language. Two contenders:

  – *floccipaucinihilipilification* (Oxford English Dictionary), "the action of estimating as worthless."

  – *pneumonoultramicroscopicsilicovolcanoconiosis* (Webster's Third International), "a lung disease common to miners."

• Many dictionaries do agree on the longest word in *common* use: it's *disproportionableness*.

• The oldest word in the English language that still resembles its earliest form is *land*, which is descended from *landa*, the Old Celtic word for "heath." It predates the Roman Empire (founded in 200 B.C.) by many hundreds of years.

# GOOD GRIEF, WHAT A REEF!

*It's approximately 350,000 square kilometres (135,000 square miles), over 2,000 kilometres (1,250 miles) long, has over 2,000 species of fish in it and is said to be the world's largest structure created by living creatures. No wonder the Great Barrier Reef is one of Australia's favourite tourist attractions!*

## WHAT'S IT ALL ABOUT, THEN?

The Great Barrier Reef stretches from Bundaberg up to beyond Cape York in Far North Queensland (or FNQ for those in the know). And despite its name, it's not just one big reef, oh no. In fact it's made up of approximately 2,900 individual little reefs, as well as 90 islands. Some of these islands are deserted, some are rocky and sandy, while others are more established with luxury five-star resorts.

In addition to all those reefs and islands, the Great Barrier Reef is also home to:
- 2,000 species of fish
- 400 species of coral
- 5,000 species of molluscs, such as clams and sea slugs
- 800 species of echinoderms, such as starfish and sea urchins
- 150 species of shark
- 500 species of seaweed
- 12 species of sea grasses
- 500 types of algae
- 215 species of birds
- 16 species of sea snakes
- 6 breeding species of turtles
- some of the largest populations of dugong (sea cow) in the world
- breeding humpback whales

Not surprisingly, it gets a lot of visitors—over one million people per year from all around the world.

The most dangerous ant in the world is the Australian bulldog ant which kills three people a year.

## A THORNY TALE

Since the early 1960s, a prickly foe called the crown-of-thorns starfish has invaded parts of the reef. These animals feed on coral and have destroyed large portions of the reef. The Australian government has made efforts to limit destruction of the coral, although scientists say it's a natural phenomenon and that outbreaks have been occurring for the last 3,000 to 7,000 years.

## GOING GLOBAL

The Great Barrier Reef is the largest of the world's 730 World Heritage sites—and is actually larger than the states of Victoria and Tasmania put together and longer than the west coast of America! The Great Barrier Reef World Heritage Area is also one of the few areas that meet all four natural criteria for a World Heritage site. In order for an area to be listed as a World Heritage site it must satisfy any one of the following:
• Be an outstanding example that shows a major stage of the earth's evolutionary history; or
• Be an outstanding example that shows significant ongoing ecological/biological evolution and man's involvement with the environment; or
• Contain unique natural phenomena or areas of exceptional natural beauty; or
• Provide a natural habitat for populations of threatened species.

A site only needs to fulfil one of these criteria to be listed, but in the case of the Great Barrier Reef, it covers the lot. Now that's what I call a reef!

\*    \*    \*    \*

### BUMPER STICKER WISDOM

Borrow money from a pessimist: he doesn't expect to be paid back.

How much deeper would the ocean be without sponges?

Ninety-nine percent of lawyers give the rest of us a bad name.

The severity of the itch is inversely proportional to the ability to reach it.

# UNEXPECTED ENCOUNTERS

*"East is east, and west is west, and never the twain shall meet." When we were kids, that seemed to make sense—except the 'twain' part. That wasn't even a word, as far as we knew. Anyway, here are some examples of people you'd never expect to see together.*

## CHARLIE CHAPLIN & MAHATMA GANDHI

**When:** 1931, in London

**Who:** Chaplin, the "Little Tramp," was the world's most famous comedian. Gandhi, a tiny figure in a loincloth, was one of the world most revered political and religious leaders.

**What Happened:** As they posed for photographers, Chaplin tried to figure out what to say. In his autobiography, he writes about his terror: "The room was suddenly attacked by flashbulbs from the camera as we sat on the sofa. Now came that uneasy, terrifying moment when I should say something astutely intelligent upon a subject I know little about...I knew I had to start the ball rolling, that it was not up to the Mahatma to tell me how much he enjoyed my last film...I doubted he had ever even seen a film." He finally got up the courage, and the two men politely exchanged political views. Then Chaplin stayed and watched Gandhi at his prayers.

## GORGEOUS GEORGE & MUHAMMAD ALI

**When:** 1961, at a radio studio in Las Vegas

**Who:** Gorgeous George, with his permed blonde hair and purple robes, was one of TV wrestling's original superstars. He sold out arenas wherever he played, and was named Mr. Television in 1949; but by 1961 his career was almost over. Cassius Clay (aka Muhammad Ali) was a young boxer who'd just turned pro.

**What Happened:** In 1961 George made a wrestling appearance in Las Vegas. To promote it, he went on a local radio show, shouting, "I am the greatest!" As it happened, the other guest on the program was a young Cassius Clay, who was so impressed with George's theatrics that he went to the wrestling match that evening. The place was packed. "That's when I decided I'd never been shy about talking," Ali remembers, "but if I talked even

---

**Home video sales and rentals are the biggest source of income for movie studios.**

more, there was no telling how much money people would pay to see me."

## NICHELLE NICHOLS & MARTIN LUTHER KING, JR.

**When:** 1967, at a party

**Who:** King was America's greatest civil rights leader, and the recipient of the Nobel Peace Prize. Nichols was playing Lt. Uhura in *Star Trek*'s first (low-rated) season. She was considering quitting the show because Paramount wouldn't give her a contract.

**What Happened:** According to one source: "A friend came up to Nichols at a party and said someone wanted to meet her. She expected a gushing Trekkie...but when she turned around, she was looking at Martin Luther King...who actually *was* a fan. He said he'd heard she was considering leaving *Star Trek*, and urged her not to; she was too important a role model for blacks—and the only black woman on TV with real authority. 'Do you realise that you're fourth in command on the *Enterprise*?' he asked. Nichols didn't. The next day she checked and found he was right...She stayed with the show and finally got her contract the next season."

## HARPO MARX & GEORGE BERNARD SHAW

**When:** 1931, at the Villa Gallanon in the south of France

**Who:** Shaw was "the most important British playright since Shakespeare." Marx was part of the world's most popular slapstick team.

**What Happened:** Here's how Harpo described the meeting in his autobiography: "I went down the cliff to the little sheltered cove we used for nude bathing, took off my clothes, and went for a swim. I came out of the water and stretched out on a towel to sunbathe...I was startled out of my doze in the sun by a man's voice, blaring from the top of the cliff. 'Halloo! Halloo! Is there nobody home?'

"I wrapped the towel around myself and scrambled up the cliff to see who it was. It was a tall, skinny, red-faced old geezer with a beard, decked out in a sporty cap and knicker suit. There was a lady with him. 'Who the devil are you?' I told him I was Harpo Marx. 'Ah, yes, of course,' he said. He held out his hand. 'I'm Bernard Shaw,' he said. Instead of shaking hands with me, he made a sudden lunge for my towel and snatched it away, and exposed me naked to the world. 'And this,' he said, 'is Mrs. Shaw.' From the moment I met him, I had nothing to hide from George Bernard Shaw." They became good friends.

# THE GENUINE ARTICLE

*A random sampling of authentic articles, dialogue, commentary.*
*You are there.*

**O**UTRAGE OVER ELVIS
*In 1956, Elvis Presley appeared on the "Ed Sullivan Show."*
*We think of it as a great moment in TV history, but at the time, critics (and other grown-ups) didn't. These comments appeared in the* New York Times:

"Last Sunday on the 'Ed Sullivan Show,' Mr. Presley made another of his appearances and attracted a record audience. In some ways, it was the most unpleasant of his recent three performances. Mr. Presley initially disturbed adult viewers with his strip-tease behaviour on last spring's Milton Berle's program…On the Sullivan program he injected movements of the tongue and indulged in wordless singing that were singularly distasteful… Some parents are puzzled or confused by Mr. Presley's almost hypnotic power; some are concerned; [but] most are a shade disgusted and [will be] content to let the Presley fad play itself out."

## CHARLIE CHAPLIN'S FAVOURITE JOKE
*At lunch one afternoon, Charlie Chaplin was asked to relate the funniest joke he'd ever heard. You'd think that "the world's greatest comic genius" would tell something hilarious. But…well…you decide.*

"A man in a tea shop orders a cup of coffee and a piece of shortbread. On paying the bill, he compliments the manager on the quality of the shortbread and asks if it could be custom-made in any shape. 'Why, certainly.'

" 'Well, if I come back tomorrow, could you make me a piece shaped like the letter "e"?'

" 'No trouble,' says the manager. Next day, on returning to the shop, the man looks aghast.

" 'But you've made it a capital "E"!' He arranges to come back another day, and this time expresses himself completely satisfied.

---

" 'Where would you like me to send it?' asks the manager.

" 'Oh, I won't give you the trouble to send it anywhere,' says the customer. 'I'll sit down here, if I may, and eat it now.' And he does."

*No one at lunch thought it was funny, either. (Neither do we.)*

## HISTORIC RECIPE
*In 1770, American revolutionaries published these detailed directions for tarring and feathering, which was, at the time "a mob ritual."*

### How to Tar and Feather Someone
"First, strip a person naked, then heat the tar until it is thin & pour it upon naked flesh, or rub it over with a tar brush.

"After which, sprinkle decently upon the tar, whilst it is yet warm, as many feathers as will stick to it.

"Then hold a lighted candle to the feathers, & try to set it all on fire."

## GREAT MOMENTS IN CENSORSHIP
*In 1937, Mae West was barred from radio after she engaged in a slightly risqué dialogue on NBC's Edgar Bergen/Charlie McCarthy Show. The conversation was with McCarthy, a ventriloquist's dummy!*

**Mae West:** "Why don't you come home with me now honey? I'll let you play in my woodpile."

**Charlie McCarthy:** "Well, I don't feel so well tonight. I've been feeling nervous lately...."

**West:** "You can't kid me. You're afraid of women. Your Casanova stuff is just a front, a false front."

**McCarthy:** "Not so loud, Mae, not so loud! All my girlfriends are listening...."

**West:** "You weren't so nervous when you came up to see me at my apartment. In fact, you didn't need any encouragement to kiss me."

**McCarthy:** "Did I do that?"

**West:** "You certainly did. I got marks to prove it. And splinters, too."

*Protests poured in from church groups, ostensibly because the show had aired on a Sunday (more likely reason: they objected to West's general "promiscuity"). The sponsor agreed it was "inappropriate," and apologised on the air; Hollywood disavowed both the skit and West; NBC declared she would never appear on radio again.*

## IMMACULATE CONCEPTION

*On Nov. 4, 1874, this article allegedly appeared in* The American
Weekly. *It was quoted in an 1896 book,* Anomalies and Curiosities
of Medicine, *but it's really just an early urban legend.*

"During the fray [between Union and Confederate troops], a
soldier staggered and fell to earth; at the same time a piercing cry
was heard in the house nearby. Examination showed that a bullet
had passed through the scrotum and carried away the left testicle.
The same bullet had apparently penetrated the left side of the
abdomen of a young lady...and become lost in the abdomen.
The daughter suffered an attack of peritonitis, but recovered.

"Two hundred and seventy-eight days after the reception of the
minie ball, she was delivered of a fine boy weighing eight pounds,
to the surprise of herself, and the mortification of her parents and
friends.

"The doctor concluded that...the same ball that had carried
away the testicle of his young friend...had penetrated the ovary
of the young lady and, with some spermatozoa upon it, had
impregnated her. With this conviction, he approached the young
man and told him of the circumstances. The soldier appeared
skeptical at first, but consented to visit the young mother; a
friendship ensued, which soon ripened into a happy marriage."

## NIXONIA

*You think Richard Nixon was "a little" stiff and formal? Here's a
memo he sent to **his wife** on January 25, 1969.*

**To:** Mrs. Nixon
**From:** The President
With regard to RN's room, what would be the most desirable is
an end table like the one on the right side of the bed, which will
accommodate two dictaphones as well as a telephone. RN has
to use one dictaphone for current matters and another for
memoranda for the file, which he will not want transcribed at this
time. In addition, he needs a bigger table on which he can work at
night. The table which is presently in the room does not allow
enough room for him to get his knees under it.

---

Is it the cause or the result? Married men are twice as likely to be obese as single men.

# CARTOON NAMES

*How did our favourite cartoon characters get their
unusual names? Here are a few answers.*

**B**ugs Bunny: Warner Brothers cartoonist Bugs Hardaway
submitted preliminary sketches for "a tall, lanky, mean
rabbit" for a cartoon called "Hare-um Scare-um"—and
someone labelled the drawings "Bugs's Bunny." Hardaway's mean
rabbit was never used—but the name was given to the bunny in
the cartoon "A Wild Hare."

**Casper the Friendly Ghost:** Cartoonist Joe Oriolo's daughter was
afraid of ghosts—so he invented one that wouldn't scare her. "We
were looking for a name that didn't sound threatening," he says.

**Chip 'n' Dale:** Disney animator Jack Hannah was meeting with
colleagues to pick names for his two new chipmunk characters.
His assistant director happened to mention Thomas Chippendale,
the famous furniture designer. "Immediately," Hannah remembers,
"I said 'That's it! That's their names!'"

**Mickey Mouse:** Walt Disney wanted to name the character
*Mortimer* Mouse—but his wife hated the name. "Mother couldn't
explain why the name grated; it just did," Disney's daughter Diane
remembers. Disney wanted the character's name to begin with the
letter M (to go with Mouse)—and eventually decided on Mickey.

**Porky Pig:** According to creator Bob Clampett: "Someone
thought of two puppies named Ham and Ex, and that started me
thinking. So after dinner one night, I came up with Porky and
Beans. I made a drawing of this fat little pig, which I named
Porky, and a little black cat named Beans."

**Rocky & Bullwinkle:** Rocky was picked because it was "just a
square-sounding kid's name"; Bullwinkle was named after
Clarence Bulwinkel, a used-car dealer from Berkeley, California.

**Elmer Fudd:** Inspired by a line in a 1920s song called "Mississippi
Mud." The line: "It's a treat to meet you on the Mississippi Mud—
Uncle Fudd."

**Foghorn Leghorn:** Modelled after Senator Claghorn, a fictional
politician in comedian Fred Alien's radio show.

# MORE LEFT-HANDED FACTS

*Here's more info for lefties. Why devote two more pages to the subject? Okay, okay. We admit it—Uncle John is left-handed.*

**L**EFT-HANDED STATS
• Lefties make up about 5% to 15% of the general population—but 15% to 30% of all patients in mental institutions.
• They're more prone to allergies, insomnia, migranes, schizophrenia and a host of other things than right-handers. They're also three times more likely than righties to become alcoholics. Why? Some scientists speculate the right hemisphere of the brain—the side left-handers use the most—has a lower tolerance for alcohol than the left side. Others think the stress of living in a right-handed world is responsible.
• Lefties are also more likely to be on the extreme ends of the intelligence scale than the general population: a higher proportion of mentally retarded people *and* people with IQs over 140 are lefties.

**LEFT OUT OF SCIENCE**
• For centuries science was biased against southpaws. In the 1870s, for example, Italian psychiatrist Cesare Lombroso published *The Delinquent Male*, in which he asserted that left-handed men were psychological "degenerates" and prone to violence. (A few years later he published *The Delinquent Female*, in which he made the same claims about women.)
• This theory existed even as late as the 1940s, when psychiatrist Abram Blau wrote that left-handedness "is nothing more than an expression of infantile negativism and falls into the same category as...general perverseness." He speculated that lefties didn't get enough attention from their mothers.

**LEFT-HANDED TRADITIONS**
• Why do we throw salt over our left shoulders for good luck? To throw it into the eyes of the Devil, who, of course, lurks behind us to our left.

- In many traditional Muslim cultures, it is extremely impolite to touch food with your left hand. Reason: Muslims eat from communal bowls using their right hand; their left hand is used to perform "unclean" tasks such as wiping themselves after going to the toilet. Hindus have a similar custom: they use their right hand exclusively when touching themselves above the waist, and use only the left hand to touch themselves below the waist.
- What did traditional Christians believe was going to happen on Judgement Day? According to custom, God blesses the saved with his right hand—and casts sinners out of Heaven with his left.
- Other traditional misbeliefs:
  – If you have a ringing in your left ear, someone is cursing you. If your right ear rings, someone is praising you.
  – If your left eye twitches, you're going to see an enemy. If the right twitches, you're going to see a friend.
  – If you get out of bed with your left foot first, you're going to have a bad day.
  – If your left palm itches, you're going to owe someone money. If your right palm does, you're going to make some money.

### LEFT-HANDED MISCELLANY
- Why are lefties sometimes called "southpaws"? In the late 1890s, most baseball parks were laid out with the pitcher facing west and the batter facing east (so the sun wouldn't be in his eyes). That meant left-handed pitchers threw with the arm that faced south. So Chicago sportswriter Charles Seymour began calling them "southpaws."
- Right-handed bias: Some Native American tribes strapped their children's left arms to the mother's cradleboard, which caused most infants to become predominantly right-handed. The Kaffirs of South Africa achieved similar results by burying the left hands of left-handed children in the burning desert sand.
- The next time you see a coat of arms, check to see if it has a stripe running diagonally across it. Most stripes are called *bends* and run from the top left to the bottom right. A stripe that runs from the bottom left to the top right, is called a "left-handed" bend or a *bend sinister*—and means the bearer was a bastard.

# KAY COTTEE—FIRST LADY OF SAIL

*Kay Cottee's first solo sailing trip was at the age of four on a mattress in the swamp near her parents' house. From that inauspicious beginning she went on to break a number of records in solo sailing— records that still stand to this day.*

## MESSING ABOUT IN BOATS

Kay was only two weeks old when she had her first taste of sailing with her father on a yacht. When Kay was nine, her father built his own boat and her whole family would race it on Sydney Harbour. Two years later, her father bought Kay and her three sisters an old Vee Jay sailing dinghy. Since Kay was the only one really interested in sailing, she had it almost exclusively for her own use. She started going out either with friends or alone—the solo sailing bug had started to bite.

Kay left school at 16, was engaged at 17, and married just after she turned 18. After her second anniversary, Kay and her husband bought an old gaff rigger and spent a year refitting the interior. They sold it, bought and refitted another boat, and then another. The building/refitting bug had also bitten Kay.

## LAUNCHING OUT ON HER OWN

Next, Kay joined her sister's charter business. Using a mould, she built her first boat at the age of 27, which she would charter out but her greatest ambition was to sail her own yacht across the oceans. In 1985, Kay purchased the hull and deck of a Cavalier 37 and started fitting it out. Shortly after, the two-handed Trans Tasman race to New Zealand and the solo Trans Tasman race back to Australia was announced. Kay knew she had to enter and approached Marcus Blackmore, the Chairman of Blackmores Laboratories Ltd, to ask his company to sponsor her with a boat. A sailor himself, Marcus told Kay that it would be much better if she sailed her own Cavalier 37 with the backing of his company. There were three small problems—Kay's boat wasn't ready, she didn't know how to navigate, and she had to sail over 500 miles solo in order to qualify.

---

**Australia is the only English-speaking country to have compulsory voting.**

## GOING SOLO

With immense tenacity, early in 1986 Kay Cottee set out on her qualifying sail with her mascot, Teddy the bear. When she returned she entered the Transfield Two-Handed Trans-Tasman race on March 8, 1986, with her friend Linda for crew. Despite the rough weather, they won their division.

On April 5, 1986, the Solo Trans-Tasman race started. This was Kay Cottee's first long solo trip. By the end of the race, the solo sailing bug had truly bitten Kay and she decided to pursue her greatest dream—to be the first woman to sail solo and non stop around the world. Blackmores Laboratories sponsored her again.

Kay Cottee sailed *Blackmores First Lady* from Sydney Harbour on November 29, 1987, and returned on June 5, 1988—189 days, zero hours, and 32 minutes later, having achieved her dream and set a number of records. On that day she became the first woman to:

• Sail solo, non-stop and unassisted around the world from west to east.
• Sail south of the five southernmost capes (Good Hope, Leeuwin, South-East Cape, South-West Cape, and the Horn).
• Complete a solo circumnavigation in record time and speed.
• Spend the longest period alone at sea and cover a record distance.

But wait, there's more! Kay Cottee also:

• Raised single-handed, more than one million dollars for the Reverend Ted Noffs' Life Education Program.
• Was named the 1988 Bicentennial Australian of the Year and became an Officer of the Order of Australia.
• Is the first Australian and second-only recipient of the Cutty Sark Medal presented by the Duke of Edinburgh.
• Was made a Paul Harris Fellow by Rotary International.
• Became an honorary international Zontian—a life member of the Cruising Yacht Club of Australia.
• Was made Honorary Life Member of the Royal Prince Alfred Yacht Club.

Where is Kay Cottee now? Today she lives on the NSW North Coast where she has a business building luxury yachts. With her love of the sea and of sailing she showed the world what a determined Australian woman could achieve.

---

Bob Hawke once held the world beer-drinking record for sculling 1.5 litres of beer in 11 seconds.

# MORE STRANGE LAWSUITS

*More bizarre doings in the halls of justice, from news reports.*

**THE PLAINTIFF:** James Hooper, a 25-year-old student at Oklahoma State University.

**THE DEFENDANT:** The Pizza Shuttle, a Stillwater, Oklahoma, pizza restaurant.

**THE LAWSUIT:** Hooper ordered an "extra cheese, pepperoni, sausage, black olive and mushroom pizza." Instead, he said, the Pizza Shuttle delivered "a pizza with something green on it, maybe peppers." He sued the restaurant for $7.00 in damages ($5.50 for the pizza and $1.50 for the delivery boy's tip).

**VERDICT:** The court found in favour of the Pizza Shuttle—and ordered Hooper to pay $57 in court costs.

**THE PLAINTIFF:** Widow of Walter Hughes, who died in 1991.

**THE DEFENDANTS:** McVicker's Chapel on the Hill and Kevin Robinson, Hughes's son-in-law and former director of the Longview, Washington, funeral home.

**THE LAWSUIT:** Mrs. Hughes sued the funeral home when she learned that it had buried her husband without his favourite cowboy hat.

**VERDICT:** She was awarded $101,000 in damages.

**THE PLAINTIFF:** Seven patrons of Charley Brown's, a Concord, California, restaurant.

**THE DEFENDANT:** The restaurant.

**THE LAWSUIT:** In 1992, the restaurant hired an actor to stage a mock robbery as part of a dinner show called "The Suspect's Dinner Theatre." The actor, dressed as a masked gunman, burst into the restaurant shouting "All you m——, hit the floor!" Dinner guests, thinking the robbery was real, cowered under their tables while the man shouted threats and fired several blank rounds from his .45-calibre pistol. (One patron, an investigator with the county district attorney's office, fought with the gunman until restaurant employees told him the robbery was part of the

---

Pet lovers: 21% of cat owners and 27% of dog owners include their pets in their wills.

show.) "When the hostess said it was all just an episode of Mystery Theatre," another diner told reporters, "I said, 'Mystery Theatre, my a—. You're going to hear from my lawyer.'" He and six others sued the restaurant, claiming assault and intentional infliction of emotional distress.

**VERDICT:** The restaurant offered to settle the case by paying $3,000 to each of the plaintiffs—and later went out of business.

**THE PLAINTIFF:** Andrea Pizzo, a 23-year-old former University of Maine student.
**THE DEFENDANT:** The University of Maine.
**THE LAWSUIT:** Apparently, Pizzo was attending a class in livestock management one afternoon in 1991, when a cow attacked her. (It butted her into a fence.) She sued, claiming the school "should have known that the heifer had a personality problem."
**VERDICT:** Unknown.

**THE PLAINTIFF:** William and Tonya P., who booked a room at a Michigan Holiday Inn during their honeymoon in 1992.
**THE DEFENDANT:** The Holiday Inn.
**THE LAWSUIT:** William and Tonya claim that a hotel employee walked into their room on their wedding night while they were having sex. They filed a $10,000 lawsuit against the hotel, claiming the unannounced visit ruined their sex life. Holiday Inn does not dispute the charge but says they should have hung up a "Do Not Disturb" sign.
**VERDICT:** Unknown.

**THE PLAINTIFF:** John M., a 50-year-old Philadelphia teacher.
**THE DEFENDANT:** His wife, Maryann K., a 46-year-old receptionist.
**THE LAWSUIT:** One day after her divorce from John became final, Ms. K. turned in a lottery ticket that was about to expire and won $10.2 million. Her lawyer claims that "Lady Luck" led her to find the ticket and turn it in two weeks before it expired— but Mr. M. thinks she deliberately waited until after the divorce was finalised to turn it in. He sued to get his share.
**VERDICT:** Pending.

---

**Clear priorities:** More than 50% of teenage boys say they'd "rather be rich than smart."

# AUNT LENNA'S PUZZLES

*More conversations with my favourite aunt.*
*Answers are on page 486.*

## MONEY MINDED

My Aunt Lenna is a little unreliable when it comes to money. So I wasn't surprised when she came to me and asked, "Nephew, why are 1993 dollar bills worth more than 1992 dollar bills?"

"Aunt Lenna, don't be silly, they—"

"Tut, tut, Nephew. Think before you answer."

*What's the answer to her question?*

## TRAIN OF THOUGHT

Aunt Lenna and I went down to the train station to pick up a friend. On the way, she came up with a little puzzle for me.

"Let's say that two sets of train tracks run right alongside one another...until they get to a narrow tunnel. Both tracks won't fit, so they merge into one track for the whole length of the tunnel... then go back to being parallel tracks. One morning a train goes into the tunnel from the east end...and another goes into the tunnel from the west end. They're travelling as fast as they can go, in opposite directions, but they don't crash. Can you tell me why not?"

"Really, Aunt Lenna. I know I'm not the brightest guy in the world, but even I can figure this one out."

*What's the story?*

## GREETINGS

"What have you got there, Aunt Lenna?"

"Oh, it's just the card I'm sending this year."

"Let's see." I looked at the card. It read:

ABCDEFGHIJKMNOPQRSTUVWXYZ

"Very cute, Aunt Lenna."

*What did it say?*

---

European country with the most auto-related fatalities: Portugal. Great Britain has the least.

## THE BLACK STONES

Aunt Lenna had a puzzle for me:

"Once there was a beautiful woman whose family owed money to an evil moneylender. 'I'll give you a chance to rid yourself of the debt,' the evil guy told her. 'How?' 'I'll put two stones in this bag,' he said—'one white, one black. You reach in and take one. If you pick the white one, your debt is wiped out. If you pick the black one, you marry me.' "

"I suppose he laughed maniacally at that point."

"Why, yes, how did you know? Where was I? Oh, yes—the girl agreed, and watched as the man put two stones in the bag. But she realised he had put two black stones in, and there was no chance of picking a white stone. How could she win the bet?"

*How did she win?*

## QUICK CUT

Aunt Lenna loves to bake. One day she was busy rolling out dough for a cake when she turned to me and said, "Nephew, I've got a little puzzle for you. How is it possible to cut a cake into eight equal parts...with just three straight cuts with a knife?"

I thought for a minute. "It's not."

"Oh yes it is. Think about it awhile."

*How can it be done?*

## TIME TO GO

Aunt Lenna was reminiscing. "When I was a teenager, there was a boy who kept coming around, asking me to the movies and such. I didn't want to hurt his feelings, but finally one day, I had to do something. So I asked him if he'd heard about the nine O's. He said no, so I drew nine O's, like this: O O O O O O O O O.

Then I added five vertical lines to the Os...and he got the message and stopped bothering me."

*What did Aunt Lenna do with the lines?*

---

How about you? 64% of women sleep on the left side of the bed.

# Q & A:
# ASK THE EXPERTS

*More random questions…and answers from leading trivia experts.*

## VISIONARIES

**Q:** *Can animals see in colour?*
**A:** "Apes and some monkeys [see] the full spectrum of colour, as may some fish and birds. But most mammals see colour only as shades of grey." (From *The Book of Answers*, by Barbara Berliner)

## YOURS, MINE, AND HOURS

**Q:** *Why are there 24 hours in a day?*
**A:** "To the ancients, 12 was a mystical number. It could be evenly divided by 2, 3, 4, and 6 (that's one of the reasons we still use dozens today). Twenty-four hours is made up of two 12s—12 hours before noon, and 12 hours after." (From *Know It All!*, by Ed Zotti)

## GR-R-R

**Q:** *Why does your stomach rumble when you're hungry?*
**A:** "Every 75–115 minutes, your stomach's muscles contract. When no food is present, their rhythm is a wave-like stretching and contracting that moulds the air, mostly digestive gases, in the stomach cavity. No one understands exactly why this makes the tummy-rumble noise, but it surely does." (From *Why Can't You Tickle Yourself?* by Ingrid Johnson)

## FAR A-FIELDS

**Q:** *Did W.C. Fields actually say, "Anyone who hates dogs and children can't be all bad?"*
**A:** Nope, it was Leo Rosten.

## GOLD DISC

**Q:** *What was the first gold record?*
**A:** Glenn Miller got it for "Chattanooga Choo-Choo." The first certified million-selling album was the soundtrack from *Oklahoma*.

It took 1,700 years to complete the Great Wall of China.

## ROCKIN' ROBIN
**Q:** *Why do birds sing?*
**A:** No, it's not because they're happy. "The vast majority of bird songs are produced by males and break down to two kinds: first, a call from male to male, proclaiming territory and warning other males away, and second, a call to females, advertising the singer's maleness...if he's not already committed." (From *Do Elephants Swim?*, compiled by Robert M. Jones)

## OVER THE HUMP
**Q:** *How long can a camel go without water?*
**A:** "A camel can go for 17 days without drinking any water.... There is a secret to this: the camel carries a great deal of fat in its hump and has the ability to manufacture water out of this hump by oxidation. This is not to say that the camel doesn't get thirsty. When it gets the chance to drink after a long drought, it can suck down 114 litres (25 gallons) of water." (From *Science Trivia*, by Charles Cazeau)

## BOXED RAISINS
**Q:** *Why don't the raisins in Raisin Bran cereal fall to the bottom of the box?*
**A:** "Raisins are added to boxes only after more than half of the cereal has already been packed. The cereal thus has a chance to settle and condense. During average shipping conditions, boxes get jostled a bit...so the raisins actually sift and become evenly distributed throughout the box." (From *Why Do Clocks Run Clockwise, and Other Imponderables*, by David Feldman)

## CHOCOLATE
**Q:** *Who brought chocolate from the New World to Europe?*
**A:** When the Spanish conquistador Hernan Cortés wrote to Emperor Charles V of Spain from the New World, he described a "divine drink...which builds up resistance and fights fatigue." Cortés was speaking of *chocolatl*, a drink the Aztecs brewed from the native *cacao* bean, which was valued so highly that it was used as currency. He brought some home to Spain and it became popular instantly.

# EVERYDAY PHRASES

*More origins of common phrases.*

## TOO MANY IRONS IN THE FIRE
**Meaning:** Working on too many projects at once.
**Origin:** "Refers to the blacksmith's forge, where if the smith had too many irons heating in the fire at the same time he couldn't do his job properly, as he was unable to use them all before some had cooled off." (From *Everyday Phrases*, by Neil Ewart)

## THE NAKED TRUTH
**Meaning:** The absolute truth.
**Origin:** Comes from this old fable: "Truth and Falsehood went swimming. Falsehood stole the clothes that Truth had left on the river bank, but Truth refused to wear Falsehood's clothes and went naked." (From *Now I Get It!*, by Douglas Ottati)

## TO GIVE SOMEONE THE COLD SHOULDER
**Meaning:** Reject, or act unfriendly toward, someone.
**Origin:** Actually refers to food. In England, a welcome or important visitor would be served a delicious hot meal. A guest "who had outstayed his welcome, or an ordinary traveller" would get a cold shoulder of mutton. (From *Rejected!* by Steve Gorlick)

## READ SOMEONE THE RIOT ACT
**Meaning:** Deliver an ultimatum.
**Origin:** Comes from an actual Riot Act, passed by the British Parliament in 1714, that made it unlawful for a dozen or more people to gather for "riotous or illegal purposes." An authority would literally stand up and read out the terms of the Act, so that the rioters knew what law they were breaking: "Our Sovereign Lord the King chargeth and commandeth all persons assembled immediately to disperse themselves and peacefully to depart to their habitations or to their lawful business." If the crowd didn't disperse, they were arrested. (From *Why Do We Say It?*, by Nigel Rees)

---

Edgar Allen Poe's *The Murders in the Rue Morgue* was the first detective story ever written.

## PASS THE BUCK
**Meaning:** Blame someone else; avoid accepting responsibility.
**Origin:** "The original buck was a buckhorn knife passed around the table in certain card games. It was placed in front of the player whose turn it was to deal the cards and see that the stakes for all the players were placed in the pool." Someone who "passed the buck" literally passed that responsibility to the person next to him. (From *Everyday Phrases*, by Neil Ewart)

## A BITTER PILL TO SWALLOW
**Meaning:** An experience that's difficult or painful to accept.
**Origin:** Refers to taking medicine in the time before doctors had any way to make pills more palatable. "The bark of a New World tree, the cinchona, was effective in fighting malaria. But the quinine it contains is extremely bitter. Widely employed in the era before medications were coated, cinchona pellets caused any disagreeable thing to be termed a bitter pill to swallow." (From *Why You Say It*, by Webb Garris)

## HE'S TIED TO HER APRON STRINGS
**Meaning:** A man is dominated by his wife.
**Origin:** In England several hundred years ago, if a man married a woman with property, he didn't get title to it, but could use it while she was alive. This was popularly called *apron-string* tenure. A man tied to his wife's apron strings was in no position to argue; hence, the phrase came to stand for any abnormal submission to a wife or mother." (From *I've Got Goose Pimples*, by Marvin Vanoni)

\*   \*   \*   \*

### Credit Where Credit Is Due
The name "credit card" was coined in 1888 by futurist author Edward Bellamy, who wrote a fictional account of a young man who wakes up in the year 2000 and discovers that cash has been dumped in favour of "a credit corresponding to his share of the annual product of the nation…and a credit card is issued to him with which he procures at the public storehouses…whatever he desires, whenever he desires it." Sixty years later, his vision (in slightly altered form) came true.

The first hot aeroplane meals were served on a Pan Am flight in 1935.

# AUSSIE JOKES

*There is nothing better than a good belly laugh to start the day!
Aussie jokes often mock others (particularly New Zealanders),
but we are also very good at laughing at ourselves.*

A Texas farmer goes to Australia for a vacation. There, he meets an Aussie farmer and gets talking. The Aussie shows off his big wheat field and the Texan says, "You call that a wheat field? We have wheat fields that are at least twice as large." Then they walk around the farm a little, and the Aussie shows off his herd of cattle. The Texan immediately says, "We have longhorns that are at least twice as large as your cows." The conversation has, meanwhile, almost died when the Texan sees a herd of kangaroos hopping through the field. He asks, "And what are those?" The Aussie replies with an incredulous look, "Don't you have any grasshoppers in Texas?"

It is a dark and stormy night on Saturday, 2 September, in Melbourne.

A guy walks into the main bar of a central city hotel with a rare jet-black dachshund under his arm. The dog is kitted out entirely in black and has a black patch over his right eye. "Could you turn on the telly please mate?" the customer asks the barman. "Me little friend here is a mad one-eyed All Black supporter and we wanna see the second round of the Bledisloe."

"Huh? The Bledisloe? What's that?" asks the barman. (Well, he is a Melbourne barman.) "Never mind just stick it on channel Seven!" says the customer, who orders a Guinness and pours some into a black ashtray for his rugby-mad, black-clad canine. During the first few minutes of the match Andrew Mehrtens kicks a penalty goal from mid field and the black-clad dog goes ballistic, howling, turning cartwheels, punching holes in the stratosphere and executing precision pelvic thrusts (which have a high degree of difficulty when you're a dachshund).

"Shit," says the barman. "That's awesome! What does he do when they win?"

"Dunno," says the customer. "Only 'ad him four years."

An Englishman, an Irishman, an Australian and a New Zealander were in a plane, getting ready to make their first parachute jump. The Englishman's exit was spectacular—he leapt out of the plane with the cry, "I am doing this for my country…" The Irishman leapt out immediately afterwards, calling out the same words. Then the Australian ripped the parachute off the New Zealander, pushed him out of the plane and cried, "I'm doing this for my country…"

There's an old swaggy walking down a dusty outback road. A cocky pulls up in an old beat-up ute and says, "Would you like a lift, mate?" The swaggy replies, "No way! You can open and close your own bloody gates."

Q: What's the definition of bad luck?
A: Sitting in Afghanistan holding your return ticket with Ansett, your travel insurance through HIH, and trying to call out on your One.Tel mobile.

Q: What's a barbecue?
A: A line of people waiting for a haircut.

Q: What do you call a field full of Australians?
A: A vacant lot.

A blonde is terribly overweight so her doctor puts her on a diet. "I want you to eat regularly for two days, then skip a day, and repeat this procedure for two weeks. The next time I see you, you'll have lost at least three kilograms."

When the blonde returns, she's lost nearly ten kilograms. "That's amazing!" the doctor says. "Did you follow my instructions?"

The blonde nods. "I'll tell you though, I thought I was going to die on that third day."

"From hunger, you mean?"

"No, from skipping."

Nearly 40% of the people who get plastic surgery are between 35 and 55 years old.

# CHILDHOOD WISDOM

*Quotes from classic children's books.*

We are all made of the same stuff, remember, we of the Jungle, and you of the City. The same substance composes us—the tree overhead, the stone beneath us, the bird, the beast, the star—we are all one, all moving to the same end....Bird and beast and stone and star—we are all one, all one—Child and serpent, star and stone—all one."

**—The Hamadryad, *Mary Poppins***

"If I can fool a bug, I can fool a man. People are not as smart as bugs."

**—Charlotte, *Charlotte's Web***

"Money is a nuisance. We'd all be much better off if it had never been invented. What does money matter, as long as we all are happy?"

**—Dr. Doolittle, *Dr. Doolittle***

"Winter will pass, the days will lengthen, the ice will melt in the pasture pond. The song sparrow will return and sing, the frogs will awake, the warm wind will blow again. All these sights and sounds and smells will be yours to enjoy, Wilbur—this lovely world, these precious days."

**—Charlotte, *Charlotte's Web***

"Don't be angry after you've been afraid. That's the worst kind of cowardice."

**—Billy the Troophorse, *The Jungle Book***

"Time flies, and one begins to grow old. This autumn I'll be ten, and then I guess I'll have seen my best days."

**—Pippi Longstocking, *Pippi Goes on Board***

# LOOK IT UP!

*Every bathroom reader knows the value of a good record book, or
a volume of quotes, in a pinch. Here are the stories of the originals.*

**B**ARTLETT'S FAMILIAR QUOTATIONS.
John Bartlett was 16 years old when he left school in 1836
and got a job as a clerk at the University Bookstore across
the street from Harvard.

Over the next 13 years he saved enough money to buy the
store—and in that time managed to read nearly every book it
contained. He became so well-known as a "quotation freak" that
whenever someone asked where a familiar saying came from, or
needed a quote to dress up a term paper, the answer would be,
"Ask John Bartlett." By the mid-1850s, his reputation had grown
beyond even his own remarkable abilities; no longer able to recite
everything from memory, he began writing things down.

In 1855 he printed up 1,000 copies of his 258-page list of quotes,
and began selling them at the store. "Should this be favourably
received," he wrote in the preface, "endeavours will be made to
make it more worthy of the public in a future edition." Sixteen
editions and nearly 140 years later, *Bartlett's Familiar Quotations* is
the most frequently consulted reference work of its kind.

## THE GUINNESS BOOK OF WORLD RECORDS.
In 1954 Sir Hugh Beaver, an avid sportsman and managing
director of Arthur Guinness, Son and Company (brewers of
Guinness Stout beer), shot at some game birds in the Irish
countryside...but they all got away. Looking for an excuse, he
exclaimed that he'd missed because the breed of birds—plovers—
were "the fastest game bird we've got" in the British Isles. But
were they? He had no idea, and no reference he consulted could
tell him.

He never found out for sure about the plovers. But the
experience *did* give him the idea for a book of world records.
He commissioned two researchers, Norris and Ross McWhirter, to
write it for Guinness. Four months later, they were finished, and
four months after that the first *Guinness Book of World Records* was
#1 on the British best-seller list.

---

Some names rejected for Disney's seven dwarfs: Gaspy, Doleful, Awful, Gabby, and Helpful.

# A HANDY GUIDE TO THE END OF THE WORLD (Part II)

*Here are more "end of time" predictions—this time*
*from three Native American sources.*
*Part I is on page 64.*

## HOPI

**Background:** A Pueblo tribe that today occupies several mesa villages in northeast Arizona. Their stories are passed on orally. Frankly, if they are really from ancient times, and not "backdated" by someone to make them sound more accurate, they're pretty amazing.

**Signs the End Is Near:** According to many Hopi tribal elders (such as Dan Evehama, Thomas Banyacya, and Martin Gashwaseoma), the coming of "white-skinned men" and "a strange beast, like a buffalo but with great long horns" that would "overrun the land" (cattle) were predicted as precursors to the end of time. They also say their prophecies include:

• "The land will be crossed by snakes of iron and rivers of stone. The land shall be criss-crossed by a giant spider's web. Seas will turn black."

• "A great dwelling-place in the heavens shall fall with a great crash. It will appear as a blue star. The world will rock to and fro."

• "The white man will battle people in other lands, with those who possess the first light of wisdom. Terrible will be the result. There will be many columns of smoke in the deserts. These are the signs that great destruction is here."

**When the World Ends:** Many will die, but those "who understand the prophecies…and stay and live in the places of my people (Hopi) shall also be safe."

• Pahana, the True White Brother will return to plant the seeds of wisdom in people's hearts and usher in the dawn of the Fifth World.

**For More On the Hopi:** www.timesoft.com/hopi/

---

## MAYANS

**Background:** An ancient Meso-American civilisation with a highly developed, extraordinarily accurate system of mathematics and astronomy. Many people think the Mayan calendar ends at around 2012 or 2013, and assume that's the scheduled date for the end of the world.

**Signs the End Is Near:** According to *The Mayan Prophecies*, the earth will be destroyed by environmental disasters—earthquakes, tidal waves, you name it. Civilisation will collapse; then Kulkulcan (Quetzalcoatl)—a feathered serpent deity who represents the forces of good and light—will arrive.

**When the World Ends:** Again, according to *The Mayan Prophecies:* "The end of artificial time signals…the return to natural time, a time in harmony with the Earth and with the natural cycles….It holds within it the potential to reinstate a balanced, positive love and unity."

**For More On the Mayans:** www.halfmoon.org/

## SIOUX

**Background:** A confederation of several Native American Plains tribes. They also have an oral tradition.

**Signs the End Is Near:** According to an Ogalala (Sioux) medicine man, a "darkness descends over the tribe…the world is out of balance. There are floods, fires and earthquakes. There is a great drought." A White Buffalo will be born and the White Buffalo Calf Woman (according to legend, a representative of the spirit world) will return.

**When the World Ends:** White Buffalo Calf Woman will purify the world. "She will bring back harmony again, and balance, spiritually."

**Note:** A white buffalo was born in 1994…and another in 1995. Many tribal elders feel these are clear signs that their prophecy is being fulfilled. "Yes indeed, it is a sign," says one. "The important ones are the last two. These were created with the influence of the Masters."

**For More On the Sioux:** www.blackhills-info.com/lakota_sioux/

# MORE PEOPLE-WATCHING

*Here are more findings about human behaviour, gleaned from
Bernard Asbell's* The Book of You and People Watching:
Downtown Los Angeles, *by Bob Herman.*

**O**N MARRIAGE...
• According to a University of Michigan researcher,
if you think you're starting to look like your spouse, you
might be right.
• His study went something like this: Wedding photos of couples
that were now in their 50s and 60s were collected, along with
current pictures of the same couples. Students were then asked
to match pictures of individuals with pictures of their spouses.
• In the younger wedding pictures, students weren't able to
match the couples any better than chance. However, with the
contemporary pictures, the students did significantly better.
• Conclusion: Apparently, married individuals are good at
mimicking their partners. This can produce similar laugh or frown
lines around the eyes and mouth as we age, changing our
expressions and making us appear more like our spouses.

**Another hint about what's going on in your marriage:** Research
shows that the less comfortable you are with your spouse, the more
you'll look at one another. If you're comfortable in your marriage,
you'll talk more frequently without glancing at one another. Why?
Apparently, people who aren't relaxed in their marriage tend to
monitor their spouses for reactions to what they say and do.

## ON JOGGING...
• Research tells us that if you're a guy out running for exercise,
and you pass a woman—any woman—you'll actually speed up
significantly as you pass her...*if* she's facing your direction. Even
if she's buried in a book, or completely preoccupied and looking
through you, your performance will increase as you pass.
• But if her back's towards you, you won't change your pace.

## ON PORNOGRAPHY...
- Whether you're male or female, looking at *Playboy*, *Penthouse*, or similar magazines won't improve your sex life.
- Studies find that after eyeing nude photos, people of *both* sexes will rate their partners as less sexually appealing.
- According to research, people also report that they feel less in love with their partners after reading a nudie rag.

## ON LOITERING...
- Loitering's not as easy to do as it may seem—security is pretty tight in some places. But people-watching has proven time and again that some people get away with it more often than others.
- One trick—if you carry something, or if you're standing in an entranceway, you're less likely to be hassled by authorities.
- You're also less likely to attract attention if you're holding an umbrella or a briefcase rather than standing around empty-handed. Reading, working on something, or at least pretending to do either, while using a library or park bench will buy you a lot more resting time than if you simply reclined for a nap in the same spot.

## ON "PERSONAL SPACE"...
- According to Asbell's *The Book of You*, personal space can be a vertical issue: "If you observe a stranger in a room gradually moving closer to you, you'll show symptoms of alertness or anxiety sooner if the ceiling is low than if it's high."
- When the "room" is an elevator, however, there are special rules:
    - If you're male, you'll stand closer to a female in an elevator than to another man.
    - If you're female, either a man or woman stranger can stand close to you in an elevator, but they stand a better chance of squeezing in if they're to your sides, than in front of you.
    - Whether male or female, if a stranger in an elevator smiles at you, you're much more likely to stand closer than if they don't smile.

**The War Between the Sexes continues:** You have a 5-to-1 chance of winning the elbow-rest between the seats on an aeroplane if you're male.

**Eighty percent of adults say they "believe in an afterlife."**

# THE MONA LISA

*It's the most famous painting in the world—even Uncle John has heard of it. But what else do you know about this mysterious lady?*

**B**ACKGROUND. Sometime between 1501 and 1506—no one is sure exactly when—Leonardo da Vinci, the great Renaissance artist, scientist, and thinker, painted his masterpiece *La Joconde*, better known as the Mona Lisa. Hardly anything is known about the painting. Da Vinci kept extensive records on many of his *other* paintings, but none on the Mona Lisa. He never once mentioned it in any of his notebooks, and never made any preliminary studies of it.

However, historians believe the painting was one of Leonardo's favourites. Unlike most of his other paintings, which he painted on commission and turned over to their owners as soon as they were finished, da Vinci kept the Mona Lisa for more than 10 years—and still had it in his possession when he died in 1519.

## WHO'S THAT GIRL?

*No one knows who really modelled for the Mona Lisa—but some of the popular candidates are:*

• **Mona Lisa Gherardini**, wife of Francesco del Giocondo, a Florentine silk merchant. After da Vinci's death, Gherardini was so widely believed to have been the model for the painting that it was named after her. But art historians now doubt she was the model, because the source of this rumour was Giorgio Vasari, da Vinci's biographer—who never even saw the painting in person.

• **Another noblewoman** da Vinci knew—or perhaps a composite painting of two or more of them.

• **No one.** Some historians think the painting was a *finzione* or "feigning"—a fictional woman not based on any particular person.

• **Himself.** The painting is a feminine self-portrait. This theory is strange but surprisingly plausible. In 1987, computer scientists at AT&T Bell Laboratories took da Vinci's 1518 *Self-Portrait*, reversed the image (it faces right, not left like the Mona Lisa), enlarged it to the same scale, and juxtaposed it against the Mona Lisa, the similarities were too striking to be accidental...or so they say.

## MONA LISA FACTS

- The Mona Lisa is considered one of the most important paintings of the Renaissance period—but King Francis I of France, who took possession of the painting after da Vinci died, hung it in the palace bathroom.
- Napoleon, on the other hand, was a big fan of the painting; he called it "The Sphinx of the Occident" and kept it in his bedroom.
- Why is Mona Lisa wearing such a strange smile? Some art historians suspect that this most famous feature may actually be the work of clumsy restorers who tried to touch up the painting centuries ago. Da Vinci may have intended her to wear a much more ordinary expression. Dozens of other theories have been proposed to explain the strange grin, including that Mona Lisa has just lost a child, has asthma or bad teeth, or is really a young man. Sigmund Freud theorised that da Vinci painted the smile that way because it reminded him of his mother.
- Mona Lisa may be "in the family way." According to writer Seymour Reit, "the lady is definitely pregnant, as shown by the slightly swollen hands and face, and her 'self-satisfied' expression." Other historians disagree—they think that Mona Lisa is just chubby.

## THE THEFT

- According to a 1952 Paris study, there are at least 72 excellent 16th- and 17th-century replicas and reproductions of the Mona Lisa in existence—leading conspiracy theorists to speculate that the painting in the Louvre is itself a replica.
- One of the most interesting forgery theories has to do with a theft of the painting that occurred in 1911. On August 21 of that year, the Mona Lisa vanished from the Louvre in what was probably the biggest art heist of the century. French authorities conducted a massive investigation, but were unable to locate the painting. Two years later, an Italian carpenter named Vincenzo Perugia was caught trying to sell the masterpiece to an Italian museum.

The official story is that Perugia wanted to return the work to Italy, da Vinci's (and his) birthplace. But Seymour Reit, author of *The Day They Stole The Mona Lisa*, theorises that the plot was the work of Marqués Eduardo de Valfierno, a nobleman who made his living selling forged masterpieces to unsuspecting millionaires. He wanted to do the same with the Mona Lisa—but knew that no one would buy a forgery of such a famous painting unless the original were stolen from the Louvre first. So de Valfierno paid a forger to paint half a dozen fakes, and then hired Perugia to steal the real Mona Lisa.

Reit argues that de Valfierno had no plans for the original masterpiece—he didn't want to sell it or even own it himself—and was only interested in selling his forgeries. He never even bothered to collect the original from Perugia, who hid it in the false bottom of a dirty steamer trunk for more than two years waiting for de Valfierno to come and get it. But he never did, so Perugia finally gave up and tried to sell the Mona Lisa to an Italian museum. As soon as he handed over the painting, he was arrested and the painting was returned to France. Perugia was tried and convicted, but spent only 7 months in prison for his crime. De Valfierno was never tried.

## PROTECTING THE PAINTING
• The Mona Lisa isn't painted on canvas—it's painted on a wood panel made from poplar. This makes it extremely fragile, since changes in the moisture content of the wood can cause it to expand and shrink, which cracks the paint.
• Because of this, the Louvre goes to great lengths to protect the Mona Lisa from the elements—and from vandals. Since 1974, the painting has been stored in a bulletproof, climate-controlled box called a *vitrine* that keeps the painting permanently at 68° Fahrenheit and at 50–55% humidity.
• Once a year, the painting is removed from its protective case and given a checkup. The process takes about an hour and requires almost 30 curators, restorers, laboratory technicians, and maintenance workers.
• Despite nearly 500 years of accumulated dust, dirt, and grime, the risks associated with cleaning the masterpiece are so great that the museum refuses to do it—even though the filth has changed the appearance of the painting dramatically. Pierre Rosenberg, the Louvre's curator, says: "If we saw the Mona Lisa as da Vinci painted it, we would not recognise it….Da Vinci actually painted with bright, vivid colours, not the subdued tones that are visible today."

But he's adamant about leaving the painting in its present state. "The Mona Lisa is such a sacrosanct image that to touch it would create a national scandal."

---

The five most popular garden veggies: tomatoes, capsicums, onions, cucumbers, beans.

# LAWRENCE DOWN UNDER

*Kangaroo jumps from D.H. Lawrence's few weeks in Australia.*

## WESTERN AUSTRALIA

It's May, 1922, in the dusty, rocky, rural quiet of the Darlington area above Perth in Western Australia. Winter is beginning to bite. It's drizzling and chilly. David Herbert Lawrence, the British novelist, poet and painter, famed for the smouldering sexy bits in *Women in Love* and *The Rainbow*, and his excitable German-born wife, Frieda, are having one of their many daily rows. They're both so loud, angry and passionate that their quarrels are pretty public.

Lawrence and Frieda arrived at Freemantle on 4 May, 1922, after sailing south through the Indian Ocean from Ceylon (now Sri Lanka). "We're going to Australia," he wrote in a letter a week earlier while still aboard the ship. "Heaven knows why: because it will be cooler, and the sea is wide...Don't know what we'll do in Australia—don't care."

## MAN IN LOVE

Lawrence was born in 1885 into a dysfunctional coalmining family near Nottingham, in the damp smoky midlands of Britain. Assisted by his overbearing mother, he managed to steer clear of life at the coalface. Instead he took an office job and eventually trained for teaching and started scribbling. It was while he was studying part-time at Nottingham University that he met Frieda, the love of his life. But there were problems. She was a mother of two children, *and* she was married to Lawrence's professor. Her elopement with Lawrence was the scandal of the times. And after abandoning her children, Frieda wasn't permitted to see them again until they were grown up.

Nothing was straightforward for Mr and the new Mrs Lawrence. Her German background made her unwelcome in Britain during the 1914–18 war. Although his books sold well from *The White Peacock* in 1911 onwards, he was constantly harried for obscenity.

---

Peter Finch and Geoffrey Rush are the only Australians to have won Academy Awards for Best Actor.

There were health difficulties, too. Lawrence was a life-long tuberculosis sufferer, although it didn't kill him until 1930. In spite of the obsession with sexuality in his writing, Lawrence was impotent for much of his life and Frieda entertained lots of lovers. No wonder there were raised voices!

## A PAIR OF NOMADS

They quit Britain in 1919 and quarrelled their way round the world—the Americas, Mexico, Europe, Ceylon, Australia—for the remainder of Lawrence's life, staying at places cheaply rented or lent by friends. Lawrence earned a reasonable income from writing and his austere tastes didn't cost much—no smoking, very little alcohol and plain food.

On reaching Australia they stayed for two days in sedate Perth before settling down for a fortnight in the Darlington region. All the time he watched people, observed Australian life and made notes. Then it was off to New South Wales for three months.

## AUSTRALIAN LEGACY

At Thirroul on the south coast, he and Frieda rented "an awfully nice bungalow with one big room and three small bedrooms, a kitchen and wash-house, a plot of grass, and a low bushy cliff, hardly more than a bank, and the sand and the sea." It only costs 30 shillings a week—the equivalent of $3 in today's money.

"Frieda loves it here," he told a friend in a letter and it was certainly conducive to writing. Lawrence began writing his eighth novel, *Kangaroo*, at his usual breakneck speed, completing the first draft in 45 days.

"Australia has a marvellous sky and air and blue clarity and a hoary sort of land beneath it, like a sleeping princess on whom the dust of ages has settled. Wonder if she'll ever get up," he writes in a letter when he can tear himself away from his work in progress.

Lawrence and Frieda sailed away in August 1922. Destination: San Francisco via Wellington and Tahiti. "I'll go round it once more—the world—and if I ever get back here I'll stay," he wrote. He didn't. He died in the south of France eight years later aged only 45. But there's a "He was here" plaque at Circular Quay in Sydney to commemorate D.H.L.'s four months in Oz.

# WHAT IS HYPNOTISM?

*You are getting sleepy...sleepy...you will do anything we tell you. Now listen carefully: When you leave the bathroom, you will experience an irresistible urge to give everyone you know copies of Uncle John's Great Big Australian Bathroom Reader. Do you understand? Good. When you emerge from the bathroom, you won't remember anything we've said. Now resume reading.*

**B**ACKGROUND. The history of hypnotism—drawing someone into an "altered state of consciousness" in which they are more susceptible to suggestion than when fully conscious—dates back thousands of years and is as old as sorcery, medicine, and witchcraft. The first person in modern times to study it was Franz Mesmer, an 18th-century Viennese physician. In 1775 he devised the theory that a person could transmit "universal forces," known as *animal magnetism*, to other people.

Critics derisively named this practice "Mesmerism," and chased him out of Vienna for practising witchcraft. He then resettled in Paris, where a royal commission dismissed Mesmerism's "cures" as the product of his patients' imaginations.

Viewed as a crackpot science by the entire medical establishment, mesmerism might have died out, except for one thing: anaesthesia hadn't been invented yet, and physicians were desperately looking for something to kill pain during surgical procedures. Mesmer himself had performed surgery using mesmerism as anaesthesia as early as 1778, and other doctors soon began trying it.

One of the most successful was John Elliotson, a London surgeon who used it successfully on thousands of patients—but at great personal cost: he was booted out of his professorship and became a laughingstock of English medical society. John Elsdaile, a medical officer with the East India Company, had better luck— he performed hundreds of operations, including amputations, "painlessly and with few fatalities" using mesmerism. At about the same time, James Braid, another English physician experimenting with the procedure renamed it "hypnosis," after Hypnos, the Greco-Roman god of sleep.

In the 1880s Sigmund Freud visited France and decided to experiment with hypnosis in the fledgling field of psychology. He used it to treat neurotic disorders by helping patients remember events in their past that they had either forgotten or repressed. But as he developed his method of psychoanalysis, he lost interest in hypnosis and eventually dumped it entirely.

Despite Freud's rejection, hypnotism continued to grow in popularity. By the mid-1950s the British and American Medical Associations had approved its use. Although hypnotism is seldom used as an anaesthetic in surgery today—except in combination with painkilling drugs—it is widely used to prepare patients for anaesthesia, ease the pain of childbirth, lower blood pressure, combat headaches, ease the fear associated with dental appointments, and has a variety of other applications. More than 15,000 physicians, dentists, and psychologists currently incorporate hypnotherapy into their practices.

## BENEFITS

According to *U.S. News and World Report*, as many as 94% of hospital patients who are hypnotised as part of their therapy "get some benefit" from it. Some examples cited by the magazine:
• "Cancer patients can undergo chemotherapy without the usual nausea if they are first hypnotised."
• "Burn patients recover faster and with less medication if they are hypnotised within two hours of receiving their burns and told they will heal quickly and painlessly. Researchers think hypnotherapy gives them the ability to will the release of anti-inflammatory substances that limit the damage."
• "J. Michael Drever, a cosmetic surgeon, finds that postsurgical hypnotic suggestions can see his patients through breast reconstructions and tummy tucks with less bleeding, fewer complications and quicker recovery."

## NONBELIEVERS

One of hypnotism's most outspoken critics is Las Vegas performer "The Amazing Kreskin," who dismisses it as "just a figment of the imagination." Kreskin worked as a hypnotherapist under the supervision of a New Jersey psychologist in the 1960s. But he ultimately became a skeptic: "Anything I ever did with a patient who was supposedly under hypnosis I was able to do without putting them in the slightest trance—by persuading them, encouraging them, threatening them, browbeating them or just giving them an awful lot of confidence….All that's happening is what Alfred Hitchcock does every time he terrifies you and changes the surface of your skin with goosebumps. You're using your imagination."

## HYPNOSIS FACTS

• It is impossible to hypnotise someone against their wishes.
• A hypnotised person, even when they appear to be asleep or in a trance, is physiologically awake at all times. Unlike sleepwalkers, their brain waves are identical to those of a person who's fully awake.
• A hypnotised person is always completely aware of his or her surroundings—although they can be instructed to ignore surrounding events, which creates the appearance of being unaware of them.

## ANOTHER FORM OF HYPNOSIS?

*Here's some background on America's most pervasive credit cards.*

**American Express.** Formed by American Express in 1958 to complement its lucrative travellers-cheque business. According to *American Heritage* magazine, "American Express came to dominate the field partly because it could cover the credit it was extending with the float from its traveller's cheques, which are, after all, a form of interest-free loan from consumers to American Express."

**Visa.** California's Bank of America began issuing its Bank Americard in 1958. At first it was intended to be used at stores near Bank of America branches, but it was so profitable that the bank licenced banks all over the country to issue it. However, other banks hated issuing a card with B of A's name on it. So in 1977 the card's name was changed to Visa.

**MasterCard.** Originally named Master Charge, the card was formed in 1968 by Wells Fargo Bank and 77 other banks, who wanted to end BankAmericard's dominance of the credit card business. They succeeded: thanks to mergers with other credit cards, it became the biggest bank card within one year. Can you remember why it changed its name to MasterCard in 1979? According to company president Russell Hogg, they wanted to shed the card's "blue collar" image.

---

Sir Francis Bacon died of pneumonia—he was freezing a chicken by stuffing it with snow.

# STAR WARS

*"There's a whole generation growing up without any kind of fairy tales. And kids need fairy tales—it's an important thing for society to have for kids."—George Lucas*

**B**ACKGROUND. In July 1973, George Lucas was an unknown director working on a low-budget 1950s nostalgia film called *American Graffiti*. He approached Universal Studios to see if they were interested in a film idea he called *Star Wars*. Universal turned him down.

It was the biggest mistake the studio ever made.

Six months later, Lucas was the hottest director in Hollywood. *American Graffiti*, which cost $750,000 to make, was a smash. It went on to earn more than $117 million, making it the most profitable film in Hollywood history.

While Universal was stonewalling Lucas, an executive at 20th Century-Fox, Alan Ladd, Jr., watched a smuggled print of *American Graffiti* before it premièred and loved it. He was so determined to work with Lucas that he agreed to finance the director's new science fiction film.

*Star Wars* opened on May 25, 1977, and by the end of August it had grossed $100 million—faster than any other film in history. By 1983 the film had sold more than $524 million in tickets worldwide—making it one of the 10 best-selling films in history.

## MAKING THE FILM

• It took Lucas more than two years to write the script. He spent 40 hours a week writing, and devoted much of his free time to reading comic books and watching old Buck Rogers and other serials looking for film ideas.

• Lucas insisted on casting unknown actors and actresses in all the important parts of the film—which made the studio uneasy. Mark Hamill had made more than 100 TV appearances, and Carrie Fisher had studied acting, but neither had had much experience in films. Harrison Ford's biggest role had been as the drag racer in *American Graffiti*, and when he read for the part of Han Solo he was working as a carpenter.

## THE CHARACTERS

**Luke Skywalker.** At first Lucas planned to portray him as an elderly general, but decided that making him a teenager gave him more potential for character development. Lucas originally named the character Luke Starkiller, but on the first day of shooting he changed it to the less violent Skywalker.

**Obi-Wan Kenobi.** Lucas got his idea for Obi-Wan Kenobi and "the Force" after reading Carlos Castaneda's *Tales of Power*, an account of Don Juan, a Mexican-Indian sorcerer and his experiences with what he calls "the life force."

**Darth Vader.** David Prowse, a 2 metre (6'7") Welsh weightlifter, played the part of Darth Vader. But Lucas didn't want his villain to have a Welsh accent, so he dubbed James Earl Jones's voice over Prowse's. Still, Prowse loved the part. "He took the whole thing very seriously," Lucas remembers. "He began to believe he really was Darth Vader."

**Han Solo.** In the early stages of development, Han Solo was a green-skinned, gilled monster with a girlfriend named Boma who was a cross between a guinea pig and a brown bear. Solo was supposed to make only a few appearances in the film, but Lucas later made him into a swashbuckling, reckless human (allegedly modelled after film director Francis Ford Coppola).

**Chewbacca.** Lucas got the idea for Chewbacca one morning in the early 1970s while watching his wife Marcia drive off in her car. She had their Alaskan malamute, Indiana, in the car (the namesake for Indiana Jones in *Raiders of the Lost Ark*), and Lucas liked the way the large shaggy mutt looked in the passenger seat. So he decided to create a character in the film that was a cross between Indiana, a bear, and a monkey.

**Princess Leia.** Carrie Fisher was a beautiful 19-year-old actress when she was cast to play Princess Leia, but Lucas did everything he could to tone down her femininity. At one point, he even ordered that her breasts be strapped to her chest with electrical tape. 'There's no jiggling in the Empire," Fisher later joked.

**R2-D2.** Lucas got the name R2-D2 while filming *American Graffiti*. During a sound-mixing session for the film, editor Waiter

Murch asked him for R2, D2 (Reel 2, Dialogue 2) of the film. Lucas liked the name so much that he made a note of it, and eventually found the right character for it.

**C-3PO.** This droid's name was inspired by a robot character in Alex Raymond's science-fiction novel, *Iron Men of Mongo*. Raymond's robot was a polite, copper-coloured, robot who was shaped like a man and who worked as a servant. Lucas intended that C-3PO and R2-D2 be a space-age Laurel and Hardy team.

## SPECIAL EFFECTS
• The spaceship battles were inspired by World War II films. Before filming of the special effects began, Lucas watched dozens of war movies like *Battle of Britain* and *The Bridges of Toko-Ri*, taping his favourite air battle scenes as he went along. Later he edited them down to a 10 minute black-and-white film, and gave it to the special effects team—which re-shot the scenes using X-wing and TIE fighter models.
• None of the spaceship models ever moved an inch during filming of the flight sequences. The motion was an optical illusion created by moving the cameras around motionless models. The models were so detailed that one of them even had Playboy pinups in its cockpit.

## MISCELLANEOUS FACTS
• The executives at 20th Century-Fox hated the film the first time they saw it. Some of the company's board of directors fell asleep during the first screening; others didn't understand the film at all. One executive's wife even suggested that C-3PO be given a moving mouth, because no one would understand how he could talk without moving his lips.
• The underwater monster in the rubbish compactor was one of Lucas's biggest disappointments in the film. He had planned to have an elaborate "alien jellyfish" in the scene, but the monster created by the special-effects department was so poorly constructed that it reminded him of "a big, wide, brown turd." Result: The monster was filmed underwater during most of the scene—so that moviegoers wouldn't see it.

# Q & A:
# ASK THE EXPERTS

*More random questions...and answers from leading trivia experts.*

**HIC!**
**Q:** *What are hiccups...and why do we have them?*
**A:** "Hiccups...involve an involuntary contraction of the diaphragm, the muscle separating the abdomen and chest. When the diaphragm contracts, the vocal chords close quickly, which is what makes the funny 'hiccuping' sound." Hiccups seem to be induced by many different factors. No one's sure *why* people hiccup, but in some circumstances, hiccups are predictable: for example, eating or drinking too fast, nervousness, pregnancy, or alcoholism.

"Most of the time hiccups...stop in a few minutes whether you do anything about them or not....There was, however, one case of hiccups listed in the *Guinness Book of World Records* that lasted for 60 years. Charles Osborne of Iowa, USA, started hiccuping in 1922 after slaughtering a pig, and he must have hiccuped at least 430 million times. He said he was able to live a fairly normal life, during which he had two wives and eight children. He did have some difficulty keeping his false teeth in his mouth." (From *Why Doesn't My Funny Bone Make Me Laugh?*, by Alan Xanakis, M.D.)

## BIRD POOP
**Q:** *What's the black dot in the middle of bird droppings?*
**A:** "The black dot is faecal matter. The white stuff is urine. They come out together, at the same time, out of the same orifice. The white stuff, which is slightly sticky, clings to the black stuff." (From *Why Do Clocks Run Clockwise, and Other Imponderables*, by David Feldman)

## ONCE IN A BLUE MOON
**Q:** *Is there really a such thing as a blue moon?*
**A:** Yes, occasionally it *looks* blue "because of dust conditions in the atmosphere. The most famous widely observed blue moon of

recent times occurred on September 26, 1950, owing to dust raised by Canadian forest fires." (From *The Book of Answers*, by Barbara Berliner)

## A BIRD ON THE WIRE

**Q:** *Why don't birds get electrocuted when they perch on electric wires?*
**A:** Because they're not grounded. "There must be a completed circuit in order for the current to go through its body. If the bird could stand with one leg on the wire, and one on the ground, the circuit would be completed. In all cases where a person has been electrocuted, part of the body touched the wire and another part touched an uninsulated object, such as the ground, or something touching the ground." (From *How Do Flies Walk Upside Down?*, by Martin M. Goldwyn)

## GRIN AND BEAR IT

**Q:** *Do bears really hibernate?*
**A:** Some insects, reptiles, amphibians, and mammals do hibernate, but though the bear is known for it, it's not a "true" hibernator. "It does gain fat and, when winter arrives, sleeps for long periods, but not continuously. At irregular intervals, it arouses and wanders about, but doesn't eat much." (From *Science Trivia*, by Charles Cazeau)

## ABOUT FIBRE

**Q:** *What is fibre, and why is it good for you?*
**A:** Fibre—the 'roughage' found in fruits, vegetables, grains and beans—helps food move through the body. It's been credited with a long list of preventive health benefits, including lowering blood cholesterol levels and reducing the risk of colon cancer.

There are two types of fibre: Insoluble fibre is found mainly in whole grains and the outside, or skin, of seeds, fruits, and beans. Studies show that this fibre may help prevent colorectal cancer. It absorbs food like a sponge and moves it through the bowel, decreasing the amount of cancer-causing substances that come in contact with the bowel wall. Soluble fibre is found in fruits, vegetables, seeds, brown rice, barley, and oats. It may lower cholesterol by adhering to fatty acids and reducing the amount of fat absorbed into the bloodstream.

---

**What's so special about Elvis's 1957 film *Loving You*? Both of his parents were extras in it.**

# WHERE DOES IT HURT?

*Going for a drive in the bush? Best buckle up, keep your wits about you, and pay attention to the wind socks.*

**FLYING HIGH**
Other than the locals, drivers on the Stuart Highway north of Glendambo could be in for a shock when they discover they're sharing the road with an aeroplane. Despite all of the many strange, unique features of Australia's flora, fauna, myths and realities, and despite the isolation and barrenness of that particular stretch of land, the aeroplane is no mirage. Actually, it's rather special.

When drivers learn the truth, they're often mightily comforted. The aeroplane is part of Australia's Royal Flying Doctor Service (RFDS). This stretch of highway was deliberately widened to provide a landing strip and lay-by for RFDS aircraft.

**WINGING IT**
Lots of countries have doctors who fly about to administer to their patients, but no country other than Australia can promise a doctor on hand to provide treatment within two hours of a reported need. Compare that to a situation reported from Canada's Far North—a tall story, one hopes—of a dentist who flew into a remote Inuit community, diligently pulled molars, bicuspids, and what have you, and promised to return the following year with dental plates for everyone. Guess what? He never showed up again. The word "haphazard" isn't in the RFDS vocabulary.

**HOUSE CALLS**
In Australia the middle of nowhere is a very big middle. Some call it inland, most call it outback. The flying doctors call it their service area and it's more than 7 million square kilometres. This may explain why the RFDS logged nearly 16.5 million air kilometres in 2002, managing to visit nearly 200,000 patients. Back in 1928, the first year of operation, the RFDS flew only 18,000 kilometres, visiting 225 patients. With headquarters in Sydney, the RFDS presently flies 40 aeroplanes and has 410 full-time staff at its 22 bases around Australia.

## HOSPITAL IN THE SKY

This is no crotchety old country doctor with his little black bag, no dinosaur from the days when doctors often as not doubled as undertakers, if on hand at all. This is modern medicine on the wings of a snow-white turbo prop. Some of the RFDS aircraft are fitted as flying intensive care units. They are armed with Global Positioning Systems and regularly carry specialists.

Most of the cost to provide these top-flight services is paid by the Australian government. In 2002, this amounted to over twenty-one million dollars with donations and other grants providing the balance of two and a half million dollars.

## HELLO, IS ANYBODY LISTENING?

In 1917, Australians John Flynn and twenty-three-year-old Clifford Peel floated the idea of flying doctors to isolated patients. The idea sank faster than a stone in a billyabong.

However, John Flynn was an authority who could not be ignored. As a Presbyterian clergyman, he established the Australian Inland Mission in 1912, setting up hostels and hospitals in the outback. These were few and far between and Flynn made sure everyone knew it, including Peel, a young medical student at Melbourne University who already had an interest in the work of the Mission and who also had an interest in flying. Peel had a solution, and in a famous letter to Flynn in 1917, written en route to the war zone with the Australian Flying Corps, he laid out the solution to Flynn, even including the estimates costs.

Clifford Peel was killed in the last days of World War I, however John Flynn persisted and, finally, in 1928, the idea of a flying doctor service took off.

## WE COPY THAT!

However, success needed more than pilots and doctors—it needed communication. Radio was the best bet, but the radios of the day were cumbersome, expensive and short-range. By 1929, the problem was solved. Another Australian, Alf Traeger, came up with the Pedal Radio. The Pedal Radio was relatively small, cheap, and had a longer range. Most important, one person could operate it—a technology breakthrough because previously a second person had been needed to operate the radio power generator. These little radios soon popped up all over the outback. People who lived in year-round isolation could now access medical care.

## YOU DON'T SAY!
Always resourceful, isolated settlers in the outback began the "Galah Sessions"—probably the first electronic chat groups in history. By 1951, the Galah Sessions were operating on a much higher plane than mere gossip and recipe exchanges. The RFDS systems were put to use providing formal distance education to children far removed from town and city schools. Augmented now by the Internet and more sophisticated radios, the program still continues.

## WHERE DOES IT HURT?
By then RFDS radio communication also had a useful diagnostic function. "Where does it hurt?" could be answered and, often, treated from inexpensive medicine chests distributed by the RFDS to remote outback stations. Every item in each chest was numbered and could be prescribed by number over the radio. This treatment technique became more efficient when numbered body charts were also included in the chests. Some 3,000 of these chests are still out there and still very much in use.

## DOING THE SUMS
One of the more enduring tales about the medicine chests is that of a station manager who, having run out of the prescribed Number Nine tablets, gave his wife a Four and a Five. He reported that the combination worked fine.

## X-TREME MEDICINE
The work of the RFDS remains risky at times. Remote quasi-landing strips may still be lit by flickering kerosene lamps or truck headlights. Others must be driven over before the plane gets in to ensure obstructions haven't materialised since the last emergency.

Apart from the risk, of course there is adventure and the satisfaction of a job well done. A recent annual report from the

RFDS Yulara medical centre lists several rescues at Uluru (Ayers Rock), likely all the cause of saving tourists from the sad fate of the legendary blue-tongued lizard men, Mita and Lungkata, who perished and became boulders.

**"HEAL 'EM,"**
To a couple of generations in North America, the RFDS is well-known with thanks to Hollywood. For several seasons, Tinseltown aired the Service's fictional exploits in television's *The Flying Doctor* series. No fiction required, as the series star, Richard Denning, probably learned. He was to change his career path from doctor to politician, becoming Hawaii's Governor in the *Hawaii Five-O* series. Surely there should have been more satisfaction in doing hands-on doctoring than spending years doing nothing but ordering McGarrett to hunt down miscreants and political enemies. "Heal 'em" has a better ring to it than "Book 'em."

\*    \*    \*    \*

## ON GUARD!

They are probably not the first animals you would think of to guard sheep. They are probably not even the second, or third…

Australian sheep farmers have always had problems protecting their sheep from foxes and feral dogs. New-born lambs are an easy target for hungry jaws. But some farmers have found a very unusual and effective way to keep predators away from their sheep—alpacas!

Looking like gangly adolescents in a preschool playground, these woolly South American animals stand tall against a herd of sheep, their long necks craning above their stumpy legs. They can see beyond the herd to any approaching danger, or possible threat of attack. And dogs won't come near an alpaca—they know a formidable opponent when they see one.

High in their Andes homeland, alpacas have long had a reputation of being protective animals. They can easily outrun dogs or foxes, and then inflict some nasty damage with their hoofs.

So the next time you have sheep to protect, forget the ubiquitous Australian blue heeler and get yourself an alpaca instead!

---

The most venomous snake in Australia is the Inland Taipan—one bite can kill 115 men.

# WHO KILLED MARILYN?

*Ever wondered what really happened to Marilyn Monroe? You're not alone. Here's a version that appeared in* It's A Conspiracy, *by the National Insecurity Council. It's great bathroom reading!*

At 4:25 a.m. on August 5, 1962, Sergeant Jack Clemmons of the West Los Angeles Police Department received a call from Dr. Hyman Engelberg. "I am calling from the house of Marilyn Monroe," he said. "She is dead."

When Clemmons arrived at 12305 Helena Drive, he found Marilyn's body lying face down on the bed. The coroner investigating the case ruled that Monroe, 36, had died from "acute barbiturate poisoning due to ingestion of overdose…a probable suicide."

## THE OFFICIAL STORY
• The night before, Monroe had gone to bed at about 8:00 p.m., too tired to attend a dinner party at actor Peter Lawford's beach house. A few hours later, Monroe's housekeeper, Eunice Murray, knocked on the star's bedroom door when she noticed a light was on inside, but got no response. Assuming that Monroe had fallen asleep, Murray turned in.
• When Murray awoke at about 3:30 a.m. and noticed the light still on in Monroe's room, she went outside to peek into the window. She saw Monroe lying nude on the bed in an "unnatural" position. Alarmed, Murray called Dr. Ralph Greenson, Monroe's psychiatrist, who came over immediately and broke into the bedroom. She also called Dr. Engelberg, Monroe's personal physician. After Engelberg pronounced her dead, they called the police.

## SUSPICIOUS FACTS
*From the start, there were conflicting versions of what had happened.*

### When Did Monroe Die?
Although Murray told the police she'd found the body after 3:30 a.m., there's evidence that Monroe died much earlier.

- Murray first told the police that she'd called Dr. Greenson at midnight; she later changed her story and said she'd call at 3:30 a.m. Sgt. Clemmons claims that when he first arrived on the scene, Engelberg and Greenson agreed that Murray had called them at about midnight. But in their official police statements, the doctors said they, were called at 3:30 a.m.
- According to Anthony Summers in his book *Goddess*, Monroe's press agent, Arthur Jacobs, may have been notified of Monroe's death as early as 11:00 p.m., when he and his wife were at a Hollywood Bowl concert. According to Jacob's wife, Natalie, "We got the news long before it broke. We left the concert at once."
- In 1982, Peter Lawford admitted in a sworn statement that he learned of Monroe's death at 1:30 a.m., when her lawyer, Milton Rudin, called from the house to tell him about it.
- The ambulance crew summoned by the police noticed that Monroe's body was in "advanced rigor mortis," suggesting that she had been dead for 4 to 6 hours. That would mean she died about midnight.

**Where Did Monroe Die?**
*Monroe supposedly died in her bedroom. But did she?*
- Monroe's body was stretched out flat on the bed, with the legs straight—not typical for a person who had overdosed on barbiturates. According to Sgt. Clemmons, barbiturate overdoses often cause a body to go into convulsions, leaving it contorted. "You never see a body with the legs straight. And I've seen hundreds of suicides by drug overdose." He speculated that she had been moved. (*The Marilyn Conspiracy*, by Milo Speriglio)
- William Shaefer, president of the Shaefer Ambulance Service, insists that "in the very early morning hours"—well before 3:00 a.m—one of his ambulances was called to Monroe's house. She was comatose; the ambulance took her to Santa Monica Hospital, where she died. "She passed away at the hospital. She did not die at home." And he was certain it was Monroe. "We'd hauled her before because of [earlier overdoses of] barbiturates. We'd hauled her when she was comatose." (ibid.)

**How Did Monroe Die?**
- Though Deputy Medical Examiner Thomas Noguchi speculated that Monroe had swallowed roughly 50 Nembutal pills, a common barbiturate, he found "no visual evidence of pills in the stomach

---

Vincent Van Gogh was able to sell only one painting (The Red Vineyard) during his lifetime.

or the small intestine. No residue. No refractile crystals." Yet, as Noguchi recounted in his book *Coroner*, toxicological reports of Monroe's blood confirmed his suspicions of an overdose.

• Why was there no pill residue in Monroe's body? Noguchi said that some "murder theorists" have suggested that an injection of barbiturates would have killed her without leaving pill residue. Other theorists have suggested that a suppository with a fatal dose of barbiturates would also leave no residue in her stomach. Or, at some point after the overdose, Monroe's stomach may have been pumped.

## MISSING EVIDENCE
*Why has so much evidence pertaining to Marilyn Monroe's case disappeared or been destroyed?*

### Phone Records
• Did Monroe try to call anyone the night she died? When a reporter for the *Los Angeles Herald Tribune* tried to get her phone records and find out, a phone company contact told him, "All hell is breaking loose down here! Apparently you're not the only one interested in Marilyn's calls. But the tape [of her calls] has disappeared. I'm told it was impounded by the Secret Service…. Obviously somebody high up ordered it." (*Goddess*)

• In 1985, a former FBI agent claimed, "The FBI did remove certain Monroe records. I was on a visit to California when Monroe died, and became aware of the removal of the records from my Los Angeles colleagues. I knew there were some people there, Bureau personnel, who normally wouldn't have been there—agents from out of town. They were there on the scene immediately, as soon as she died, before anyone realised what had happened. It had to be on the instruction of somebody high up, higher even than Hoover…either the Attorney General or the President." (ibid.)

### Monroe's Diary
• Monroe supposedly kept a detailed diary. According to Robert Slatzer, a longtime friend of the actress, "For years, Marilyn kept scribbled notes of conversations to help her remember things." What things? Slatzer said the diary included her intimate discussions with people like Robert Kennedy. Monroe supposedly

told Slatzer, "Bobby liked to talk about political things. He got mad at me one day because he said I didn't remember the things he told me." (*The Marilyn Conspiracy*)

• After Monroe's death, Coroner's Aide Lionel Grandison claimed that the diary "came into my office with the rest of Miss Monroe's personal effects" during the investigation. But by the next day the diary had vanished—and, according to Grandison, someone had removed it from the list of items that had been brought in for investigation. (ibid.)

**The Original Police Files**

• In 1974, Captain Kenneth McCauley of the Los Angeles Police Department contacted the Homicide Department to ask about the files. They wrote back that the department had no crime reports in its files pertaining to Monroe's death. Even the death report had vanished.

• The files on Monroe may have disappeared as early as 1966. That year, Los Angeles Mayor Sam Yorty requested a copy of the files from the police department. The police declined, saying that the file "isn't here."

• What happened to the files? Lieutenant Marion Phillips of the Los Angeles Police Department claimed that he was told in 1962 that a high-ranking police official "had taken the file to show someone in Washington. That was the last we heard of it."

**MONROE AND THE KENNEDYS**

• As part of his research for *Goddess*, the most authoritative book on Marilyn Monroe, Anthony Summers interviewed more than 600 people linked to her. He quotes friends, acquaintances, reporters, and politicians who confirm what many Americans already suspected—that Monroe had affairs with both John and Robert Kennedy.

• Apparently, John Kennedy met her through his brother-in-law, Peter Lawford. According to Lawford's third wife, Deborah Gould, "Peter told me that Jack...had always wanted to meet Marilyn Monroe. It was one of his fantasies." Quoting Lawford, Gould says "Monroe's affair with John Kennedy began before he became president and continued for several years." (*Goddess*)

• According to Gould, JFK decided to end his affair with Monroe early in 1962. He sent his brother Robert to California to give her

the news. "Marilyn took it quite badly," says Gould, "and Bobby went away with a feeling of wanting to get to know her better. At the beginning it was just to help and console, but then it led into an affair between Marilyn and Bobby." (ibid.)
• It didn't last long. By the summer of 1962, RFK began having second thoughts and decided to break off the affair. Monroe, already severely depressed, began acting erratically after being dumped by Bobby. She began calling him at home; when he changed his unlisted phone number to avoid her, she began calling him at the Justice Department, the White House, and even at the Kennedy compound in Hyannisport. When Bobby still refused to take her calls, Monroe threatened to go public with both affairs.

## WAS IT A CONSPIRACY?
**THEORY #1: Monroe was distraught about her affairs and committed suicide. To protect the Kennedys from scandal, someone tried to cover up the suicide and cleaned up Monroe's house.**
• Monroe may have become frantic when Robert Kennedy cut her off, perhaps—as some theorists guess—because she was pregnant.
• Fred Otash, a Hollywood private detective, claimed that a "police source" told him that weeks before her death Monroe had gone to Mexico to have an abortion. According to Otash, "An American doctor went down to Tijuana to do it, which made Monroe safe medically, and made the doctor safe from U.S. law," since at that time abortion was illegal in the United States. But author Summers disagrees, noting: "There was no medical evidence to support the theory that Monroe had been pregnant." (*Goddess*)
• In any event, if Monroe was threatening to embarrass the Kennedys by going public about their affairs, it was cause for alarm. According to several reports, Robert Kennedy—who was vacationing with his family near San Francisco—flew to Los Angeles on August 4 to meet with Monroe and try to calm her down. It didn't work.
• Terribly depressed, Monroe took a massive dose of sleeping pills, but not before calling Peter Lawford and saying, in a slurred

voice, "Say goodbye to Pat [Lawford's wife], say goodbye to Jack
[JFK], and say goodbye to yourself, because you're such a nice guy."
The call may have frightened Lawford so badly that he—and
perhaps RFK—drove to Monroe's home. There he may have
found her comatose and called an ambulance. (This would explain
the Shaefer Ambulance claim of having taken Monroe to the
hospital that night.) If Monroe had been taken to a hospital
emergency room because of an overdose, her stomach would
almost certainly have been pumped—which would account for
the coroner's finding no "pill residue" in her stomach. When
even the hospital's best attempts could not save Monroe, perhaps
her body was returned to her bedroom in an effort to avoid
controversy.

**The Cleanup**
• No suicide note was ever found, nor was Monroe's personal
phone book. Someone had probably "sanitised" her bedroom
before the police came. The most likely person was Peter Lawford.
His second wife claimed, "He went there and tidied up the place,
and did what he could, before the police and the press arrived."
She also claimed Lawford had found a suicide note and
destroyed it.
• Lawford may also have hired detective Fred Otash to finish the
cleanup. According to a security consultant who worked with
Otash, Lawford hired him on the night of the death to "check her
house, especially for papers or letters, that might give away her
affairs with the Kennedys."

**THEORY #2: The Mob killed Monroe to embarrass—or even
frame—Attorney General Robert Kennedy.**
• The Mob almost certainly knew of Monroe's affairs with the
Kennedys—in fact, several reputable accounts claim that the star's
house had been bugged by the Mob. By recording intimate
moments between Monroe and Robert Kennedy, the syndicate
may have hoped to blackmail the attorney general and thus end
his prosecution of Teamsters boss Jimmy Hoffa and other
gangsters.
• In their book *Double Cross*, Chuck and Sam Giancana—the
brother and godson of Mob godfather Sam "Mooney" Giancana—
allege that the Mafia eventually decided to kill Monroe as they

figured the public would decide that Monroe had killed herself over RFK. They figured a sex and suicide scandal would force him to resign. So the Mob waited for Kennedy to visit Monroe in response to her desperate phone calls.

Finally, Kennedy took the bait. According to the authors of *Double Cross*, when Sam Giancana learned that Bobby would be in California the weekend of August 4, he arranged the hit on Marilyn. The authors allege he chose Needles Gianola, an experienced killer, for the mission. Needles selected three men of his own to help him. Together they travelled to California "under Mooney's orders, to murder Marilyn Monroe."

• According to *Double Cross*, the mob had already bugged Marilyn's home, and the hit men were waiting at their secret listening post nearby when Kennedy arrived late Saturday night. They heard Bobby and another man enter the home and begin talking to Marilyn, who was extremely upset. Marilyn, the authors report, "became agitated—hysterical, in fact—and in response, they heard Kennedy instruct the man with him, evidently a doctor, to give her a shot to 'calm her down.' Shortly afterwards, RFK and the doctor left."

• *Double Cross* claims that the four killers waited until nightfall and then sneaked into Monroe's home to make the hit. Marilyn resisted, but was easily subdued because of the sedatives: "Calmly, and with all the efficiency of a team of surgeons, they taped her mouth shut and proceeded to insert a specially 'doctored' Nembutal suppository into her anus. According to the authors, the killers waited for the lethal combination of barbiturates and chloral hydrate to take effect. Once she was totally unconscious, the men carefully removed the tape, wiped her mouth clean, and placed her across the bed. Their job completed, they left as quietly as they had come."

• Unfortunately for the conspirators, however, Kennedy's close friends and the FBI so thoroughly cleaned up Monroe's house and commandeered her phone records that any proof of the romance was eliminated. The Giancanas say that J. Edgar Hoover protected the Kennedys because, after keeping their secrets, he knew that they'd never fire him. *Double Cross* also alleges that the CIA was also in on the hit, but its reasoning is not convincing.

**FOOTNOTE**
In 1982, after reinvestigating Marilyn Monroe's death, the Los Angeles District Attorney's Office released the following statement: "Marilyn Monroe's murder would have required a massive, in-place conspiracy covering all of the principals at the death scene on August 4 and 5, 1962; the actual killer or killers; the Chief Medical Examiner-Coroner; the autopsy surgeon to whom the case was fortuitously assigned; and almost all of the police officers assigned to the case, as well as their superiors in the LAPD...Our inquiries and document examination uncovered no credible evidence supporting a murder theory."

\* \* \* \*

## YOU HAVE TO LOVE AUSTRALIANS

1. The shorter your nickname, the more popular you are.

2. The bigger your hat, the smaller your farm.

3. Whether it is a federal election or a wake, no event can't be improved by a sausage sizzle.

4. All our favourite heroes are losers.

5. At the beach, all Australians hide their wallet and keys inside their shoes or wrapped up in their towel. No thief has ever worked this out.

6. If you can't fix it with pantyhose and fencing wire it's not worth fixing.

7. We refer to our best friend as a "total bastard." By contrast, our worst enemy is "a bit of a bastard."

8. All Australians will one day realise that Aerogard® is worse than flies.

9. In the country, the bitumen road always ends just after the councillor's house.

10. The wise Australian bloke chooses a partner who is not only attractive to himself, but also to mosquitoes.

# FRANK HURLEY— AN ENDURING PHOTOGRAPHER

*Australia's answer to Ansel Adams, Frank Hurley changed the face of photography forever with his brilliant visual portrayal of Antarctica and World War I.*

## A NATURAL TALENT

Born in 1885 in Sydney, Frank Hurley ran away from home at the age of 14 and went to work in an engineering firm. It was this early introduction into a practical discipline that shaped the young Hurley into an extraordinarily competent and confident individual. With his innate capacity for sheer hard work and a natural desire for adventure, it was obvious from an early age that Frank Hurley was destined for great things.

Rough and abrasive in nature, Hurley had an artistic side, which found expression in the burgeoning art of photography. Hurley quickly taught himself the technical aspects of photography and put himself into debt in order to purchase his first camera.

In 1910, after hearing that Douglas Mawson was planning an expedition to Antarctica, Hurley tracked him down and convinced Mawson to take him as expedition photographer even though Hurley had no prior experience.

## A KODAK MOMENT

During this expedition, Hurley achieved new heights in expedition photography due to his technical brilliance and his ability to capture the landscapes and scenery in such breath-taking grandeur that on his return to Australia, Kodak sponsored an Australia-wide tour of his expedition photographic works.

Also on this expedition, Hurley shot a film, *Home of the Blizzard*, which received critical acclaim throughout the world. Ernest Shackleton, on seeing this film, hired Hurley to be the photographer on his upcoming Antarctic expedition to be the first men to cross

the Antarctic continent. They came within 129 kilometres
(80 miles) of their destination when their ship, the *Endurance*, was
trapped in pack ice. It was during this now world-famous, 22-month
ordeal, that Hurley's courage and steadfastness made his fellow
expeditioner, Lionel Greenstreet, remark that, "Hurley is a warrior
with his camera and would go anywhere or do anything to get
a picture."

## AN ENDURING LEGACY

Hurley was fearless and single-minded in his efforts to effectively
portray the *Endurance* expedition in all its tragedy and pathos.
Showing an extraordinary amount of innovation, Hurley would
climb masts, trek across unstable ice and hang off the bowsprit in
crashing seas to get the picture that he wanted. When the
*Endurance* was crushed by pack ice, Hurley dived under the
submerged decks to retrieve his photographic plates. After five
and a half months adrift on the sea ice, Shackleton made the
decision to take to the life rafts and Hurley was only allowed
to take 120 of his photographic plates with him, the rest he
smashed on the ice so he wouldn't change his mind about his
final selection.

In all aspects of the expedition, Hurley risked his life in the
pursuit of the ultimate photographic representation of what came
to be known as the "ultimate adventure."

It was because of Hurley's skill with the camera that decades on
we can all still appreciate, through his photographs, the desolation
and hardship that those on the *Endurance* expedition suffered.

## "MY CAMERA IS PACKED"

The *Endurance* expedition whet Hurley's appetite for the life of a
peripatetic photographer. No sooner had he returned home from
Antarctica that he volunteered as a frontline photographer for the
Australian Imperial Force in World War I where he managed to
capture, in haunting detail, the sheer desolation of the war zone
and the frailness of the human condition in such an environment.

Frank Hurley died in 1962, at the age of 76, having just
returned home from a photographic assignment.

# WORDPLAY

*We use these phrases everyday but where did they come from?*
*Here are the origins of some of them.*

## THE BEE'S KNEES
**Meaning:** "The best there is."
**Background:** The phrase, "The be all and the end all of everything" was once popular in Britain in the 18th century but being fairly long, this was shortened to "the B's and E's" which eventually became "the bee's knees".

## GET THE SACK/GET SACKED
**Meaning:** "Get fired/lose your job."
**Background:** When you worked on assembly lines in the old days, you had to bring your own tools—which most people carried in sacks—to work with you. If your boss fired you, he literally *gave you the sack*—handed you your tool bag and told you to get lost.

## OUT OF TOUCH
**Meaning:** "A person is out of physical or mental contact with others."
**Background:** In the 18th century it became fashionable among European military leaders to have their soldiers march as close together as possible. "As a practical way of regulating his space," one observer notes, "the soldier in the ranks had to be sure that his swinging elbows would touch those of comrades on each side." When gaps in the line formed, it was a sure sign that somewhere a soldier was—literally—*out of touch*.

## BEHIND THE SCENES
**Meaning:** "In the background; out of view."
**Background:** It was common in Elizabethan theatre to leave important actions and events out of plays entirely, and instead just report to the audience that the event had taken place between acts. Audience members joked that the actions had taken place *behind the scenes*—behind the props and backdrops on the stage—where no one could see them.

# ACRONYMANIA

*An acronym is "a word formed from the initial letters of a name."*
*Here are some acronyms you may have heard—without realising they*
*were acronyms. See if you know (or can guess) what they stand for.*
*(Answers are on page 487.)*

1. ACCC
2. DNA
3. DOA
4. EST
5. QANTAS
6. INTERPOL
7. KISS (a business axiom)
8. LASER
9. UNIVAC (the 1950s computer)
10. NABISCO
11. NASA
12. SES
13. NIMBY
14. SAS
15. OPEC
16. ASAP
17. QUASAR
18. HAND

19. FYI
20. REM
21. SCUBA tank or diver
22. SWAK
23. TNT
24. UNESCO
25. UNICEF
26. CAT scan
27. AWACS
28. AWOL
29. CD-ROM
30. M*A*S*H
31. WILCO (as in "Roger-wilco, over and out")
32. SONAR
33. SNAFU
34. NATO
35. SALT (as in "SALT agreement")

36. RADAR
37. SCUD
38. SAC
39. WYSIWYG (computer term)
40. WHO
41. SEALS
42. MS-DOS (computer term)
43. GMTA
44. TASER
45. RAM (computer term)
46. WOMBAT
47. AKA
48. CANOLA (the oil)
49. IVF
50. STD
51. FAQ

# CLOUDMASTER ELVIS

*So you thought Elvis was just a rock'n'roll singer? Maybe not.*
*Maybe he had special powers over nature…and was an expert*
*on embalming. Here are two bizarre stories told in Elvis, What*
*Happened? by Steve Dunleavy.*

## CONTROLLING THE CLOUDS

As Elvis got more famous, he came to believe that he was no ordinary human being. How did he know? Well, for one thing, he believed he could move clouds.

"I remember one day in Palm Springs," says former aide Dave Hebler. "It was hotter than hell, over a hundred degrees, and Elvis wanted to go shopping. So we all jam into this car…Elvis was talking about the power of metaphysics, although I'm not quite sure he knew the real definition of the word."

The sky in the desert was cloudless, except for one small, far-off cloud. "Suddenly Elvis yells out, 'Stop the car. I want to show you what I mean, Dave. Now see that cloud? I will show you what my powers really are. Now I want you all to watch. All of you, look at that cloud.'

"Well, we all look at the damn little cloud up there like a bunch of goats. Elvis is staring a hole through the damn thing. Well, the perspiration is dripping off us. Not a sound in the car, just a whole bunch of dummies dying of heat stroke looking up at the cloud.

"I'm near dying and I am praying that the sonofabitch would blow away. At the same time, I'm really having a problem not to burst out laughing. After about ten minutes, thank God, the damn thing dissipated a little. I saved the day by noticing it first…
I said, 'Gee, Elvis, you're right. Look, it's moving away.' [He] gave me one of those sly little smiles that told me he had done it again. 'I know, I moved it,' he says. Then we drive off."

## COMMUNING WITH THE DEAD

"You never knew where a night out with Elvis would end up," says Sonny West, Elvis's bodyguard. "Worst of all were the trips to the funeral home." Elvis had a particular fondness for visiting the

---

For the past 150 years, Bolivia has averaged about one new government a year.

Memphis funeral home where his mother's body had been "laid out".

One night, Elvis and some of his troupe went to the funeral home. Elvis began wandering around, trying doors and poking his head into various rooms. He seemed to be looking for something.

Meanwhile, Sonny had his gun out, expecting a security guard to come charging in, thinking "we're grave robbers or something and start blazing away." But no one else seemed to be around.

West recalls: "Then I get the shock of my life. We come into this big room with heads sticking from under the sheets. They were bodies, and they were sort of tilted upward, feet first. This was the damn embalming room. I'm horrified. But this was apparently what Elvis was looking for. He is happy he has found this room."

Elvis started checking out the bodies, explaining to his companions how people get embalmed. "He is walking around and lifting up sheets looking at the bodies, and he is telling us all the cosmetic things the morticians do when people are in accidents. He is showing us the various veins…how a body is bled. Then he shows us where the bodies were cut, and because the cuts don't heal, there is only the stitches holding the body together."

"[Some of us] hated those trips, but that's what Elvis wanted and you just went along with it."

\*　　\*　　\*　　\*

## STRANGE LAWSUITS: JAPANESE VERSION

**THE PLAINTIFF:** Reiko Sekiguchi, 56, a Japanese sociology professor

**THE DEFENDANT:** The University of Library and Information Science in Tsukuba, Japan

**THE LAWSUIT:** In 1988, the university stopped paying Sekiguchi's research expenses and travel allowances because she signed official documents using her maiden name instead of her married name. So she sued the university, arguing that "women should have the right to use their maiden names in professional activities and in daily life."

**THE VERDICT:** She lost.

# THE PENCIL

*Ever wondered how the pencil got its lead? We did too.*

## IS THERE REALLY LEAD IN A PENCIL?

Not anymore. The ancient Greeks, Romans and Egyptians used small lead disks for drawing guidelines on papyrus before writing with brushes and ink, and artists in Europe used metallic rods of lead, silver, and zinc to make very light drawings centuries ago. But all that changed in 1564, when a graphite deposit was unearthed in Borrowdale, England.

Using graphite for writing wasn't new; the Aztecs did it long before the arrival of Columbus. But it was new to the Europeans. They discovered that the soft graphite—a form of carbon—made rich, dark lines. They began carving pointed "marking stones" out of it and using the stones to write with.

The problem was that the stones marked the writer's hands as much as the paper. Eventually, people figured out that they could wrap a string around the stick to keep their hands clean, unwinding the string as the graphite wore down. That was the first version of the modern pencil.

## HOW THEY GET THE "LEAD" INTO THE PENCIL

*Now, of course, the graphite comes in a wood casing. But how does it get in there?*

• First the graphite is ground up and mixed with fine clay. The more clay added, the harder the lead.

• Then the mixture is forced through an "extruder" to make a long, thin rod.

• The rod is fired at an extremely high temperature to harden it and then is treated with wax for smooth writing.

• The wood is sawed into small boards that are the length of one pencil, the width of seven pencils, and the thickness of half a pencil.

• Seven tiny grooves are cut lengthwise. Then the lead is laid into each of them, and an identical board is glued on top. A machine cuts the boards into seven individual pencils.

• Last step: They're painted with nontoxic paint.

---

**Heavy thought: Hailstones can weigh as much as 700 grams (1½ lbs).**

# THE FINGERPRINT FILE

*It seems like law enforcement agencies have been catching criminals
using fingerprints for ages…but actually the practice is less than a
century old. Here's a little background on one of the most important
crime fighting techniques of the 20th century.*

**W**HERE THERE'S A WILL…
In 1903 a convicted criminal named Will West was
being processed for entry into an American
penitentiary when prison officials realised that they already had
a man matching his name and description at the prison. After
double-checking their records (including a photograph of the
inmate), they confirmed that the man being processed was the
same Will West who was supposedly already behind bars. What
was he doing on the outside?

Prison officials assumed he had escaped without anyone
noticing…until they checked Will West's cell and found he was
still in it. The men looked like twins.

At the time, the standard method for criminal identification
was the "Bertillon System," a system based on physical
descriptions and anatomical measurements. Robert Listen
describes the theory behind it in his book, *Great Detectives*:

> If one measurement was taken of a man, his height, for
> example, the chance of another man having exactly the
> same height was four to one. If a second measurement
> was added, his head circumference, say, the chances
> increased to 16 to 1. If eleven measurements were
> taken, the odds against a duplication were 4,191,304
> to 1. If fourteen measurements were kept, the odds were
> 286,435,456 to 1.

It seemed foolproof. But now the Wests had proved it fallible.
They resembled each other so closely that the system concluded
they were the *same individual*.

## WHAT HAPPENED

Left with no alternative, prison officials turned to a new system
being developed by England's Scotland Yard. They *fingerprinted*
the men and discovered that, although the men appeared to be
identical, their fingerprints had almost nothing in common.

---

**The moon weighs about 81 billion tonnes, give or take a tonne.**

## FINGERPRINT HISTORY

In 1858 William Herschel, an English civil servant working in India, began collecting his friends' fingerprints as a hobby. Carefully studying the prints over the years, he made two discoveries: no two fingerprints were the same, and each subject's fingerprints remained identical throughout their life. He brought his hobby to work with him. Put in charge of paying out pensions to Indian subjects, Herschel—a bigot who thought all Indians looked alike—required each Indian to place their thumbprint on the payroll next to their signature. He figured he could more easily spot fraudulent claimants if he took their fingerprints.

In 1880 Dr. Henry Faulds, a Scottish missionary in Japan, published an article describing how the Japanese had been signing legal documents with their fingerprints for generations. He reported another important discovery: Even when their fingers were perfectly clean, people left fingerprints on every surface they touched. Faulds called on British law enforcement agencies to make fingerprint searches a standard part of police investigations; Scotland Yard finally took his advice in 1901.

## FINGERPRINT FACTS

• The FBI didn't begin fingerprinting until the 1920s; but by the late 1980s it had more than 140 million sets of prints on file, including those of every government employee and member of the military. An estimated 2,700 criminals per month are identified using the FBI's files.
• It is possible to have your fingerprints removed, but it's painful and pretty pointless. Even if you do burn or slice off your prints, the scars that are left behind are as unique as the prints they replaced. There is no known case of a criminal successfully concealing his identity by mutilating their fingertips.
• It's just about impossible to get a set of fingerprints from a handgun; experts place the odds as low as 1 in 1,000. All that stuff you see in movies about cops picking up guns by inserting a pencil under a trigger guard are hooey—there simply aren't enough smooth, flat surfaces on most handguns to get a good print.
• No one fingerprint is *necessarily* unique; scientists figure there's a 1 in 2 quadrillion (about 1 million times the Earth's population) chance that someone on Earth has the same fingerprint you do.

# THE LOST TIGER

*It was a shy, secretive animal with stripes on its body and a bounty on its head.*

The Tasmanian tiger or thylacine is not a mammal, as its name would suggest, but a marsupial. Its scientific name *Thylacinus cynocephalus* means "pouched dog" with a wolf's head. However, with 13–20 brown-black stripes down its side, it is hardly surprising that it was known as the Tasmanian tiger. It was once the largest known marsupial carnivore in Australia, until its extinction in 1936.

## BORN FREE
Fossil records dating back around 4,000 years confirm that the Tasmanian tiger once roamed the open forests and woodlands of the entire Australian continent and New Guinea. Two thousand years later they were only to be found in Tasmania. Predation and competition from the dingo may have contributed to their disappearance from the mainland and New Guinea, but they thrived in Tasmania, protected from the mainland by Bass Strait.

## A NEW PREDATOR ARRIVES
The good life changed for it when Europeans settled in Tasmania in 1803. Wallabies were their main prey, but occasionally sheep were now taken too. Tasmanians waged war. In 1830, Van Diemens Land Company introduced a Tasmanian tiger bounty and in 1888 the Tasmanian Parliament placed a price on its head.

By 1900, some 2,000 bounties had been paid. The Tasmanian tigers' numbers had also plummeted due to an increasing loss of habitat as settlers cleared land for agriculture and livestock. The bounty scheme was terminated in 1909 and zoos around the world paid top dollars for the rare Tasmanian tiger. The last known Tasmanian tiger, named Benjamin, died in Hobart Zoo in 1936.

## BACK TO LIFE
In 1999, DNA was extracted from an ethanol-preserved Tasmanian tiger pup. It is now the dream of the Evolutionary Biology Unit at the Australian Museum in Sydney to clone a Tasmanian tiger and reverse the extinction caused by humans.

---

**Number of heartbeats in an average lifetime: approximately 2.5 billion.**

# TIPS FOR TEENS

*Here are some classic "how-to" tips for teenagers from the 1950s. We're sure you'll find the information as "valuable" now as it was then.*

## BOYS' DATING DO'S AND DON'T'S

### How to Ask a Girl for a Date

*When a boy wants to ask a girl for a date, there are several rules to follow and pitfalls to avoid.*

**First of all,** he invites her specifically for a particular occasion, giving her the time, the place, and the nature of the affair. He says, for example, "May I take you to a school dance at two next Saturday afternoon?" Knowing all the relevant facts, she has a basis upon which to refuse or to accept.

**In the second place,** he is friendly and acts as though he really wants her to accept his invitation. He looks at her with a smile while he waits for her reply.

**If she accepts,** he seems pleased and arranges definitely for the time at which he will call for her. If she refuses, he says that he is sorry and suggests that perhaps another time she will go with him.

### How Not to Ask Her

**Boys find that** girls do not like the indirect approach that starts, "What are you doing next Friday night?" That puts the girl "on a spot."

**Boys should not** act as though they expect to be refused, as Amos does when he says, "I don't suppose you'd like to go on a date with me, would you?" This can make the girl feel uncomfortable and is a mark of the boy's feeling of insecurity, too.

**Girls do not like** to be asked for dates at the last minute. It is no compliment to call a girl up the very evening of an affair.

**Since asking a girl** for a date is both a compliment and an invitation, a boy needs have no fear of using the simplest, most direct approach he can muster. He might be surprised to know how eager the girl has been to hear the words he is struggling to say!

---

First vehicle to use inflatable rubber tyres: Queen Victoria's carriage, in 1846.

# LOONEY LAWS

*America sure has some funny laws.*
*Believe it or not, these laws are real.*

In Las Vegas, Nevada, it's against the law to pawn your dentures.

In Natoma, Kansas, it's illegal to throw knives at men wearing striped suits.

It's illegal to sleep with your boots on in Tulsa, Oklahoma.

Michigan law forbids pet owners from tying their crocodiles to fire hydrants.

If you're 88 years of age or older, it's illegal for you to ride your motorcycle in Idaho Falls, Idaho.

It's against the law in Tuscumbia, Alabama, to have more than eight rabbits per city block.

It's against the law (not to mention impossible) to whistle under water in Vermont.

In Alabama, it's illegal to play dominoes on Sunday.

It's illegal to eat snakes in Kansas.

In Barber, North Carolina, it's illegal for a cat to fight a dog (or vice versa).

It's illegal to sleep with chickens in Clawson City, Michigan…and illegal to walk your elephant without a leash in Wisconsin.

The law prohibits barbers in Omaha, Nebraska, from shaving the chests of customers.

In California, it's illegal to hunt whales from your automobile. It's also against the law to use your dirty underwear as a dust rag.

In St. Louis, Missouri, it's illegal for you to drink beer out of a bucket while you're sitting on a curb.

Cotton Valley, Louisiana, law forbids cows and horses from sleeping in a bakery.

The maximum penalty for double parking in Minneapolis, Minnesota, is working on a chain gang with nothing to eat but bread and water.

---

**Man of the world:** Both China and Russia have their own "Tarzan" legends.

# THE GRIMM PHILOSOPHY

*The Brothers Grimm are among the most famous storytellers in history. During the 1800s, they collected such classic folk tales as* Rumpelstiltskin *and* Cinderella. *But these weren't the Disney versions—the view of life portrayed in Grimm tales was...well...grim. Here's an example.*

## THE CAT AND THE MOUSE

**A certain cat made** the acquaintance of a mouse, and said so much about the great love and friendship she felt for her, that the mouse agreed that they should live and keep house together. "But we must put some food aside for winter, or we'll go hungry," said the cat; "And you, little mouse, can't venture out alone, or you'll be caught in a trap some day."

**This good advice** was followed, and a pot of fat was bought—but they didn't know where to put it. The cat gave it a lot of thought, and said: "I know no place where it will be safer than in the church, for no one dares take anything from there. We'll set it beneath the altar, and not touch it until we really need it."

**So the pot was placed** in safety, but it wasn't long before the cat had a great yearning for it, and said: "Little mouse; my cousin has brought a little son into the world, and has asked me to be godmother; he is white with brown spots, and I am to hold him over the font at the christening. Let me go out today, and you look after the house by yourself."

"Yes," answered the mouse, "by all means go, and if you get anything very good to eat, think of me, I should like a drop of sweet red christening wine myself."

**All this, however, was untrue;** the cat had no cousin, and had not been asked to be godmother.

She went straight to the church, stole the pot of fat, began to lick at it, and licked the top of the fat off. Then she stretched herself in the sun. She didn't get home until evening. "Well, here you are again," said the mouse. "No doubt you've had a merry day." "All went well," answered the cat. "What name did they give the child?" "Top-off!" said the cat quite coolly. "Top-off!" cried the mouse, "What an unusual name. Is it a family name?" "What does that matter," said the cat, 'it's no worse than Crumb-stealer, as your godchildren are called."

---

**Built-in bias? 96.1% of all television writers are white.**

Before long the cat was seized by another fit of yearning. She said to the mouse: "You must do me a favour, and once more manage the house for a day alone. I am again asked to be godmother, and, as the child has a white ring round its neck, I cannot refuse." The good mouse consented, but the cat crept to the church and devoured half the pot of fat. When she went home the mouse inquired: "And what was this child named?" "Half-done," answered the cat. "Half-done?" replied the mouse, "Why, I never heard such a name in all my life!"

The cat's mouth soon began to water again. "All good things go in threes," said she, "I am asked to stand godmother again. The child is quite black, except for its paws. This only happens once every few years; you will let me go, won't you?" "Top-off! Half-done!" mused the mouse, "they are such odd names, they make me very thoughtful." "You sit at home," said the cat, "in your dark-gray fur coat and long tail, and are filled with fancies, that's because you do not go out in the daytime."

During the cat's absence the mouse cleaned the house and put it in order, but the greedy cat entirely emptied the pot of fat. She did not return home till night. The mouse at once asked what name had been given to the third child. "It will not please you more than the others," said the cat. "He is called All-gone." "All-gone!" cried the mouse, "That's the most suspicious name of all! I have never seen it in print. All-gone; what can that mean?" She shook her head, curled up, and lay down to sleep.

After this, no one invited the cat to be godmother, but when the winter came and there was no longer any food to be found outside, the mouse said: "Come, cat, let's go to the pot of fat which we've stored up for ourselves—we shall enjoy that."

"Yes," answered the cat, "you'll enjoy it as much as you'd enjoy sticking that dainty tongue of yours out of the window." They set out on their way, but when they arrived, they found that the pot of fat was empty.

"Alas!" said the mouse, "now I see what has happened! You are a true friend! You have devoured all when you were pretending to be godmother. First Top-off, then Half-done, then—" "Hold your tongue," cried the cat. "One word more, and I'll eat you too." "All-gone" was already on the poor mouse's lips; scarcely had she spoken it before the cat sprang on her, seized her, and swallowed her down.

Verily, that is the way of the world.

---

From 1950 to 1971, owning a Chinese stamp was considered "trading with the enemy."

# ZAP!

*Frank Zappa was one of the first rock musicians to admit publicly
that he could think. Here are a few of his thoughts.*

"In the fight between you and the world, back the world."

"One of my favourite philosophical tenets is that people will agree with you only if they already agree with you. You do not change people's minds."

"Without deviation, progress is not possible."

"In the old days your old man would say 'Be home by midnight' and you'd be home by midnight. Today parents daren't tell you what time to be in. They're frightened you won't come back."

"Most rock journalism is people who can't write interviewing people who can't talk for people who can't read."

"Everyone has the right to be comfortable on his own terms."

"Most people wouldn't know good music if it came up and bit them in the arse."

"Pop is the new politics. There is more truth in pop music than in most political statements rendered by our leaders, even when you get down to the level of really simplified pop records. What I'm saying is that's how bad politics is."

"If your children ever found out how lame you are, they'd kill you in your sleep."

"Politics is a valid concept but what we do is not really politics…it's a popularity contest. It has nothing to do with politics. What it is, is mass merchandising."

"I can't understand why anybody would want to devote their life to a cause like dope. It's the most boring pastime I can think of. It ranks a close second to television."

"I think cynicism is a positive value. You have to be cynical. You can't not be cynical. The more people that I have encouraged to be cynical, the better job I've done."

---

In Bangkok, Thailand, ice skates are known as "hard water shoes."

# Q & A:
# ASK THE EXPERTS

*Everyone's got a question or two they want answered—basic stuff like
"Why is the sky blue?" Here are a few of those questions, with
answers from books by some top trivia experts.*

## NAVEL ENCOUNTER

**Q:** *Where does belly-button lint come from?*
**A:** "Your navel is one of the few places on your body
where perspiration has a chance to accumulate before evaporating.
Lint from your clothing, cottons especially, adheres to the wet
area and remains after the moisture departs." (From *The Straight
Dope*, by Cecil Adams)

## MYTH-INFORMATION

**Q:** *Why do the symbols Γ and E represent male and female?*
**A:** "They're related to Greek mythology. The female symbol E
is supposed to represent a woman holding a hand mirror, and is
associated with Aphrodite, the Greek goddess of beauty. The male
symbol Γ represents a spear and a shield and is associated with
the Greek god of war, Ares. The male and female symbols also
represent the planets Mars (the Roman god of war) and Venus
(the Roman goddess of beauty)." (From *The Book of Totally Useless
Information*, by Don Voorhees)

## CIRCULAR LOGIC

**Q:** *Why do clocks run clockwise?*
**A:** No one knows for sure, but here's one answer: "Before the
advent of clocks, we used sundials. In the Northern Hemisphere,
the shadows rotated in the direction we now call 'clockwise.'
The clock hands were built to mimic the natural movements of
the sun. If clocks had been invented in the Southern Hemisphere,
[perhaps] 'clockwise' would be in the opposite direction." (From
*Why Do Clocks Run Clockwise? and Other Imponderables*, by
David Feldman)

---

Brazilian fans are so rowdy that many of the country's sports fields are surrounded by moats.

## DON'T WORRY, BEE HAPPY
**Q:** *We've all heard the phrase "busy as a bee." Are bees really busy?*
**A:** Judge for yourself: "In order to fill its honey sac, the average worker bee has to visit between 1,000 and 1,500 individual florets of clover. About 60 full loads of nectar are necessary to produce a mere thimbleful of honey. Nevertheless, during a favourable season, a single hive might store nearly a kilogram (2 pounds) of honey *a day*—representing approximately five million individual bee journeys." (From *Can Elephants Swim?* compiled by Robert M. Jones)

## STAYING COOL
**Q:** *Does iced tea or iced coffee really cool you off?*
**A:** "Contrary to popular belief, neither iced tea nor iced coffee will really cool you off because they contain caffeine, which constricts the blood vessels. Because of this effect, coffee or tea, either iced or hot, can cause you to become overheated...so it's best to avoid these drinks on hot days. But don't substitute a cola drink for them; colas also contain caffeine. Instead, drink water or juice." (From *FYI, For Your Information*, by Hal Linden)

## GONE TO THE DOGS
**Q:** *Is a dog year really the equivalent of seven human years?*
**A:** "No—it is actually five to six years. The average life expectancy of a dog is 12–14 years. However, most dogs mature sexually within six to nine months, so in a sense there is no strict correspondence to human years." (From *The Book of Answers*, by Barbara Berliner)

## TO PEE OR NOT TO PEE?
**Q:** *Why does people's pee smell funny after eating asparagus?*
**A:** "The odour is caused by an acid present in the vegetable, and it doesn't happen to everybody. Whether you produce the odour or not is determined genetically." In a British study using 800 volunteers, only 43% of the people "had the characteristic ability to excrete the six sulphur alkyl compounds that combine to produce the odour in urine. This inherited ability is a dominant trait. If one of your parents had it, so will you." (From *Why Do Men Have Nipples?* by Katherine Dunn)

---

**Legal logic:** In 19th-century England, attempting suicide was a crime punishable by death.

# IT LOSES SOMETHING IN THE TRANSLATION

*Have you ever thought that you were communicating brilliantly,
only to find out other people thought you were speaking nonsense?
That's a particularly easy mistake when you're speaking
a foreign language. A few classic examples:*

**B**UT HE'S NOT SQUEEZING THEM
When President Jimmy Carter arrived in Poland in 1977,
he made a brief speech to press and officials. But his
interpreter delivered a slightly different speech. Carter said he
had "left the United States that day." His interpreter said he'd
"abandoned" it. Carter referred to the Poles' "desires for the
future." His interpreter translated this as "lusts for the future."
And, finally, the interpreter explained to the crowd: "The
president says he is pleased to be here in Poland grasping your
private parts."

## LOOKING FOR PROTECTION
**Shannon, Ireland** (UPI)—"A young Russian couple caused an
embarrassing mix-up at Shannon Airport when they were
mistaken for political defectors.

"The pair, on a technical stopover on the Havana-Moscow
Aeroflot route, approached a counter at the big Shannon duty-free
store Monday. In halting English, the man asked for "protection,"
according to an airport spokesman.

"He was quickly whisked away for questioning by immigration
authorities. But after 20 minutes, officials determined it was not
political protection he was after, but sexual protection. He just
wanted to buy some condoms."

## MORE BIRTH CONTROL
In one campaign to introduce its ballpoint pens to Mexico, the
Parker Pen Co. used the slogan "It won't leak in your pocket and
embarrass you." The company's translators mistakenly used the
verb *embarazar*, which sounds like "to embarrass" but actually

---

Japan has only half the population of the U.S., but buys 10 times as many comic books.

means "to become pregnant." The ad appeared to suggest that the pen could prevent unwanted pregnancies.

## CULTURAL THAI'S

"Thais still talk about President Lyndon Johnson's visit in the mid '60s, when, seated next to King Bhumibol Adulyadej on national television, the lanky Texan hitched his foot up over his thigh and pointed his shoe directly at the king—a common obscene gesture in that country. It didn't relieve tensions when, on the same telecast, the American president gave the Thai queen a big "hi, honey" hug. Solemn tradition in Thailand demands that nobody touches the queen."

—*The Washington Post*

## COMIC DELIVERY

According to Roger Axtell, in his book *Do's and Taboos of Hosting International Visitors*, a high-ranking insurance company executive visiting Japan in the 1980s delivered a speech that began with a joke. It went over well...but later on he learned that it was translated something like this:

> American businessman is beginning speech with thing called joke. I am not certain why, but all American businessmen believe it necessary to start speech with joke. [Pause] He is telling joke now, but frankly you would not understand it, so I won't translate it. He thinks I am telling you joke now. [Pause] Polite thing to do when he finishes is to laugh. [Pause] He is getting close. [Pause] Now!

"The audience not only laughed," Axtell says, "but in typical generous Japanese style, they stood and applauded as well. After the speech, not realising what had transpired, the American remembered going to the translator and saying, 'I've been giving speeches in this country for several years and you are the first translator who knows how to tell a good joke.'"

## WHAT A GUY!

When the Perdue Chicken Co. translated its slogan—"It takes a tough man to make a tender chicken"—into Spanish, they ended up with "It takes a hard [sexually aroused] man to make a chicken affectionate."

That white half-moon under your fingernail is an air pocket. No one knows why it's there.

# SYDNEY'S COLOURFUL ECCENTRICS

*Every city has them—people who just stand out from the norm. We call them characters, or eccentrics, or maybe even peculiar, odd or queer. Sydney has been blessed with its fair share over the years*

Sydney is a city of dazzling harbour views and beaches with golden sand that stretch the length of the coastline. It's had a colourful past, and here are just a few of its colourful characters.

## BEATRICE MILLER (1902–73)

"Unconventional" is the word that was used to describe Bea Miller. From a wealthy family on the North Shore of Sydney, Bea was heading for a notable career as a doctor. But this was not the life she chose to lead. Abandoning her studies and the comfort of her North Shore home, she decided to become a bohemian. And in the early twentieth century, this was a choice not often made by women from middle-class families.

Bea soon began to be a figure around town. She appeared in court hundreds of times charged with "unconventional behaviours". This included sitting on the steps of the State Library, dressed in an old overcoat and an eyeshade. A placard around her neck said that she would recite pieces from Shakespeare for prices ranging from sixpence to three shillings. At other times, she surprised taxi drivers by jumping into their taxis at intersections and refusing to get out. The only way to make her leave was for the taxi driver to hose her out.

Bea spent the last years of her life in a home where she read up to 14 books a week. Her unpublished manuscript, *Dictionary by a Bitch*, is kept in the State Library of New South Wales. Kate Grenville's book, *Lilian's Story*, is a fictionalised account of her life.

## DULCIE DEAMER (1890–1972)

In the 1920s, Kings Cross was a steamy scene for artists and writers. And Dulcie Deamer was in the thick of it. Her name became synonymous with the "roaring twenties" and the social changes taking place in Sydney. She wrote articles for various Sydney newspapers and magazines. One of her most famous exploits was performing the splits at the 1923 Artists' Ball in a leopard-skin costume.

## ARTHUR STACE (1884–1967)

As the last minutes of the twentieth century slipped away under Sydney skies, thousands of people gathered beneath the Sydney Harbour Bridge and at vantage points all around the harbour. On the stroke of midnight, millions of dollars of fireworks exploded in the sky.

The crowning display was the Harbour Bridge. Every year, a word is illuminated in fireworks. This year was especially important—the end of the millennium (and quite possibly the beginning of Y2K!) When the word "Eternity" blazoned in the sky, it seemed that Arthur Stace finally had his wish. But who was Arthur Stace?

He was an alcoholic who heard the word "Eternity" spoken by an evangelist. Inspired by the word, he stopped drinking and decided to change his life. He began to write the word "Eternity" on pavements, first in yellow chalk and then in marked crayon. Over 35 years, he wrote it more than half a million times.

Arthur Stace died of a stroke in a nursing home. He left his body to Sydney University.

## WILLIAM KING (1807–73)

Billy King liked to walk. But it was never just a stroll—he was a strong practitioner of pedestrianism. Billy King travelled everywhere on foot. Sometimes he even carried a goat, a dog, or even a pig on each shoulder!

He became known as "The Flying Pieman" when he began to combine his walking feats with selling pies. Once he sold pies to passengers getting on the Parramatta River steamer and then outwalked them to Parramatta, a distance of about 29 km (18 miles) to sell them pies again. He was also said to have walked 2,630 km (1,635 miles) in 39 days.

Mark Twain coined the phrase "gossip column" in 1893.

# DISASTER FILMS

*Some films, like* The Poseidon Adventure *and* The Towering
Inferno, *are about disasters. Other films are disasters.*
*Take these losers, for example:*

## ISHTAR (1987)

**Description:** Dustin Hoffman and Warren Beatty starred as
inept singer-songwriters who travel to the Middle East looking
for work.

**Dollars and Sense:** Budgeted at $27.5 million, *Ishtar* wound up
costing $45 million...and losing $37.3 million.

**Wretched Excess:** Director Elaine May decided the desert's
natural sand dunes didn't look authentic—so workers spent nearly
10 days scraping away the dunes to make the desert flat. *Ishtar*'s
crew spent days looking for a suitable animal to play a blind
camel. They found the perfect camel, but when they came back to
pick it up, the owner had eaten it. Dustin Hoffman and Warren
Beatty each received $6 million—roughly the cost for filming the
entire film *Platoon*.

**The Critics Speak:** "It's interesting only in the way that a traffic
accident is interesting."—Roger Ebert

## INCHON (1982)

**Description:** A 140-minute epic about General Douglas
Mac-Arthur's military excursion into Korea. Bankrolled by
Reverend Sun Myung Moon, who shipped the entire cast and
crew to South Korea to film on location.

**Dollars and Sense:** "They wasted tremendous amounts of money
in every way imaginable," said one crew member. "Always in cash.
I got the feeling they were trying to make the film cost as much as
possible." The film ultimately cost $48 million...and *lost*
$48 million, making it the biggest bomb of the 1980s.

**Wretched Excess:** At first *Inchon* was dismissed as just another
weirdo cult project, but then Moon began to sign big names to the
project, including Jacqueline Bisset, Ben Gazzara...and Sir
Laurence Olivier as General Douglas MacArthur. "People ask me
why I'm playing in this picture," Olivier told a critic. "The answer

is simple: Money, dear boy." He was paid $1.25 million for the part…and later sued for an additional $1 million in overtime when the film ran months behind schedule. Terence Young received $1.8 million to direct.

Cast and crew waited for two months for their equipment to clear customs—at a cost of $200,000 a day!

A typical day of shooting featured a fleet of ships, six fighter bombers, and a bagpipe marching band. The film's opening was hyped with "The *Inchon* Million Dollar Sweepstakes." Prizes included a Rolls Royce, paid vacations to Korea, MacArthur-style sunglasses and "50,000 beautifully illustrated *Inchon* souvenir books."

**The Critics Speak:** "Quite possibly the worst movie ever made… stupefyingly incompetent."—Peter Rainer, *L.A. Herald Examiner* "A larger bomb than any dropped during the Korean police action."—*Variety*

## HEAVEN'S GATE (1981)

**Description:** Written and directed by Michael Cimino, whose *Deer Hunter* had won Oscars for best director and best film the previous year. Kris Kristofferson starred as an idealistic Harvard graduate who became a U.S. marshall in the Wyoming territory.

**Dollars and Sense:** Studio executives put Cimino's girlfriend in charge of controlling expenses; he wound up spending nearly $200,000 a day. Originally budgeted at $7.8 million, the film cost $44 million to make. It lost over $34.5 million.

**Wretched Excess:** Harvard refused to let Cimino shoot the film's prologue on their campus, so for an additional $4 million, the director took his crew and cast to England and shot the scene at Oxford. In the final version, it was less than 10 minutes of the film.

They picked Glacier National Park as their ideal location, then painted vast areas of unspoiled grassland there with green and yellow paint to make it look more "natural." Two hundred extras were hired for a roller skating scene, given a cassette with their skating music, and sent home for six months to practise.

**The Critics Speak:** "*Heaven's Gate* fails so completely," Vincent Canby wrote in *The New York Times*, "that you might suspect Mr. Cimino sold his soul to the Devil to obtain the success of *The Deer Hunter*, and the Devil has just come around to collect."

---

In case you were wondering: The average rhino's horn grows at a rate of 8 cm (3 inches) per year.

# BOW-WOW...OR WANG-WANG?

*It's a truism we all learn as kids: A dog goes bow-wow...a cat goes meow...etc. A universal language, right? Nope. Believe it or not, animal sounds vary from language to language. Here are some examples.*

## PIGS
*English:* Oink Oink!
*Russian:* Kroo!
*French:* Groin Groin!
*German:* Grunz!

## ROOSTERS
*English:* Cock-a-doodle-doo!
*Arabic:* Ku-ku-ku-ku!
*Russian:* Ku-ka-rzhi-ku!
*Japanese:* Ko-ki-koko!
*Greek:* Ki-ki-ri-koo!
*Hebreeo:* Ku-ku-ri-ku!

## DUCKS
*English:* Quack Quack!
*Swedish:* Kvack Kvack!
*Arabic:* Kack-kack-kack!
*Chinese:* Ga-ga!
*French:* Guahn Quahn!

## FROGS
*English:* Croak!
*Spanish:* Croack!
*German:* Quak-quak!
*Swedish:* Kouack!
*Russian:* Kva-kva!

## TWEETY-BIRDS
*English:* Tweet Tweet!
*French:* Kwi-kwi!
*Hebrew:* Tsef Tsef!
*Chinese:* Chu-chu!
*German:* Tschiep Tschiep!

## GEESE
*English:* Honk Honk!
*Arabic:* Wack Wack!
*German:* Schnatter-schnatter!
*Japanese:* Boo Boo!

## OWLS
*English:* Who-whoo!
*Japanese:* Ho-ho!
*German:* Koh-koh-a-oh!
*Russian:* Ookh!

## CATS
*English:* Meow!
*Hebrew:* Miyau!
*German:* Miau!
*French:* Miaou!
*Spanish (and Portuguese and German):* Miau!

## DOGS
*English:* Bow-wow!
*Swedish:* Voff Voff!
*Hebrew:* Hav Hav!
*Chinese:* Wang-wang!
*Japanese:* Won-won!
*Swahili:* Hu Hu Hu Huuu!

## CHICKENS
*English:* Cluck-cluck!
*French:* Cot-cot-cot-codet!
*German:* Gak-gak!
*Hebrew:* Pak-pak-pak!
*Arabic:* Kakakakakakakak

---

**Boris Karloff's real name was William Henry Pratt.**

# "LET ME WRITE SIGN— I SPEAK ENGLISH"

*When signs in a foreign country are written in English, any combination of words is possible. Here are some real-life examples.*

"It is forbidden to steal hotel towels please. If you are not person to do such thing is please not to read notis."
—*Japanese hotel*

"You are invited to take advantage of the chambermaid."
—*Japanese hotel*

"Do not enter the lift backwards, and only when lit up."
—*Leipzig hotel elevator*

"To move the cabin, push button for wishing floor. If the cabin should enter more persons, each one should press a number of wishing floor. Driving is then going alphabetically by national order."
—*Belgrade hotel elevator*

"Please leave your values at the front desk."
—*Paris hotel elevator*

"Our wines leave you nothing to hope for."
—*Swiss restaurant menu*

"Visitors are expected to complain at the office between the hours of 9 and 11 a.m. daily."
—*Athens hotel*

"The flattening of underwear with pleasure is the job of the chambermaid."
—*Yugoslavia hotel*

"The lift is being fixed for the next day. During that time we regret that you will be unbearable."
—*Bucharest hotel lobby*

"Not to perambulate corridors in the hours of repose in the boots of ascension."
—*Austrian hotel for skiers*

"Salad a firm's own make; limpid red beet soup with cheesy dumplings in the form of a finger; roasted duck let loose; beef rashers beaten up in the country people's fashion."
—*Menu at a Polish hotel*

**The average person laughs seven to eight times a day.**

# PHRASE ORIGINS

*Here are the origins of some more famous phrases.*

## THE HANDWRITING IS ON THE WALL

**Meaning:** The outcome (usually negative) is obvious.

**Background:** The expression comes from a Babylonian legend in which the evil King Belshazzar drank from a sacred vessel looted from the Temple in Jerusalem. According to one version of the legend, "A mysterious hand appeared after this act of sacrilege and to the astonishment of the king wrote four strange words on the wall of the banquet room. Only the Hebrew prophet, Daniel, could interpret the mysterious message. He boldly told the ruler that they spelled disaster for him and for his nation. Soon afterward, Belshazzar was defeated and slain, just as Daniel said." The scene was a popular subject for tapestries and paintings during the Middle Ages.

## OLD STOMPING GROUND

**Meaning:** Places where you spent a lot of time in your youth or in years past.

**Background:** The prairie chicken, which is found in Indiana and Illinois, is famous for the courtship dance it performs when looking for a mate. Large groups of males gather together in the morning to strut about, stamp their feet, and make booming noises with their throats. The original settlers used to get up early just to watch them; and the well-worn patches of earth became known as *stomping grounds.*

## JIMINY CRICKET

**Meaning:** The name of the cricket character in the Walt Disney film *Pinocchio*; also a mild expletive.

**Background:** The name Jiminy Cricket predates *Pinnochio*...and has nothing to do with crickets. It is believed to have originated in the American colonies as "a roundabout way of invoking Jesus Christ." (Since the Puritans strictly forbade taking the Lord's name in vain, an entire new set of kinder, gentler swear words— darn, dang, heck, etc.—were invented to replace them.

---

If a pack-a-day smoker inhaled a week's worth of nicotine all at once, they would die instantly.

## THE BITTER END
**Meaning:** The very end—often an unpleasant one.
**Background:** Has nothing to do with bitterness. It's a sailing term that refers to the end of a mooring line or anchor line that is attached to the *bitts*, the sturdy wooden or metal posts that are mounted to the ship's deck.

## HAVE A SCREW LOOSE
**Meaning:** Something is wrong with a person or mechanism.
**Background:** The phrase comes from the cotton industry and dates back as far as the 1780s, when the industrial revolution made mass production of textiles possible for the first time. Huge mills sprang up to take advantage of the new technology (and the cheap labour), but it was difficult to keep all the machines running properly; any machine that broke down or produced defective cloth was said to have "a screw loose" somewhere.

## MAKE THINGS HUM
**Meaning:** Make things run properly, smoothly, quickly, and efficiently.
**Background:** Another cotton term: the guy who fixed the loose screws on the broken—and thus *silent*—machines was known as the person who *made them hum* again.

## IF THE SHOE FITS, WEAR IT
**Meaning:** "If something applies to you, accept it."
**Background:** The term is a direct descendant of the early 18th-century term "if the cap fits, put it on," which referred specifically to *fool's caps*.

## PLEASED AS PUNCH
**Meaning:** Delighted.
**Background:** Believe it or not, the expression has nothing to do with party beverages—it has to do with the rascally puppet character Punch (of Punch and Judy fame), who derived enormous sadistic pleasure from his many evil deeds. The phrase was so popular that even Charles Dickens used it in his 1854 book, *Hard Times*.

Attila the Hun bled to death from a nosebleed on his wedding night.

# SPORT CRAZED

*Australians watch it, play it and obsess about it. They paint themselves in green and gold, and chant in warlike fury. It's primitive, it's impassioned, it's...SPORT!*

Australians love the thrill of competition. And whatever the sporting occasion, there's always a bet to be had and some drinking to be done. Some Australians, however, just take their sporting achievements to the limit!

## A BLISTERING PACE

Queenslander Ron Grant made a name for himself by running extraordinary distances in blistering conditions. In June 1981, he ran across the desert from Oodnadatta to Birdsville, a mere 380 km (236 miles), in four-and-a-half days. Determined to outdo even himself, he upped the stakes by running the same distance in January 1985—in the ferociously hot conditions of summer. He covered the distance 14 hours quicker!

## TWO FEET DOWN UNDER

Potato farmer Cliff Young led a quiet life. He didn't drink and he didn't smoke. Mostly he chased cows around his paddocks wearing gumboots. At the age of 61, however, all that suddenly changed when he entered one of the most challenging road races in the world—the 875-km (544-mile) marathon from Sydney to Melbourne. This tough event is a total endurance test. Over five to six days, competitors suffer from heat exhaustion, hyperthermia and hallucinations. They sleep only a few hours and run through the night in order to take advantage of the cooler night air and to try to gain an advantage over their rivals. This race is as much a mental endurance as a physical one.

Cliff Young seemed an unlikely contender for such a race. In a baggy old tracksuit, with plenty of holes to keep him cool, he shuffled along the road, happy to chat to interviewers about his life. And the public loved him. By the time Cliff Young reached Melbourne to become the winner of one of the most gruelling races in the world, he was already a sporting legend!

# MUMMY'S THE WORD

*Mummies are as much a part of American pop culture
as they are a part of Ancient Egyptian culture.
But how much do you know about them?*

**RAG TIME**
As long as there have been people in Egypt, there have been mummies—not necessarily *man-made* mummies, but mummies nonetheless. The extreme conditions of the desert environment guaranteed that any corpse exposed to the elements for more than a day or two dried out completely, a process that halted decomposition in its tracks.

The ancient Egyptian culture that arose on the banks of the Nile River believed very strongly in preserving human bodies, which they believed were as necessary a part of the afterlife as they were a part of daily life. The formula was simple: no body, no afterlife—you couldn't have one without the other. The only problem: As Egyptian civilisation advanced and burial tombs became increasingly elaborate, bodies also became more insulated from the very elements—high temperatures and dry air—that made natural preservation possible in the first place.

The result was that a new science emerged: artificial mummification. From 3100 B.C. to 649 A.D., the ancient Egyptians deliberately mummified the bodies of their dead, using methods that became more sophisticated and successful over time.

## MUMMY SECRETS
Scientists have yet to unlock all of the secrets of Egyptian mummification, but they have a pretty good idea of how the process worked:
• When a king or other high official died, the embalmers slit open the body and removed nearly all the organs, which they preserved separately in special ceremonial jars. A few of the important organs, like the heart and kidneys, were left in place. The Egyptians apparently thought the brain was useless and in most cases they shredded it with small hooks inserted through the nostrils, pulled it out the nose using tiny spoons, and then threw it away.

- Next, the embalmers packed the body in oil of cedar (similar to turpentine) and natron, a special mineral with a high salt content. The chemicals slowly dried the body out, a process that took from 40 to 70 days.
- The body was now completely dried out and "preserved," but the process invariably left it shrunken and wrinkled like a prune, so the next step was to stuff the mouth, nose, chest cavities, etc., with sawdust, pottery, cloth, and other items to fill it out and make it look more human. In many cases the eyes were removed and artificial ones put in their place.
- Then the embalmers doused the body with a waterproofing substance similar to tar, which protected the dried body from moisture. In fact, the word mummy comes from the Persian word *mumiai*, which means "pitch" or "asphalt," and was originally used to describe the preservatives themselves, not the corpse that had been preserved.
- Finally, the body was carefully wrapped in narrow strips of linen and a funerary mask resembling the deceased was placed on the head. Afterwards it was placed in a large coffin that was also carved and painted to look like the deceased, and the coffin was placed in a tomb outfitted with the everyday items that the deceased would need in the afterlife.

## THE MUMMY GLUT

Pharaohs weren't the only ancient Egyptians who were mummified—nearly anyone in Egyptian society who could afford it had it done. The result: By the end of the Late Period of Ancient Egypt in the seventh century A.D., the country contained an estimated 500 million mummies, far more than anyone knew what to do with.

They were too numerous to count, too disconnected from modern Egyptian life to have any sacred spiritual value, and in most cases, were thought to be too insignificant to be worthy of study. Egyptians from the 1100s onward thought of them as more of a natural resource than as the bodies of distant relatives, and treated them as such.

Well into the 19th century, mummies were used as a major fuel source for locomotives of the Egyptian railroad, which bought them by the ton (or by the graveyard). They were cheaper than wood and burned very well.

There's enough salt in the world's oceans to cover the entire U.S. with a layer 2.5 km deep.

For more than 400 years, mummies were one of Egypt's largest export industries, and the supply was so plentiful that by 1600 you could buy a pound of mummy powder in Scotland for about 8 shillings. As early as 1100 A.D., Arabs and Christians ground them up for use as medicine, which was often rubbed into wounds, mixed into food, or stirred into tea.

By the 1600s, the medicinal use of mummies began to decline, as many doctors began to question the practice. "Not only does this wretched drug do no good to the sick," the French surgeon Ambrose Paré wrote in his medical journal, "…but it causes them great pain in their stomach, gives them evil smelling breath, and brings on serious vomiting which is more likely to stir up the blood and worsen haemorrhaging than to stop it." He recommended using mummies as fish bait.

By the 1800s, mummies were imported only as curiosities, where it was fashionable to unwrap them during dinner parties.

Mummies were also one of the first sources of recycled paper: During one 19th-century rag shortage (in the days when paper was made from *cloth* fibres, not wood fibres), one Canadian paper manufacturer literally imported Egyptian mummies as a source of raw materials: he unwrapped the cloth and made it into sturdy brown paper, which he sold to butchers and grocers for use as a food wrap. The scheme died out after only a few months, when employees in charge of unwrapping them began coming down with cholera.

**Note:** What happened when the supply of mummies became scarce? A grisly "instant mummy" industry sprang up in which fresh corpses of criminals and beggars were hastily embalmed and sold as real mummies.)

### MUMMY FACTS

• Scientists in South America have discovered mummies from the ancient civilisation of Chinchorros that are more than 7,800 years old—nearly twice as old as the oldest Egyptian mummy. And, just as in Egypt, the mummies are plentiful there. "Every time we dug in the garden or dug to add a section to our house, we found bodies," one elderly South American woman told *Discover* magazine. "But I got used to it. We'd throw their bones out on a hill, and the dogs would take them away."

• The average Egyptian mummy contains more than 20 layers of cloth that, laid end-to-end, would be more than four football fields long.

• In 1977, an Egyptian scientist discovered that the mummy of Pharaoh Ramses II, more than 3,000 years old, was infested with beetles. So they sent it to France for treatment, complete with an Egyptian passport describing his occupation as "King, deceased."

• What's the quickest way to tell if an Egyptian mummy still has its brains? Shake the skull—if it rattles, the brain is still in there.

• The Egyptians were also fond of mummifying animals. To date, scientists have discovered the preserved remains of bulls, cats, baboons, birds, crocodiles, fish, scorpions, insects…even wild dogs. One tomb contained the remains of more than one *million* mummified birds.

• Some mummies have been discovered in coffins containing chicken bones. Some scientists believe the bones have special religious meaning, but (no kidding) other experts theorise that the bones are actually leftover garbage from the embalmer's lunch.

\*     \*     \*     \*

## CELEBRITY MUMMIES

**Jeremy Bentham and his "Auto Icon."** Bentham was a famous 19th-century English philosopher. When he died in 1832, he left instructions with a surgeon friend that his body be beheaded, mummified, dressed in his everyday clothes, and propped up in a chair, and that a wax head be placed on his neck to give the corpse a more realistic appearance. He further instructed that his real head also be mummified and placed at his feet, and that the whole arrangement be put on public display. The corpse and its head(s) can still be seen at University College in London, where they sit in a glass case specially built for that purpose.

**Vladimir Lenin.** When the Soviet leader died on January 21, 1924, the Communist Party assembled a team of top embalmers to preserve his corpse for all eternity. Unlike the embalming processes of the ancient Egyptians, which prevented decomposition by removing body fluids, the Soviets *replaced* cell fluids with liquids that inhibited deterioration.

*Some Egyptian mummies wore dentures.*

# KNITTING WITH DOG HAIR

*When we heard about this "hobby," we couldn't believe it. But sure*
*enough, it's real. First we found a book called* Knitting with Dog
Hair, *by Kendall Crolius...then several web pages on the subject.*
*All are apparently serious, so here are some ideas if you're*
*interested in "Putting on the dog."*

**MY DOG HAS FLEECE**
"Let's be honest," writes Kendall Crolius in her book
*Knitting with Dog Hair,* "everything in your house is
probably covered with a fine coat of pet hair. Now all that fuzz
that used to clog up your vacuum cleaner can be put to good use.
In fact, you'll probably want to brush your dog more often—you'll
not only have gorgeous new clothes but a better-groomed pet and
a cleaner house."

Gorgeous new clothes? Is she really suggesting we make clothes
out of dog hair? You bet. And why not? After all, before there
were sheep in Scandanavia and on the American continent, there
were canines. While other animals were killed for their fur,
prehistoric natives on both continents considered dogs too
valuable as hunters and companions for that. So, she informs us,
they saved dog hair and knitted it into fabrics.

**PUBLIC OPINION**
Dedicated dog hair knitters have learned from experience that
other people think they're weird.

"When you first tell your friends that the garment you're
wearing was previously worn by your dog, you're bound to get
some raised eyebrows, not to mention a few shrieks of horror,"
Crolius writes. That's why most of them have learned that it's a
better idea not to say "dog hair" at all when showing off a new
hand-knitted jumper. After all, most people immediately think
of fleas, itching and doggy smells when they think of canine fur.

Some even ask, with eyes wide, "How many dogs have to be
killed to make a jumper?"

---

Among many other things, Thomas Jefferson is the inventor of the calendar clock.

## DOG HAIR BY ANY OTHER NAME SMELLS AS SWEET
• Faced with such reactions from friends, family and neighbours, knitters have dealt with the issue…by avoiding it—they've come up with a new name.

• Combining the French word for "dog" with the name of another natural hair fibre, angora, they've coined a fashion euphemism that's nearly as good as the day that furriers discovered that "ermine" sounds more luxurious than "white weasel." The new name for dog-hair creations is…"chiengora."

• In fact, in her *Merry Spinster* web page, Patty Lee Dranchak insists that dog hair should be considered a luxury fibre, like all the others that come from humble origins including cashmere and angora (goat) and mohair (rabbit).

### Reasons to Bark
• The hardcore dog-lovers who practise the art have created jumpers, hats, mittens and pantsuits from the hair of their beloved pets.

• They report that chiengora is—to quote Dranchak—"soft and fluffy, lovely and lustrous, incredibly warm and it sheds water. This furry look just seems to invite touching. Wearing it invites comments, questions and even an occasional pat on the back to see if it is really as soft as it looks."

• Besides that, Dranchak says, dog lovers have sentimental reasons: "By having a pet's hair spun, dog lovers will always have a part of their treasured companion with them—a reminder of the love, loyalty and good times they shared together."

• Jerilyn Monroe, who makes yarn out of her half-wolf dogs, agrees: "Having a scarf, blanket or hat made from a special pet can be a lovely way to remember them."

### A SHAGGY DOG YARN
• The key to knitting with dog hair is its length. "Rule number one is that you should never shear, cut, or shave fur from your pet," says Crolius. "Not only would such a radical approach seriously humiliate your companion and render him exceedingly unattractive, it is counterproductive. To spin a really nice yarn, you need the longest, softest fibres your pet can grow. It's best if the hair is 5 cm (2 inches) or longer if you want a pure chiengora yarn, so collies, Afghans, poodles, samoyeds, golden retrievers, sheepdogs and huskies work better than basset hounds or chihuahuas."

---

A column of air 6.5 cm (1 inch) square and 965 km (600 miles) high weighs about 7 kg (15 lbs).

- Shorter hair has to be blended with wool, silk or other fibres to hold it together. "Properly blended and spun, it's difficult to tell that the resulting yarn isn't all dog hair," observes Dranchak.

## THE HARVEST
However, unlike sheep, you don't shear your dog—you merely collect hair from brushes and combs. So even with the hairiest dog, it can take several years to collect enough hair for a major project like a jumper or a blanket.
- After you gather it, you should store it dry in a paper bag—never plastic, say some dog hair experts.
- However, other experts disagree, saying it should be stored tightly sealed in a plastic bag to keep out fleas and moths. "Moths love dog hair," says one, who recommends zip-lock bags.
- Regardless, paper grocery bags make a good standard of measure: a knitted jumper takes about two bags, a vest about one and a hat about $1/3$ of a bag. Crocheting adds another 33% for each garment; weaving about 33% less.

## WARP AND WOOF...WOOF...WOOF
- Once you have your big bags of hair, how do you turn it into yarn? Dog hair requires gently hand-spindling with a weighted drop spindle—none of these newfangled machines like the spinning wheel. The result comes from twisting the hairs around each other.
- The good thing about fibres like dog hair is that if the yarn breaks, you just fluff up the end and begin again, adding fibres. "This is a craft that the whole family can participate in," suggests Crolius. "The younger kids can help brush the dog, and the older kids can help prepare the fibre for spinning. It's a terrific way to spend time together."

## ODDS & ODDS
- If you have a multi-coloured dog, experts suggest keeping the colours somewhat separate to give an interesting graduated colour effect.
- Mixing the hair together yields a uniform grey-beige colour.
- Like the dogs it came from, dog-hair garments should be hand-washed—not thrown into a washing machine. Unlike the dogs, the fabrics can be dry-cleaned. Dog-hair garments can last 20 years.

If your dog has fleas, put flea powder in your vacuum cleaner bag. (Lots of flea eggs there.)

# SPARE A THOUGHT FOR BLUEBOTTLES

*They're a part of summer, their sting hurts like crazy and can even kill you, but have you ever given much thought to the life of a bluebottle?*

## DIRECTIONLESS

Think you're having a tough time, struggling for some direction? Then spare a thought for bluebottles or Portuguese man-of-wars (*Physalia*). Although not unique to Australia, these little fellows that inhabit our beaches all year round, but particularly during the warmer months, are at the mercy of the waves and currents. They have no control over where they go and they reproduce asexually through a process called "budding." This means no sex! And to add injury to insult, sea turtles love them. Can you imagine being outrun and eaten by a turtle!

## SAFETY IN NUMBERS

The float (or bottle) that supports the colony of tentacles is a pear-shaped sac that can exceed 15 cm (6 inches). It is mainly blue, though its upper margin may show delicate shades of green or pink.

Bluebottles float in groups of up to one thousand. Unlike fish and jellyfish, that are single organisms, bluebottles are colonies of organisms and can have several hundred tentacles.

Theoretically, the life span of a bluebottle is infinite, but realistically, due to the perils of the sea, they are unlikely to live forever. The most common way for a bluebottle to meet its maker is for it to be washed up on the beach, to be bashed against rocks by waves, or to be eaten by a predator.

Once beached, all but the organism that controls the stinging cells die—so a beached bluebottle can still emit its stinging cells if someone comes in contact with its nearly invisible tentacles.

But can you blame the little guys for wanting to lash out with the odd sting once in a while? No sex and no way to run—it's no life. And yet they might live forever!

One in 500 humans has one blue eye and one brown eye.

# PIRATE LORE

*We've all got an idea of what it was like to be a pirate in the 1700s—*
*but a lot of it is pure Hollywood fiction. Here are a few of our most*
*common misconceptions about pirates…and the truth about them.*

## NICKNAMES

Why did so many pirates have colourful nicknames like
"Blackbeard" and "Half Bottom"? The main reason was
to prevent government officials from identifying and persecuting
their relatives back home. (How did "Half Bottom" get his
nickname? A cannonball shot half his bottom off.)

## WALKING THE PLANK

Few (if any) pirate ships ever used "the plank." When pirates took
over a ship, they usually let the captured crewmembers choose
between joining the pirate crew or jumping overboard. Why go to
all the trouble of setting up a plank to walk off? As historian Hugh
Rankin put it: "The formality of a plank seems a bit absurd when
it was so much easier just to toss a prisoner overboard."

## BURIED TREASURE

Another myth. No pirate would have trusted his captain to bury
treasure for him. According to pirate expert Robert Ritchie,
"The men who turned to piracy did so because they wanted
money. As soon as possible after capturing a prize they insisted
on dividing the loot, which they could then gamble with or carry
home. The idea of burying booty on a tropical island would have
struck them as insane."

## BOARDING A SHIP BY FORCE

It's a scene from the movies: A pirate ship pulls up alongside
another ship, and then the pirates swing across on ropes and storm
the ship. But how realistic is this scene? Not very, experts say.
Most ship captains owned their cargos, which were usually fully
insured. They preferred to surrender the minute they were
approached by a pirate ship, seeing piracy as one of the costs
of doing business.

---

The average cat brain is as big as a marble; the average ostrich's eyes are as big as tennis balls.

## THE JOLLY ROGER (SKULL AND CROSSBONES)

Pirates used a variety of flags to communicate. The Jolly Roger was used to coerce nearby ships into allowing the pirates to board. But it wasn't the only flag of choice—some pirate ships preferred flags with hourglasses on them (to let would-be victims know that time was running out); others used black or red flags. How did the Jolly Roger get its name? Nobody knows for sure—although some historians believe it comes from the English pronunciation of *Ali Raja*, the Arabic words for "King of the Sea."

## PIRATE SHIPS

In the movies they're huge—but in real life they were much smaller. "Real pirates," one expert writes, "relied on small, swift vessels and hit-and-run attacks."

## ROWDINESS

Not all pirate ships were rough-and-tumble. Pirates often operated under a document that had some similarity to a constitution. Here are a few of the articles from an agreement drawn up by the crew of Captain John Phillips in 1723.

1. Every man shall obey civil Command; the Captain shall have one full Share and a half in all prizes; the Master, Carpenter, Boatswain, and Gunner shall have one share and a quarter.

2. If any man shall offer to run away, or keep any Secret from the Company, he shall be maroon'd with one Bottle of Powder, one Bottle of Water, one small Arm, and Shot.

3. If any Man shall steal any Thing in the Company, or game, to the Value of a Piece of Eight, he shall be maroon'd or shot.

4. That Man that shall strike another whilst those Articles are in force, shall receive Moses's Law (that is 40 stripes lacking one) on the bare Back.

5. That Man that shall not keep his Arms clean, fit for an Engagement, or neglect his Business, shall be cut off from his Share, and suffer such other Punishment as the Captain and the Company shall think fit.

6. If any Man shall lose a Joint in time of an Engagement, shall have 400 Pieces of Eight; if a limb 800.

7. If at any time you meet with a prudent Woman, that Man that offers to meddle with her, without her Consent, shall suffer Death.

---

**Good news?** Marriages lasting more than 13 years are more likely to end in death than in divorce.

# TIPS FOR TEENS

*More advice from a teen guidebook of the 1950s.*

## GOOD GROOMING FOR GIRLS

**YOU'RE YOUR OWN SHOW!**
*Rest, relaxation, and good food all* help *keep a clear skin, shiny hair, good teeth and bones, but they aren't the* whole *story...*
**Let's start with posture.** Think about walking tall; it's surprising how much better clothes look! There'll be fewer backaches, or even headaches, too. Don't slouch as you walk, nor slump as you sit. Relax! Lift your head and shoulders, then walk as if you're going *somewhere.*
**Look at yourself** in the mirror! Have you a regular night-time, morning and weekly cleanliness program? Soon you'll be at college or on your own; no family to remind you of the toothbrush, nail file, comb, or soap and water. Yet regular attention to teeth, nails and hair is a habit just as important to good health as food.
**Give that room** of yours the "once-over." Of course you meant to hang things up after last night's party, but did you *do* it? It's only smart to hang, clothes in your closet

immediately—they need less pressing and laundry care that way. And tidy, wrinkle-free clothing is an important part of the shined-and-polished look!
**In actuality,** beauty is lots more than skin deep. Beauty is as deep as you are. Beauty is all of you, your face, your figure, your skin. More than any other part, though, your skin will be the barometer of your beauty weather. It will tell you how well you are keeping to a beauty schedule. A broken-out complexion is a sure sign that you have slipped up somewhere. It is an indication that you have eaten too many sweets or skimped on cleanliness. Be diligent in your daily habits, and your reward will be a smooth, silken complexion (and, not incidentally, a fine face and figure).
**Just remember,** most of us wouldn't take the first prize in a beauty contest. Yet it's possible, with some time and attention, to improve the looks we have. So form good grooming habits *now*—for the rest of your life.

# SOUND EFFECTS

*Jurassic Park and Star Wars—two of the most popular and profitable
films of all time—got a big boost from their unusual sound effects.
Here are a few of the secrets behind them.*

## STAR WARS

Ben Burtt, *a talented university student, recorded most of the
sounds needed for the film. Some of his secrets:*
• Chewbacca's voice was created from a combination of walrus,
badger, sea lion, three different bears, and bear cub recordings.
After mixing the sounds together, Burtt changed the pitch and
slowed them down to "match" a Wookie photo Lucas had sent
him.
• The light sabers were a combination of humming film
projectors and static from Burtt's TV set.
• The Jawas spoke a mixture of sped-up Swahili and Zulu dialects.
• R2-D2's "voice" was Burtt's own voice combined with sounds of
bending pipes and metal scraping around in dry ice.

## JURASSIC PARK

• The *Tyrannosaurus rex's* voice is an assortment of animal
noises—elephants, tigers, dogs, penguins, and alligators, etc—and
the thudding sound of his feet are recordings of trees falling in a
forest.
• The sound of a sick *Triceratops* was recorded at a farm for
"retired" performing lions. Sound designers went to the farm
looking for sounds for the t-rex, but they found that the "wheezy,
pained breathing" of the old lions was perfect for the triceratops.
• The *Velociraptors* used 25 different animals sounds…but not all
at once: a "very old" horse was used to provide the breathing
sounds they make when stalking prey; dolphin sounds were used to
make the "attack" screeches; and mating tortoises provided the
hooting call that raptors make to each other.
• The sound designers wanted to use whale sounds for the
*Brachiosaurus* (the veggie-munching, long-necked dinosaur)—but
they couldn't get the right recording…so they recorded a donkey
braying, slowed it down, and played it backwards. The end result
was practically indistinguishable from a whale.

---

**The stirrup, the tiniest bone in your body (it's in your ear), is smaller than an ant.**

# HOW TO TAKE A SHOWER-BATH

*Showers are so commonplace today that it's hard to think of them as a novelty. But this article by W. Beach, M.D., printed in an 1848 magazine, shows that 150 years ago, dripping water on your head was still a weird and exotic practice.*

**Reprinted from The American Practice of Medicine, 1848.**

**The shower bath** is a species of cold bath, an invention by which water falls from a height through numerous holes or apertures, on the head and body. It may be conveniently made by boring numerous small holes through a tub or half barrel, which must be fastened a few feet above the head of the person.

**Another tub,** of a sufficient size to contain two pails of water, must be suspended over the other, and made to turn upon an axis. A rope or cord must be fastened to this, so that it can be inverted or turned downward at pleasure.

**The person taking** the shower bath must place himself beneath, uncovered; and, having filled the tub with water, he will suddenly pull upon the cord, when almost instantaneously the contents of the upper tub or bath will fall into the lower one containing the holes, and the water will thus be conveyed in numerous and copious streams upon the head and body.

**The apparatus should be** enclosed, as well as the body, in a box or frame a few feet square, or large enough to enable the person to stand or turn round with convenience. A few boards or planks enclosed in a small frame is sufficient for the purpose. Rub the body well with a dry towel after the bathing.

**This bath may be** used in all diseases of the head, epilepsy, nervous complaints, headache, melancholy, hypo-chondriasis, obstruction of the menses, and such complaints as arise therefrom, delirium, general debility, &c.

**Dr. Sylvester Graham,** who has become very celebrated on account of his lectures on temperance and diet, recommends, I am told,

---

**The automobile "population" of Seoul, South Korea, increases by 800 cars every day.**

the shower bath for numerous complaints.

**A writer in *Zion's Herald*,** over the appropriate signature "Comfort," has the following interesting remarks on the shower bath, and his own experience in applying the same:

I had a shower bath made at the expense of ten dollars, and it makes a neat article of furniture in one corner of my chamber. On the top a box, that holds about a pail of water, swings on a pivot, and a string from it communicates inside; and underneath, to catch the water, is a snug-fitting drawer.

Immediately on rising in the morning I shut myself in this enclosure, and receive the contents of the box at the top, let it drip off a moment, and then apply briskly a crash towel, and immediately a fine healthy glow is produced all over the body.

The time occupied does not exceed five minutes: I have often done it conveniently in three or four minutes, particularly when the wind has been in a cold corner, and all cheerless out of doors; but in these melting times it is too great a luxury to be hurried through with.

I hope all will be induced to try this plan who can possibly raise ten dollars to pay for the bath. I can assure them they will never put this article aside as useless, or sell it for less than cost. I certainly would not part with mine for ten times its cost, if another could not be procured.

**The portable shower** bath may be constructed at a small expense, and placed in a bedroom or other place. Both the bath and the water may be drawn to the desired height by means of a cord or rope running over the pulleys, and fastened to the ceiling.

**The person taking** the shower bath is placed within, surrounded partially or wholly by curtains, when he pulls a wire or cord which inverts the vessel overhead containing the water, and lets it fall in copious streams over the whole body.

**"The warm, tepid, cold,** or shower bath," says Dr. Combe, "as a means of preserving health, ought to be in as common use as a change of apparel, for it is equally a measure of necessary cleanliness." A bath on the above plan can be purchased for eight dollars.

# MISSED IT BY THAT MUCH

*It's bizarre to think that the outcome of some of the most momentous events in Western history have hinged on one detail. But that's the case. Here are three examples of what we mean.*

## THE TITANIC

**Near Miss:** With an extra pair of binoculars, the *Titanic* might have been saved.

**What Happened:** After the *Titanic* was launched, but before it left on its maiden voyage in 1912, one of the ship's lookouts reported that two pairs of binoculars—used by the deck crew to spot icebergs—were missing. He put in a request for a new pair, but the request was denied. So the deck crew kept watch for icebergs with their naked eyes. On April 1912, the *Titanic* struck an iceberg and sank, drowning more than 1,500 people. Lookout Frederick Fleet, one of only 705 survivors, told investigators that the binoculars would have allowed the crew to see the iceberg in time to avoid it.

## PEARL HARBOR

**Near Miss:** The U.S. almost learned of the attack on Pearl Harbor in time to defend against it.

**What Happened:** At 7 a.m. on the morning of December 7, 1941, radar operators Joseph Lockhard and George Elliott had just finished their shift at a radar station on the island of Oahu, Hawaii. But the truck that was supposed to pick them up was late, so they stayed at their consoles a few minutes longer, and at 7:02 Elliott picked up the biggest blip either man had ever seen. They tried to call the control room, but according to John and Claire Whitcomb in their book *Oh Say Can You See*, "the line was dead—the men in the control room had gone to breakfast."

Elliott tried the regular phone circuit and got through to Lieutenant Kermit Tyler, a pilot who was the only person on duty. "There's a large number of planes coming in from the north, three degrees east." Lieutenant Tyler was unimpressed. Lockhard got on

the line and tried to convince the lieutenant that it
was important—he had never seen so many planes on
the screen. "Well, don't worry about it," Tyler finally
said. At 7:45 a.m. the truck came and the two
privates shut down the station and left. At 7:55 a.m.
the first bombs fell on Pearl Harbor.

## A PRESIDENT'S LIFE

**Near Miss:** President Franklin Delano Roosevelt was almost
assassinated in 1943, during World War II...by the U.S. Navy.
**What Happened:** On November 14, 1943, the battleship *Iowa*
was carrying President Roosevelt and his joint chiefs of staff to
Cairo for a secret conference with Winston Churchill and Chiang
Kai-shek. According to one account, "In one of the U.S. Navy's
most embarrassing moments, the destroyer *William D. Porter*,
making a simulated torpedo attack during defensive exercises,
inadvertently fired a live 'fish' directly at the *Iowa*. Five minutes
of pure panic ensued. The *Iowa*'s skipper desperately executed a
high-speed turn, trying to get his ship out of the line of fire.
However, as the torpedo entered the *Iowa*'s churning wake,
it exploded, set off by the extreme turbulence of the sea."

\*     \*     \*     \*

## THE TROUBLE WITH ENGLISH

There is no egg in eggplant, no ham in hamburger and no pine or
apple in pineapple.

Quicksand swallows you up slowly; boxing rings are square and
guinea pigs aren't from Guinea and aren't pigs.

If love is blind, why is lingerie so popular?

Why is it that the person who invests all your money is called a
broker?

If people from Poland are called "Poles", why aren't people from
Holland called "Holes"?

Why do you wind up a watch to start it but wind up a story to
finish it?

# TRAIN WHISTLE BLOWING!

*It's not the Orient Express, but throw in your glad rags anyway
for a bit of glamour and mystique on the Ghan.*

**R**AILWAY BAZAAR
There's something about trains and train journeys.
They've inspired writers as diverse as Paul Theroux (*The
Great Railway Bazaar*) and Agatha Christie (*Murder on the Orient
Express*). Even Arthur Conan Doyle featured trains in several
Sherlock Holmes stories. And don't forget the *Hogwart's Express*
in J.K. Rowling's popular series, *Harry Potter*. But the *Ghan*, which
runs from Adelaide to Alice Spring, has its own story—one that is
embedded in Australian history.

## I'D WALK A MILE FOR A CAMEL

The *Ghan* takes its name from a slice of Australian history. Nearly
150 years ago, Afghan camel drivers and their camel "trains" criss-
crossed the long distances through the harsh Australian interior—
a land that was unforgiving and hostile, and too tough for bullock
or horse teams. The camels carried supplies and essential
equipment for the outback cattle and sheep stations, the telegraph
and railways. Without them, the permanently parched lands of
Central Australia would have been inaccessible. Aptly, the
emblem on the *Ghan* is that of an Afghan on a camel.

## ON TRACK

It was a bold decision to build a trans-continental railway.
Without a ready supply of water and trees, and amid withering
temperatures, the new tracks slowly inched along the terrain.
In 1929, the first train carrying passengers and goods left the
Adelaide railway station. It was bound for the centre of Australia.
Two days later, it arrived in Alice Springs. As is the Australian
way, *The Afghan Express* was quickly shortened to the *Ghan* and,
as such, it soon became part of the Australian outback tradition.
In its early history, however, the *Ghan* was neither reliable nor

The G in g-string stands for "groin."

speedy. The two-day journey from Adelaide to Alice could take up to six weeks. Delays were often caused by termite damage, or by rails that buckled helplessly in the outback heat. Then there were the floods that wiped out tracks and railway bridges. On one such occasion, the *Ghan* was marooned on the bank of a flooded river for two weeks. When the supplies of fresh food ran out, the driver calmly took his gun and shot wild goats to feed his passengers.

In 1935, the *Ghan* made a different kind of headline when "The Great *Ghan* Gold Robbery" caused a stir through the country. On a lonely stretch of railway linking Alice with Quorn, 34 lb of gold (worth £4,000) disappeared from a locked safe in the brake van of the *Ghan*. The booking clerk at Quorn discovered the theft and two detectives were brought in from Adelaide. They fingerprinted the safe and interviewed the passengers, but all leads came to nothing. The gold was never found.

## ALL ABOARD!

Today, you can board the *Ghan* in Sydney, Melbourne, Adelaide or Alice Springs to experience one of the great train journeys of the world—a journey through the heart of the Australian continent. The scenery en route is spectacular. The colours of the outback are framed by startlingly blue skies and dimmed by dramatic sunsets. Spinifex plains are backdropped by majestic mountain ranges, while all kinds of native wildlife scurry across the ochre soil.

If you really want to experience the *Ghan* in complete style—the Prince of Wales car, which was built originally by the Commonwealth Railways for visiting royalty, is now available for a mere $8,000 for a one-way fare!

\*  \*  \*  \*

## LIFE'S LIKE THAT

**Q:** How can you tell when a train is gone?
**A:** It leaves its tracks behind.

**Q:** Why do you have to wait so long for a ghost train to come along?
**A:** Because they only operate on skeleton staff.

The can-opener was invented 48 years after the can was.

# THE BIRTH OF THE COMIC BOOK

*A story for people who read comics in the bathroom.*

The modern comic book was born at the Eastern Colour Printing Company in Waterbury, Connecticut.

In the late 1920s, Eastern printed the Sunday comic sections for a number of East Coast newspapers. Eastern's sales manager, Harry Wildenberg, was looking for ways to increase the company's profits and keep the printing presses busy. He came up with a clever idea: bind some of the comics into a "tabloid-sized book," and sell them as a premium.

He convinced the Gulf Oil Company to give it a shot. They bought the books, gave them to customers…and were pleased with the results. Eastern had a new product to sell.

Meanwhile, Wildenberg was trying to make the package more practical. He noticed that if he shrank the comic strips to half-size, he could fit two complete strips on each tabloid-sized page. He played with the idea, and figured out how to produce a 64-page book of comics on Eastern's presses.

## A NEW PRODUCT

This new creation was a big hit with companies whose products were geared to kids. Procter & Gamble, Kinney Shoes, Canada Dry, and other businesses gave away anywhere from 100,000 to 250,000 copies at a time.

Then it occurred to people at Eastern that if the product was so popular as a premium, maybe it could be sold directly to kids. So in 1934, they printed 200,000 copies of a "comic book" called *Famous Funnies*, put a price on them (10¢), and got them onto newsstands around the country.

*Famous Funnies* was an instant hit. Eastern sold 180,000 copies—90% of the first print run. And by the 12th issue, they were making as much as $30,000 a month from it.

The comic book was established as a profitable part of American pop culture.

# GROUNDS FOR DIVORCE

*Think you're in a bad relationship? Take a look at these folks.*

In Loving, New Mexico, a woman divorced her husband because he made her salute him and address him as "Major" whenever he walked by.

One Tarittville, Connecticut, man filed for divorce after his wife left him a note on the refrigerator. It read, "I won't be home when you return from work. Have gone to the bridge club. There'll be a recipe for your dinner at 7 o'clock on Channel 2."

In Lynch Heights, Delaware, a woman filed for divorce because her husband "regularly put itching powder in her underwear when she wasn't looking."

In Honolulu, Hawaii, a man filed for divorce from his wife, because she "served pea soup for breakfast and dinner…and packed his lunch with pea sandwiches."

In Hazard, Kentucky, a man divorced his wife because she "beat him whenever he removed onions from his hamburger without first asking for permission."

In Frackville, Pennsylvania, a woman filed for divorce because her husband insisted on "shooting tin cans off of her head with a slingshot."

One Winthrop, Maine, man divorced his wife because she "wore earplugs whenever his mother came to visit."

A Smelterville, Idaho, man won divorce from his wife on similar grounds. "His wife dressed up as a ghost and tried to scare his elderly mother out of the house."

In Canon City, Colorado, a woman divorced her husband because he made her "duck under the dashboard whenever they drove past his girlfriend's house."

No escape: In Bennettsville, South Carolina, a deaf man filed for divorce from his wife because "she was always nagging him in sign language."

*The Last Straw:* In Hardwick, Georgia, a woman actually divorced her husband because he "stayed home too much and was much too affectionate."

---

Q: **What do you call a person who assembles the underparts of pianos? A: The "belly builder."**

# THE NATURAL HISTORY OF THE UNICORN

*Today we know that there's no such thing as unicorns. But back in the 1500s, they were a sort of respectable version of Bigfoot. Although only a few people had ever "seen" them, it was widely believed that they existed. So when Topsell's* Historie of Four-footed Beastes, *the first illustrated natural history in English, was published in 1607, unicorns were included. Here are some excerpts from the original version of the book. Remember, as you read, that these descriptions were considered science, not fantasy.*

## ABOUT THE HORN

• "We will now relate the true history of the horn of the unicorn. The horn grows out of the forehead between the eyelids. It is neither light nor hollow, nor yet smooth like other horns, but hard as iron, rough as a file. It is wreathed about with divers spires. It is sharper than any dart, and it is straight and not crooked, and everywhere black except at the point."

• "The horn of the unicorn has a wonderful power of dissolving and expelling all venom or poison. If the unicorn puts his horn into water from which any venomous beast has drunk, the horn drives away poison, so that the unicorn can drink without harm. It is said that the horn being put upon the tables of kings and set among their junkets and banquets reveals any venom if there be any such therein, by a certain sweat which comes over the horn."

• "The horn of a unicorn being beaten and boiled in wine has a wonderful effect in making the teeth white or clear. And thus much shall suffice for the medicines and virtues arising from the unicorn."

## THE WILD CREATURE

• "Unicorns are very swift. They keep for the most part in the deserts and live solitary in the tops of mountains. There is nothing more horrible than the voice or braying of the unicorn, for his voice is strained above measure."

**The Mona Lisa has no eyebrows.**

- "The unicorn fights with both the mouth and his heels, with the mouth biting like a lion's and with the heels kicking like a horse's. He is a beast of an untamable nature. He fears not iron nor any iron instrument."
- "What is most strange of all other is that he fights with his own kind (yea, even with females unto death, except when he burns in lust for procreation), but unto stranger-beasts, with whom he has no affinity in nature, he is more sociable and familiar, delighting in their company when they come willingly unto him, never rising against them, but proud of their dependence and retinue, keeps with them all quarters of league and truce."
- "With his female, when once his flesh is tickled with lust, he grows tame, gregarious, and loving, and so continues till she is filled and great with young, and then returns to his former hostility."

## NATURAL ENEMIES

- "The unicorn is an enemy to the lion, wherefore, as soon as ever a lion sees a unicorn, he runs to a tree for succor, so that, when the unicorn makes force at him, he may not only avoid his horn but also destroy the unicorn, for, in the swiftness of his course, the unicorn runs against the tree wherein his sharp horn sticks fast."
- "Then, when the lion sees the unicorn fastened by his horn, he falls upon him and kills him."

## CAPTURING THE UNICORN

- "It is said that unicorns above all other creatures do reverence virgins and young maids, and that many times at the sight of them, unicorns grow tame, and come and sleep beside them, for there is in their nature a certain savor by which the unicorns are allured and delighted."
- "The Indian and Ethiopian hunters are said to use a stratagem to take the beast. They take a goodly strong and beautiful young man, whom they dress in the apparel of a woman, besetting him with divers odoriferous flowers and spices."
- "The man so adorned, they set him in the mountains or the woods where the unicorn hunts, so as the wind may carry the savor to the beast, and in the mean season, the other hunters hide themselves."

Commonsense fact: Animals that lay eggs don't have belly buttons.

- "Deceived by the outward shape of a woman and the sweet smells, the unicorn comes unto the young man without fear and so suffers his head to be covered and wrapped within his large sleeves, never stirring but lying still and asleep, as in his most acceptable repose."
- "Then when the hunters by the sign of the young man perceive the unicorn fast and secure, they come upon him and by force cut off his horn and send him away alive."

## PROOF THAT UNICORNS EXIST

*Why was Edward Topsell so sure that unicorns roamed the earth? A matter of faith. Although he'd never seen a unicorn, Topsell believed that to doubt its existence was to deny the very existence of God:*

- "That there is such a beast Scripture itself witnesses, for David thus speaks in Psalm 92: 'My horn shall be lifted up like the horn of a unicorn.'"
- "All divines that have ever written have not only concluded that there is a unicorn, but also affirm the similitude between the kingdom of David and the horn of the unicorn, for as the horn of the unicorn is wholesome to all beasts and creatures, so should the kingdom of David be in the generation of Christ."
- "Do we think that David would compare the virtue of his kingdom and the powerful redemption of the world unto a thing that is not or is uncertain and fantastical? Likewise, in many other places of Scripture, we will have to traduce God, Himself, if there is no unicorn in the world."

\*     \*     \*     \*

## AND NOW FOR A COUPLE OF BAD JOKES

**Q:** Why was the idiot staring at a carton of orange juice?
**A:** Because it said concentrate.

**Q:** What do you call a paddock full of Australians?
**A:** A vacant lot.

**Q:** Why did the jellybean go to school?
**A:** To learn how to be a smartie.

# LLOYD'S OF LONDON

*Insurance companies are probably the last subject you'd expect to read
about in the* Bathroom Reader. *But Lloyd's of London is special.
They insure stuff like people's legs and performing insects and floating
bathtubs. Here's the story of Lloyd's, courtesy of BRI alum
Jack Mingo, author of* How the Cadillac Got Its Fins *and
numerous other books.*

**ORIGIN.** Today most business is conducted over the
phone or in company offices, but in the 17th century the
most popular place for businesses and their clients to meet
was in coffee houses—many of which were built specifically to the
business trade. Lloyd's Coffee House, opened by Edward Lloyd in
London in 1688, was just such a place. Lloyd wanted to take
advantage for the maritime insurance trade, so he built his coffee
house near the London docks.

Lloyd never personally got involved in the insurance business,
but he provided a congenial business atmosphere, semi-enclosed
booths, and even writing materials for his patrons. The cafe
developed a reputation as a source of accurate shipping news and
quickly became the hub of London's maritime insurance industry.

Long after Lloyd's death in 1723, his coffee house remained an
important business meeting place.

## A GROWING BUSINESS

In the 17th and 18th centuries, merchants with a ship or cargo to
insure didn't buy insurance from companies—they hired a broker
to go from one wealthy person to another, selling a share of the
risk in exchange for a share of the insurance premium.

This was considered a respectable profession. But covering
wagers on things like who would win a particular sports contest
or war, or when the current king would die, was not. These less
respectable brokers began frequenting Lloyd's, too.

In 1769, a number of "high-class" brokers decided they didn't
want to be associated with their seamier brethren anymore. So
they set up their own coffee house and called it the "New Lloyd's
Coffee House." They allowed business dealings in maritime

---

Birth of the dimpled ball: Golfers noticed that old, dented balls flew farther than new ones.

insurance only. The new building soon proved too small, so
79 brokers, underwriters, and merchants each chipped in £100 to
finance new headquarters. When they moved this time, they left
the coffee business behind. Over the following century, the
Lloyd's society of underwriters evolved into its modern
incarnation, expanding to all forms of insurance except life
insurance. As one broker put it, "Everybody dies, so what's the
fun of writing life insurance?"

## RISXY BUSINESS
*Lloyd's will insure just about anything. Here are some of the weirder items:*
• **Celebrity anatomy.** Bruce Springsteen has insured his voice for
£3.5 million; Marlene Dietrich had a $500,000 policy on her legs;
and supermodel Suzanne Mizzi was insured for £10 million against
any "serious injury" that left her unable to model underwear.
During filming of the movie *Superman*, man of steel Christopher
Reeves was insured for $20 million.
• **Whiskers.** Forty members of the Derbyshire, England,
"Whiskers Club" insured their facial hair "against fire and theft."
Cost: £20 a head.
• **Laughter.** One theatre group took out a policy "against the risk
of a member of their audience dying from laughter."
• **Space debris.** Before Skylab, the space laboratory, crashed to
earth, Lloyd's offered coverage of up to £2.5 million for property
damage and £500,000 for death coverage to anyone who wanted
it. (No takers.)
• **The weather.** Lloyd's insures the opera festival of Verona, Italy,
for £1 million against bad weather. Reason: When outdoor
performances get cancelled due to rain, the festival has to refund
ticket holders.
• **Souvenirs.** When Charles and Diana announced they were
tying the knot, Lloyd's insured commemorative souvenir makers…
just in case the wedding got called off.
• **A floating bathtub.** When a 20-year-old merchant navy officer
sailed from Dover, England, to Cap Gris Nez, France, in a
bathtub, Lloyd's insured it for £100,000 on one condition: that the
tub's drain plug "remain in position at all times."

- **Dead rats.** Lloyd's once insured an entire boatload of dead rats (which were en route to a Greek research lab) for £110,000 against their condition deteriorating any further.
- **A tiny portrait.** A grain of rice with a portrait of Queen Elizabeth and Prince Philip engraved on it was insured for £20,000.
- **Nessie.** Cutty Sark Whiskey once offered £1 million to anyone who could capture the Loch Ness monster alive, and took out two £1 million policies with Lloyd's…just in case.
- **The King.** When a Memphis radio station offered $1 million to anyone who could prove Elvis was really alive, Lloyd's backed them up 100 percent.

## THE NAME GAME
**How Lloyd's works.** Lloyd's of London isn't a company at all: It's a "society" of thousands of members (called Names because they put their "name," or full reputation and worth, behind the risk), who underwrite insurance policies with their personal assets. As was the case three centuries ago, each Name is personally liable for claims. The Name never has to turn over the money he "invests" with Lloyd's—he just has to prove that he *has* it and can surrender it on demand to pay claims.

## HARD TIMES
The system worked great for hundreds of years, but disaster struck in the late 1980s, after more than a decade of excessive policy writing in which Lloyd's Names insured asbestos manufacturers, the Exxon *Valdez*, and the San Francisco earthquake of 1989. Between 1988 and 1990 the company had to pay out more than $10 billion in claims, which meant that by 1991 each of the company's 32,000 Names owed more than $312,500 to policyholders, with the total expected to climb still further. More than 21,000 of the Names sued Lloyd's, claiming that Lloyd's underwriters were negligent in writing insurance contracts. Lloyd's admitted as much in 1994, and offered a $1.3 billion settlement to the Names, but, at the time this was written, the lawsuits were still pending.

# HUMPBACKS IN THE OUTBACK

*Known in Africa as "ships in the desert," these strange, exotic animals can survive for about 20 days without water. They are ideal desert animals. For more on camels in Australia see* Will That Be One Hump or Two? *on page 58.*

In the heart of Australia you will find the world's only wild single-hump camels, or dromedaries. Their imported ancestors were freed after playing an important role in exploring and settling the outback.

## CAMEL LOT

The first three camels in Australia arrived at Port Adelaide from the Canary Islands in 1840. Twenty years later, camels were arriving by the shipload, many bound for Beltana Station, a camel stud established by pastoralist Thomas Elder. They were needed to meet the growing demand for transport and exploration. Camels were used on the ill-fated Burke and Wills trip when they left Melbourne in August 1860 to cross Australia from south to north. Their team reached the Gulf of Carpentaria in February 1861, but Burke and Wills died on the return journey through a series of mishaps and misjudgements. However camels were used more successfully, in equally harsh terrain, when Warbuton travelled from Alice Springs to Perth in 1873 and when Ernest Giles led a return trip from South Australia to Perth in 1875.

## HERE COME THE CAMELEERS

More than 10,000 camels were imported up until 1907, and with them came the Afghan cameleers (later known as Ghans). Camels became a familiar sight across inland Australia. A camel team would be made up of around seventy camels and four Afghans. They would travel between 32–40 km (20–25 miles) a day, with a large bull camel carrying up to 600 kg (1,323 lb).

Camel teams carried supplies to inland towns, mining camps, sheep and cattle stations, and Aboriginal communities. They also

**The box jellyfish has killed more people than sharks, stonefish and crocodiles combined.**

carried pipe sections for the Goldfields Water Supply and helped build the Overland Telegraph Line, the Canning Stock Route, major fence lines throughout outback Australia and the Trans–Australia and Central Australian railways.

## ROAMING FREE
Although outback police, boundary riders and postmen continued to use camels right up to World War II, motor transport in the 1920s took over many of the camels' tasks. Camels that once sold for about $600–$1000 were now worthless. Some were destroyed and others were released and established "free-range" herds in the semi-arid desert areas of Australia. Today, there are around 500,000 camels roaming free.

\*　　\*　　\*　　\*

## FUNNY 'OL DUNNY
Originally, the word "dunny" referred to an outside toilet, a little distance from the house, in an unsewered area. It was the butt of a great many stories, real or otherwise, for the uninitiated. They were warned of the dangers of encountering red-back spiders, snakes, frogs, blowflies, bull ants, flies, mosquitoes…and whatever other nasties might be around at the time.

Some dunnies were simply built over large dug-out holes in the ground. Dunnies in the town and cities had cans that were regularly collected by the "night carter."

The "flaming fury" was a very special type of dunny. When this very large pit was full, kerosene was poured onto it. Once lit, furious flames certainly ensured that the dunny was out of order for a while.

Australian toilets are a little more refined today, but the word "dunny" still has an enduring spot in the Australian language. If you're "all alone like a country dunny," you're in a very bad way! And you know someone is REALLY mad at you if they yell: "I hope your chooks turn into emus and kick your dunny down!"

The first royal to visit Australia was Prince Alfred, Duke of Edinburgh in 1867–1868.

# THE NUMBERS GAME

*This is a tough game—very few people can solve more than a few of these equations on the first try. But don't look at the answers on page 488 right away. People often come up with them later, when their minds are relaxed. And you can work on this page for a number of "sittings".*

## INSTRUCTIONS

Each equation contains the initials of words that will make it a correct statement. Your job is to finish the missing words. For example:

26 = L. of the A. would be 26 = *Letters of the Alphabet*. Good luck.

1. 7 = W. of the A. W.
2. 1001 = A. N.
3. 12 = S. of the Z.
4. 54 = C. in a D. (with the J.)
5. 9 = P. in the S. S.
6. 88 = P. K.
7. 13 = S. on the A. F.
8. 32 = D. F. at which W. F.
9. 90 = D. in a R. A.
10. 99 = B. of B. on the W.
11. 18 = H. on a G. C.
12. 8 = S. on a S. S.
13. 3 = B. M. (S. H. T. R.)
14. 4 = Q. in a G.
15. 1 = W. on a U.
16. 5 = D. in a Z. C.
17. 24 = H. in a D.
18. 57 = H. V.
19. 11 = P. on a F. T.
20. 1000 = W. that a P. is W.
21. 29 = D. in F. in a L. Y.
22. 64 = S. on a C.
23. 40 = D. and N. of the G. F.
24. 2 = T. T.
25. 76 = T. in a B. P.
26. 8 = G. T. in a L. B. C.
27. 101 = D.
28. 23 = S.
29. 4 = H. a J. G. F.
30. 16 = M. on a D. M. C.
31. 12 = D. of C.
32. 5 = G. L.
33. 7 = D. S.
34. 2.5 = C. in a T. A. F.
35. 1, 2, 3 = S. Y. O.
   at the O. B. G.
36. 3 = M. in a T.
37. 13 = B. D.

**Doctors in ancient China were paid when patients were healthy, not sick.**

# IT LOSES SOMETHING IN THE TRANSLATION

*Mongo teep robinek. Pargo meep, kiga lorb. Squarp? Neegah!*
*Sheerik sot morbo. Pid rintu…guira—gop fibge. Here are more*
*nonsense that seems perfectly understandable to the person who's*
*speaking. For the first batch see page 371.*

## PARDON ME…

"I once observed a foreign gentleman with halting English at a subway station asking for the correct time," author Roger Axtell recalls in his book *Do's and Taboos of Hosting International Visitors.* "He was repeatedly rebuffed by brusque New Yorkers. Edging closer, I heard the patient but tiring visitor finally say to the fifth or sixth passerby, 'Pardon me, sir, but do *you* have the correct time…or should I go screw myself, as the others have suggested?' "

## ADVENTURES IN THE EAST
• In China, Kentucky Fried Chicken's slogan "finger-lickin' good" was translated as "eat your fingers off" and a phonetic adaptation of Coca-Cola came out as "Bite the Wax Tadpole."
• In Taiwan, Pepsi's "Come Alive with Pepsi" came out as "Pepsi Will Bring Your Ancestors Back from the Dead."
• Japan's second-largest tourist agency, Kinki Nippon Tourist Co., had to change the name of its overseas division because the word "Kinki" was too close to the English word "kinky." The company was worried about attracting the "wrong kind of customer."

## NO HABLO ESPANOL
• Many of the T-shirts made for Pope John Paul II's visit to Miami were in Spanish. They were supposed to say "I saw the Pope." Instead, they said, "I saw the potato."
• Braniff Airlines once wanted to promote the fact that its leather seats were comfortable. According to reporters, when they did ads for Hispanic customers, they "used a slang term for leather which means a person's hide as well as a cowhide. Rather than asking people to fly Braniff on leather seats, the airline asked them to fly in the nude."

Ever wonder what we call these things at the bottom of the page? They're "running feet."

- A frozen foods manufacturer used the word *burruda* to describe its burrito line. They didn't realise that the word is slang for "huge mistake."

## JUST DO WHAT?
In one of its shoe commercials, Nike showed a Kenyan Samburu looking into the camera and speaking Maa, his native language. The subtitle read "Just do it," Nike's advertising slogan…but it wasn't until after the commercial hit the airwaves that company officials realised he was saying, "I don't want these. Give me big shoes."

## NO SEX, PLEASE
- The Swedish company that makes Electrolux vacuum cleaners once tried to market their products in the United States using the slogan "Nothing sucks like an Electrolux." (The company's translators talked them out of it at the last minute.)
- What Brazilian would have admitted to driving a Ford Pinto? Pinto, it turns out, is slang in Portuguese for "small male genitals." Ford changed the name in Brazil to "Corcel," which means *horse*.

\*     \*     \*     \*

## AND FUNNY MONEY, TOO
- WELLINGTON, New Zealand—March 4, 1992.
Lance Aukett, a 13-year-old boy, found a 10,000-yen note in a box of schoolbooks while he was cleaning his bedroom. Unsure of its value, he decided to check with some banks. One bank said that it might be worth $8; another valued it at $26. But the best deal came from the National Bank of New Zealand, which accepted the note and gave Aukett $78 for it.

Two weeks later the bank realised they had purchased a piece of Monopoly money (from a Japanese version of the game).
- "Since 1971, any money lost through bribery has been tax deductible." According to the IRS's official taxpayers' guide, "bribes and kickbacks to governmental officials *are* deductible unless the individual has been convicted of making the bribe or has entered a plea of not guilty or *nolo contendere*."

**—2201 Fascinating Facts, by David Louis**

Yuck! 70% of the dust in your house is skin your family members (including pets) have shed.

# A GAGGLE OF GEESE

*You've used the terms a "pack" of wolves and a "flock" of sheep...
here are some animal terms you probably haven't even heard of.*

**MAMMALS**
A shrewdness or troop of apes (also monkeys)
A pace of asses
A cete of badgers
A sloth of bears
A colony of beavers
A singular of boars
A clouder of cats
A brood of chickens
A rag of colts
A cowardice of curs
A gang of elk
A business of ferrets
A skulk or troop of foxes
A trip of goats
A drift of hogs
A troop of kangaroos
A kindle of kittens
A leap of leopards
A nest of mice
A barren of mules
A string of ponies
A nest of rabbits
A crash of rhinoceroses
A bevy of roebucks

A dray of squirrels
A sounder of swine
A pod or gam of whales

**BIRDS**
A murder of crows
A dole or piteousness of doves
A paddling of duck (swimming)
A raft of duck (in the water, but *not* swimming)
A team of ducks (in the air)
A charm of finches
A gaggle of geese (on the ground)
A skein of geese (in the air)
A siege of herons
A deceit of lapwings
An exaltation or bevy of larks
A parliament of owls
A covey of quail
An ostentation of peacocks

A nye or covey of pheasants (on the ground)
A bouquet of pheasants (taking to the air)
An unkindness of ravens
A murmuration of sandpipers
A rafter of turkeys
A descent of woodpeckers

**INSECTS**
An army of caterpillars
A business of flies
A cluster of grasshoppers
A plague or swarm of locusts

**OTHER**
A shoal of bass
A clutch of eggs
A bed of snakes
A knot of toads
A bale of turtles
A nest of vipers

**Scientists say:** An average person gives off about as much heat in an hour as a 100-watt lightbulb.

# DISASTER FILMS II

*Here are more of the worst losers Hollywood has ever produced.*

**C**LEOPATRA (1963)
**Description:** It started out as a low-budget "tits-and-togas" epic, but became a high-cost extravaganza when studio executives offered Liz Taylor the lead. "Sure," she supposedly replied, "I'll do it for a million dollars." She was joking—no one had *ever* been paid that much for a single film role before—but 20th Century-Fox took the bait and made her the first million-dollar star in Hollywood history.

**Dollars and Sense:** Adjusted for inflation, *Cleopatra* is believed to be the biggest money loser in the history of film. It had a $6 million budget when Taylor was signed, but cost $44 million—the equivalent of nearly $200 million dollars. Twenty years after it was released, the film was still an estimated $46.2 million in the hole.

**Wretched Excess:** More than three hectares (eight acres) of sets were built near London, and the Thames River was diverted to create a "mini Nile" for the film. But the fog made filming impossible. "On a good day," said the director, "whenever a word was spoken, you could see the vapour coming from the actors' mouths. It was like a tobacco commercial." Taylor almost died of pneumonia during the filming and couldn't return to the damp London sets for more than six months. Overhead costs piled up at $45,000 a day. Finally the studio gave up and shut the London studios down. Total cost: $6 million for 12 minutes of usable film.

**The Critics Speak:** "After [the London premiere], I raced back to the Dorchester and just made it to the downstairs lavatory and vomited."—Elizabeth Taylor

## THE GREATEST STORY EVER TOLD (1965)
**Description:** In 1954, 20th Century-Fox paid $100,000 for the film rights to *The Greatest Story Ever Told*, a novel about the life of Jesus Christ. The studio set out to make a big-budget Bible epic along the lines of *Samson and Delilah* (1949) and *The Ten Commandments* (1956).

**Dollars and Sense:** The film cost more than $20 million to make; five years later it had still only earned $8 million worldwide.

**Wretched Excess:** Director George Stevens insisted on building a fake Holy Land in Arizona, arguing that the *real* Holy Land wasn't good enough. "I wanted to get an effect of grandeur as a background to Christ," he explained, "and none of the Holy Land areas shape up with the excitement of the American Southwest." Six months into the film, a blizzard pounded the 9-hectare (22-acre) Jerusalem set and buried it in snow. Stevens just moved to Los Angeles, where he built a whole *new* Jerusalem.

Filming fell so far behind schedule that two members of the cast and crew died, and the actress who played Mary Magdalene became pregnant (forcing Stevens to film her standing behind furniture and in other odd angles). Stevens handed out so many cameo roles to Hollywood celebrities that "it made the road to Calvary look like the Hollywood Walk of Stars." In one scene, John Wayne played a centurion who barked out the now-famous line, "Truly, this man *wuz* the Son of Gawd!!"

## MOHAMMED: MESSENGER OF GOD (1977)

**Description:** A cinematic biography of the prophet Mohammed, *Mohammed: Messenger of God* was intended by the producer to be Islam's *The Ten Commandments*.

**Dollars and Sense:** Two different versions of the film were made: one with Islamic actors for the Islamic world, and one with Western actors. Both versions bombed; in fact, every Islamic country except Turkey banned the Islamic version. The film(s) cost $17 million and earned less than $5 million.

**Wretched Excess:** When rumours spread that Peter O'Toole— and then Charleton Heston—had been signed to play Mohammed, angry protests broke out all over the Middle East. Saudi Arabia's King Faisal had granted permission to film on location in Mecca, but changed his mind and kicked the director out of the country. The director then moved to the desert outside of Marrakash, Morocco, and spent hundreds of thousands of dollars building a detailed replica of Mecca. Six months after filming began, King Faisal "communicated his displeasure" over the film to King Hassan of Morocco by threatening to cut off oil shipments to the kingdom and banning all Moroccan pilgrims from entering Saudi Arabia. The Director had to move to the Libyan desert and build a *third* Mecca.

Yum yum! Half a kilogram of houseflies contains more protein than half a kilogram of beef.

# BAD HAIR DAYS

*Think you've ever had a bad hair day? Just be glad you never had one like these folks.*

**B**ACKGROUND
"One kind of day that everyone dreads is the widely known and feared *bad hair day*," wrote columnist William Safire when a reader asked him about the term. Safire speculated that it started with comedian Gary Shandling. "Irritated with his coverage in *Us* magazine, Shandling (who used to begin his routine with 'Is my hair all right?') told the *Seattle Times* in January 1991: 'I was at a celebrity screening of *Misery* and they made up a quote for me.

They said I told them I was having a *bad hair* day. They didn't even talk to me.' "

A month later the phrase appeared in the *L.A. Times*, then the *Toronto Star* ("Was Robert DeNiro caught in a crosswind, or was he just having a bad hair day?"), and now it's a part of our lexicon.

## SIX REAL BAD HAIR DAYS
### 1. Michael Jackson
In February 1984, Jackson and his brothers were filming a $1.5 million commercial for Pepsi-Cola in which he walked down a staircase as a pyrotechnic display went off behind him. They shot the scene four times, but according to *Time* magazine, "The effect was not quite right for Director Bob Giraldi...He asked the singer to move more slowly and ordered the fireworks 'heated up' a bit. The combination proved volatile: On the fiery fifth take...sparks from a smoke bomb ignited Jackson's hair, sending the singer to the hospital with second- and third-degree burns on his scalp.
### 2. Albert Anastasia
Anastasia was head of the Mangano crime family, one of the infamous "five families" of the New York mafia. On the morning of October 25, 1957, he went for a haircut at the Park Sheraton Hotel. While his bodyguard parked the car, Anastasia sat down in the barber chair and fell asleep. Minutes later, two men wearing scarves over their faces walked up to him, drew their guns, and opened fire. Anastasia jumped out of the chair and tried to attack the gunmen, but he was too badly wounded and collapsed dead on the floor.

As a person ages, the first sense to go is the sense of smell.

### 3. Hans Steininger

Steininger was a 16th-century Austrian man famous for having the longest beard in the world. In September 1567, he tripped on his beard as he was climbing the stairs to the council chamber of Brunn, Austria. He fell down the stairs and died.

### 4. Hans Hoffman

In 1993, Hoffman, a 31-year-old vagrant, robbed a Rotterdam (Netherlands) bank of $15,000, telling the teller he needed the money to get a haircut and buy a piece of cheese. A few hours later he showed up at the Rotterdam police department, surrendered, and handed over a bag full of cash. Police counted the money and it was all there—minus the price of a haircut and a piece of cheese.

### 5. King Louis VII of France

King Louis had a beard when he married Eleanor of Aquitaine in 1137, but when he shaved it off, Eleanor thought he looked ugly without it and insisted he grow it back. Louis refused—so she left him and married King Henry II of England. However, Louis refused to give back Aquitaine, Eleanor's ancestral lands, which had become part of France when the couple got married. King Henry declared war. "The War of the Whiskers" lasted 301 years, until peace was finally signed in 1453.

### 6. President Bill Clinton

In May 1993, President Clinton received a $200 haircut on Air Force One. The only problem: At the time, Air Force One was parked on the tarmac, and according to a Federal Aviation Administration official, the trim shut down two of LAX's four runways for 56 minutes. The scene generated so much bad publicity that the hair stylist, Christophe, held a press conference to deny that Clinton was as smug, self-important, or stylish as the incident suggested.

"I am not saying this in a negative way," he told reporters, "but from what you can see, do you really think that Hillary or Bill Clinton, are very concerned about their appearance?"

The whole thing may have been the work of a political trickster. Subsequent checks of the records at LAX showed that the haircut had actually caused no problems. Runways were not shut down, and no planes were kept waiting.

---

71% of university-educated women, but only 44% of non-university-educated women, breastfeed.

# AUSSIE SPEAK

*Blow me down mate, Bluey is shooting through to the Top End.
Why not come round this arvo for a farewell barbie. Bring
some snags, tinnies, the anklebiters and cozzies, but not that
bloody bitzer or your dipstick brother-in-law!*

**H**OME-GROWN LINGO
This may sound like another language to many English-speaking people, but not to the Aussies. It makes perfect sense. This is their own, home-grown lingo. If you are new to the land of Oz these words might help you.

**aerial ping-pong** Australian Rules
**airy-fairy** insubstantial; hare-brained; in your dreams
**anklebiter** a child
**arvo** afternoon

**back of Bourke** any remote outback region
**bananabender** a barbecue
**barney** a fight or scuffle
**battlers** honest, hardworking folk
**beaut** very good; excellent
**bickie** a biscuit
**bit o' all right** someone who is lovely or even beautiful
**bitzer** mongrel dog
**bloody** difficult
**bloody oath!** expression of agreement
**blow me** astonishment
**blue** a mistake; row
**Bluey** a nickname for someone with red hair
**bob's your uncle** it's all right
**boogie board** a small, flexible, lightweight surf board
**Buckley's chance** a very slim chance
**bush** the country
**bush telegraph** the local gossip network
**bush telly** campfire

**chinwag** a chat; conversation
**chuffed** pleased; delighted

**cocky** a farmer; a cockatoo or other parrot
**come a gutser** to fall over; to fail as a result of an error of judgement
**crook** not feeling well or not going well
**cut lunch** sandwiches prepared at home and to be eaten elsewhere

**dag** a bit of a fool; not very well presented
**dead-set** certain; assured
**dipstick** an idiot
**dingbat** someone odd; crazy
**drop kick** an obnoxious person

**ear bashing** talking too much
**exie** expensive

**fair dinkum** true; genuine
**fairy floss** spun sugar often served on a stick
**flat out like a lizard drinking** exerting yourself to the utmost
**footy** Australian Rules or other football code
**fruit loop** someone of unsound mind

**galah** a fool; a silly person
**garbo, garbologist** garbage collector
**g'day, gidday** hello!
**gee-gees** horses; horse racing
**get a Guernsey** to succeed; win approval

**happy as Larry** extremely happy; without a care in the world
**homestead** main residence on a sheep or cattle station
**hooly-dooly** an expression of surprise
**hoon** a loutish, aggressive, or surly youth
**hooroo** goodbye; see you later

**iffy** doubtful; depending on circumstances

**lippie** lipstick

**jack off** sick of; fed up with
**jackaroo** a male farm hand, usually on a cattle station
**jillaroo** a female farm hand, usually on a cattle station
**john** toilet
**jumback** sheep

Four health clinics around the world specialise in bad breath. (Two are in America.)

**mates rates** specially cheap rates for friends
**mozzie** mosquito
**mug** a fool; gullible person

**nipper** young surf lifesaver
**not the full quid** mentally challenged; dull-witted
**not within cooee** far from achieving a given goal

**o.s.** overseas
**owyergoin** a greeting, "How are you going?"

**plonk** any alcoholic liquor, especially cheap wine
**possie** a place; position
**prezzie** a gift

**right** all right; okay
**ripper** great; fantastic

**shoot through** to leave
**shout** to pay for something for another person; treat
**sickie** a day taken off with pay, because of genuine or feigned illness
**snag** a sausage
**spit the dummy** to give up on something before there is reasonable cause to do so; to throw a tantrum
**sport** a more general way of referring to someone other than mate
**strewth** an exclamation, often of surprise
**stubbie** a small beer bottle

**tall poppy** a person who is outstanding in any way, especially someone with great wealth or status
**tinnie** a can of beer; small aluminium boat
**Top End** the top end of the Northern Territory of Australia
**veg out** relax in front of the TV

**wallop** to beat soundly; thrash
**whinge** to complain; whine
**within cooee** within calling distance
**wog** a cold or stomach upset
**Woop Woop** an imaginary remote and insignificant town

**yabber** to talk
**yobbo** an uncouth person

The world's fastest typist can type 216 words per minute.

# LIMERICKS

*Limericks have been around since the 1700s.
And our readers have been sending them in since 1988.
Here are a few more of their favourites.*

There was a faith-healer
of Deal,
Who said, "Although pain
isn't real,
If I sit on a pin,
And it punctures my skin,
I dislike what I fancy I feel."

There were once two young
people of taste
Who were beautiful, down to
the waist.
So they limited love
To the regions above,
And thus remained perfectly
chaste.

There was an old man
of Blackheath,
Who sat on his set of false
teeth;
Said he, with a start,
"O Lord, bless my heart!
I've bitten myself
underneath!"

There was a young man
of Montrose,
Who had pockets in none of
his clothes.
When asked by his lass
Where he carried his brass,
He said: "Darling, I pay
through the nose."

There was a young student
called Fred,
Who was questioned on
Descartes and said:
"It's perfectly clear
That I'm not really here,
For I haven't a thought in my
head."

Dr. Johnson, when sober
or pissed,
Could be frequently heard
to insist,
Letting out a great fart:
"Yes, I follow Descartes—
I stink, and I therefore exist."

A cute secretary,
none cuter,
Was replaced by a clicking
computer.
T'was the wife of her boss
Who put the deal across;
You see, the computer
was neuter.

There was a young lady
named Jeanie,
Who wore an outrageous
bikini,
Two wisps light as air,
One here and one there,
With nothing but Jeanie
betweenie.

# FIVE PET FADS

*An informal study by the BRI has shown that many bathroom readers
are also pet aficionados. Uncle John himself keeps a piranha in his
bathtub. And he's trying to convince Mrs. Uncle John to keep
a fainting goat in the bedroom.*

**A**QUARIUMS
Fish tanks were popular in the United States as far back
as the early 1800s, but for the most part only the wealthy
had them. The reason: Water quickly became deprived of oxygen,
and fish died unless the water was constantly changed. No one
wanted to take on that responsibility...unless they could afford to
pay someone to do it for them.

It wasn't until 1850 that Robert Warington, a chemist,
announced to the world that he'd kept a pet fish alive for a year in
a tank without changing the water. His secret: He added plants to
the tank, which replenished the oxygen supply. His contribution
was so significant that the first aquariums were known as
Warrington [sic] cases.

Not long afterward, British naturalist Philip Gosse published
*The Aquarium*, a how-to book that quickly became a bestseller.
Soon, American and British fish lovers had made aquarium-
keeping one of the largest and most popular pet fads in the world.

### COLLIES
For centuries, collies were common in the Scottish Lowlands, but
virtually unknown everywhere else in the world. A working dog
used to guard the large flocks of sheep that roamed the area, the
collie might still be uncommon today if it hadn't been for Queen
Victoria. She happened to notice some of the dogs outside of
Balmoral Castle and was so charmed by them that she brought a
few back to London. The British upper classes, quick to take a
royal hint, made the collie one of the most popular breeds in the
country...and eventually in the world.

### THE MAKECH BEETLE
A short-lived fad of the 1960s, the "makech" was a gilded and
stone-encrusted living beetle that was attached to a pin by a thin
gold chain. The wearer attached the pin to their shirt, and let the

beetle walk over their shoulder and neck. Phyllis Diller wore a
makech emblazoned with gold lace and white seed pearls. "How
else," she asked at the time, "am I going to get ten men standing
around looking at my chest?" Not everyone liked the fad.
"A makech's appeal is primarily to the screwball fringe," said a
customs agent in charge of breaking up illegal beetle-smuggling
rings. "It takes some kind of nut to wear a bug."

## PIRANHAS

Another weird pet craze of the 1960s was the piranha.
Enterprising pet store owners skirted laws banning importation
and possession of the meat-eating fishes, claiming they were
actually friendly pets, not the flesh-eating meanies they were
reputed to be. "We got very attached to ours," one owner told
reporters about her aquatic carnivore. "He had a personality that
most tropical fish don't seem to have." But state and federal
officials held the line—to date it is still illegal to import or own a
piranha. According to one biologist with the California Fish and
Game Department, "Piranhas eat people."

## FAINTING GOATS

Fainting goats aren't much different from normal goats…except
that they have a genetic trait that causes them to stiffen up and
fall over when someone (usually the owner or the owner's friends)
frightens them. Fainting faddists rank their pets' "skill" on a scale
of one to six, with "six being the highest, meaning they lock up
most of the time and fall over," says Kathy Majewski, founder of
The American Tennessee Fainting Goat Association (TATFGA).
First observed in Tennessee in the 1800s, the goats were nearly
driven extinct by coyotes, who (for obvious reasons) preferred
them to regular goats. But TATFGA was formed to save them.

The group boasts more than 200 members, but not everyone
thinks their motives are pure. "To raise animals with an
abnormality for use as entertainment is sick," says Lisa Landres of
the Tennessee Humane Society. "The whole phenomenon is
mind-boggling." She may not have to worry, though—the fad may
die out on its own because it gets increasingly harder to scare the
goats once they get to know you…which defeats the purpose of
owning them in the first place.

# FAMILIAR PHRASES

*More inside info on the origins of phrases we use every day.*

## THE SEAMY SIDE
**Meaning:** The unsavory or worst part.
**Background:** Originally used to refer to the inside part of a sewed garment: If the garment was turned inside out so that the *wrong* side was showing, the stitched *seams* were clearly visible.

## TOP DRAWER
**Meaning:** The best quality.
**Background:** Traditionally, the top drawer of a dresser is the place where jewellery and other valuables are kept.

## ALL OVER BUT THE SHOUTING
**Meaning:** Any situation in which victory is clear before a final decision is reached.
**Background:** Rather than hold formal elections to decide local issues, for centuries in England it was common practice to call an assembly of townspeople and decide matters with a simple voice vote. The assemblies themselves were known as "shoutings," and when the outcome of an issue was known before the meeting, the situation was described as *all over but the shouting.*

## GUM UP THE WORKS
**Meaning:** Screw something up.
**Background:** Believe it or not, the phrase has a pre-industrial inspiration: the red gum or sweet gum tree, which is found in the eastern United States. The early settlers chewed the sticky sap, especially kids, who loved its sweet taste. The only problem: Getting the stuff out of the tree was virtually impossible to do without getting it all over yourself. So was getting it out of your hair and clothes—if you weren't careful, you could really *gum up the works.*

## TAKE BY STORM
**Meaning:** Make a big impression; become famous or popular virtually overnight.
**Background:** Today's politicians, movie stars, and war heroes take the world by storm...but the term itself dates back to the days when soldiers took fortified enemy positions *by storming them*.

## TO BE BESIDE YOURSELF
**Meaning:** Under great emotional stress.
**Background:** The ancient Greeks believed that when a person was under intense pressure, the soul literally left the body and was *beside itself*. (The word *ecstasy* has a similar meaning: Its Greek root means "to stand out of.")

## GET YOUR SEA LEGS
**Meaning:** To adjust to a new situation.
**Background:** The term dates back to the days when sailing ships ruled the high seas: a new sailor was said to have "gotten his sea legs" when he could walk steadily across the deck of a ship in stormy weather.

## TO RUN AMOK
**Meaning:** To behave in a wild, uncontrolled manner.
**Background:** The Malay word for "a person who has gone crazy" is *moq*. The first English sailors to visit Malaysia associated the word with the occasional insane people they saw there...and brought the word home with them.

## DOUBLEHEADER
**Meaning:** Two baseball games in a single afternoon.
**Background:** The name was borrowed from railroading—a train with two engines on it is also known as a doubleheader.

## FLAG SOMETHING DOWN
**Meaning:** To stop a moving vehicle, usually a taxi cab.
**Background:** Another train term: Railroad employees used to literally flag trains down—they stopped them by waving flags at the engineers.

There really is an insect called the love bug. It spends 56 hours—more than its life—mating.

# TO TELL THE TRUTH

*Are polygraphs accurate crime-fighting tools...or little more than modern-day witchcraft? You be the judge.*

C an we ever *really* know for sure if someone is telling a lie? Most experts agree that the answer is no—but that hasn't stopped society from cooking up ways to sort out the liars from the honest people.

## ANCIENT METHODS
• The Bedouins of the Arabian peninsula forced suspected liars to lick red-hot pokers with their tongues, on the assumption that liars would burn their tongues and truth tellers wouldn't. The method was primitive and barbaric—but it may have also been *accurate*, since the procedure measures the moisture content of the suspect's mouth—and dry mouths are often associated with nervousness caused by lying.
• The ancient Chinese forced suspected liars to chew a mouthful of rice powder and spit it out; if the rice was still dry, the suspect was deemed guilty.
• The ancient British used a similar trick: they fed suspects a large 'trial slice' of bread and cheese, and watched to see if he could swallow it. If a suspect's mouth was too dry to swallow, he was declared a liar and punished.
• The preferred method in India was to send the suspects into a dark room and have them pull on the tail of a sacred donkey, which was supposed to bray if the person was dishonest...at least that's what the suspects thought. The way the system *really* worked was that the investigators dusted the donkey's tail with black powder (which was impossible to see in the unlit room). Innocent people, the investigators reasoned, would pull the tail without hesitation...but the guilty person, figuring that no one could see them in the darkness, would only pretend to pull the tail but would not touch it at all.

## MODERN METHOD
The first modern lie detector was invented by Cesare Lombroso, an Italian criminologist, in 1895. His device measured changes in

pulse and blood pressure. Then, in 1914, another researcher named Vittorio Benussi invented a machine that measured changes in breathing rate. But it wasn't until 1921 that John A. Larson, a medical student at the University of California, invented a machine that measured pulse, blood pressure, and breathing rate simultaneously. His machine became known as a polygraph, because it measured three types of physiological changes. Today's polygraphs use these methods, as well as more sophisticated measurements.

## THE QUESTIONS

The most common questioning method is called the Control Question Test (CQT), in which the polygraph operator asks three types of questions: neutral questions, key questions, and control questions.

• **Neutral questions** like "What kind of car do you drive?" are designed to measure the suspect's general level of nervousness, because nearly anyone who takes a polygraph test is going to be nervous.

• **Key, or "guilty," questions** quiz the suspect on information that only the guilty person would know. (For example: If the person taking the test was suspected of murdering someone, and the murder weapon was a knife, questions about knives would be considered key questions.)

• **Control, or "innocent," questions** would be indistinguishable from key questions by someone who did not have knowledge of the crime—but the guilty person would know. Questions about weapons not used in a murder would be considered control questions.

An innocent person with no knowledge of the murder weapon would show the same level of nervousness during all the weapon questions—but the guilty person would be more nervous during questions about knives—and would be easy to identify using a polygraph...at least in theory.

## BEATING THE SYSTEM

Modern-day lie detectors are pretty sophisticated, but they have the same flaw that the ancients methods did—they all assume that the liar, out of guilt or fear of discovery, will have some kind of

---

The "first electronic computer" was built in 1889 for the U.S. Census Bureau.

involuntary physical response every time they lie...but that isn't necessarily the case, according to most experts. "I don't think there's any medical or scientific evidence which tends to establish that your blood pressure elevates, that you perspire more freely or that your pulse quickens when you tell a lie," says William G. Hundley, a defence lawyer.

Still, many people believe that the polygraph is a useful tool when used in concert with other investigative methods, especially when they're used on ordinary people who don't know how to cheat. "It's a great psychological tool," says Plate Cacheris, another defence lawyer. "You take the average guy and tell him you're going to give him a poly, and he's concerned enough to believe it will disclose any deception on his part." (Note: Cacheris is famous for having represented non-average guy Aldrich Ames, a CIA spy who passed a lie detector test in 1991 and then went on to sell more than $2.5 million worth of secrets to the Russians before he was finally caught in 1994.)

## FAKIN' IT
Two tricks to help you beat a lie detector:
• Curl your toes or press your feet down against the floor while answering the "innocent" questions. It can raise the polygraph readings to the same range as the "guilty" questions, which can either make you appear innocent or invalidate the results.
• Stick a tack in your shoe and press your big toe against the sharp point during the "innocent" questions.

Both toe-curling and stepping on a tack during the innocent questions have the same effect: they raise the stress level of your body.

\* \* \* \*

Police in Radnor, Pennsylvania, interrogated a suspect by placing a metal colander on his head and connecting it with a metal wire to a photocopy machine. The message, "He's lying," was placed in the copier and police pressed the copy button each time they believed the suspect wasn't telling the truth. Believing the "lie detector" was working, the suspect confessed.

—*News of the Weird*

# SIR DOUGLAS MAWSON

*Most of us know him as the bloke in the balaclava on the front
of the original $100 note, but who was this man Mawson
and what did he achieve?*

## THE ICE CALLS

Douglas Mawson was two years old when he arrived in Australia from Yorkshire, England. From a young age he was captivated by the deserts and coastline of his adopted country. He pursued this interest by studying engineering and science at Sydney University. He followed with a Doctorate of Science from Adelaide University in 1909 where he was also a lecturer in mineralogy and petrology.

Mawson was keen to visit Antarctica. His chance came when he was asked to join Ernest Shackleton's 1907 Antarctic expedition. It was during this expedition that Mawson and his team achieved two firsts—the first to climb Antarctica's only active volcano, Mount Erebus, and the first to reach the Magnetic South Pole.

## HOME OF THE BLIZZARD

This initial time in Antarctica captivated Mawson and at the age of 29, he returned as leader of the first Australasian expedition of Antarctica on the ship *Aurora*. After travelling through 2,414 km (1,500 miles) of pack-ice to get there, Mawson and his crew of 18 set up base on the Antarctic mainland in the spring of 1912. They named their campsite "Home of the Blizzard" due to prevailing winds of up to 200 kms (125 miles) per hour that blew incessantly. The chief objective of this expedition was to investigate a stretch of essentially unknown coastline, mapping and conducting experiments along the way.

## AGAINST ALL ODDS

It was on one of these expedition forays that Mawson performed one of the most extraordinary feats of lone polar survival ever

---

Why did Japanese scientists invent "square" watermelons? They stack better.

recorded. Five hundred kilometres (310 miles) from base camp, one of his two travelling companions, most of their provisions and the strongest sledge dogs were lost down a crevasse. Mawson and his remaining companion, Mertz, with no food, had to turn back and try and make base camp. The remaining huskies were progressively killed and eaten in order for Mawson and Mertz to survive.

One hundred and sixty kilometres (100 miles) from base camp Mertz became increasingly weak and soon died. (His death was later attributed to a toxic level of Vitamin A from eating the livers of the dogs.)

On Mertz's death, Mawson wrote, "My physical condition was such that I felt I might collapse at any moment…several of my toes commenced to blacken and fester near the tips causing the nails to work loose. There appeared to be little hope…It was easy to sleep in the bag, and the weather outside was cruel."

Mawson however found the strength to go on. Ten days later he too fell down a crevasse, only to be saved by his rope harness. Delirious and exhausted, Mawson struggled to pull himself out. Time and time again he would reach the lip of the crevasse only to fall back down again. But he was a man of remarkable courage and with sheer determination, he finally made it out of the crevasse. He would later write in his diary that during his time in the crevasse he was sorely tempted to give up and cut the rope that held him.

Mawson, exhausted and starving, dragged himself for a further 150 kilometres (93 miles) until he finally reached the expedition base camp only to arrive to see the supply vessel *Aurora* departing. Mawson had to wait for another year before being rescued.

## COME IN ANTARCTICA
Douglas Mawson, on the Australasian Antarctic Expedition of 1911–14, also set up Macquarie Island's first scientific station. The expedition made studies of the plants, animals, geology and meteorology as well as magnetic observations. Importantly, the expeditioners established the first ever radio link with Antarctica from Wireless Hill. The scant remains of the Wireless Hill mast are the only physical reminder of Mawson's expedition, however it was his research papers that marked a change in attitude from exploitation to conservation of the island's natural resources.

After Mawson's return to Australia he lobbied strongly for the declaration of Macquarie Island as a wildlife sanctuary. Sealing licences were revoked in 1919, and sanctuary status was conferred in 1933. In 1948, the Australian National Antarctic Research Expedition, ANARE, set up a permanent station on the island that has remained staffed ever since.

Mawson later served in World War I before resuming an academic career in science and exploration. He went on to lead the British Australian New Zealand Antarctic Research Expedition in 1929–1931 where he charted over 1,600 km (1,000 miles) of previously unknown Antarctic coast.

## A GLITTERING CAREER

In his three Antarctic trips between 1907 and 1931, Mawson claimed over 5.7 million square kilometres (2.2 million square miles) of Antarctic territory for Australia (42% of the total Antarctic territory).

As well as receiving a knighthood in 1914, Mawson received other glittering prizes from around the world including the King's Polar Medal, the American Geographical Society Gold Medal and the Paris Geographical Society Gold Medal. He became a Foundation Fellow of the Royal Academy of Science in 1954, and had an Australian Antarctic base named after him (Mawson base).

## AN ADMIRABLE AUSTRALIAN

Sir Douglas Mawson should be remembered by all Australians as a great scientist and explorer and also as a man of unusual courage and endurance. His love and pride for his adopted country can be felt in his speech to the Royal Geographical Society in London in 1911 when he was discussing his first expedition: "Australia will reap an advantage from this expedition…It will moreover afford the whole world an opportunity of seeing what Australians can do…it is a big project which has had the effect of bringing Australia prominently before European countries…it presents Australia in a new light. Australia gains the prestige of being strong enough to investigate and claim new territory."

Mawson died in 1958 at the age of 76, leaving a wife and two daughters.

Seventy-six percent of teenagers say they believe in angels. That's up from 64% in 1978.

# VIVE LA DIFFERENCE!

*Researchers say that males and females are naturally different
from one another in a number of unexpected ways.
Here are a few of the things they've found out.*

Women are more likely to smile than men when delivering bad news.

Toddler girls as young as two years old maintain eye contact with adults nearly twice as long as toddler boys do.

At the age of four months, infant girls can distinguish between photographs of people they know and don't know; most boys can't.

Did you have a nightmare last night? Women are twice as likely as men to say they did.

In households that have them, males control the TV remote control 55% of the time; women have control 34% of the time.

Doctors consider men obese when 25% of their body is composed of fat, and women obese when 30% is fat.

Boys fight more than girls do. The difference begins at about age two.

Fifty-nine percent of females—but only 4% of males—say they didn't enjoy the first time they had sex.

The average male brain is 14 percent larger than the average female brain.

Seventy-one percent of car-accident victims are male; only 29% are female.

On average, a man's skin ages 10 years more slowly than a woman's does.

In the year following a divorce, the average woman's standard of living falls 73%; the man's standard of living actually *rises* by 43%.

Male snow skiers are more likely to fall on their faces; female skiers are more likely to fall on their backs.

In one recent study, 36% of husbands surveyed said their wife "is like a god." Only 19% of women said the same thing about their husbands.

Women cry about five times as much as men; a male hormone may actually suppress tears.

# Q & A:
# ASK THE EXPERTS

*More random questions…and answers…from leading trivia experts.*

## SEEING THE LIGHT
Q: *What is a hologram? How is it different than a regular picture?*
A: "A hologram is a three-dimensional image produced with the use of laser light. Contrary to what you might think, when you look at something, you are not really viewing the object itself, but are instead looking at the light coming from the object. Because photographs are only able to record part of this light, the images they produce are limited to two dimensions. Using a laser, an object's illumination can be completely recorded, enabling it to be reproduced later in three dimensions." (From *Ask Me Something I Don't Know*, by Bill Adler, Jr. and Beth Pratt-Dewey)

## DELICIOUS QUESTION
Q: *Why is New York called the Big Apple?*
A: "It appears more than likely that jazz musicians deserve the credit. Musicians of the 1930s, playing one night stands, coined their own terms not only for their music…but also for their travels, the people they met, the towns they stayed in. A town or city was an "apple." At that time a man named Charles Gillett was president of the New York City Convention and Visitors Bureau. Learning of the jazz term, he bragged, 'There are lots of "apples" in the U.S.A., but we're the best and the biggest. We're The Big Apple.'" (From *All Those Wonderful Names*, by J. N. Hook)

## ABOUT YOUR BODY
Q: *How heavy are our bones?*
A: Our bones are a remarkable combination of strength and lightness. "In a 73-kg (160-lb) man, only about 13 kg (29 lbs)—less than 20 percent—represent bone weight. Steel bars of comparable size would weigh at least four or five times as much." (From *Can Elephants Swim?* compiled by Robert M. Jones)

---

Crocodiles kill more people in the jungle than any other animal.

## BURNING QUESTION

**Q:** *What are first-, second-, and third-degree burns?*
**A:** "Burns are always serious because of the danger of infection while the damaged tissues are healing. In a first-degree burn, no skin is broken, but it is red and painful. In a second-degree burn, the burned area develops blisters and is very painful. One must try to avoid opening the blisters. In a third-degree burn, both the outer layer of the skin and the lower layer of flesh have been burned. This is the most serious of the three types, as the possibility of infection is greatest." (From *How Does a Fly Walk Upside Down*, by Martin M. Goldwyn)

## BUSY THOUGHTS

**Q:** *Why doesn't a busy signal stop as soon as the person you're calling gets off the phone?*
**A:** "There's both a technical and a business reason that you can't just stay on the line and wait for the busy signal to stop. The technical reason is that the sound isn't coming from your friend over there on the other side of town, it's coming from the central switching office of the phone company. (The tone is generated by a gadget sensibly called the tone generator.) That said, the main reason you can't stick on the line is that the phone company doesn't want you to. You're tying up a line. So get off the phone." (From *Why Things Are, Volume II*, by Joel Aschenbach)

## COLD FLASHES

**Q:** *Why do people get headaches when they eat ice cream too fast?*
**A:** "No one is quite sure what causes an ice cream headache (the official name for it). One likely guess is that it happens when ice cream (or other cold stuff) causes the blood vessels on the roof of your mouth to contract (i.e., shrink) a bit. Since the blood can't flow through these vessels as quickly as before, it backs up into the head, causing the other blood vessels to stretch. The result: pain." (From *Know It All*, by Ed Zotti)

\*     \*     \*     \*

Man only dies when he stops dreaming.

**—Aboriginal proverb**

# THE BERMUDA TRIANGLE

*It's as famous as UFOs, as fascinating as the Abominable Snowman,*
*as mysterious as the lost city of Atlantis. But is it real?*

**B**ACKGROUND
The next time you're looking at a map of the world, trace
your finger from Key West, Florida, to Puerto Rico; from
Puerto Rico to the island of Bermuda; and from there back to
Florida. The 362,600-square-kilometre (140,000-square-mile)
patch of ocean you've just outlined is the Bermuda Triangle.
In the past 50 years, more than 100 ships and planes have
disappeared there. That may sound like a lot, but it's actually
about standard for a busy stretch of ocean.

"Besides," says Larry Kuche, author of *The Bermuda Triangle
Mystery Solved*, "hundreds of planes and ships pass safely through
the so-called triangle every day....It is no more logical to try to find
a common cause for all the disappearances in the triangle than to
try to find one cause for all the automobile accidents in Arizona."

Experts agree that the only real mystery about the Bermuda
Triangle is why everyone thinks it's so mysterious.

## THE DISAPPEARANCE THAT STARTED IT ALL
**The "Lost Squadron."** On December 15, 1945, Flight 19, a group
of five U.S. Navy Avenger planes carrying 14 men, took off from
the Fort Lauderdale Naval Air Station at 2 p.m. for a three-hour
training mission off the Florida coast. Everything went well until
about 3:40 p.m., when Lt. Charles C. Taylor, the leader of
Flight 19, radioed back to Fort Lauderdale that both of his
compasses had malfunctioned and that he was lost. "I am over
land, but it's broken," he reported to base. "I am sure I'm in the
Keys, but I don't know how far down and I don't know how to get
to Fort Lauderdale." Shortly afterward he broke in with an eerier
transmission: "We cannot see land....We can't be sure of any
direction—even the ocean doesn't look as it should."

Over the next few hours, the tower heard numerous static-filled
transmissions between the five planes. The last transmission came

at 6:00 p.m., when a Coast Guard plane heard Taylor radio his colleagues: "All planes close up tight…will have to ditch unless land-fall. When the first plane drops to 46 litres (10 gallons) of fuel we all go down together." That was his last transmission— that evening all five planes disappeared without a trace.

A few hours later, a search plane with a crew of 13 took off for the last reported position of the flight…and was never seen again. No wreckage or oil slick from any of the planes was ever found, prompting the Naval Board of Inquiry to observe that the planes "had disappeared as if they had flown to Mars."

## A MYTH IS BORN
The Lost Squadron would probably be forgotten today if it hadn't been for a single news story published on September 16, 1950. An Associated Press reporter named E.V.W. Jones decided to occupy his time on a slow day by writing a story about the Lost Squadron and other ships and planes that had disappeared into the Atlantic Ocean off the Florida coast.

Dozens of newspapers around the country picked it up…and for some reason, it captured people's imaginations. Over the next few years the story was reprinted in tabloids, pulp magazines, pseudo-science journals, and "unexplained mysteries" books.

## IT GETS A NAME
In 1964, Vincent Gaddis, another journalist, gave the story its *name*. He wrote an article in *Argosy* magazine called "The Deadly Bermuda Triangle" and listed dozens of ships that had disappeared there over the centuries, starting with the *Rosalie* (which disappeared in 1840) and ending with the yacht *Conne-mara IV* (which vanished in 1956). He also offered an explanation for the disappearances, speculating that they were caused by "space-time continua [that] may exist around us on the earth, inter-penetrating our known world," a pseudo-scientific way of suggesting that the planes and ships had disappeared into a third dimension.

Interest in the Bermuda Triangle hit a high point in 1974, when Charles Berlitz (grandson of the founder of Berlitz language schools) authored *The Bermuda Triangle: An Incredible Saga of Unexplained Disappearances*. Without presenting a shred of real evidence, he suggested the disappearances were caused by electromagnetic impulses generated by a 122-metre (400-foot) tall pyramid at the bottom of the ocean. The book shot to the top of the bestseller list, inspiring scores of copycat books, TV specials, and movies that kept the Bermuda Triangle myth alive for another generation.

## DEBUNKING THE MYTH

Is there anything to the Bermuda Triangle theory? The U.S. government doesn't think so—the Coast Guard doesn't even bother to keep complete statistics on the incidents there and attributes the disappearances to the strong currents and violent weather patterns.

In 1985 an air-traffic controller named John Myhre came up with a plausible theory about the Lost Squadron's strange fate. A few years earlier he had been flipping through a book on the subject, when he came across a more complete record of the last radio communications between the five planes. Myhre was a pilot and had logged many hours flying off the coast of Florida. "When I ran across a more accurate version of Taylor's last transmissions," Myhre recounts, "I realised what had happened…The lead plane radioed that he was lost over the Florida Keys. Then he said he was over a single island and there was no land visible in any direction." Myhre believes the island Lt. Taylor reported "had to be Walker's Cay," an island that is not part of the Florida Keys:

> "I've flown over it dozens of times and it's the only one of the hundreds of islands around Florida that's by itself out of sight of other land. And it's northwest of the Abacos, which, in fact, look very much like the Keys when you fly over them. Clearly if he thought he was in the Keys, he thought he could reach mainland by flying northeast. But if he was in the Abacos, a northeast course would just take him farther over the ocean."

\*      \*      \*      \*

## MOVIE NOTE

The original Lost Squadron story became so embellished with new "facts" (Taylor's last words were reported to have been "I know where I am now…Don't come after me!…They look like they're from outer space!"), that filmmaker Steven Spielberg included the Lost Squadron in a scene in *Close Encounters of the Third Kind*. The crew reappears on board the mother spaceship after being missing in action for decades.

---

G.I. blues: Elvis received 10,000 letters a week during his stint in the U.S. Army.

# INCOMPETENT CRIMINALS

*A lot of people are worried about the growing threat of crime.
Well, the good news is that there are plenty of crooks who are
their own worst enemies. Here are a few true-life examples.*

**ARE WE HIGH YET?**
When Nathan Radlich's house was burgled on June 4,
1993, thieves left his TV, his VCR, and even his watch.
All they took was a "generic white cardboard box" of greyish
white powder. A police spokesman said it looked similar to
cocaine.

"They probably thought they scored big," he mused.

The powder was actually the cremated remains of Radlich's
sister, Gertrude, who had died three years earlier.

**—From the *Fort Lauderdale Sun-Sentinel***


**POOR PENMANSHIP**
In 1992, 79-year-old Albert Goldsband walked into a San
Bernardino, California, bank and handed the teller a note
demanding money. When she couldn't read the note, he pulled
out a toy gun. But the teller had already taken the note to her
supervisor for help deciphering it.

Goldsband panicked and fled...to a nearby restaurant that was
frequented by police officers. He was arrested immediately.

**—From the *San Francisco Chronicle***


**STUCK ON GLUE**
RIO DE JANEIRO—Nov. 5, 1993. "A thief was found stuck to
the floor of a factory Thursday after trying to steal glue in Belo
Horizonte, 280 miles north of Rio, newspapers reported.

"Edilber Guimaeares, 19, stopped to sniff some of the glue he
was stealing when two large cans fell to the floor, spilling over.

"When police were called Thursday morning, Guimaeares was
glued to the floor, asleep."

**—From the *San Francisco Examiner***

---

A blue whale's sound can be heard from more than 800 km (500 miles) away.

## MISTAKEN IDENTITY

"Warren Gillen, 26, was arrested for trying to rob a bank in Glasgow. Police put him in a lineup, but no one identified him. He was booked anyway after calling out from the lineup, 'Hey, don't you recognise me?'"

—**From** *More News of the Weird*

## A CASE OF NERVES?

Lee W. Womble, 28, was spotted and picked up a few minutes after robbing the Lafayette Bank in Bridgeport, Connecticut.

Police said that even if they hadn't seen him, he would have been easy to identify; he had written his name on the note he handed the teller demanding money.

"He wrote his name on it twice—once on top of the other," said police. "He could have been trying to kill time. He could have been nervous or something. Who knows?"

—**From the** *Oakland Tribune*

## WRONG TURN

"An alleged drunk driver who led police on a wild midnight chase landed in jail even before his arrest. His car crashed into the jail building.

" 'He didn't have too far to go from there,' said Police Capt. Mike Lanam. 'It was like a drive-up window.' "

—**From the** *Chicago Tribune*

## EMPLOYMENT OPPORTUNITY

"A man accused of stealing a car was easy to track, police said, especially after they found his resume under one of the seats.

"Police discovered the handwritten resume when they looked through the stolen 1985 Chevrolet Celebrity they had recovered.

"Police then telephoned an employer listed on the resume for a different sort of reference."

—**From the Associated Press**

# SHARK ATTACK!

*We all saw Jaws, and didn't go swimming in the sea for a year.*
*The theme music is still enough to send shivers up your spine.*
*But what are the real shark facts in Oz?*

Worldwide, there are probably from 70 to 100 shark attacks a year. Of those, about 10 are fatal. Almost any shark 2 metres (6.5 feet) or longer is a potential danger to humans. However, three shark species in Australia and worldwide have been identified repeatedly in attacks: the bull, tiger and great white shark. All three species reach large sizes and eat large prey, such as marine mammals, sea turtles and fish. Great white sharks can grow as long as 5 metres (16 feet) and weigh 2,500 kg (5,555 lb). For a shark this size, a little nibble can be a big chunk off a human!

## SWIMMER BEWARE

The International Shark Attack File reports that Australia's coastline is the most dangerous in the world. New South Wales has had the most fatal attacks, but Queensland has had the most recent.

|  | Total Attacks | Fatal Attacks | Last Fatality |
|---|---|---|---|
| New South Wales | 123 | 62 | 1993 |
| Queensland | 102 | 48 | 2003 |
| South Australia | 30 | 16 | 2000 |
| Western Australia | 28 | 9 | 2000 |
| Victoria | 20 | 8 | 1970 |
| Tasmania | 16 | 6 | 1993 |
| Northern Territory | 1 | 1 | 1934 |

## THE TERRIBLE TRIO

The bull shark, also known in Australia as freshwater whaler, Swan River whaler and river whaler, is found in all Australian water systems, except along the Southern coastline. It is responsible for a large number of attacks and deaths, particularly around river and harbour inlets.

The tiger shark likes warmer waters and stays clear of the

The first car, a Peugeot, was stolen in Paris in 1896.

southern coastline and the lower eastern coastline of Australia. It feeds mostly at night and is indiscriminate in what it eats. Garbage is often found in the stomachs of tiger sharks that have been caught in harbours and rivers inlets. One infamous tiger shark that was caught alive off Coogee Beach in 1935, vomited up a severed arm. It turned out to be the arm of a man that had been murdered, cut up and dumped at sea. Two men were eventually charged with what is now known as the "shark arm murder case."

The great white shark is a widespread, but scarce species. Found in most temperate waters, the southern coastline of Australia is recognised as being one of the last areas of high abundance. Game fishing has seriously reduced its numbers and the great white is now a protected species in Australian waters.

## FEEDING TIME

Based on research done in the late 1950s, a timetable was drawn up for the key months of shark attacks in Australia. These findings still apply today.

North of Tropic of Capricorn:    all year
Southern Queensland:    November–May
Newcastle:    December–April
Sydney:    December–April
Adelaide:    December–March
Melbourne:    January–March
Bass Strait and Tasmania    January

## MISTAKEN IDENTITY

Why do sharks attack people? There are a number of theories:
• Sharks may now be hunting closer to shore because of overfishing.
• People are more exposed to sharks because of increased water activities and because they spend longer amounts of time in the water.
• Sharks may mistake the silhouette of divers in wetsuits, surfers on short surfboards, and perhaps even kayakers, for marine mammals.

Apparently the odds of dying in a shark attack in Australia are less than being killed by a crocodile or struck by lightning. So get back out there and remember—*Jaws* was only a movie!

# MONTHS OF THE YEAR

*Here's where the names of the months come from.*

**JANUARY.** Named for the Roman god *Janus*, a two-faced god who "opened the gates of heaven to let out the morning, and closed them at dusk." Janus was worshiped as the god of all doors, gates, and other entrances. Consequently, the opening month of the year was named after him.

**FEBRUARY.** The Roman "Month of Purification" got its name from *februarius*, the Latin word for purification. February 15 was set aside for the Festival of Februa, in which people repented and made sacrifices to the gods to atone for their wrongdoings.

**MARCH.** Named for Mars, the Roman god of war. The Roman empire placed great emphasis on wars and conquest, so until 46 B.C. this was the first month of the year.

**APRIL.** No one knows the origin of the name. One theory: it comes from *Aprilis* or *aphrilis*, which are corruptions of *Aphrodite*, the Greek name for Venus, the goddess of love. However, many experts think the month is named after the Latin verb *aperire*, which means "to open." (Most plants in the Northern Hemisphere open their leaves and buds in April.)

**MAY.** Some people think the month is named after *Maia*, the mother of the god Mercury; other people think it was named in honour of the *Majores*, the older branch of the Roman Senate.

**JUNE.** It may have been named in honour of *Juno*, the wife of Jupiter; or it may have been named after the *Juniores*, the lower branch of the Roman Senate.

**JULY.** Named after Julius Caesar.

**AUGUST.** Named after Gaius Julius Caesar Octavianus, heir and nephew of Julius Caesar. The Roman Senate gave this Caesar the title of "Augustus," which means "revered," and honoured him further by naming a month after him.

**SEPTEMBER** Comes from the Latin word *septem*, which means "seven." September was the seventh month until about the year 700 B.C., when Numa Pompilius, the second Roman king, switched from a 304-day calendar to a 355-day lunar calendar.

---

Experts say: Elephants are the only animals in the world that can't jump.

**OCTOBER.** From *octo*, the Latin word for "eight." When Romans changed the calendar, they knew October was no longer the eighth month, and tried to rename it. Some candidates: *Germanicus* (after a general), *Antonius* (an emperor), *Faustina* (the emperor's wife), and *Herculeus* (after Emperor Commodus, who had nicknamed himself the "Roman Hercules.") None of the new names stuck.

**NOVEMBER.** From *novem*, the Latin word for "nine." November was also referred to as "blood-month." Reason: It was the peak season for pagan animal sacrifices.

**DECEMBER.** From *decem*, the Latin word for "ten." Attempts to rename it *Amazonius* in honour of the mistress of Emperor Commodius failed.

## DAYS OF THE WEEK

*When Anglo-Saxons invaded the British Isles, they brought their language and pagan gods with them. The names of the days of the week are a legacy.*

**SUNDAY.** Originally called *Sunnan daeg*, which, like today, meant "sun day."

**MONDAY.** Originally called *Monan daeg*, "moon day."

**TUESDAY.** *Tiwes daeg* was named in honour of Tiw, the Anglo-Saxon and Norse god of war.

**WEDNESDAY.** Named *Wodnes daeg* and dedicated to Woden, the king of the gods in Valhalla.

**THURSDAY.** *Thu(n)res daeg* commemorated Thor, the god of thunder, and the strongest and bravest god of them all.

**FRIDAY.** Originally named *Frige daeg* after Thor's mother Frigga, the most important goddess in Valhalla. (That's one theory: the day may be also named after Freyja, the Norse goddess of love.)

**SATURDAY.** Named *Saeter daeg* in honour of Saturn, the Roman god of agriculture. It's the one day of the week whose name *isn't* derived from Anglo-Saxon/Norse myths.

The Pinta was pint-sized: Columbus's third ship was only 15 metres (50 feet) long.

# INTERNATIONAL LAW

*And you thought the Australian legal system was strange…*

Paris law forbids spinning tops on sidewalks…and staring at the mayor.

19th-century Scottish law required brides to be pregnant on their wedding day.

In England it's against the law to sue the queen—or to name your daughter "Princess" without her permission.

The law in Teruel, Spain, forbids taking hot baths on Sunday. (Cold baths are OK.)

In Rio de Janeiro, it's illegal to dance the samba in a tunnel.

Gun control: In Switzerland, the law *requires* you to keep guns and ammunition in your home.

Swedish law prohibits trained seals from balancing balls on their noses.

If you're arrested for drunken driving in Malaysia, you go to jail. (So does your wife.)

In Reykjavik, Iceland, it's illegal to keep a dog as a pet.

If you curse within earshot of a woman in Egypt, the law says you forfeit two days' pay.

In pre-Islamic Turkey, if a wife let the family coffee pot run dry, her husband was free to divorce her.

The opposite was true in Saudi Arabia, where a woman was free to divorce her husband if he didn't keep her supplied with coffee.

Horses in Mukden, China, are required to wear nappies; their owners are required "to empty them at regular intervals into specially constructed receptacles."

Toronto, Canada, law requires pedestrians to give hand signals before turning.

English law forbids marrying your mother-in-law.

Red cars are outlawed in Shanghai, China…and other automobile colours are assigned according to the owner's profession.

…did you know in Australia it's illegal to hire a woman under the age of 45 to work as a chorus girl?

---

**For the birds:** The Swiss Army keeps 20,000 carrier pigeons for emergency communications.

# WORD ORIGINS

*You already know these words. But did
you know where they come from?*

**Gossip:** From *godsib*, which meant "godparent." (*Sibling* has the same root.) According to Morton S. Freeman in *The Story Behind the Word*, "The idea of gossip grew out of the regular meetings and intimate conversations of the *godsibbes*. What they talked about came to be called *godsibbes* or (as slurred) *gossip*."

**Ignoramus:** The Latin word which means "we do not know." By the 17th century the term referred almost exclusively to "ignorant, arrogant attorneys," thanks in large part to a 1615 play in which the main character was a stupid lawyer named Ignoramus.

**Minimum:** Comes from the Latin word *minium*, meaning "red lead." "In medieval times," the book *Word Mysteries and Histories* reports, "chapter headings and other important divisions of a text were distinguished by being written in red, while the rest of the book was written in black....Sections of a manuscript were also marked off with large ornate initial capital letters, which were often decorated with small paintings. *Miniatura* was used to describe these paintings as well. Since the paintings were necessarily very tiny, *miniatura* came to mean 'a small painting or object of any kind.'"

**Boor:** Originally meant "farmer." (A "neighbour" was a near-farmer.) Originally the term had no pejorative meaning...but over time city dwellers, who fancied themselves as being more refined than their country cousins, interpreted the word to mean "ill-mannered," "unrefined," or "rude'—so much so that the original meaning was lost entirely.

**Nickname:** From the Middle English word *ekename*, which meant "additional name." Where did the "n" come from? From the definite article an, which frequently proceeded the word. Over time "an ekename" became "a nekename"...and then finally "a nickname."

Pirates thought that wearing an earring in a pierced ear improved their eyesight.

# THE NAKED TRUTH

*People get very strange when they take their clothes off.*
*Check out these excerpts from newspaper articles*
*contributed by BRI correspondent Peter Wing.*

**A BIG SURPRISE**
A male motorist told authorities yesterday that a naked, red-haired woman—'the largest woman you ever saw'—jumped out of the woods and attacked his car on a dark country road in northern Michigan.

After briefly terrorising the motorist, the woman disappeared into the woods."

**—United Press International**

**AND WHAT ABOUT KETCHUP?**
LANSING, MICHIGAN—Oct. 16, 1981. "Two sisters who described their nude mustard-smeared joyride in a parcel delivery truck as a religious experience have been set free…A third sister was found mentally ill; sentencing in her case has been postponed.

"The three were arrested after driving off—nude except for their shoes and smeared with mustard—in a parked United Parcel Service truck. 'We were trying to find God,' one of the sisters explained."

**—San Francisco Chronicle**

**THE CRISCO KID**
"A Tifton, Georgia, man has been convicted of public indecency and placed on probation for slinging chunks of lard at women while driving a car in the nude."

**—Associated Press**

**HOPPING AROUND THE NEIGHBOURHOOD**
SANTA CRUZ, CALIFORNIA—"A city police officer was investigating a complaint of a disturbance at a man's home when he spotted what looked like a tall, chocolate rabbit coming 'hippity hoppity' out of the yard. After a closer look, the officer discovered it was a 30-year-old female neighbour who had covered her nude body in chocolate glaze. She was disguised as the Easter bunny."

**—Associated Press**

Q: Where are the world's largest sculptures? A: Mt. Rushmore in the U.S.

# "FORTUNATE" SONS

*We often assume that the children of rich or famous parents have
it made. Maybe not. Here are a few stories to consider.*

**W.C. FIELDS, JR.,** son of comedy great W.C. Fields.
As a child, Claude Fields hardly ever saw his father...or
his father's money. W. C. Fields was as cheap as he was
successful. He paid his estranged wife a paltry $60-a-week
allowance and refused to contribute a cent to Claude's education.
When he died, he left his wife and son only $10,000 each from his
$800,000 estate, instructing that the rest be spent founding the
W. C. Fields College for Orphan White Boys and Girls, Where
No Religion of Any Sort Is to Be Preached. Claude, by then a
successful lawyer, contested the will and won.

**WILLIAM FRANKLIN,** son of Benjamin Franklin. William
picked up pro-British sentiments while living in London with
his father in the 1750s and became an outspoken Royalist and
opponent of American independence. Through his connections in
the English aristocracy, he had himself appointed Royal Governor
of New Jersey. In 1776, he was arrested for trying to rally
opposition to the Declaration of Independence in the New Jersey
colonial assembly. He languished in prison until 1778, then
returned to London in 1782 when it became obvious that England
was going to lose the war. Disinherited and shunned by his father
(who died in 1790), William died in England in 1813.

**HARILAL GANDHI,** son of Mahatma Gandhi. "Men may be
good," Mahatma Gandhi once observed, "but not necessarily their
children." He was talking about Harilal Gandhi, his oldest son.
But the Mahatma, who was as terrible a father as he was a great
leader, had virtually abandoned his son by the time the lad was in
his teens. Estranged from his father, widowed, and left to raise his
four children alone, Harilal became a womaniser and an alcoholic.
In 1936, he converted to Islam, which so deeply embarrassed the
elder Gandhi that he issued a public letter condemning the
conversion. "Harilal's apostasy is no loss to Hinduism," the letter
read, "and his admission to Islam is a source of weakness to it, if
he remains the same wreck that he was before." Harilal remained

---

A dragonfly, the fastest flying insect, can move up to 56 km (35 m.p.h.).

a drunk in spite of his embracing a religion that forbade the consumption of alcohol, showing up drunk and disoriented at both his mother's funeral in 1944 and his father's in 1948. He died of tuberculosis six months after his father's death.

**ALBERT FRANCIS CAPONE, JR.,** son of Al Capone. Believe it or not, Little Al was actually pretty honest. In the 1940s he even quit his job as a used-car salesman when he caught his boss turning back odometers. When the family assets were seized by the IRS after Big Al died in 1947, he had to drop out of college and make a living. So he opened a Miami restaurant with his mother.

In 1965, he was arrested for stealing two bottles of aspirin and some batteries from a supermarket. He pled no contest, telling the judge, "Everybody has a little larceny in him, I guess." A year later, still smarting from the publicity, Capone changed his name to Albert Francis.

**ROMANO MUSSOLINI,** son of Italian dictator Benito Mussolini. He was only 18 years old when his father fell from power at the end of World War II. So Romano spent much of his life in exile going to school, working as a poultry farmer, playing the piano, and developing a taste for jazz music. He eventually formed his own band, "The Romano Mussolini Jazz Band," and either because of talent or novelty, was able to book performances around the world.

**WILLIAM MURRAY,** son of American Madalyn Murray O'Hair, the atheist whose 1963 Supreme Court case resulted in outlawing school prayer. His mother's famous lawsuit was filed on William's behalf, so he wouldn't have to join in prayers with the rest of his ninth-grade class. But he converted to Christianity in the late 1970s after finding God in an Alcoholics Anonymous support group. William later became a Baptist preacher...and on at least one occasion was barred from preaching in a school auditorium by principals citing his own Supreme Court case.

**RICHARD J. REYNOLDS II,** R.J.Reynolds tobacco fortune heir. Died of emphysema in 1964. His son, Richard J. Reynolds III, died of emphysema in 1994. Patrick Reynolds (R. J. III's half-brother) sold his R.J. Reynolds stock and became an antismoking activist.

# THE PENTAGON

*It isn't one of the Seven Wonders of the World, but it probably deserves to be. Here's the story of what was for decades the world's largest office building...and what remains today "the most easily recognised building on Earth."*

## AMERICA GOES TO WAR

As the United States geared up for World War II in the late 1930s, military planners were concerned by the fact that the War Department was located in 17 buildings spread out all over Washington, D.C. Officers wasted hours each day travelling around town from one office to another. This made it almost impossible to plan America's defence quickly and efficiently. And the problem was expected to get much worse: In the second half of 1941 alone, the Department of the Army was expected to grow by 25%, enough to fill four more office buildings.

## GETTING IN SHAPE

In July 1941, General Brehon Somervell, the army's chief of construction, gave a team of architects one weekend to come up with a plan for a building that would house the entire military, to be built on a compact site adjacent to Arlington National Cemetery. The architects probably would have preferred a traditional square design, but because a road cut through one corner of the property there wasn't enough room for a square building. So they designed a building with a pentagonal shape instead.

At first it looked like all of their work had been for nothing. When President Roosevelt learned of the intended site for the Pentagon, he insisted that it be moved farther away from Arlington National Cemetery so as not to desecrate the hallowed burial ground. The architects selected another site about one kilometre ($^3/_4$ of a mile) away, larger than the first site, but stuck with the original pentagonal shape. Why? According to historian R. Alton Lee:

> The original Pentagon pattern was retained for a number of reasons: it already was designed and there was the pressure of time; Army officers liked it because its shape was reminiscent of a 17th-century

fortress; and any pattern close to a circular shape would permit the greatest amount of office area within the shortest walking distance…Roosevelt agreed to the new site, but disliked the architectural design. Why not build a large, square, windowless building that could be converted during peace time into a storage area for archives or supplies? However, [Gen. Brehon Somervell, the officer in charge of construction] liked the pentagonal concept and, as time was vital, told the contractors to proceed…When the President discovered what was happening, construction had already begun.

## THE HEIGHT

The architects also decided on a long, flat building instead of a tall, thin one like a skyscraper. Reason: it was faster and cheaper to build a building without elevators. Also, given that 20,000 to 30,000 people an hour would enter and leave the building during peak traffic times, connecting the floors with wide ramps enabled more people to get where they were going than stairs, elevators, or escalators ever could.

## BUILDING THE BEHEMOTH

Because it seemed likely that the United States might enter the war at any moment, what took place next was one of the fastest and most massive construction projects ever attempted. Groundbreaking took place on August 11, 1941; soon afterward workers moved more than 4.2 million cubic metres (5.5 million cubic yards) of earth onto the site and then hammered 41,491 massive concrete piles (more than one for each person scheduled to move into the Pentagon) into the ground to form the foundation. Then they built the Pentagon building itself using more than 332,558 cubic metres (435,000 cubic yards) of concrete made from sand and gravel dredged from the nearby Potomac River. Because speed was essential, 13,000 workers worked around the clock to get the building finished as quickly as possible. The pace was so rapid that rather than take the time to remove all of the heavy equipment after excavating the basement, contractors left some of it in place and entombed it in cement. And given the frantic pace of construction, the architects' drawings barely kept ahead of the construction crews.

The building wasn't built all at once: each of the Pentagon's five sides was built independently of the others in clockwise order, with the occupants of each section moving in as soon as it was finished.

The last section was finally completed on January 15, 1943, just 16 months after the ground-breaking.

## RANDOM PENTAGON FACTS

• Originally budgeted at $35 million, the building ultimately cost $70 million in 1942, about as much as a battleship. Despite the huge cost overruns and the last-minute changes in the plans, Congress barely let out a whimper when it authorised the additional funds needed to complete the building. World War II was in full swing, and even the most penny-pinching politicos kept silent out of fear of jeopardising—or being *accused* of jeopardising—the war effort.

• When the Pentagon was in its planning stages, Franklin Roosevelt insisted that the outside of the building not have any windows, believing it would look more dramatic. Furthermore, a windowless building would be easier to convert to civilian government use once the war was over. But munitions experts talked him out of it, explaining that walls with "blow-out" windows survive bombings better than solid masonry walls, which collapse entirely.

• The Pentagon is designed so that the offices are as close together as they possibly can be—even so, when the building first opened it quickly earned the nickname "Pantygon" because people walked their pants off getting from one place to another.

• To deal with the immense amount of vehicle traffic each working day, architects designed an elaborate system of over- and underpasses arranged into cloverleaf shapes, which enabled thousands of vehicles to drop off passengers and leave again without ever once stopping for a traffic light. The innovative cloverleaf over and underpasses were so successful that they became a standard feature of the interstate highway system.

• The Pentagon has enough cafeterias and dining rooms to serve more than 17,500 meals a day…but has only 230 toilets.

• It has 28 km (17.5 miles) of corridors, 150 stairways, 4,200 clocks, 22,500 telephones connected by 160,000 km (100,000 miles) of telephone cable, 25,000 employees, 2 hospitals, its own power and sewage plants, and the world's largest pneumatic tube system. But it only has one passenger elevator: the one that the Secretary of Defence uses to get from his parking space in the basement to his office.

It took Einstein five weeks to write his Theory of Relativity.

# FAMOUS AUSSIEISMS

*More of the low down on our colourful language.*

Aussies are famous for their colourful brand of English. Concocting words and phrases that ring with a particularly Australian twang is practically a national pastime. Here are some of the better-known Aussieisms that could be handy to know, lest someone tries to come the raw prawn and make a galah out of you.

**barbie**  barbecue
**billabong**  water hole
**bingle**  motor car accident
**bizzo**  business
**blokes and sheilas**  men and women
**boomer**  something large
**clobber**  clothing
**cooee**  a prolonged, clear call
**corker**  an outstanding thing or person
**forty winks**  a short sleep or nap
**fossick**  to search unsystematically
**laughing gear**  mouth
**nick off**  to leave
**no worries**  no problems
**piss-weak**  inadequate
**pommy**  a person hailing from England
**purler**  anyone or anything of top quality
**shonky**  unreliable, dubious
**skin tuxedo**  naked body
**stonkered**  defeated; exhausted; drunk
**strides**  trousers
**tucker**  food
**whingeing pom**  an English person who complains excessively
**wowser**  prudish teetotaller

And some colourful phrases…
**a few chops short of a barbie**  an expression of someone's mental incapacity

---

The shortest serving Australian Prime Minister, Francis Forde, was in power for 7 days.

**act the goat**  to behave like a fool
**arse over tit**  to fall forward in an awkward fashion
**as fit as a Mallee bull**  very fit and strong
**bit on the side**  to have an extra-marital affair
**bite the dust**  to fall down dead
**blind as a wombat**  very blind
**boots and all**  wholeheartedly
**bung it on**  to behave temperamentally
**come the raw prawn**  to try to deceive
**drop a bundle**  to give birth
**every man and his dog**  a lot of people
**fair crack of the whip**  be fair; give me a break
**fair suck of the sav**  an exhortation to be fair (a "sav," or saveloy, is a kind of sausage)
**feed the fishes**  to be seasick
**go for broke**  to take a risk, usually with money
**go to billyo**  an expression of dismissal
**have a lend of**  to take advantage of somebody's gullibility
**home and hosed**  finished successfully
**horizontal cha-cha**  sexual intercourse
**in the nick**  in the nude
**kangaroos loose in the top paddock**  intellectually inadequate
**like a blue-arse fly**  to do something in a frenzied fashion
**mad as a cut snake**  completely insane
**no good to gundy**  worthless
**on ya bike**  an expression of dismissal
**piss into the wind**  to embark on a futile course of action
**round the bend**  insane
**run like a hairy goat**  to run very slowly
**stir the possum**  to instigate a debate on a controversial topic
**stone the crows**  an expression of shock, amazement or annoyance
**strike me lucky (or dead)**  to be surprised, indignant
**useful as tits on a bull**  useless; an incompetent person
**whacko-the-diddle-oh**  an expression of delight
**wrap your laughing gear (around that)**  to suck or bite into something

---

Australian women were first granted the right to vote in 1902.

# A HANDY GUIDE TO THE END OF THE WORLD (Part III)

*Here are the end of time prophesies of another three familiar religions, Part I begins on page 64 and Part II begins on page 325.*

CHRISTIANITY
**Background:** A 2000-year-old religion based on the teachings of Jesus Christ, considered the Son of God.

**Signs Of The End:** According to Dr. Douglas Ottati, an eminent Christian scholar, signs of the end are "very diverse…and can be very deceptive. One question that has to be answered," he says, "is how dependable are they in the first place? Jesus Himself is often interpreted as having said that they're not very dependable." But not everyone agrees with that view; a number of events are regarded by many contemporary Christians as signs, based on *Revelation* and other parts of the *Bible*. A few examples:

• *The return of Jews to Israel.* Many consider the existence of the modern state of Israel to be a sign of the impending apocalypse.

• *The rise of China. Revelation* says an army of 200 million people will attack Israel at Armageddon. According to some sources, that's the current size of the Chinese army.

• *Development of computer technology. Revelation* says that in the end-times, only people with the mark of the Beast will be able to buy and sell goods. Some people think this could refer to computer technology such as bar codes.

• *The European Economic Community.* Many believe that the Antichrist must emerge from a united Europe.

**When the World Ends:** After much turmoil and strife, Christ will return and reign for a thousand-year period of peace. The battle of Armageddon will occur, evil will be defeated, and Judgment Day will arrive.

## JUDAISM

**Background:** A 6,000-year-old monotheistic religion based on the Talmud (Jewish Oral Law) and the Torah (Written Law)—the first five books of the Old Testament.

**Signs the End Is Near:** The Messiah arrives. According to Rabbi Chaim Richman, this will be obvious, because "the world [will] be so drastically changed for the better that it [will] be absolutely incontestable!" For signs, he offers a list of "basic missions of the Messiah," including:

- "Cause the world to return to God and His teachings"
- "Oversee the rebuilding of Jerusalem, including the Temple, in the event that it has not yet been rebuilt."
- "Gather the Jewish people from all over the world and bring them home to the land of Israel."

**When the World Ends:** "Jews don't think in terms of the end of the world," says one scholar. "They think in terms of a new beginning. There's no cataclysm that marks this beginning. After the Messiah comes, people work in partnership with the Divine to bring about a better world."

## ISLAM

**Background:** A religion founded in the 7th century by the prophet Muhammed. He experienced a series of divine visions which he wrote down in the *Koran*.

**Signs The End Is Near:** Mohammed Ali Ibn Zubair Ali says in *Signs of Qiyamah* that after the arrival of the Enlightened One, Imam Madhi, "the ground will cave in, fog or smoke will cover the skies for forty days. A night three nights long will follow the fog. After the night of three nights, the sun will rise in the west. The Beast from the Earth will emerge. The Beast will talk to people and mark the faces of people. A breeze from the south causes sores in the armpits of Muslims which they will die from. The Qur'an will be lifted from the hearts of the people."

**When the World Ends:** "The Imam…will create a world state….He will teach you simple living and high thinking. With such a start he will establish an empire of God in this world. He will be the final demonstration and proof of God's merciful wish to acquaint man with the right ways of life."

# TO SHAVE, OR
# NOT TO SHAVE?

*Calling all men: It may come as a surprise, but shaving your beard is more than a social obligation. It's a grooming ritual that men have been messing around with since prehistoric times. Here are a few facts to ponder the next time you whip out that razor and start scraping.*

**P**REHISTORIC SHAVING
• According to *Razor House*: "Cave paintings have shown that, contrary to popular opinion, early man went about his work clean-shaven, making good use of pieces of sharpened flint." *Shaving historian Eleanor Whitty adds:*
• "The earliest razors discovered were flint blades made possibly as far back as 30,000 B.C. Flint could provide an extremely sharp edge for shaving. These were the first disposable shavers because flint becomes dull rather quickly."
• "Not only did early man cut and/or shave off body hair with flint, he also seemed to enjoy carving unusual artistic designs into his skin. If he added natural dyes and colours to these cuts, he ended up with a tattoo. Other stone shaving tools found were made during the Neolithic Period, or Late Stone Age."
• "With the Bronze Age and primitive metalworking, came razors made from iron, bronze and even gold."

**ANCIENT SHAVING**
• Egyptian pharaohs (around 4000 B.C.) were clean-shaven. All body hair, including beards, were considered a sign of "uncleanliness and negligence."
• The civilizations of Rome and Greece used iron blades with a long handle and developed the shape of the "open" or "cut-throat" razor which was the only practical razor until the 19th century.
• In Greece (around 500 B.C.) men cropped their hair very short and shaved their faces. Alexander the Great was largely responsible for this. Historians call him "obsessed with shaving." One reason: good military strategy. "He didn't want the enemy to be able to grab his soldiers' beards with one hand while

---

Car accidents are most likely at 1 a.m. on Sunday and least likely at 5 a.m. on Friday.

stabbing them with the other." However, it was also a matter of aesthetics. Alexander even shaved during wartime, and "would not allow himself to be seen going into battle with a five o'clock shadow."

• Whitty reports that professional barbers were introduced to Rome about 300 B.C. by a businessman named Publicus Ticinius Maenas who brought a few barbers with him from Sicily. It started a fad that lasted for hundreds of years.

• During this time, Whitty writes, "young Roman men about 21 years of age were actually *required* to have their first shave. To celebrate this official entry into manhood, they had an elaborate party-like ritual." Male friends were invited to watch, and brought gifts. The only Romans not required to go through this ritual were soldiers and young men training to become philosophers.

## MODERN SHAVING
*Razor House* reports:

• "Advances in razor technology changed shaving habits in the 20th century. In 1900, most men were either shaved by the local barber (your trusted confidante, wielding a cut-throat razor), or periodically at home when required, rather than regularly. The barber's better-off customers would have personal sets of seven razors, labelled 'Sunday' to 'Saturday'."

• "The first 'safety' razor, a razor where the skin is protected from all but the very edge of the blade, was invented by a Frenchman, Jean-Jacques Perret, who was inspired by the joiner's plane. An expert on the subject, he also wrote a book called *Pogonotomy or the Art of Learning to Shave Oneself*. In the late 1820s, a similar razor was made in Sheffield and from the 1870s, a single-edge blade, mounted on a hoe-shaped handle was available in Britain and Germany."

• "The idea of a use-once, disposable blade (which didn't need resharpening) came from King Camp Gillette in 1895. It was suggested to him that the ideal way to make money was to sell a product that had to be replaced constantly—an early example of built-in obsolescence. However, producing a paper-thin piece of steel with a sharpened edge strong enough to remove a beard was a near technical impossibility at that time. Although patents were filed in 1901, it was not until 1903 that Gillette could go into business, with the assistance of his technical adviser, MIT's William Nickerson. He produced a grand total of 51 razors and 168 blades in that year.

## SHAVING AND THE PRESIDENCY
• US presidents were clean-shaven for the first half of the 19th century.
• Lincoln famously grew a beard just before taking office in 1860, and except for his successor, Andrew Johnson, who was clean-shaven, and Grover Cleveland, who had only a moustache, beards held sway for the rest of the century.
• For the record, Rutherford Hayes (1877–81) had the longest beard, and the last bearded president was Benjamin Harrison (1889–1892). (The public health experts at the turn of the last century believed that beards carried germs into the home.)

## FEAR OF SHAVING
*New York Times* in 1879 under the headline "Barbers Terrorize Public," which begins:
    "The records of our insane asylums show the fearful effects wrought by the conversation of barbers. No less than 78 percent of the insane patients in public institutions in this state were in the habit of being shaved by barbers before they became insane. If this does not mean that to be shaved by a barber is to incur the risk of being talked into madness, statistics have no meaning."

## HAIR FACTS
*According to the* Portland Oregonian:
• "Human beings have three times more body hair than chimpanzees."
• "Men's whiskers grow 13 to 15 centimetres (5 to 6 inches) a year."
• "The average guy devotes 2,965 hours over his lifetime to standing in front of a mirror and shaving—the equivalent of four months."
• In the matter of total facial-hair follicles, "people from Europe and the Middle East are hairiest, Asians the least hairy and Africans fall somewhere in between."

---

Twelve most-often-used letters in the alphabet: E, T, A, O, I, N, S, H, R, D, L, U.

# NAME YOUR POISON

*Here are the stories of how two popular
alcoholic drinks got their names.*

**D**RAMBUIE
Originally the personal liqueur of Prince Charles Edward
(history's "Bonnie Prince Charlie"), who tried to
overthrow King George II (1727–1760) in 1745. Charles's
Scottish troops made it to within 128 km (80 miles) of London,
but they were ultimately beaten back and Charles was driven into
hiding. In 1760 a member of the Mackinnon clan helped the
prince escape to France. Charles was so grateful that he presented
the man with the secret formula for his personal liqueur, which he
called *an dram budheach*—which is Gaelic for "the drink that
satisfies." The Mackinnons kept the drink to themselves for nearly
a century and a half, but in 1906 Malcolm Mackinnon began
selling it to the public under the shortened name Drambuie.
**Historical Note:** The recipe for Drambuie remains a family secret
as closely held as the recipe for Coca-Cola—only a handful of
Mackinnons know the recipe; to this day they mix the secret
formula themselves.

## CHAMPAGNE
Accidentally invented by Dom Perignon, a 17th-century monk in
the Champagne region of France. Technically speaking, he didn't
invent champagne—he invented *corks*, which he stuffed into the
bottles of wine produced at his abbey in place of traditional cloth
rag stoppers.

The cloth allowed carbon dioxide that formed during
fermentation to escape, but the corks didn't—they were airtight
and caused bubbles to form in the wine. Amazingly, Dom
Perignon thought the bubbles were a sign of poor quality—and
devoted his entire life to removing them, but he never succeeded.

Louis XIV took such a liking to champagne that he began
drinking it exclusively. Thanks to his patronage, by the 1700s
champagne was a staple of French cuisine.

# WHO HELPED HITLER?

*Remember those movies about World War II, when all the allies pitched in together to fight the Nazis? Well, here's some more amazing info from* It's a Conspiracy!, *by The National Insecurity Council.*

While most Americans were appalled by the Nazis and the rearming of Germany in the 1930s, some of America's most powerful corporations were more concerned about making a buck from their German investments. Here are some examples of how U.S. industrialists supported Hitler and Nazi Germany.

## GENERAL MOTORS

**The Nazi connection:** GM, which was controlled by the DuPont family during the 1940s, owned 80% of the stock of Opel AG, which made 30% of Germany's passenger cars.

**Helping Hitler:** When Hitler's panzer divisions rolled into France and Eastern Europe, they were riding in Opel trucks and other equipment. Opel earned GM a hefty $36 million in the ten years before war broke out, but because Hitler prohibited the export of capital, GM reinvested the profits in other German companies. At least $20 million was invested in companies owned or controlled by Nazi officials.

## THE CURTISS-WRIGHT AVIATION COMPANY

**The Nazi connection:** Employees of Curtiss-Wright taught dive-bombing to Hitler's *Luftwaffe*.

**Helping Hitler:** When Hitler's bombers terrorised Europe, they were using American bombing techniques. The U.S. Navy invented dive-bombing several years before Hitler came to power, but managed to keep it a secret from the rest of the world by expressly prohibiting U.S. aircraft manufacturers from mentioning the technique to other countries. However, in 1934, Curtiss-Wright, hoping to increase aeroplane sales to Nazi Germany, found a way around the restriction: instead of *telling* the Nazis about dive-bombing, he *demonstrated* the technique in air shows. A U.S. Senate investigation concluded, "It is apparent that American aviation companies did their part to assist Germany's air armament."

## STANDARD OIL

**The Nazi connection:** The oil giant developed and financed Germany's synthetic fuel program in partnership with the German chemical giant I.G. Farben.

**Helping Hitler:** As late as 1934, Germany was forced to import as much as 85 percent of its petroleum from abroad. This meant that a worldwide fuel embargo could stop Hitler's army overnight. To get around this threat, Nazi Germany began converting domestic coal into synthetic fuel using processes developed jointly by Standard Oil and I.G. Farben.

• Standard taught I.G. Farben how to make tetraethyl-lead and add it to gasoline to make leaded gasoline. This information was priceless; leaded gas was essential for modern mechanised warfare. An I.G. Farben memo stated, "Since the beginning of the war we have been in a position to produce lead tetraethyl solely because, a short time before the outbreak of the war, the Americans established plants for us and supplied us with all available experience."

• A congressional investigation conducted after World War II found evidence that Standard Oil had conspired with I.G. Farben to block American research into synthetic rubber, in exchange for a promise that I.G. Farben would give Standard Oil a monopoly on its rubber-synthesising process. The investigation concluded that "Standard fully accomplished I.G.'s purpose of preventing the United States production by dissuading American rubber companies from undertaking independent research in developing synthetic rubber processes."

## HENRY FORD, founder of the Ford Motor Company

**The Nazi connection:** Ford was a big donor to the Nazi party.

**Helping Hitler:** Ford allegedly bankrolled Hitler in the early 1920s, at a time when the party had few other sources of income. In fact, the party might have perished without Ford's sponsorship. Hitler admired Ford enormously. In 1922, the *New York Times* reported, "The wall beside his desk in Hitler's private office is decorated with a large picture of Henry Ford." Ford never denied that he had bankrolled the Führer. In fact, Hitler presented him with Nazi Germany's highest decoration for foreigners, the Grand Cross of the German Eagle.

## CHASE NATIONAL BANK (later Chase Manhattan Bank)

**The Nazi connection:** Chase operated branches in Nazi-occupied Paris and handled accounts for the German embassy as well as for German businesses operating in France.

**Helping Hitler:** As late as six months before the start of World War II in Europe, Chase National Bank worked with the Nazis to raise money for Hitler from Nazi sympathisers in the United States.

• Even after America entered the war, "the Chase Bank in Paris was the focus of substantial financing of the Nazi embassy's activities, with the full knowledge of [Chase headquarters in] New York. To assure the Germans of its loyalty to the Nazi cause…the Vichy branch of Chase at Chateauneuf-sur-Cher were strenuous in enforcing restrictions against Jewish property, even going so far as to refuse to release funds belonging to Jews because they anticipated a Nazi decree with retroactive provisions prohibiting such a release."

## INTERNATIONAL TELEPHONE AND TELEGRAPH

**The Nazi connection:** IT&T owned substantial amounts of stock in several German armaments companies, including a 28% stake in Focke-Wolf, which built fighter aircraft for the German army.

**Helping Hitler:** Unlike General Motors, IT&T was permitted to repatriate the profits it made in Germany, but it chose not to. Instead, the profits were reinvested in the German armaments industry. According to *Wall Street and the Rise of Hitler*: "IT&T's purchase of a substantial interest in Focke-Wolf meant that IT&T was producing German planes used to kill Americans and their allies—and it made excellent profits out of the enterprise."

• The relationship with the Nazis continued even after the U.S. entered the war. According to *Trading with the Enemy*, the German army, navy, and air force hired IT&T to make "switchboards, telephones, alarm gongs, buoys, air raid warning devices, radar equipment, and 30,000 fuses per month for artillery shells used to kill British and American troops" *after* the bombing of Pearl Harbor. "In addition, IT&T supplied ingredients for the rocket bombs that fell on London…high frequency radio equipment, and fortification and field communication sets. Without this supply of crucial materials, it would have been impossible for the German air force to kill American and British troops."

# THE STORY BEHIND THE NAMES

**S**YDNEY
Named by Captain Arthur Phillip on 26 January, 1788, after Lord Thomas Townshend Sydney, the British Secretary of State for the Colonies.

**BRISBANE**
Named after Sir Thomas Brisbane, who was Governor of New South Wales in 1823. He sent John Oxley, the Surveyor General, to explore new terrain for a penal settlement. The site eventually chosen was the site of Brisbane.

**MELBOURNE**
This was originally known as Dutigalla or Bearbrass until 1837 when the New South Wales Governor, Sir Richard Bourke, visited the area and renamed it Melbourne. This was in honour of Lord Melbourne, who was Prime Minister of England at the time.

**PERTH**
Perth was proclaimed a city by Queen Victoria in 1856. It was named after the Scottish city Perth, which was the capital of Scotland until 1437.

**ADELAIDE**
Named after Queen Adelaide, wife of the British monarch William IV (1830–1837).

**HOBART**
Named after Lord Hobart, the British Secretary of State of the Colonies 1801–04.

**CANBERRA**
Joshua Moore established a stock station in 1824 near the present site of Canberra Hospital. He named it *Canberry*, after what he

The world's heaviest man, Robert Hughes, weighed 484 kg when he died in 1958.

thought was the Aboriginal name for place. With usage, it evolved into Canberra, and 90 years later it was chosen as the national capital's name.

## DARWIN

The crew of the *Beagle* first sighted Darwin's harbour in 1839. The ship's captain named it after Charles Darwin, the British naturalist, who had sailed with him on an earlier expedition on the *Beagle*.

\*　　\*　　\*　　\*

## EVER WONDERED HOW SYDNEY'S BLUE MOUNTAINS GOT THEIR NAME?

The Blue Mountains National Park consists of over 250,000 hectares (617,764 acres) of spectacular mountains and valleys just 60 kilometres (37 miles) west of Sydney.

The area is densely forested with native eucalyptus and it is these trees that cause the mountains to appear blue. During the day, eucalypt trees emit eucalyptus oil into the atmosphere. This oil causes the blue light rays of the sun to be scattered more effectively thus intensifying the usual light. This phenomenon is known as Rayleigh Scattering and causes all distant objects to appear blue. This process is temperature dependent—the hotter the weather the more oil is dispersed into the air and the bluer the mountains appear.

\*　　\*　　\*　　\*

## LIFE'S LIKE THAT

A bloke is looking for a new caddy. His friend says, "I know a great one—he's 90 years old but has eyes like a hawk."

"Okay, tell him I'm playing next week."

A week later they head for the first hole. The golfer slices badly and his ball heads for the rough.

"Caddy, did you see where it went?"

"Yes, I did."

"Okay, where is it?"

"I forget."

# ELVIS: TOP GUN

*Like many Americans some of Elvis's favourite toys were his guns. And when he wasn't shooting, he liked to pretend he was a karate champ. Some details:*

**S**HOT OFF THE CAN
You never knew when Elvis might get the urge to engage in a little shooting practice, so it paid to be on guard at *all* times.

On one memorable night, Elvis and some friends were relaxing in the Imperial Suite on the 30th floor of the Las Vegas Hilton after his show. "The very elegant Linda Thompson [Elvis's girlfriend] was sitting in the well-appointed and luxurious bathroom," writes Steve Dunleavy in *Elvis: What Happened?*, "when her reverie was rudely interrupted by a resounding blast. At the same time, a tiny rip appeared in the toilet paper on her right side [and] the mirror on the closet door splintered into shards of glass."

"I think Elvis was trying to hit a light holder on the opposite wall," explains Sonny West, Elvis's bodyguard. "Well, he's a lousy shot and he missed. The damn bullet went straight through the wall and missed Linda by centimetres. If she had been standing up next to the toilet paper holder, it would have gone right through her leg. If it had changed course or bounced off something, it could have killer her, man."

**PLAYING IT SAFE**
Elvis had hundreds of guns, and he liked to keep them loaded at all times. But he always left the first bullet chamber empty. "It is a habit he got from me," says Sonny West. "I had a friend who dropped his gun. It landed on the hammer…fired and hit him right through the heart, killing him instantly."

But Elvis had another reason. "Elvis knew what a real bad temper he had," says Sonny. "When he flashed, anything could happen. If he pulled the trigger in a rage, it would come up blank and give him just enough time to realise what on earth he was doing."

It paid off. One evening when the Elvis entourage was at the movies (Elvis rented the entire movie theatre and brought his friends with him), Elvis went to the men's room and stayed there for a while. One of the group—a visitor who wasn't part of the regular "Memphis mafia"—started joking around, pounding on the bathroom door. West recalls:

"Elvis yells back 'Okay, man, okay.'

"But this guy just kept banging on the door....Apparently Elvis flashed. 'Goddammit!' he yelled as he charged out the door. Then he screamed, 'Who do you think you are, you m—f—r?,' whipped out his gun, pointed it right at the guy and pulled the trigger. Jesus, thank God, he didn't have a bullet in that chamber; otherwise, he would have blown the man's head clean off his shoulders."

### CHOP! CHOP!

Elvis was fascinated with karate. He dreamed of making his own karate movie, starring himself as the evil karate master, and liked to drop in at various karate studios to shoot the breeze and work out.

Dave Hebler, a seventh-degree black-belt, remembers their first sparring session in *Elvis: What Happened?*:

"He came in with his usual entourage and shook hands all around. Then he wanted to show-off some moves. Within seconds ...it was obvious to me that one, Elvis didn't know half as much about karate as he thought he did; and two, he hardly knew where he was.

"He was moving very sluggishly and lurching around like a man who'd had far too much to drink...I mean he was actually tripping over and damn near falling on his butt.

"While I couldn't make him look like an expert, I tried to react to his moves in such a way that he wouldn't look half as bad as he could have." Hebler became a regular member of Elvis's entourage.

\* \* \* \*

### GOOD ADVICE

"Keep your temper. Do not quarrel with an angry person, but give him a soft answer. It is commanded by the Holy Writ, and, furthermore, it makes him madder than anything else you could say."

—*Anonymous*

# TIPS FOR TEENS

*Teenage girls need all the advice they can get…so here's
more priceless advice from a 1950s teen self-help book.*

## BLUE-RIBBON BABY-SITTING

*Remember, mothers have a
remarkable way of comparing
notes on sitters. If you are serious
about earning a few dollars,
shape up!*

**A baby-sitting job** is no time
for watching TV programs not
permitted at home. Act as if
this is business. You are being
paid. Arrange a definite time
for sitting, and inform your
family when they may expect
you home.

**Arrive on time,** or a few
minutes early to check facts
before parents depart. Be sure
you have a telephone number
where parents, or a responsible
adult, may be reached in an
emergency.

**Bring a book,** your homework
or knitting. Don't arm yourself
with a long list of telephone
numbers for a four-hour gab
session. Don't treat your
employer's refrigerator as a free
raid on the local drive-in.
Don't glue your nose to TV
and overlook sleeping children.
Check them every half hour.

**Before bed,** little ones often
need a bottle. No cause for
panic. The wiggles, small cries
and faces are baby ways of
saying, "Where's my nightcap?"
Be prepared a few minutes
before feeding time to avoid a
long hungry roar.

**Once the children** are bedded
down, stay fairly near the
telephone. Light sleepers are
frequently awakened by its
ring.

**Should the phone ring,** answer
as your employer directed. Be
sure to write down messages.
Never say, "This is Ann. The
family is out, and I am baby-
sitting with the children" to
a stranger. Sad but true, this
occasionally leads to harm to
you or the children.

**The Blue Ribbon** Baby-Sitter
is dependable and completely
aware of her responsibility for
others. Expect to be out of a
job if you eat four hot dogs,
two bottles of chilled cola,
three packs of snacks, run
up the phone bill with
unnecessary calls to friends,
or permit boy or girl friends
to join you without permission!

---

**Watch your step:** A male spider's reproductive organ is located at the end of one of his legs.

# DANGER: LEAVE YOUR GIRLFRIEND'S BOYFRIEND ALONE!

*Are you the kind of girl who would dream up an elaborate and ridiculous plot to steal your girlfriend's boyfriend?*

**Perhaps the compulsion** comes to you one day during a geometry test after you have borrowed a pencil from him because something is wrong with your ballpoint pen. You flunk the test. His darling smile keeps coming between you and the angles. At the end of the period, you return the pencil. He hands it back.

"Keep it," he says with a smile. "You'll probably need it in your next class, and I have another." Another smile! The light in his eyes! You tremble with excitement. This is it! He loves you, and you love him. No one, not even your dearest girlfriend must stand between you.

**After school you walk** half a block behind him until both he and you are away from the crowds. Then you catch up and "just happen" to appear and join him. In a moment you "just happen" to stumble over nothing so that he must catch you in his arms. He releases you quickly, a strange expression on his face, and then he strides ahead. You turn back toward your own home on the other side of town, overcome by the wonder of it all. You are sure the boy is too overcome by emotion to speak—that is why he went away so fast.

**Unhappily, that evening** you see him with your girlfriend. They are so engrossed in each other, neither sees you. Evidently the boy has spoken of your afternoon pursuit, however, for your girlfriend is cool toward you. In fact, you find yourself very lonely these days. You are a pitiful case because you are not only dishonest but ignorant.

## SHOULD GIRLS TELEPHONE BOYS?

**Careful, girls:** In a poll of high-school boys more than two-thirds said they do not like to have girls call them on the telephone. They feel that this is a boy's privilege, and that a girl seems forward when she phones a boy. In fact, most say their families *tease* them about girls who call them at home.

---

40% of Australians take music lessons at some point in their lives; 7% take acting lessons.

# THE DUMBEST WESTERN EVER MADE

*There are plenty of worthless Westerns. But few can match this combination of two—count 'em—hilariously lousy films in one. Director Bill "One-Shot" Beaudine managed to capture the worst elements of both dumb Westerns and cheesy monster movies and roll them into a single feature film.*

**J**ESSE JAMES MEETS FRANKENSTEIN'S DAUGHTER,
*Starring Narda Onyx, John Lupton, Cal Bolder, Estelita, Jim Davis and Steven Geray. Directed by William Beaudine.*

**Background:** William Beaudine was a film pioneer who began working for legendary director D.W. Griffith in 1909. During the the golden age of silent films, he became a director himself and churned out some of Hollywood's biggest hits. But he specialised in Westerns. In *Incredibly Strange Films*, Jim Morton writes:

Beaudine hit his stride during the early days of Hollywood when studios were less devoted to big-budget productions and more interested in getting as many films as possible out to the American public. In those days, a western had an immediate audience. If it was a *Western*, it couldn't fail. These took anywhere from two days to two weeks to make. Beaudine dutifully churned them out, rarely lavishing much attention on any of them....One of the ways Beaudine kept his costs down (and his speed up) was by avoiding retakes whenever possible. He became so notorious for his refusal to reshoot a scene that he earned the nickname "One-Shot Beaudine." If a boom mike dipped into the frame, if a cowboy started to fall *before* he was shot—*oh well.*

Once, when told that he was behind schedule with a film, he responded: "You mean someone's actually waiting for this c—p?"

During the latter part of his career, Beaudine directed mostly TV shows—including more than 70 episodes of "Lassie." But in 1965, he directed two last films (both flicks in a drive-in double-feature). The first was called *Billy the Kid Meets Dracula.* This second, and worst, was *Jesse James Meets Frankenstein's Daughter.*

Beaudine, who wound up directing over 150 films, died in 1970.

At age 78, he was Hollywood's oldest working director...and he has the unusual distinction, for a B-film-meister, of having a star on the Hollywood Walk of Fame.

He certainly didn't get it for this movie.

**The Plot:** Dr. Maria Frankenstein and her brother Rudolf have settled in a small town in the Southwest. It's the perfect location—there's plenty of lightning to power her experiments, there are plenty of fresh young boys to experiment on, and the Austrian police will never find her there. (Seems she's been experimenting in Europe, too).

As the film opens, all the Mexican peasants are leaving town—mostly to get away from Maria. Only one family remains, waiting for their son—who works at the Frankenstein hacienda—to get over "the sickness." Actually, Maria has operated on the boy, giving him the artificial brain her grandfather (she's really Frankenstein's *grand*daughter) created.

Rudolf is spooked by all this mad scientist stuff; he gives the boy poison rather than letting Maria succeed. Maria doesn't know what's going on—so she decides the boy was too weak; she needs a big, strong man to experiment on.

Well, it just so happens that Jesse James is riding around the countryside with a hulking doofus named Hank...and Hank has been shot during a robbery. He needs a doctor...so he and Jesse conveniently wind up at Frankenstein's hacienda.

To make a long story mercifully short: Maria gives Hank a new brain and calls him—what else?—Igor. Then she gets Igor to kill her brother. Then Igor kills Maria. Then Juanita, Jesse's girlfriend, kills Igor. Then the sheriff takes Jesse away. The End.

**Don't Miss:**
• *The Frankenstein "hacienda"* overlooking town. Viewed from main street, it's an obvious 6-metre (20-foot) high painting. You've gotta see this one to appreciate it.
• *The generic poison bottle.* Rudolph poisons the boy with a beaker full of red water, labelled POISON. What kind of poison? Who cares?
• *The Indians riding by.* Blissfully pointless footage cut in from some other B-film.

---

In 1658 an American legislature passed a law outlawing lawyers.

- **The helmet.** Maria uses it to activate the artificial brain. But it looks like a Rastafarian chemistry experiment, topped with a wire fence. Should win some sort of prize for low-budget props.
- **Juanita.** Played by actress Estelita Rodriguez, supposed to be a beautiful young girl…"even though she looks everyone of her thirty-eight years."

## IMMORTAL DIALOGUE

**Maria:** "What a fool I've been! I've allowed the duo-thermal impulsator to be attached only to the body! Let's see what Grandfather's notation says.... You see? The duo-thermal impulsator must also be attached to a living brain, to transmit living vibrations to the artificial brain!"

**Rudolph:** "But such a powerful electric impulse might prove fatal to the brain of a living person!"

**Maria:** "That chance I am willing to take!"

**Maria:** "It's because we've been forced to use the brains of children that we've failed. What we need is a man—a powerful man—a giant! Then we will succeed!"

**Rudolph:** "But what—what good will it do to succeed?"

**Maria:** "Imagine! We'll have someone to do our bidding who can't be put to death! Just as we have given it life, only we can take its life away!"

**Rudolph:** "Maria, we've already caused the deaths of three children, and violated the graves of others, just to make the experiments!"

**Maria:** "My, you're a humanitarian! You should have stayed in Europe and given pink pills to sweet old ladies!"

**Maria:** "This is the last artificial brain Grandfather Frankenstein made. The secret of how to make them died with him. If I fail in this last attempt, I too am willing to die!"

**Rudolph:** "Is it so terrible to fail?"

**Maria:** "You're a fool, Rudolph! We hold the secret of life in our hands!

**Rudolph:** "Maria, Maria! This has already cost Grandfather his life!"

---

Taxi drivers and chauffeurs are more likely to be murdered on the job than anyone else.

# WOMBAT ON THE LOOSE

*It's the star of an Australian children's book called* The Muddle-Headed Wombat *by Ruth Park. It lives underground in elaborate burrows and is rarely seen. But there's more to this thick little animal with short, stumpy legs than you might first think.*

## THE WOMBAT LOWDOWN

Wombats are sturdy, stout marsupials that can grow to about 1.3 metres (4 feet) in length and can weight up to 35 kg (80 lb). They are very elusive and rarely leave their burrows before dusk. They have many different burrows, which may be up to 30 metres (98 feet) long and 5 metres (16 feet) deep. Wombats mark their burrows by leaving splashes or urine and droppings around the edges of the burrow.

There are three species of wombat:

**The southern hairy-nosed wombat** occurs in parts of southern South Australia, southeastern Western Australia and western Victoria. It is the smallest of the three species.

**The northern hairy-nosed wombat** lives in grasslands, and acacia and eucalyptus woodlands. It is the largest of the three species.

**The common wombat** occurs in southeastern Australia. It has coarse hair and a small tail, and its ears are more rounded than the northern hairy-nosed wombat.

## WHO ARE YOU CALLING A HAIRY NOSE?

The northern hairy-nosed wombat was always the least widespread of the three species, but now it is one of the rarest animals in the world. There are only about 80 known northern hairy-nosed wombats and these live in Epping Forest National Park in central Queensland.

## BURROWING DEEP

Wombats are some of the biggest animals in the world to dig burrows. They seek out natural weaknesses in the ground and then they begin. Scratching with alternate front paws, the wombat

---

The length of the small intestine: six metres. The large intestine: 1.5 metres.

loosens the soil, then scoops it backwards or sideways. The pouch of the female wombat faces backwards so that dirt can't enter it while she is digging and scooping. To dig the sides and roof of the burrow, the wombat rolls onto its side. It also uses its teeth to remove rocks and roots. Sometimes wombat burrows are large enough for people to crawl through. In 1878, a trooper hid from the notorious Ned Kelly gang in a wombat burrow.

## WANTED DEAD OR ALIVE

Up until 1971, the common wombat was considered vermin as it was thought to cause widespread destruction to farming land. As a result, the government placed a bounty on its head. In some parts of Victoria today, the common wombat is still unprotected and can be shot without prosecution.

## DON'T MESS WITH ME!

Wombats may have the reputation of being slow, clumsy creatures, but think again. They have a nasty bite and can run at speeds of up to 40 kilometres (25 miles) an hour. If a dog or a fox chases a wombat into its burrow, the wombat raises its rump and crushes the attacker's head against the roof of the burrow. This is certainly a painful, but effective, way of telling the intruder to "butt out!"

\* \* \* \*

## WORLD PRAWN EATING CHAMPIONSHIPS

These prawns definitely don't make it to the barbie. Every year in March, Tea Gardens, Hawks Nest, a sleepy little tourist town on the north coast of New South Wales, is the site of a world prawn-fest. Eaters of prawns gather to show their skill in consuming the most prawns possible. The record is 1 kg (2.2 lb) of prawns in five minutes.

Anyone for dessert?

Longest time survived by a headless chicken: 18 months.

# UNCLE JOHN'S
# GOLDEN TURKEYS

*Back in the 1980s, the Medved brothers introduced the term
"golden turkeys" for unbelievably, hilariously bad films.
Today there's a big subculture of people who love to watch them...
and Uncle John is one. Here are two of his favourite grade Z films.*

## THE BEAST OF YUCCA FLATS (1961)

*Written, directed and edited by Coleman Francis. Produced
by Anthony Cardoza. Starring Tor Johnson, Conrad Brooks.
Narration: Coleman Francis.*

**The Plot:** Joseph Javorski, a Russian rocket scientist (played by
hulking ex-wrestler Tor Johnson) escapes to America with secret
documents. Javorski's destination: "Yucca Flats. And a meeting
with top brass at the A-bomb testing grounds." When he gets
there, he's chased into the desert by 2 KGB agents. Uh-oh there's
an atomic test going on. An A-bomb goes off near the Russian
trio; the spies are vaporised, but Tor is merely turned into a
maniac. He spends the rest of the film wandering around the
desert with a stick, looking for people to beat up and/or kill.

**Commentary:**
• *From "The Beast of Yucca Flats" website:* "As a fan of bad movies
I have seen many of the greats in bad films, including the works
of Ed Wood Jr., Larry (*Mars Needs Women*) Buchanan and Jerry
(*Teenage Zombies*) Warren....But I have never seen a worse film
than this....As soon as I saw it I knew my search (for the world's
worst movie) was over. Since then I have seen it over and
over...and each time it still amazes me.

**Don't Miss:**
• *The Narrator.* There's almost no dialogue, and no synchronised
soundtrack. Instead, there's an "omniscient narrator," dubbed in
after the film was completed. Ken Begg writes in *Jabootu's Bad
Movie Universe:*
  Adding to the laughs is some of the most mind-boggling
narration this side of the master, Ed Wood himself. Getting to

watch Tor run around in ragged clothing, like TV's *Incredible Hulk*, is a treat for any Bad Movie connoisseur. The ponderous, repetitive narration about Mankind, Science, Justice and other Big Topics so solemnly intoned here is the cherry on the sundae. *Some examples:*

– "Touch a button. Things happen. A scientist becomes a beast."
– "Jim Archer. Joe's partner. Another man caught in the frantic race for the betterment of mankind. Progress."
– "Jim Archer. Wounded parachuting on Korea. Jim and Joe try to keep the desert roads safe for travellers. Seven days a week."
– "Shockwaves of an A-bomb. A once powerful, humble man. Reduced to…nothing."
– "Joseph Javorski. Respected scientist. Now a fiend. Prowling the wastelands. A prehistoric beast in a nuclear age. Kill. Kill, just to be killing."
– "Vacation time. People travel east. West. North or south. The Radcliffs travel east, with two small boys, adventurous boys. Nothing bothers some people. Not even Flying Saucers."
– "Boys from the City. Not yet caught by the Whirlwind of Progress. Feed soda pop to the thirsty pigs."

• The " 'exciting' car chase…" How many inconsistencies can *you* find? Here's Ken Begg's (Jabootu's) analysis:

The scene immediately cuts from daytime to night-time. Plus the scenery keeps changing (when the film isn't so dark that you can't see what's going on). First, they're driving through a forest. Then the desert. Then they're still in the desert, but on a road. Then on a road bordered by mountains. Then on a road where the other side's bordered by mountains. This goes on for some minutes. They drive past a plywood sign obviously made for the film (by somebody's kid, by the look of it) that reads "Yucca Flats." (Wow!)

## THE CRAWLING EYE (1958)
*Starring Forrest Tucker, Janet Munro, Laurence Payne, Jennifer Jayne, Warren Mitchell*
**The Plot:** A mysterious radioactive cloud covers Mt. Trollenberg in the Swiss Alps. Meanwhile, mountain climbers are turning up decapitated. What's going on? United Nations investigator Alan Brooks is sent to find out. He and his psychic girlfriend Anne

(who "slips in and out of unintentionally hilarious trances") discover "giant paper mache eyeballs with ultra-cheap tentacles," er, space aliens who want to take over our planet. Brooks finally figures out that the creatures like it cold, and gets rid of them with the help of a few "U.N. fire bombs" (molotov cocktails and napalm!).

**Commentary:**
*From "Rotten Tomatoes"* (Dennis Schwartz):
"May be a good film to see on late night cable TV while you're hoisting a few at the bar. In fact, every character in the film has either a brandy or a Scotch to drink at some time—when they're shook up or about to climb the mountain...or just to be sociable. So they might know something about this film [we] don't—such as, it might be best to have a few nips while viewing to enhance the "quality" of the film. Not that I'm an advocate of drinking, but what the hell...it can't hurt in this case."

*From "The Bad Movie Report":*
- "This film had a couple of things going for it, not least of which was that Anne is really attractive. Unfortunately they made this movie in 1958 so she dresses like June Cleaver.
- "Things I learned from this movie:
    - Villagers have something to say about everything
    - Clouds that are stationary and radioactive are bad news
    - Foreboding music does not belong in a scene involving empty beds
    - Do not open a [backpack] that is just lying around on a mountainside; odds are there's a head in it
    - Zombies created by freezing aliens melt away when killed."

**BONUS: Scene to Watch For.** "As the villagers flee to the observatory, a child of about four somehow manages to cover what appears to be several miles in a matter of minutes to retrieve her ball. This scene is obviously contrived so that (a) we can get our first look at the enemy and (b) Forrest Tucker can do a manly rescue in the very nick."

—*Elizabeth Burton*

---

# WORD ORIGINS

*Here are a few more words we all use—and where they come from…*

**Orangutan:** From a Malay phrase that means "man of the forest."

**Candidate:** In ancient Rome a *candidatus* was "a person clothed in white." Roman politicians wore white togas to symbolise "humility and purity of motive."

**Idiot:** From the Greek word *idiotes*, which means "private people" or "people who do not hold public office."

**Outlandish:** Described the unfamiliar behavior of foreigners, also known as *outlanders*.

**Eleven:** The Germanic ancestor of the word, *ain-lif*, translates as "one left [over]." That's what happens when you count to ten on your fingers and still have one left over.

**Twelve:** Means "two left over."

**Pirate:** From the Greek word for "attacker."

**Bus:** Shortened from the French phrase *voiture omnibus*, "vehicle for all."

**Taxi:** Shortened from *taximeter-cabriolet. Cabriolet* was the name given to two-wheeled carriages…and *taximeter* was the device that "measured the charge."

**Bylaw:** A descendant of the Old Norse term *byr log*, which meant "village law."

**Obvious:** Comes from the Latin words *ob viam*, which mean "in the way." Something that's obvious is so clear to see that you can't help but stumble across it.

**Hazard:** From the Arabic words *al-zahr*, "a die," the name of a game played with dice. Then as now, gambling was *hazardous* to your financial health.

**Scandal:** From the Greek word for "snare, trap, or stumbling block."

---

Dwight D. Eisenhower wore two watches on his left arm and one on his right. (Even to bed.)

# THE STRANGE FATE OF THE DODO BIRD

*The dodo bird has been labelled the "mascot of extinction" and the "poster child for endangered species." Here's a look at the ill-fated fowl.*

**B**ACKGROUND
You may have heard of the dodo—or been called one— but you've never seen one. *Webster's New World Dictionary* offers three definitions for dodo: "foolish, stupid"; "an old-fashioned person, a fogy"; and "a large bird, now extinct, that had a hooked bill, a short neck and legs, and rudimentary wings useless for flying."

In fact, the dodo, now synonymous with stupidity, was the first animal species acknowledged to have been forced into extinction by man. It was probably one of the fastest extinctions in history.

## MAURITIUS IS "DISCOVERED"
Portuguese mariners first landed on Mauritius, a small island 640 km (400 miles) east of Madagascar in the Indian Ocean, in about 1507. There they encountered a strange, flightless bird. Weighing more than 23 kg (50 lbs), it was slightly larger than a turkey, as sluggish as a turtle, and remarkably stupid. The Portuguese named it *duodo* or "simpleton."

Dutch settlers were the next Westerners to arrive on the island; they called the dodo *dodaers* ("fat asses") and even *Walghvögel* ("nauseus bird"), because the bird tasted terrible. "Greasie stomachs may seeke after them," one taster remarked in 1606, "but to the delicate they are offensive and of no nourishment."

## THE DODO'S SECRET
Centuries of isolation from other animals and the absence of any natural enemies on Mauritius had deprived the dodo of its instinct for survival. For example:
• The dodo didn't bother to build nests for its eggs. It just laid them on the ground wherever it happened to be at the time…and just walked off afterward, abandoning the egg to whatever fate

befell it. This wasn't a bad strategy when there were no predators around. But in time, humans brought monkeys, rats, pigs, and dogs to the island. They feasted on the eggs they found.
• It had no fear of humans. The early Mauritian settlers literally had to walk around the birds, or shove them aside with their feet when they walked around the island. If the settlers were hungry, they just killed the birds and ate them; others of the species would watch dumbly.

## THE DISAPPEARING DODO
Dodos were plentiful in 1507, when man first arrived, but by 1631 they were already quite scarce.

No one knows precisely when the dodo went extinct, but when the Frenchman Francois Leguat inventoried the wildlife of Mauritius in 1693, he made no mention of any bird resembling it—although he did note ominously that the wild boars (introduced by Western settlers) devoured "all the young animals they catch."

## MISSED OPPORTUNITY
Was the dodo's extinction inevitable? Some experts say no. They point to animals such as domesticated cows, which flourish even though they're "slow, weak, stupid, and altogether uncompetitive." They think that if dodos had lasted for one more generation, they might have been successfully domesticated.
According to one account:

> On several occasions during the 17th century, living birds were brought from the Indian Ocean to Europe, and some of these were exhibited to the public. Even during the century in which it became extinct, the species aroused great interest in Europe. Had Dodos survived for a few more decades, colonies might perhaps have established themselves in European parks and gardens. Today, Dodos might be as common as peacocks in ornamental gardens the world over! Instead, all that remains are a few bones and pieces of skin, a collection of pictures of varying quality, and a series of written descriptions [that are] curiously inadequate in the information they convey.

It takes 454,000 litres (100,000 gallons) of water to make one car, car manufacturers say.

## THE LAST DODO

Not only are there no *live* dodos, there aren't even any *dead* ones left. The last stuffed specimen, collected by John Tradescant, a 17th-century horticulturist and collector of oddities, was donated to Ashmolean Museum at Oxford University after his death. It remained there until 1755. "In that year," *Horizon* magazine reported in 1971:

> the university...considered what to do with the dodo, which was probably stuffed with salt and sand, by then altogether tatty, and, who knows, maybe lice-infested. [Museum instructions] said: "That as any particular [specimen] grows old and perishing the Keeper may remove it into one of the closets or other repository, and some other to be substituted." The dodo was removed, and burned. Some thoughtful soul preserved the head and one foot, but there was, of course, no other bird to be substituted. The dodo was extinct.

## OUT OF SIGHT, OUT OF MIND

So little was known about the dodo that by the middle of the 19th century, nearly 100 years after the Oxford University specimen was thrown out, people believed it had never existed, and had been merely "a legend like the unicorn."

It took a little digging to prove otherwise. "In 1863," recounts Errol Fuller in his book *Extinct Birds*, "a persistent native of Mauritius, George Clark, realising the island's volcanic soil was too hard to hold fossils, decided that some dodo bones might have been washed up by rains on the muddy delta near the town of Mahebourg. He led an excavation that yielded a great quantity of dodo bones, which were assembled into complete skeletons and sent to the museums of the world. Joy! The dodo lived again."

## LEWIS CARROLL'S DODO

Today, the most famous dodo bird is probably the one in *Alice in Wonderland*. Perhaps because the dodo is a symbol of stupidity, Lewis Carroll used it to parody politicians. His dodo is a windbag, runs aimlessly, and placates the masses with other people's assets...then ceremoniously gives some of them back to the original owner.

Q: On average, how long is a giraffe's tongue? A: 36 cm (14 inches).

## ALICE & THE DODO
When Alice became a giant in Wonderland, she began to cry. Her tears turned into a flood that swept away everything—including a strange menagerie of birds, mice, and other creatures. Finally the flood subsided and the dripping-wet animals wanted to get dry. First, a mouse tried reciting English history ("The driest thing I know") When that didn't work, the Dodo made a suggestion. Here's the passage in which the dodo appears:

## THE DODO SPEAKS
"How are you getting on now, my dear?" the mouse said, turning to Alice as it spoke.

"As wet as ever," said Alice in a melancholy tone. "it doesn't seem to dry me at all."

"In that case,' said the Dodo solemnly, rising to its feet, "I move that the meeting adjourn, for the immediate adoption of more energetic remedies—"

"Speak English!" said the Eaglet. "I don't know the meaning of half those long words, and, what's more, I don't believe you do either!' And the Eaglet bent down its head to hide a smile: some of the other birds tittered audibly.

"What I was going to say," said the Dodo in an offended tone, "was, that the best thing to get us dry would be a Caucus-race."

"What is a Caucus-race?" said Alice; Not that she much wanted to know, but the Dodo had paused as if it thought that somebody ought to speak, and no one else seemed inclined to say anything.

"Why," said the Dodo, "the best way to explain it is to do it." (And, as you might like to try the thing yourself some winter day, I'll tell you how the Dodo managed it.)

## THE CAUCUS RACE
First it marked out a race-course, in a sort of circle ("the exact shape doesn't matter," it said) and then all the party were placed along the course, here and there. There was no "One, two, three, and away!" but they began running when they liked, and left off when they liked, so that it was not easy to know when the race was over. However, when they had been running half an hour or so, and were quite dry again, the Dodo suddenly called out "The race is over!" and they all crowded round it, panting, and asking, "But who has won?"

**If you had to eat one food for the rest of your life, what would it be? 36% of people said pizza.**

This question the Dodo could not answer without a great deal of thought, and it stood for a long time with one finger pressed upon its forehead (the position in which you usually see Shakespeare, in the pictures of him), while the rest waited in silence. At last the Dodo said "Everybody has won, and all must have prizes."

## ALICE IS SELECTED

"But who is to give the prizes?" quite a chorus of voices asked.

"Why, she, of course," said the Dodo, pointing to Alice with one finger; and the whole party at once crowded round her, calling out, in a confused way, "Prizes! Prizes!"

Alice had no idea what to do, and in despair she put her hand in her pocket, and pulled out a box of comfits...and handed them round as prizes. There was exactly one a-piece, all round.

"But she must have a prize herself, you know," said the Mouse. "Of course," the Dodo replied very gravely. "What else have you got in your pocket?" it went on, turning to Alice.

"Only a thimble," said Alice sadly.

"Hand it over here," said the Dodo.

Then they all crowded round her once more, while the Dodo solemnly presented the thimble, saying "We beg your acceptance of this elegant thimble"; and, when it had finished this short speech, they all cheered.

Alice thought the whole thing very absurd, but they all looked so grave that she did not dare to laugh; and, as she could not think of anything to say, she simply bowed, and took the thimble, looking as solemn as she could.

*Alice begins talking about her cat, and the animals nervously slink away. The Dodo never appears again.*

\*　　\*　　\*　　\*

## NOTABLE AUSTRALIAN QUOTES

"Australia is a lucky country run mainly by second-rate people who share its luck."

**—Donald Horne**

"If Australia is a lucky country, the Aborigines must be the unluckiest people in the world."

**—Franky Hardy**

---

**Reindeer are the only species of deer in which the female grows antlers.**

# SANDBURGERS

*Thoughts from Carl Sandburg, one of America's
most celebrated poets and authors.*

"Even those who have read books on manners are sometimes a
pain in the neck."

"Put all your eggs in one basket and watch the basket."

"Everybody talks about the weather and nobody does anything
about it."

"Blessed are they who expect nothing for they shall not be
disappointed."

"Those who fear they may cast pearls before swine are often
lacking in pearls."

"May you live to eat the hen that scratches on your grave."

"A lawyer is a man who gets two other men to take off their
clothes and then he runs away with them."

"Six feet of earth make us all one size."

"I want money in order to buy the time to get the things that
money will not buy."

"Many kiss the hands they wish to see cut off."

"Time is the storyteller you can't shut up."

"We asked the cyclone to go around our barn but it didn't hear
us."

"Someday they'll give a war and nobody will come."

---

We're outnumbered: 7,000 new insect species are discovered every year.

# THE ANSWER ZONE

*Here are the solutions to our brain teasers, games, and quizzes.*

## WHAT DOES IT SAY?, PAGE 177

**1.** *John Underwood, Andover, Mass.* (JOHN under WOOD, and over MASS)

**2.** I thought I heard a noise outside, but it was *nothing after all.* (0 after ALL)

**3.** Let's have *an understanding* (AN under STANDING)

**4.** *Look around you.* (LOOK around U)

**5.** "Remember," she said to the group, *"united we stand, divided we fall."* (United WESTAND, divided WE FALL)

**6.** "Why'd he do that?" Jesse asked. "Well, son," I said, "he's a *mixed-up kid."* (DKI = kid)

**7.** Texas? I love *wide-open spaces.* (S P A C E S)

**8.** "Drat! My watch broke. Time to get it *repaired."* (RE paired)

**9.** "I remember the 1960s," she said, *looking backward.* (GNIKOOL = "looking" spelled backward)

**10.** No, we're not living together anymore. It's a *legal separation.* (L E G A L)

**11.** Haven't seen him in a while. He's *far away from home.* (FAR away from HOME)

**12.** Careful, I warned my sister. He's a *wolf in sheep's clothing.* (WOLF inside WOOL)

**13.** "How do I get out of here?" he asked. I said, "Just calm down and put the *car in reverse."* (R A C = car spelled backward)

**14.** I tried to teach her, but no luck. I guess she's a *backward child.* (DLIHC = *child* spelled backward)

**15.** When it's raining, *she meets me under an umbrella.* (SHE meets ME under AN UMBRELLA)

## THE GODZILLA QUIZ, PAGE 195

**1. C)** They added Raymond Burr, casting him as Steve Martin, a reporter who remembers the whole incident as a flashback. It starts off with Burr in a hospital bed, recalling the horror he's seen. Then, throughout the film, footage of Burr is cleverly inserted to make it seem as though he's interacting with the Japanese cast.

**2. C)** *Gigantis*; it was illegal to use the name Godzilla. Warner Bros. brought the film into America, but they forgot to secure the rights to the name Godzilla, so they couldn't legally use it. In this film, by the way, Godzilla crushes Osaka instead of Tokyo, and begins his long tradition of monster-fighting (he takes on a giant creature called Angorus).

**3. B)** A giant cockroach and a robot with a buzz saw in his stomach. The Seatopians, stationed under the sea, are using a metal bird monster with a buzz saw (Gaigan) and a giant cockroach (Megalon—described as a "metal monster insect with drill arms") to fight Godzilla on the surface. Godzilla can't take them on alone. He teams up with Jet Jaguar, a cyborg who can change size to fight monsters.

**4. B)** A giant moth. The thing is Mothra, who starred in its own film a few years earlier. Godzilla kills Mothra—but a giant egg on display at a carnival hatches, and two "junior Mothras" emerge. They spin a cocoon around Godzilla and dump him in the ocean.

**5. A)** He fought a Godzilla robot from outer space. The film was originally called *Godzilla vs. the Bionic Monster*, presumably to cash in on the popularity of the "Six Million Dollar Man" TV show. But the owners of that TV show sued, and the title was changed to *Godzilla vs. the Cosmic Monster*.

**6. C)** A three-headed dragon. To defeat them, Godzilla takes a partner again—this time Angorus, his foe from *Gigantis*.

**7. A)** The smog Monster—a 400-foot blob of garbage. The smog monster flies around, leaving a trail of poisonous vapors that cause people to drop like flies, especially at discos where teens are dancing to anti-pollution songs. Don't miss the smash tune, "Save the Earth."

**8. B)** To show a little kid how to fight bullies. The boy falls asleep and dreams he travels to Monster Island, where Godzilla and his son teach him how to defend himself.

**9. C)** A giant lobster. Actually, he might be a giant shrimp. It's hard to tell. His strength: He can regenerate a limb every time one is torn off:

**10. C)** It was Godzilla's son. Imagine that—Godzilla's a parent!

## AUNT LENNA'S PUZZLES, PAGE 253
**1.** The accountant and lawyer were women. Steve is a man's name.
**2.** The answers are WHOLESOME and ONE WORD.

## AUNT LENNA'S PUZZLES, PAGE 284
**1.** He couldn't have heard where she was going if he was deaf.
**2.** 99 99/99
**3.** His wife was on a life-support system. When he pushed the
elevator button, he realised the power had gone off.
**4.** The first man, who saw the smoke, knew first; the second man,
who heard it, knew second; the third man, who saw the bullet,
knew last. The speed of light travels faster than the speed of
sound, and the speed of sound travels faster than a bullet.
**5.** Her shoes. Check it out against the woman's laments—it
makes sense.
**6.** Let's start with the grandmothers and grandfathers. That's 4.
They're all mothers and fathers, so if there are 3 mothers and 3
fathers, we have 2 new people—1 mother, 1 father—for a total of 6.

The 2 mothers-in-law and fathers-in-law are the grandparents,
so we don't count them again. The son-in-law and daughter-in-law
are the 2 additional parents, so we don't count them again, either.

The 2 sons and 2 daughters are their children—which makes
10 people.

## AUNT LENNA'S PUZZLES, PAGE 315
**1.** She's talking about the amount of bills, not the year. 1,993 bills
are worth exactly $1 more than more than 1,992 bills.
**2.** They were travelling at different times.
**3.** Noel (No "L").
**4.** She grabbed one of the stones and quickly let it "slip" from her
hands. Then, because she "couldn't find" the stone she'd dropped,
she just looked in the bag to see what was left. It was a black
stone, of course…which meant she'd won the bet.
**5.** Cut them into quarters with two cuts…then stack the quarters
on top of each other and cut once. Eight pieces, three cuts.
**6.** She wrote:

## *g o o d g o d g o*

## ACRONYMANIA, PAGE 357

1. Australian Competition and Consumer Commission
2. Deoxyribo Nucleic Aci
3. Dead On Arrival
4. Eastern Standard Time
5. Queensland And Northern Territory Aerial Services
6. INTERnational Criminal POLice Organization
7. Keep It Simple Stupid
8. Light Amplification by Stimulated Emission of Radiation
9. UNIVersal Automatic Computer
10. NAtional BIScuit COmpany
11. National Aeronautics and Space Administration
12. State Emergency Service
13. Not In My BackYard
14. Special Air Service
15. Organization of Petroleum Exporting Countries
16. As Soon As Possible
17. QUASi-StellAR Radio Source
18. Have A Nice Day
19. For Your Information
20. Rapid Eye Movement
21. Self-Contained Underwater Breathing Apparatus
22. Sealed With A Kiss
23. TriNiTrotoluene
24. United Nations Educational Scientific and Cultural Organisation
25. United Nations International Children's Emergency Fund
26. Computerised Axial Tomography scan
27. Airborne Warning And Control System
28. Absent WithOut Leave
29. Compact Disc—Read Only Memory
30. Mobile Army Surgical Hospital
31. Will COmply
32. SOund Navigation And Ranging
33. Situation Normal, All Fouled (or F——) Up
34. North Atlantic Treaty Organization
35. Strategic Arms Limitation Talks
36. RAdio Detection And Ranging
37. Subsonic Cruise Unarmed Decoy

---

Medical studies show that intelligent people have more copper and zinc in their hair.

38. Strategic Air Command
39. What You See Is What You Get
40. World Health Organisation
41. SEa-Air-Land unitS
42. MicroSoft Disk Operating System
43. Great Minds Think Alike
44. Tele-Active Shock Electronic Repulsion
45. Random Access Memory
46. Waste Of Money, Brains, And Time
47. Also Known As
48. CANada Oil, Low Acid
49. In Vitro Fertilization
50. Sexually Transmitted Disease
51. Frequently Asked Question(s)

## THE NUMBERS GAME, PAGE 410

1. 7 = Wonders of the Ancient World
2. 1001 = Arabian Nights
3. 12 = Signs of the Zodiac
4. 54 = Cards in a Deck (with the Jokers)
5. 9 = Planets in the Solar System
6. 88 = Piano Keys
7. 13 = Stripes on the American Flag
8. 32 = Degrees Fahrenheit, at Which Water Freezes
9. 90 = Degrees in a Right Angle
10. 99 = Bottles of Beer on the Wall
11. 18 = Holes on a Golf Course
12. 8 = Sides on a Stop Sign
13. 3 = Blind Mice (See How They Run)
14. 4 = Quarts in a Gallon
15. 1 = Wheel on a Unicycle
16. 5 = Digits in a Zip Code
17. 24 = Hours in a Day
18. 57 = Heinz Varieties
19. 11 = Players on a Football Team
20. 1000 = Words That a Picture Is Worth
21. 29 = Days in February in a Leap Year
22. 64 = Squares on a Chessboard

23. 40 = Days and Nights of the Great Flood
24. 2 = To Tango
25. 76 = Trombones in a Big Parade
26. 8 = Great Tomatoes in a Little Bitty Can
27. 101 = Dalmatians
28. 23 = Skidoo
29. 4 = He's a Jolly Good Fellow (yes, it's a trick)
30. 16 = Men on a Dead Man's Chest
31. 12 = Days of Christmas
32. 5 = Great Lakes
33. 7 = Deadly Sins
34. 2.5 = Children in a Typical American Family
35. 1, 2, 3 = Strikes You're Out at the Old Ball Game
36. 3 = Men in a Tub
37. 13 = Baker's Dozen

Most, if not all, polar bears are left-handed.

# THE LAST PAGE

**B**ATHROOM READERS,
We at the Bathroom Readers' Institute do not take your quest for good and plentiful bathroom reading lightly. We sit firmly and believe that it is your inalienable right to have high-quality reading material.

So we invite you to take the plunge. Sit down and be counted by joining the Bathroom Readers' Institute. Contact us about this book's content at **unclejohn@advmkt.com**.

Visit our website at **www.bathroomreader.com**, where you can:

- Visit "The Throne Room"—a great place to read!
- Submit your favorite articles and facts.
- Suggest ideas for future editions.
- Become a BRI member.

Well, we're out of space, and when you've gotta go, you've gotta go! We hope you've enjoyed this book as much as we have. And never forget:

## *Go with the flow!*

---

It takes six months to build a Rolls Royce and 13 hours to build a Toyota.